Women and Gender in Early Modern Europe

Third Edition

This new, updated edition of Merry E. Wiesner-Hanks's prize-winning survey of women and gender in early modern Europe features an entirely new chapter on gender and race in the colonial world; expanded coverage of eighteenth-century developments including the Enlightenment; and enhanced discussions of masculinity, single women, same-sex relations, humanism, and women's religious roles within Christianity, Judaism, and Islam. All of the chapters incorporate the newest scholarship, and the book preserves the clear structure of previous editions with its tripartite division of mind, body, and spirit. Within this structure, other themes include the female life cycle, women's economic roles, artistic creations, education, and witchcraft. Coverage is geographically broad, including Russia, Scandinavia, the Ottoman Empire, and the Iberian Peninsula. This is essential reading for all students of early modern Europe and gender history and is accompanied by a Web site featuring extensive updated bibliographies, Web links, and primary source material.

Merry E. Wiesner-Hanks is a Distinguished Professor in the Department of History at the University of Wisconsin–Milwaukee. She is the coeditor of the *Sixteenth Century Journal*. Her previous publications include *Early Modern Europe 1450–1789* (2006), *Gender in History* (2001), and *Christianity and Sexuality in the Early Modern World* (2000).

The companion Web site for this textbook can be found at www.cambridge.org/womenandgender.

NEW APPROACHES TO EUROPEAN HISTORY

Series editors

WILLIAM BEIK *Emory University*
T. C. W. BLANNING *Sidney Sussex College, Cambridge*
BRENDAN SIMMS *Peterhouse, Cambridge*

New Approaches to European History is an important textbook series, which provides concise but authoritative surveys of major themes and problems in European history since the Renaissance. Written at a level and length accessible to advanced school students and undergraduates, each book in the series addresses topics or themes that students of European history encounter daily: the series embraces both some of the more "'traditional" subjects of study and those cultural and social issues to which increasing numbers of school and college courses are devoted. A particular effort is made to consider the wider international implications of the subject under scrutiny.

To aid the student reader, scholarly apparatus and annotation is light, but each work has full supplementary bibliographies and notes for further reading: where appropriate, chronologies, maps, diagrams, and other illustrative material are also provided.

For a list of titles published in the series, please see the end of the book.

CAMBRIDGE
UNIVERSITY PRESS

University Printing House, Cambridge CB2 8BS, United Kingdom

Cambridge University Press is part of the University of Cambridge.

It furthers the University's mission by disseminating knowledge in the pursuit of education, learning and research at the highest international levels of excellence.

First published 2008
10th printing 2018

Printed in the United Kingdom by Clays, St Ives plc

A catalog record for this publication is available from the British Library.

Library of Congress Cataloging in Publication Data

Wiesner-Hanks, Merry E., 1952–
Women and gender in early modern Europe / Merry E.
Wiesner-Hanks. – 3rd ed.
  p.   cm. – (New approaches to European history)
Includes bibliographical references and index.
ISBN 978-0-521-87372-7 (hardback) – ISBN 978-0-521-69544-2 (pbk.)
1. Women – Europe – History.   I. Title.   II. Series.
HQ1587.W54   2008
305.4094′0903 – dc22   2007039502

ISBN   978-0-521-87372-7 Hardback
ISBN   978-0-521-69544-2 Paperback

Women and Gender in Early Modern Europe

Third Edition

Merry E. Wiesner-Hanks

University of Wisconsin – Milwaukee

CAMBRIDGE
UNIVERSITY PRESS

University Printing House, Cambridge CB2 8BS, United Kingdom

Cambridge University Press is part of the University of Cambridge.

It furthers the University's mission by disseminating knowledge in the pursuit of education, learning and research at the highest international levels of excellence.

First published 2008
10th printing 2018

Printed in the United Kingdom by Clays, St Ives plc

A catalog record for this publication is available from the British Library.

Library of Congress Cataloging in Publication Data

Wiesner-Hanks, Merry E., 1952–
Women and gender in early modern Europe / Merry E.
Wiesner-Hanks. – 3rd ed.
 p. cm. – (New approaches to European history)
Includes bibliographical references and index.
ISBN 978-0-521-87372-7 (hardback) – ISBN 978-0-521-69544-2 (pbk.)
1. Women – Europe – History. I. Title. II. Series.
HQ1587.W54 2008
305.4094'0903 – dc22   2007039502

ISBN   978-0-521-87372-7 Hardback
ISBN   978-0-521-69544-2 Paperback

NEW APPROACHES TO EUROPEAN HISTORY

Series editors

WILLIAM BEIK *Emory University*
T. C. W. BLANNING *Sidney Sussex College, Cambridge*
BRENDAN SIMMS *Peterhouse, Cambridge*

New Approaches to European History is an important textbook series, which provides concise but authoritative surveys of major themes and problems in European history since the Renaissance. Written at a level and length accessible to advanced school students and undergraduates, each book in the series addresses topics or themes that students of European history encounter daily: the series embraces both some of the more "'traditional"' subjects of study and those cultural and social issues to which increasing numbers of school and college courses are devoted. A particular effort is made to consider the wider international implications of the subject under scrutiny.

To aid the student reader, scholarly apparatus and annotation is light, but each work has full supplementary bibliographies and notes for further reading: where appropriate, chronologies, maps, diagrams, and other illustrative material are also provided.

For a list of titles published in the series, please see the end of the book.

For Kai and Tyr

Contents

List of Illustrations

Illustrations

Map

Acknowledgments

A study like this that attempts to survey the entire life experience of half the European population from Spain to Scandinavia over 300 years would not be possible without the kind assistance of a huge number of people and the financial support of foundations and institutions. On the latter, I first thank the Regents of the University of Wisconsin, from whom I received a fellowship at the Institute for Research in the Humanities at the University of Wisconsin – Madison, which allowed me a year off from teaching to write the first edition of this book and subsequent sabbaticals to work on several other books whose ideas shaped the second and third editions. Much of the information from Germany comes from my own research in libraries and archives there over the years, which was supported by grants from the Fulbright Foundation, the Deutsche Akademische Austauschdienst, and the American Council of Learned Societies. My familiarity with women's writings in many languages was enhanced by a summer at the Center for Renaissance Studies at the Newberry Library, for which I thank the Exxon Foundation. My first venture into gender history on a global scale was supported by a fellowship from the John Simon Guggenheim Foundation.

My intellectual debts are much more difficult to acknowledge adequately. Women's history has always prided itself on sisterly camaraderie and the sharing of ideas, and my own experience over the years has certainly borne this out. In the first and even second editions of this book, I tried to thank everyone by name who provided me with information and suggestions or with whom I've discussed the ideas that emerge here, but that is now impossible, as the list would go on for pages. I would still like to acknowledge the many people who willingly read and commented on drafts of chapters for the various editions: Diana Robin, Barbara Duden, Jeffrey Merrick, Jens-Christian Johansen, Carole Shammas, Grethe Jacobsen, Suzanne Desan, Tom Broman, Susan Karant-Nunn, Jane Bowers, and David Lindbergh. I also thank a few people whose scholarship and friendship have been particularly important over the years: Darlene Abreu-Ferreira, Barbara Andaya, Judith Bennett,

xiii

Elizabeth Cohen, Natalie Zemon Davis, Katherine French, Grethe Jacobsen, Deirdre Keenan, Gwynne Kennedy, Susan Karant-Nunn, Carole Levin, JoAnn McNamara, Jeffrey Merrick, Allyson Poska, Diana Robin, Lyndal Roper, Anne Schutte, Hilda Smith, Ulrike Strasser, Susan Stuard, Gerhild Scholz Williams, and Heide Wunder.

My inability to acknowledge everyone results from what has happened with scholarship in the field. When I first began to study women in early modern Europe, I could read everything that had been published in the field in a couple of months. Now my bookshelves groan and my file cabinets burst with a spectacular array of research, and there is an entire book series (Women and Gender in the Early Modern World) and a specialized journal (*Early Modern Women*). Even surveying this research is difficult, and for this I relied on the assistance of my wonderful graduate student, Bri Smith. The extended and thorough bibliographies that are the results of her work can best be seen on the Web site that accompanies this book. As always, none of this work would have been possible without the support of my husband Neil and my sons Kai and Tyr. I dedicated my first book to my grandmothers in sisterhood and dedicate this one to my sons, in the hope that the world they shape will be one where gender will make less of a difference, where cats will be cats.

Introduction

Both man and woman of three parts consist, Which Paul doth bodie,
soule, and spirit call . . .

> Rachel Speght, *Mortalities Memorandum with a Dreame Prefixed* (London,
> by Edward Griffin for Jacob Bloome, 1621), 11. 127–8

Nothing more resembles a tomcat on a windowsill than a female cat.

> Marie le Jars de Gournay, *L'Égalitédes hommes et des femmes*
> (A la Reyne, 1622)

Since the 1970s, there has been an explosion of studies in women's history. Historians have searched for new sources that reveal the historical
experience of women and have used traditional sources in innovative
ways. They analyze the distinctive experiences of individuals and groups
and relate these histories to political, ideological, and economic developments.

Interest in women's history has resulted from several academic and
political movements. Beginning in the 1930s, some historians turned
their attention from the traditional subjects of historical inquiry such as
public political developments, diplomatic changes, military events, and
major intellectual movements to investigating the lives of more ordinary
people – what is usually termed "social history." Social history attracted
more people in the 1960s, as historians and activists used historical investigation of past incidents of racial, class, or religious oppression in support
of demands for change in present institutions and power structures.

The political movements of the 1960s also reinvigorated the feminist
movement as women involved in civil rights and antiwar causes discovered
that even their most revolutionary male colleagues did not treat them as
equals or consider their ideas or contributions as valuable as those of
men. The feminist movement that began in the 1960s – often termed the
"second wave" to set it apart from the "first wave" of feminism that began
in the nineteenth century – included a wide range of political beliefs, with
various groups working for a broad spectrum of goals, one of which was
to understand more about the lives of women in the past. This paralleled

1

a similar rise of interest in women's history that accompanied the first wave of feminism.

Students in history programs in North America and western Europe in the late 1960s and early 1970s, most (although not all) of them women, began to focus on women, asserting that any investigation of past oppression or power relationships had to include information on both sexes. Initially, these studies were often met with derision or skepticism, not only by more traditional historians who regarded women's history as a fad but also by some social historians, who were unwilling to see gender along with race and class as a key determinant of human experience. This criticism did not quell interest in women's history and may in fact have stimulated it; many women who were active in radical or reformist political movements were angered by claims that their own history was trivial, marginal, or "too political." By the late 1970s, hundreds of colleges and universities in the United States and Canada offered courses in women's history, and many had separate programs in women's history or women's studies. Universities in Britain, Australia, the Netherlands, and the Scandinavian countries added courses and programs a bit more slowly, and other developed countries were slower still. (Universities and researchers in developing countries have far fewer resources, which hampers all historical research and limits opportunities for any new direction.) Women in some countries in the early twenty-first century still report that investigating the history of women can get them pegged as less than serious and be detrimental to their future careers as historians. Thus, an inordinate amount of the work in women's history, including that which focuses on the continent of Europe and many other parts of the world, has been done by English-speaking historians, although this is changing.

Women's history therefore began in some ways as a subfield of social history, but it has widened to include investigations of intellectual, political, economic, and even military and diplomatic history. Historians of women have demonstrated that there is really no historical change that does not affect the lives of women in some way, although often differently from how it affects the lives of men of the same class or social group. Women's historians often began by fitting women into familiar historical categories – nations, historical periods, social classes, religious allegiance – and then realized that this approach, sarcastically labeled "add women and stir," was unsatisfying. Focusing on women often disrupted the familiar categories and forced a rethinking of the way that history was organized and structured. The European Renaissance and Enlightenment lost some of their luster once women were included, as did the democracy of ancient Athens or Jacksonian America.

Gender History

This disruption of well-known categories and paradigms ultimately included the topic that had long been considered the proper focus of all history – man. Viewing the male experience as universal had not only hidden women's history, it had also prevented analyzing men's experiences as those of men. The very words used to describe individuals – "artist" and "woman artist," for example, or "scientist" and "woman scientist" – encouraged one to think about how being female affected Georgia O'Keefe or Marie Curie while overlooking the ways that being male shaped the experiences of Michelangelo or Picasso or Isaac Newton. Historians familiar with studying women increasingly began to discuss the ways in which systems of sexual differentiation affected both women and men and, by the early 1980s, to use the word "gender" to describe these systems. At that point, they differentiated primarily between "sex," by which they meant physical, morphological, and anatomical differences (what are often called "biological differences"), and "gender," by which they meant a culturally constructed and historically changing system of differences. Most of the studies with "gender" in the title still focused on women – and women's history continued as its own field – but some looked equally at both sexes or concentrated on the male experience, calling their work "men's history" or "men's studies."

Historians interested in this new perspective asserted that gender was an appropriate category of analysis when looking at *all* historical developments, not simply those involving women or the family. *Every* political, intellectual, religious, economic, social, and even military change had an impact on the actions and roles of men and women, and, conversely, a culture's gender structures influenced every other structure or development. People's notions of gender shaped not only the way they thought about men and women but also about their society in general. As the historian Joan Scott put it, "gender is a primary way of signifying relationships of power." Thus, hierarchies in other realms of life were often expressed in terms of gender, with dominant individuals or groups described in masculine terms and dependent ones in feminine. These ideas in turn affected the way people acted, although explicit and symbolic ideas of gender could also conflict with the way men and women chose or were forced to operate in the world.

Along with a focus on the gendered nature of both women's and men's experiences, some historians turned their attention more fully in the 1980s to the history of sexuality. Just as interest in women's history has been part of feminist political movements, interest in the history of sexuality has been part of the gay liberation movement that began in the

1970s. The gay liberation movement encouraged the study of homosexuality in the past and present and the development of gay and lesbian studies programs, and it also made both public and academic discussions of sexual matters more acceptable. Historians have attempted to trace the history of men's and women's sexual experiences in the past and, as in women's history, to find new sources that will allow fuller understanding. The history of sexuality has contributed to a new interest in the history of the body, with historians investigating how cultural understandings of the body shaped people's experiences of their own bodies and also studying the ways in which religious, medical, and political authorities exerted control over those bodies.

Just at the point that historians and their students were gradually beginning to see the distinction between sex and gender (and an increasing number accepting the importance of gender as a category of analysis), that distinction became contested. Not only were there great debates about where the line should be drawn – were women "biologically" more peaceful and men "biologically" more skillful at math, or were such tendencies the result solely of their upbringing? – but some scholars wondered whether social gender and biological sex are so interrelated that any distinction between the two is meaningless. For example, although most people are categorized "male" or "female" at birth when someone looks at their external genitalia, some have more ambiguous sex organs. The gender polarity man/woman has been so strong, however, that such persons were usually simply assigned to the sex they most closely resembled. Since the nineteenth century, this assignment has been reinforced by surgical procedures modifying or removing the inappropriate body parts, generally shortly after birth. Thus, cultural norms about gender (that everyone *should* be a man or a woman) determine sex in such cases, rather than the other way around.

The arbitrary nature of gender has also been challenged by transsexual and transgender individuals. In the 1950s, sex-change operations became available for people whose external genitalia and even chromosomal and hormonal patterns marked them as male or female but who mentally understood themselves to be the other. Transsexual surgery could make the body fit more closely with the mind, but it also led to challenging questions: At what point in this process does a "man" become a "woman," or vice versa? With the loss or acquisition of a penis? Breasts? From the beginning? In the 1980s, such questions began to be made even more complex by individuals who described themselves as "transgendered," that is, as neither male nor female or both male and female. Should such individuals be allowed in spaces designated "women only" or "men only"? Should they have to choose between them, or should there be more than two choices? Anthropologists point out that many of the world's cultures have a third or even a fourth gender, that is, people understood to be neither men nor women, who often have (or had) specialized religious or ceremonial roles. The contemporary trans- movement points to these examples and highlights limitations in any dichotomous system of gender *or* sex, instead favoring a continuum.

Historians of women also contributed to debates about the distinction between gender and sex. They put increasing emphasis on differences among women, noting that women's experiences differed because of class, race, nationality, ethnicity, religion, and other factors, and they varied over time. Because of these differences, some wondered, did it make sense to talk about "women" at all? If, for example, women were thought to be delicate guardians of the home, as was true in the nineteenth-century United States, then were black women, who worked in fields alongside men, really "women"? If women were thought to be inferior and irrational (as was true in sixteenth-century Europe, as we see in Chapter 1), then was Queen Elizabeth of England a "woman"? Was "woman" a valid category, the meaning of which is self-evident and unchanging over time, or is arguing for a biological base for gender difference naïve "essentialism"? These historians noted that not only in the present is gender "performative," that is, a role that can be taken on or changed at will, but it was so at many points in the past, as individuals "did gender" and conformed to or challenged gender roles. Thus, it is misguided to think that we are studying women (or men, for that matter) as a sex, they argued, for the only thing that is in the historical record is gender.

All of these doubts came together at a time when many historians were changing their basic understanding of the methods and function of history. Historians have long recognized that documents and other types of evidence are produced by particular individuals with particular interests and biases that consciously and unconsciously shape their content. Most historians thus attempted to keep the limitations of their sources in mind as they reconstructed events and tried to determine causation, although sometimes these got lost in the narrative. During the 1980s, some historians began to assert that because historical sources always present a biased and partial picture, we can never fully determine what happened or why; to try to do so is foolish or misguided. What historians should do instead is to analyze the written and visuals materials of the past – what is often termed "discourse" – to determine the way various things are "represented" in them and their possible meanings. This heightened interest in discourse among historians, usually labeled the "linguistic/cultural turn," drew on the ideas of literary and linguistic theory – often loosely termed "deconstruction" or "poststructuralism" – about the power of language. Language is so powerful, argued some theorists, that it determines, rather than simply describes, our understanding of the world; knowledge is passed down through language, and knowledge is power.

This emphasis on the relationship of knowledge to power, and on the power of language, made poststructuralism attractive to feminist scholars in many disciplines, who themselves already emphasized the ways language and other structures of knowledge excluded women. The French philosopher Michel Foucault's insight that power comes from everywhere fit with feminist recognition that misogyny and other forces that limited women's lives could be found in many places: in fashion magazines, fairy tales, and jokes told at work, as well as overt job discrimination and domestic violence. Historians of gender were thus prominent exponents of the linguistic turn, and many analyzed representations of women, men, the body, sexual actions, and related topics within different types of discourses.

The linguistic/cultural turn – which happened in other fields along with history – elicited harsh responses from other historians, however, including many who focused on women and gender. They asserted that it denied women the ability to shape their world – what is usually termed "agency" – in both past and present by positing unchangeable linguistic structures. Wasn't it ironic, they noted, that just as women were learning they *had* a history and asserting they were *part* of history, "history" became just a text? They wondered whether the ideas that gender – and perhaps even "women" – were simply historical constructs denied the very real oppression that many women in the past (and present) experienced. For a period, it looked as if this disagreement would lead proponents of discourse analysis to lay claim to "gender" and those who opposed it to avoid "gender" and stick with "women." Because women's history was clearly rooted in the women's rights movement of the 1970s, it also appeared more political than gender analysis, and programs and research projects sometimes opted to use "gender" to downplay this connection with feminism.

As we enter the twenty-first century, however, it appears that the division is less sharp. Historians using gender as a category of analysis do not focus solely on discourse but treat their sources as referring to something beyond the sources themselves – an author, an event, a physical body. Historians who were initially suspicious of the linguistic turn use a wider range of literary and artistic sources than did earlier women's history, thus paying more attention to discourse. The distinction between sex and gender has not been defined – indeed, it seems to get ever more murky – but "gender" has become the accepted replacement for "sex" in many common phrases – "gender roles," "gender distinctions," and so on. Scholars describe the field as "women's and gender history" – occasionally even using the acronym WGH – thus highlighting the link between them rather than the differences.

New theoretical perspectives are adding additional complexity and bringing in still more questions. One of these is queer theory, a field that began in the 1990s as in some ways a combination of gay and lesbian studies and poststructuralism. Like women's history, gay and lesbian history challenged the assumption that sexual attitudes and practices were "natural" and unchanging. Queer theory built on these challenges and on the doubts about the distinction between sex and gender to highlight the artificial and constructed nature of all oppositional categories: men/women, homosexual/heterosexual, black/white. Some theorists celebrate all efforts at blurring or bending categories, viewing "identity" – or what in literary and cultural studies is often termed "subjectivity" – as both false and oppressive. Others have doubts about this, wondering whether one can work to end discrimination against homosexuals, women, African Americans or any other group if one denies that the group has an essential identity, something that makes its members clearly homosexual or women or African American. (A similar debate can be found within the contemporary trans- movement, with some groups arguing that gender is an "essential" aspect of identity and others that it is not or should not be.)

Related questions about identity, subjectivity, and the cultural construction of difference have also emerged from postcolonial theory and critical race theory. Postcolonial history and theory has been particularly associated with South Asian scholars and the book series Subaltern Studies and initially focused on people who have been subordinated by virtue of their race, class, culture, or language. Critical race theory developed in the 1980s as an outgrowth (and critique) of the civil rights movement combined with ideas derived from critical legal studies, a radical group of legal scholars who argued that supposedly neutral legal concepts such as the individual or meritocracy actually masked power relationships. Both of these theoretical schools point out that racial, ethnic, and other hierarchies are deeply rooted social and cultural principles, not simply aberrations that can be remedied by legal or political change. They note that along with disenfranchising certain groups, such hierarchies privilege certain groups, a phenomenon that is beginning to be analyzed under the rubric of critical white studies. (This is a pattern similar to the growth of men's studies, and there is also a parallel within queer theory that is beginning to analyze heterosexuality rather than simply take it as an unquestioned given.)

Queer theory, postcolonial studies, and critical race theory have all been criticized from both inside and outside for falling into the pattern set by traditional history, that is, regarding the male experience as normative and paying insufficient attention to gender differences. Scholars who have pointed this out have also noted that much feminist scholarship suffered from the opposite problem, taking the experiences of heterosexual white women as normative and paying too little attention to differences of race, class, nationality, ethnicity, or sexual orientation. They argue that the experiences of women of color must be recognized as distinctive and that no one axis of difference (men/women, black/white, rich/poor, gay/straight) should be viewed as sufficient. These criticisms led in the 1990s to theoretical perspectives that attempted to recognize multiple lines of difference, such as postcolonial feminism. Such scholarship has begun to influence many areas of gender studies, even those that do not deal explicitly with race or ethnicity. It appears this cross-fertilization will continue because issues of difference and identity are clearly key topics for historians in the ever-more-connected twenty-first-century world.

Early Modern History

The meaning of the first half of this book's title, "women and gender," is thus not as self-evident as it probably seemed at first glance, and the second half, "early modern Europe," has also been seen as problematic. The term "early modern" was developed by historians seeking to refine an intellectual model first devised during this very period, which saw European history as divided into three parts: ancient (to the end of the Roman Empire in the West in the fifth century), medieval (from the fifth century to the fifteenth), and modern (from the fifteenth century to their own time). In this model, the break between the Middle Ages and the Modern Era was marked by the first voyage of Columbus (1492) and the beginning of the Protestant Reformation (1517), although some scholars, especially those who focused on Italy, set the break somewhat earlier with the Italian Renaissance. As the modern era grew longer and longer, historians began to divide it into "early modern" – from the Renaissance or Columbus to the French Revolution in 1789 – and what we might call "truly modern" – from the French Revolution to whenever they happened to be writing.

As with any intellectual model, the longer this tripartite division was used, the more problematic it seemed. The voyages of Columbus may have marked the beginning of European exploration and colonization, but there was plenty of earlier contact between Europeans and other cultures, and Columbus himself was motivated more by religious zeal – generally regarded as "medieval" – than by a "modern" desire to explore the un-known. The Protestant Reformation did bring a major break in Western Christianity, but Martin Luther was seeking to reform the church, not split it, just like medieval reformers, of which there were many. Other developments traditionally regarded as marks of modernity, such as the expansion of capitalism, the growth of the nation-state, or increasing interest in science and technology, were also brought into question as scholars found both earlier precedents and evidence that these changes were slow in coming. Thus, in many aspects of life, continuities out-weighed change. More philosophical issues also emerged: What exactly do we mean by "modernity"? Will it ever end? Has it ended? What comes afterward? The thinkers who first thought of themselves as "modern" saw modernity as positive – and "medieval" as negative – but is modernity necessarily a good thing?

If "early modern" is not as clear as it seems, what about the other part of the title, "Europe"? What is "Europe"? The answer most of us learned in school – one of the world's seven continents – can easily be rejected simply by looking at a globe. If a continent is a "large land mass surrounded by water" (which we also learned in school), then surely the correct designation for what is conventionally called "Europe" is the western part of the continent of Eurasia. If we look very closely at the globe, in fact, Europe is a small northwestern part of the huge continent of Afroeurasia, a term increasingly used by geographers and world historians for what is the world's largest land mass.

The idea of "Europe" derived more from culture than geography. The word "Europe" was first used by Greek writers in the seventh century B.C.E. to designate their side of the Mediterranean (the sea whose name means "middle of the world," which it was to the ancient Greeks) from the other side, "Asia," which to the Greeks originally included Africa. They derived the word from the myth of Europa, the daughter of Agenor, a Phoenician king. In the myth, Europa was awakened by a dream in which two continents that had taken the shape of women argued over who should possess her: Asia said she had given birth to her and so owned her, but the other as-yet-unnamed continent asserted that Zeus would give Europa to her. Right on cue, Zeus fell in love with the beautiful Europa as she gathered flowers with her friends and carried her away after changing into a bull. He took her to Crete, where she bore him a number of sons, including two who later became judges of the dead, and gave her name to the continent. In a tamer version of the myth, told by the ancient Greek historian Herodotus and repeated by later Christian writers, merchants from Crete carried Europa away in a ship shaped like a bull to marry their king. Herodotus notes that the (Asian) Trojans later abducted Helen, wife of the Greek king Menelaus – an event that led to the Trojan War – in part to avenge Europa. Like all mythology, either version of this story raises questions of interpretation: Crete is actually located between Asia and Europe; does this represent Greek ambivalence about Europe's separation from Asia? Is Zeus's abduction (some scholars use the word "rape") of Europa a demonstration and justification of men's rights over women and mothers' lack of rights to their own children, both of which were law in ancient Athens? Why were Zeus's children from this affair given such powers, rather than his children by his wife, Hera? And where was Hera during all this, anyway? If Europa was snatched away by merchants rather than Zeus, why didn't her father come after her?

Whatever we may think of this myth, it is clear that the idea of "Europe" came from Greeks asserting their distinction from people who lived on the other side of the Aegean or Mediterranean. In this it is much like the notion of "modern," that is, a term used consciously by people to differentiate themselves from others, to create a boundary between "us" and "them." But what are Europe's boundaries? Is Iceland part of Europe? Does it become part of Europe once the Vikings get there? Does Greenland? Where is the eastern boundary of Europe? That boundary is often set at the Ural Mountains and the Ural River, which flows into the Caspian Sea, but most discussions of "European" history focus only on the western part of this area. So, are some parts of Europe more European than others?

This questioning of terminology may seem both paralyzing and pedantic – don't we all basically know what "modern" and "Europe" mean, in the same way that we know what "women" means? In fact, just as historians who have problematized "women" and "gender" still use the words, historians who note the issues surrounding "early modern Europe" continue to use the term. Being conscious about terminology can lead to important insights, however – many in the realm of women's and gender history. As we have just seen, exploring the roots of the word "Europe" highlights the gendered nature of what seems at first to be an objective geographical designation. Similarly, discussions of the implications of "modern" have suggested that its meaning was different for men and women and that gender was a key element of modernity, however it is defined.

Early Modern Women's and Gender History

Insights into women's and gender history have come from new theoretical perspectives, but, more important, from a huge amount of basic research. Europe in the early modern period has been an important area of research in women's and gender history since it began. Women's history of this era, as of most eras, began by asking what women contributed to what were already judged to be the key developments, in a search for what Natalie Davis has termed "women worthies." Who were the great women artists/musicians/scientists/rulers/religious figures? How did women's work serve capitalist expansion? What was women's role in the Reformation? In political movements such as the English Civil War or other seventeenth-century revolts? Along with this, historians investigated what effects the developments of the early modern period had on women, a line of questioning that has resulted in the rethinking of several major historical issues. Joan Kelly, for example, began with a simple question, "Did women have a Renaissance?" Her answer of "No, at least not during the Renaissance" has not only led to more than three decades of intensive historical and literary research, as people have attempted to confirm, refute, modify, or nuance her answer, but has also contributed to the broader questioning of the whole notion of historical periodization. If a particular development had little or, indeed, a negative effect on women, can we still call a period a "golden age," a "Renaissance," or an "Enlightenment"? Can we continue to view the seventeenth century, during which hundreds or perhaps thousands of women were burned as witches on the European continent, as the period of "the spread of rational thought"? Kelly's questioning of the term "Renaissance" for women's history has been joined by doubts about the term "early modern." Judith Bennett, among others, challenges "the assumption of a dramatic change in women's lives between 1300 and 1700" and asserts that historians must pay attention to continuities as well with changes.

Both the original lines of questioning in women's history for this period – women's role in general historical developments and the effects of these developments on women – continue, particularly for parts of Europe or groups of women about which we have as yet little information: eastern Europe, Jewish women, peasant women in most parts of Europe. They have been augmented by quite different types of questions, as historians realized the limitations of the "add women and stir" approach. Such questions often center on women's physical experiences – menstruation, pregnancy, motherhood – and the ways in which women gave meaning to these experiences, and on private or domestic matters, such as friendship networks, family devotional practices, or unpaid household labor. Because so little of this was documented in public sources during the early modern period, this research has required a great amount of archival digging and the use of literary and artistic sources.

This emphasis on women's private and domestic experiences has been challenged by some historians, who warn of the dangers of equating women's history with the history of the family or of accepting without comment a division between public and private in which women are relegated to the private sphere. They see a primary task of early modern historians as the investigation of how divisions between what was considered "public" and what was considered "private" were developed and contested. Some scholars hold that this period is one of the exclusion of women from many areas of public life and power at the very time larger groups of men were given access, although others emphasize that this exclusion was more theoretical than real. Linked to issues of public/private are questions about the symbolic role of gender, that is, how qualities judged masculine and feminine are differently valued and then used in discussions that do not explicitly relate to men and women but that still reinforce women's secondary status. For example, Martin Luther's labeling of the pope as the "Whore of Babylon" has previously been viewed as an expression of his negative attitude about the papacy, and James I of England's description of himself as the "father of his country" as an expression of his ideas about his power vis-à-vis his subjects. These phrases are now also recognized as expressions of attitudes about women and gender relations, for the fact that both men use gendered language was not accidental. These investigations of the real and symbolic relations between gender and power have usually not been based on new types of sources but have approached some of the most traditional types of historical sources – political treatises, public speeches by monarchs, state documents – with new questions.

All of these studies have resulted in three somewhat contradictory conclusions. First: the historical experience of early modern women was much less uniform than we thought it was several decades ago. Women's experience differed according to categories that we had already set out based on male experience – social class, geographic location, rural or urban setting – but also categories that had previously not been taken into account – marital status, health, number of children. Historians are thus much less comfortable talking about the "status of women" in general without sharply qualifying exactly what type of women or in what type of sources; we can make conclusions about, for example, the legal status of women in theoretical treatises or the role of widows in a particular craft guild, but statements about the status of women rising or falling are too vague to have any meaning.

Second: the role of gender in determining the historical experiences of men and women varied over time and from group to group. For some people, such as the very poor, social class was probably more important than gender, although this "equality of misery" was certainly not much consolation to the women experiencing it. Women at the very top of the social scale sometimes had opportunities to exert great power and influence. For women in the middle, however, the early modern period may have been a time when gender became a more important determinant of experience than class, at least in people's perceptions of the world. At the same time, new contacts between peoples brought about primarily – although not only – by European voyages made race an increasingly important category, at least in the minds of Europeans looking at the rest of the world. Every one of these global interactions was gendered, and new scholarship is beginning to make clear how gender and race intersected to shape the intellectual, legal, and political structures within which people lived and gave meaning to their world.

Third: every question that has been asked and is being asked about the female experience must also be asked about the male. The research on masculinity described above demonstrates that gender roles were just as prescribed for men as they were for women, and history that ignores the effects of "private" factors such as marital status, sexuality, and friendships in men's lives is incomplete. The history of masculinity is a booming field, although it has been criticized both by traditional historians who see it as trivializing "great men and their ideas" and by some women's historians who view it as simply a way to refocus historical concern back where it has always been – on men. Many historians, however, accept the idea that the status of women *and* men was at once more varied and more shaped by their gender than most historians would have concluded thirty years ago.

I have attempted in this study to keep these conclusions in mind while providing an overview of what we have discovered about women's lives and the role of gender in early modern European society. The book begins with a chapter that examines ideas about women and the laws that resulted from the notions of proper gender roles held by the dominant group in early modern society – educated men. This does not imply that women's experience was completely determined by intellectual and legal constructs, as the rest of the book makes clear, but simply the fact that male intellectual structures and institutions formed the most important frameworks for thought and action in early modern society. It also reflects the way the field of women's history has developed because many of the early studies of women actually discussed male opinions and views, although sometimes the authors did not explicitly recognize this.

After the initial chapter, the book is divided into three sections that correspond to the three parts of the self traditional in Western philosophy – body, mind, and spirit. This tripartite division is particularly appropriate when studying women, who were often regarded as dominated by one part to the exclusion of the other two: married women and prostitutes by their bodies; learned women and artists by their minds; nuns and witches by their spirits. Perhaps because of this, early modern women who reflected on the condition of women in general such as Rachel Speght, the seventeenth-century English poet quoted earlier, emphasized that men were not the only ones with complex and multifaceted selves. Each of these three sections has two chapters: the section on the body a chapter on sexuality and the female life cycle and one on women's economic role; that on the mind, a chapter on literacy and learning and one on women and the production of culture; that on the spirit, a chapter on religion and spirituality and one on witchcraft.

The book ends with another two-chapter section, one on gender and power and one on gender and colonialism. The chapter on gender and power examines the public political roles of women; the relations among ideas about femininity, masculinity, and social order; and the symbolic role of gender. It discusses early modern thinkers, female and male, who were conscious of gender as a social construct rather than a natural or God-given status. In the quotation above, for example, the French philosopher Marie le Jars de Gournay succinctly and humorously states the insight of modern anthropologists and historians that gender identification involves the suppression of similarities. The final chapter is one new to this third edition and reflects the growing sense that European history, like the "continent" of Europe itself, is intimately connected to the rest of the world. In the early modern era, the lives of European women were shaped by developments beyond Europe more than they had been earlier, and European notions and patterns of gender were spread throughout much of the world.

I hope that this book will not only provide you with information about the lives of early modern European women and men but also will allow you to discover how a historical field develops and lines of inquiry connect and influence each other, how old assumptions are revised, and how totally new areas become accepted topics for historical inquiry. This field continues to grow in both descriptive studies and analytical interpretations, so quickly that the bibliographies in the second edition were both enormous and already out of date when the book was published. For that reason, I have moved the long bibliographies to the Web site that accompanies this book and included only brief suggestions for further reading in the printed text. The Web site contains all of the references from the previous edition and full details on hundreds of new books and articles. Reflecting (and further expanding) the explosion of original source materials now available in published form and electronically, it also includes sources and links to other sources.

In addition to the new chapter on gender and colonialism, I have made changes in each of the chapters to reflect the newest scholarship.

These changes vary from minor to substantive, for research in some areas, such as sexuality, masculinity, and women's writings, has been extensive, whereas other areas have seen fewer new studies. In particular, information on eighteenth-century developments, such as the Enlightenment and the pietist movement in Christianity, has been expanded. Like the first and second editions, this is certainly not the final word but rather an introduction and progress report.

For Further Reading

There are several theoretical studies that underlie much of contemporary women's and gender history. These include Joan Kelly, "Did Women Have a Renaissance?" in Renate Bridenthal and Claudia Koonz, eds., *Becoming Visible: Women in European History* (Boston, Houghton-Mifflin, 1977), 137–64; and Joan Scott, "Gender: A Useful Category of Historical Analysis," *American Historical Review* 91/5 (1986), 1053–75 (and widely reprinted). The development of women's and gender history as a field has been examined in Judith Zinsser, *History and Feminism: A Glass Half Full* (New York, Twayne, 1992); and Laura Lee Downs, *Writing Gender History* (London, Hodder/Arnold, 2004). Karen Offen, Ruth Roach Pierson, and Jane Rendell (eds.), *Writing Women's History: International Perspectives* (Bloomington, Indiana University Press, 1990) is an excellent survey of trends in women's history around the world.

The best place to begin in considering the socially constructed nature of gender is still Suzanne J. Kessler and Wendy McKenna, *Gender: An Ethnometholodogical Approach* (New York, Wiley, 1978). Judith Butler's works, especially *Gender Trouble: Feminism and the Subversion of Identity* (New York, Routledge, 2nd ed., 2000), are central to thinking about sex and gender, although they can be challenging to read. Anne Fausto-Sterling's *Sexing the Body: Gender Politics and the Construction of Sexuality* (New York, Basic Books, 2000) is equally important and more approachable. Doubts about the value of "women" as an analytical category were conveyed most forcefully in Denise Riley, *"Am I That Name?" Feminism and the Category of 'Women' in History* (Minneapolis, University of Minnesota Press, 1988), although they have primarily been associated with the work of Joan Scott, such as *Gender and the Politics of History* (New York, Columbia University Press, 1988). Elizabeth A. Clark, *History, Theory, Text: Historians and the Linguistic Turn* (Cambridge, MA, Harvard University Press, 2004), offers a broad survey of debates about history and theory.

For queer theory, a good place to begin is the aptly titled book by Annamarie Jagose, *Queer Theory: An Introduction* (Washington Square, NY, New York University Press, 1996). The best introduction to critical race feminism is Adrien Katherine Wing (ed.), *Critical Race Feminism: A Reader* (New York, New York University Press, 1997). Anne McClintock, Aamir Mufti, and Ella Shoalt (eds.), *Dangerous Liaisons: Gender, Nation and Post-colonial Perspectives* (Minneapolis, University of Minnesota Press, 1997) brings together feminist and postcolonial theory. For further discussion and longer bibliographies of these issues, see my *Gender in History* (Oxford, Blackwell, 2001).

For perspectives on "early modern" as a conceptual category, including its relevance for women and gender, see Judith M. Bennett, *History Matters: Patriarchy and the Challenge of Feminism* (Philadelphia, University of Pennsylvania Press, 2006), and Charles H. Parker and Jerry H. Bentley, (eds.), *Between the Middle Ages and Modernity: Individual and Community in the Early Modern World* (Ranham, MD, Rowman and Littlefield, 2007). A special twentieth-anniversary issue of *Gender and History* (20:1, 2008) focuses on periodization in women's and gender history more broadly.

The Web site for this chapter includes, among other materials, references to many of the monographs and collections of articles and studies that focus on women and gender in one country or in Europe as a whole.

For more suggestions and links, see the companion Web site www.cambridge.org/womenandgender.

1   Ideas and Laws Regarding Women

A woman, properly speaking, is not a human being.

> Jacques Cujas, *Observationes et emendationes*, 6.21 in *Opera omnia*
> (Lyons 1606), 4, 1484

Women then being the last of creatures, the end, complement and consummation of all the works of God, what Ignorance is there so stupid, or what Impudence can there be so effronted, as to deny her a Prerogative above all other Creatures, without whom the World itself had been imperfect.

> Cornelius Agrippa von Nettesheim, *De nobilitate et praecellentia sexus foeminei*
> (1529) in *Opera* (2 vols. Lyon, 1600?, reprint Hildesheim: Olms, 1970),
> vol. 2; 533

Women are created for no other purpose than to serve men and be their helpers. If women grow weary or even die while bearing children, that doesn't harm anything. Let them bear children to death; they are created for that.

> Martin Luther, *Sämmtliche Werke* (Erlangen and Frankfurt, 1826–57),
> vol. 20; 84

There is nothing better on earth than a woman's love.

> Martin Luther, *Sämmtliche Werke* (Erlangen and Frankfurt, 1826–57),
> vol. 61; 212

Ideas about women, particularly the ideas of educated men, are in many ways the easiest thing to investigate when analyzing the experience of women in any culture. Educated men have been thinking and writing about women since the beginning of recorded history, trying to determine what makes them different from men and creating ideals for female behavior and appearance. Their ideas emerge in works of all types – religious literature, scientific treatises, plays, poetry, philosophical discussions – which have been preserved and read by subsequent generations. This not only makes them the most accessible source regarding women for modern historians, it also means that these ideas influenced all later periods. The works that contain them, especially religious, scientific, and philosophical writings, came to be considered authoritative and unquestionable, so that the ideas of educated men spread to the vast majority of women and men who could not record their own ideas and served as the basis for law codes that attempted to regulate behavior. In fact, these ideas and opinions were often no longer recognized as such but were regarded as religious truth or scientific fact, particularly when the laws that resulted from them led women to act in ways that conformed with male notions.

Before we explore the reality of women's lives in the early modern period, then, we must survey commonly held notions about women, many of which were inherited from classical and medieval writers and from Jewish and Christian religious thinkers. Although they disagreed about many other things, the vast majority of religious and secular writers before 1500 regarded women as clearly inferior to men and provided subsequent generations with countless examples of women's negative qualities. The fact that so many revered authorities agreed about "woman's nature" indicated to most people that they must be right. Only a few individuals recognized that the largely negative view of women in Western culture resulted from the fact that almost all written records came from male authors and that a very different picture might have emerged had women also left records of their thoughts. Chaucer's fictional character, the Wife of Bath, states this clearly in the *Canterbury Tales*:

> My God, had women written histories
> Like cloistered scholars in oratories
> They'd have set down more of men's wickedness
> Than all the sons of Adam could redress.[1]

Her insight was not widely shared.

Ideas changed somewhat from 1500 to 1750 with the intellectual changes of the Renaissance, the religious reformations of the sixteenth century, and the development of science in the seventeenth century, when authorities of all types began to be questioned. Dissident voices, both female and male, expressing a more positive view of women began to be a bit louder, but negative views of women were also voiced more loudly, now based on new types of authority such as the natural sciences or comparisons of legal systems rather than on the views of Aristotle or the Bible. As we shall see, many of the legal changes of the period actually restricted, rather than increased, the ability of women to act independently.

---

[1] Chaucer, *Canterbury Tales*, trans. David Wright (London, Oxford University Press, 1985), p. 236.

Inherited Traditions

Christianity was the most important source of ideas about women for early modern Europeans, and Christianity had, in turn, inherited many of its ideas from Judaism. There are two somewhat conflicting accounts of creation in Genesis, the first book of both Hebrew Scripture and the Christian Bible. In the first, God creates women and men at the same time; and in the second, a woman, Eve, is created out of the rib of the first man, Adam, after God decides Adam needs a mate. This account is the one that comes to be retold and portrayed visually much more often, so that medieval and early modern Europeans were much more familiar with it. It is also the one that goes on to describe the first human sin, in which Eve is tempted by a serpent to disobey God to gain knowledge and then tempts Adam; their disobedience gets them expelled from the Garden of Eden and comes to be described in Christian doctrine as the "fall of man" or "the original sin." Most later Jewish and Christian commentators thus chose to view Eve, and by extension all women, as the source of evil and sin in the world, although there were also a few who held Adam equally responsible, and a very few who viewed him as *more* responsible because he was a man and should have been better able to withstand the temptation. (Their reasoning thus also expresses negative opinions of the relative merits of men and women.)

Jewish traditions and commentaries contained in Hebrew Scripture and later works continued to view women in a largely negative light. Women were totally excluded from the priesthood and from many religious duties and were regarded as ritually impure for about half of each month because of menstruation. They were also viewed as unclean after giving birth, for forty days after the birth of a boy and eighty after the birth of a girl. They were responsible for some religious rituals within the household, but other parts of domestic religious life were carried out by men, so that no aspect of religious life was strictly female. The authors of Hebrew Scripture had a clear idea of the ideal woman; she was the mother of many children, up working before sunrise to provide food and clothing for her household, and made no objections when her husband brought home concubines or a second wife. In short, she was totally obedient and deferential. She was not passive, for Hebrew Scripture recounts the exploits of many women who carried out heroic actions to defend their households or Israelite society, but when the emergency had passed, these women, such as Judith or Jael, returned willingly to their quiet domestic lives. It is perhaps no wonder that by the first century A.D. Jewish men included a special thank you to God "who has not made me a woman" in their regular morning prayers. Along with Eve, Hebrew Scripture also describes other women whose actions helped create a negative stereotype for women: Delilah, whose sexuality could tempt even the strongest man; Rebekah, whose love for one of her sons led her to deceive her husband; Lot's wife (her name is not recorded), who was changed into a pillar of salt for disobeying God and her husband.

Christian ideas about women built on both the positive and the negative in Jewish tradition. Jesus himself spoke frequently to women and included them in his followers, sometimes to the embarrassment of his male associates. He preached that men and women were equally capable of achieving life after death and that women as well as men should not let their domestic responsibilities come before their spiritual well-being. Many of his parables use women as positive examples or relate things that would have more meaning for women, leading some contemporary scholars to view Jesus as a feminist. The untraditional nature of Jesus' ideas was quickly downplayed by many of his followers shortly after his death, however. The role of the twelve disciples, all of whom were male, was stressed in the books that became the Christian New Testament, and the role of his female followers, such as Mary Magdalene, was downplayed. Paul, whose letters form about half of the books of the New Testament and who in many ways transformed Jesus' teachings into a systematic set of beliefs, had a more ambivalent view about women's place; at one point, he notes that there should be no distinction on account of gender in the Christian community but says elsewhere that women should be silent in churches, although this latter statement is now held to have been written by another author and simply attributed to Paul.

Christianity gained followers quickly, and because there was no central authority in the first centuries, an enormous range of ideas and practices developed. Women were active in the early church. Some acted as missionaries or carried out priestly functions such as baptism. Although most converts married, some rejected marriage to live a life not bound by domestic concerns and to devote themselves to contemplation or to the charity that was an important aspect of Christianity from the beginning. A few men and women decided to blend marriage and virginity, living in what were termed "chaste" or "spiritual" marriages in which the spouses either rejected sexual activity from the start or else renounced it sometime during the course of the marriage.

Many of these experiments were eventually rejected by church leaders as they attempted to make Christian teachings appear less threatening to Roman authorities to gain still more followers and reduce persecution. Women were gradually excluded from church offices and priestly functions as the church became more hierarchical, using as its model Roman political structures that also excluded women from positions of authority. Chaste marriage was officially rejected, although popular accounts of saints continued to include such marriages. Virginity was accepted, however, and gradually came to be considered spiritually superior to marriage. Praise of virginity was often combined with denigration of women in the writings of the learned men whose ideas were most influential in the subsequent development of Christianity, however. These men, subsequently termed the Church Fathers, wrote harshly against women both to combat their own sexual urges and to restrict women's independent activities within the church. The second-century Church Father Tertullian, for example, linked all women with Eve, writing to women: "*You* are the Devil's gateway. *You* are the first deserter of the divine Law.... *You* destroyed so easily God's image, man. On account of *your* desert, that is death, even the Son of God had to die."[2] He praised women who chose a life of virginity but emphasized their dependence by terming them "brides of Christ" rather than the more active "virgins in the service of Christ" they chose to call themselves.

The most important early Christian philosopher, St. Augustine (354–430), asserted that the initial decision by Adam and Eve had ended human free will for all time and also created sexual desire; he saw as proof of this the fact that men cannot control the actions of their sexual organs by virtue of their will or reason alone. After Augustine, even sexuality within marriage was considered sinful by most church leaders, and both clergy and laymen were warned against the temptations of women more emphatically. Augustine also saw female subordination as intrinsic in God's original creation, for only men were fully created in the image of God, and women were intellectually, physically, and morally inferior. Augustine's contemporary, St. Jerome (ca. 347–419/20) largely agreed, although both he and his female patrons asserted that women could move up the spiritual hierarchy by choosing a life of virginity: "As long as woman is for birth and children, she is as different from man as body is from soul. But when she wishes to serve Christ more than the world, then she will cease to be a woman and will be called man."[3]

The Greek philosopher Aristotle was the most influential non-Christian source for ideas in many fields up to the seventeenth century, which had unfortunate effects for women. To Aristotle, women were

---

[2] Tertullian, *De Cultu Fem.* 1,1 quoted in Rosemary Radford Ruether, *Religion and Sexism: Images of Women in the Jewish and Christian Traditions* (New York, Simon and Schuster, 1974), p. 157.

[3] Saint Jerome, *Commentaries on the Letter to the Ephesians*, book 16, cited in Vern Bullough, *Sexual Variance in Society and History* (Chicago, University of Chicago Press, 1976), p. 365.

imperfect men, the result of something wrong with the conception that
created them – their parents were too young or too old, or too diverse in
age, or one of them was not healthy. Nature always aimed at perfection,
and Aristotle termed anything less than perfect "monstrous"; a woman
was thus "a deformity, but one which occurs in the ordinary course of
nature."[4] Aristotle was not sure exactly why imperfect men were required
in the natural scheme of things but decided that it must be because they
performed a function necessary for men, so that his fundamental question about women was "What are women *for*?" whereas about men it
was "What *is* man?" Aristotle did view the household and women's role
within it as important, but because he regarded women as fundamentally
intellectually inferior, he saw their primary function as procreation, not
companionship. The philosopher Plato agreed, for he viewed the best
love and friendship as that between men and commented in one of his
dialogues that originally all humans had been male, but some had been
reborn as women when they proved to be cowardly and wicked. In his
most important work, the *Republic*, Plato does include women among the
group of people who governed the rest, but because he also abolishes
the family for this group, these are women who, like celibate women in
early Christianity, have rejected or escaped the traditional female role and
become more like men.

Beginning in the twelfth century, theologians and religious writers generally called Scholastics attempted to bring together the teachings of
Aristotle and those of early Christian writers, creating one grand philosophical system. Thomas Aquinas, the most brilliant and thorough of
the Scholastics, synthesized classical and Christian ideas about women,
stating that women's inferiority was not simply the result of Eve's actions
but was inherent in her original creation. Even in procreation, her role
was minimal, for the mother provided simply the material substance in
the child, whereas the father supplied the active force (an idea Aquinas
drew largely from Aristotle). Women needed male assistance in everything because of their physical and intellectual weakness, although they
did have souls and so were responsible for their own salvation. Several
other Scholastics held slightly less negative views – Peter Abelard held that
sexuality was God-given and could not therefore be sinful, and Hugh of
St. Victor stressed the importance of spiritual comradeship in marriage –
but even these men did not view women as in any way equal to men. The
opinions of the Scholastics were expressed not only in complex philosophical treatises but were also communicated more broadly through public
sermons and through the university lectures they gave.

---

[4] Aristotle, *Generation of Animals*, trans. A. L. Peck, Loeb Classics (Cambridge, MA,
Harvard University Press, 1943), Book IV, vi, p. 460.

At about the same time as the growth of Scholasticism, a new emphasis on the veneration of Mary developed in Western Christianity. During its early centuries, Christianity had not stressed the role of Mary because it wanted to differentiate itself from pagan religions with female goddesses. By the twelfth century, all of Europe was more or less Christian, and many churches that were dedicated to Mary began to be built; poetry and hymns were also written in her honor. Mary's peculiar status as virgin and mother allowed her to be honored as both pure and nurturing at the same time, and she came to be viewed as the exact opposite of Eve, creating a good woman/bad woman dichotomy that would become extremely strong in European culture. The effects of the cult of Mary on the actual status of women, or even on attitudes toward women, are ambiguous, however. Because Christianity taught that there was and would be only one savior, Mary represented an unattainable ideal for all other women, for no other woman could hope to give birth to the Messiah. Yet Mary was also not divine, so that she set a standard for female behavior in a way that Jesus did not for men. Some of the men most devoted to Mary, such as Bernard of Clairvaux, were also the harshest in their condemnation of all other women. Nevertheless, Mary did provide a female focus for veneration, and although official theology always stressed her role as obedient helpmate, in popular worship she was often viewed as one member of the Trinity, one no less powerful than God or Jesus.

Secular literature of the high and late Middle Ages also reflects male opinions of women. Beginning in the twelfth century, poetry and songs no longer celebrated simply the great military deeds of warriors and fighters but also their passion and respect for women. An enormous number of romances, poems, and songs were written about what has come to be termed "courtly love," in which a knight swears loyalty to a lady, does great deeds in her honor, sings her praises, and so wins her love. Courtly love literature created many of the romantic conventions that have been part of popular and learned romance since then – the hero might die on his quest or the lovers be separated by boundaries of social class – and generally described women as pure and virtuous. It thus presented a more positive view of women than religious literature, and actual women were involved in its production both as patrons of poets and as troubadour poets themselves. We should not overemphasize its impact, however, because it is unclear whether the conventions of chivalry actually changed male behavior toward women very much. Even within the songs and poems, women often play a passive role; they bestow handkerchiefs but do not roam the world in search of dragons or villains, a passivity that continues in most contemporary romance literature. By the end of the Middle Ages as well, many writers of courtly love literature, such as Andreas Capellanus, also wrote cynical satires mocking chivalric conventions and bitterly criticizing women as devious, domineering, and demanding. Their misogyny matches that of the harshest clerical writers. Similar views of women also dominate most of the popular literature of the late Middle Ages, such as folktales and songs. Women were often the central figures in popular stories and songs, in which they represented either the positive or negative female stereotype: a patient Griselda, who put up with everything her sadistic husband did to test her loyalty, including apparently killing her children, or a shrewish wife who could only be tamed by physical violence.

The Debate about Women

Toward the end of the fourteenth century, several writers in Europe decided to answer misogynist attacks on women directly, beginning a debate about women's character and nature that would last throughout the early modern period. Around 1370, the Italian writer Giovanni Boccaccio compiled a long list of famous and praiseworthy women, *De mulieribus claris*, describing women from classical history who were exemplary for their loyalty, bravery, and morality. This was the first such list since the Roman writer Plutarch's *Mulierum virtues* and served as the model for scores of similar treatises by writers from many countries over the next 300 years, who would often add women from the Bible, Christian history, and more contemporary figures to their lists. Boccaccio's work and those modeled on it appear at first glance to be unqualified tributes to women, but they are actually more ambiguous, for the highest praise they can bestow on a woman is that she is like a man. In Boccaccio's words, "What can we think except that it was an error of nature to give female sex to a body which had been endowed by God with a magnificent virile spirit?"[5]

Christine de Pizan, a well-educated Italian woman who lived in Paris and supported her family through her writing, was the first female author to enter this debate. She was not content simply to list illustrious women but explored the reasons behind women's secondary status. Christine wrote a series of works in defense of women, the most important of which was the *City of Ladies* (1405), in which she ponders the question about why misogynist ideas are so widely held. She attacks these ideas in a sophisticated way, noting that the authorities usually cited in attacks on women are not only all men but that they also disagree among themselves, and with reason and logic, that the language of the attacks is open to

[5] Boccaccio, *Concerning Famous Women*, trans. Guido Guarino (New Brunswick, NJ, Rutgers University Press, 1963), p. 87.

interpretation and that they are often based on men's projection of their own fears and weaknesses. Instead of using extraordinary female counter-examples to argue against women's inferiority, she admits that women *are* inferior in many things but that this comes from their lack of education, economic dependence, and subordinate status. Because she explicitly discusses the historical misrepresentation of women and recognizes the social and economic bases of women's weakness, Christine is sometimes termed the "first feminist." Others have seen this label as misleading because Christine does not use her analysis to call for social change, as will the feminist thinkers of the seventeenth century whom I discuss later in this book. If we keep in mind the time in which she wrote, however, we can view her conclusion that women's oppression and suffering made them better able than men to live virtuous lives in imitation of Christ not simply as a resigned acceptance of the realities of male power but also as a positive affirmation of women's spiritual superiority.

Christine's work was not printed in France during the early modern period (although an English translation appeared in 1521), and most of the later defenses of women follow more closely the pattern set by Boccaccio, whose work was frequently printed and translated. Juan Luis Vives, Desiderius Erasmus, and Thomas Elyot, three important human-ists, all viewed women as spiritually equal and argued for the educa-tion of at least upper-class girls. None of them thought this spiritual equality should translate into political equality or even total mutuality between spouses, however, and their views of the most important human virtues were highly gender-specific. Men received the greatest praise for courage, wisdom, and power, and women, including female rulers, for piety, chastity, modesty, and obedience.

Cornelius Agrippa of Nettesheim, a German humanist, provided the most exhaustive and frequently pirated list of illustrious women in his *De nobilitate et praecellentia foeminei sexus . . . declamatio* (1529) and argued not simply that women were equal to men, but that they were superior. As the quotation that opens this chapter indicates, he cites as proof of this their place as the final act of God's creation and then goes on to list other factors drawn from theology and biology. Eve was superior to Adam because she alone was created in the Garden of Eden, and she was made out of bone (Adam's rib), which was a material superior to the clay out of which Adam was formed; only women produce milk, which nourishes human life, and only they have a natural process which rids the body of poisons (menstruation); Adam, not Eve, was responsible for bringing sin into the world, for God's commandment not to eat of the Tree of Knowledge had been given to Adam before Eve was created; the greatest human woman, Mary, far surpassed the greatest human man, whom Agrippa judged to be John the Baptist. Agrippa uses these reasons to argue that women can and should hold public office, but later writers who repeat his ideas lessen their impact by couching them as part of effusive praise for the female rulers to whom they dedicated their works, so it is difficult to ascertain their sincerity; Agrippa himself had written *De nobilitate* twenty years before he published it, deciding to publish only when a female monarch to whom he could write an appropriate dedication, Margaret of Austria, began to rule.

A number of the authors of defenses of women, such as Edward Gosyn-hille, an English hack writer, and Gedaliah ibn Yahya, an Italian Jewish historian, also wrote attacks on women, or, like Baldassar Castiglione in *The Courtier*, included both sides of the argument in a single work, so that it is difficult to gauge their actual opinions. This has led some modern analysts to view the entire debate about women as a literary game, an issue used by male writers and intellectuals to show off their rhetorical skills and classical or biblical knowledge but that did not reflect their actual opinions of women. The most extreme statements of female infe-riority, such as the argument that women were not human beings that opens this chapter – made both in an explanation of the law of homicide written by Jacques Cujas, a French jurist, and in a theological treatise probably written by Valens Acidalius, a German scholar and physician – are judged to be so outrageous that their authors could have only meant them as satirical jokes.

Many of the attacks and defenses did use satire, and many of them were motivated by hopes of personal gain on the part of their authors, but this did not mean that the issue was simply an exercise for intellectuals. Beginning in the mid-sixteenth century, popular interest in the debate about women grew, leading to frequent translations and reprints of Latin works. Acidalius's treatise and some responses defending women were published as a pamphlet in German, Italian, and French, and Agrippa's longer work was translated into English, French, German, and Italian; both were reprinted for almost 200 years.

Original vernacular works of all types also began to appear. In Italy, a number of learned women wrote spirited defenses of women that directly refuted the works of misogynist writers. Laura Terracina (1519–77) specifically criticized the Italian poet Ludovico Ariosto's characterization of women. The Venetian poet Modesta Pozzo (1555–92), writing under the pen name Moderata Fonte ("moderate fountain"), produced *The Worth of Women: Wherein Is Clearly Revealed Their Nobility and Their Supe-riority to Men* (first published 1600), the main point of which is captured in the title. Women's activities as wives and mothers have been undeval-ued, Fonte argued, and if women received the same education as men, their innate moral superiority would clearly emerge. Lucrezia Marinelli (1571–1653) agreed, penning *The Nobility and Excellence of Women and the Defects and Vices of Men* (1600). She also pointed out the problems caused by the use of illustrious women as a disproof of female inferiority among many of the writers who considered themselves defenders of women. In France, Mariele Jars de Gournay in *L'Egalité des hommes et des femmes* (1622) built on the arguments of Christine de Pizan to argue that the equality of men and women rested on divine law.

The debate spread to England in the later sixteenth and seventeenth centuries. Edward Gosynhill probably wrote *The Schoolhouse of Women*, a humorous attack in rhyme, in 1541 and *The Praise of All Women*, a sober defense, in the following year. Both of these provoked numerous satirical and serious answers for the rest of the century, the defenses usually catalogs of virtuous women based on Boccaccio and Agrippa and the attacks catalogs of women's vices; their main complaints included female pride, lasciviousness, obstinacy, desire for mastery, jealousy, talkativeness, vanity, greed, extravagance, infidelity, physical and moral inferiority, and caprice.

In 1615, Joseph Swetnam published *The Arraignment of Lewd, Idle, Froward and Unconstant Women*, which was not very original in content but was very popular because of its humor and middle-class emphasis. This provoked three direct responses, all published under the name of female authors. Rachel Speght published *A Muzzle for Melastomus* (1617) under her own name, carefully refuting all of Swetnam's charges with biblical arguments and criticizing his grammar and logic. *Esther hath Hanged Haman* (1617) appeared under the name Esther Sowernam (a clear play on Swetnam's name) and *The Worming of a Mad Dog* (1617) under the name Constantia Munda, both of which replied to Swetnam with invective and rational argument. Although the exact identity of these authors remains unknown, the spirit with which they wrote, the examples they use drawn from women's experience, the generalized nature of their attacks on men, and the fact that a male author would gain nothing from writing under a female pseudonym all argue for female authorship. Both attacks and defenses continued in England well into the eighteenth century, the latter frequently written by women, who became gradually more willing to publish their work under their own name.

Although some vernacular defenses of women were published more than once, most were not, and the serious and satirical attacks were generally republished more often. This was also the case with popular songs, jokes, jests, and stories that included examples of women's virtues and vices; misogynist sentiments find expression much more often than praises of women. In part, this is because satire is more fun to read than is

Figure 1. Abraham Bach, *Recipe for Marital Bliss*, c. 1680. This woodcut was sold as a single sheet, to be read at home or hung on the wall. The qualities on the part of the wife that merit a beating, according to the artist, are laziness, talkativeness, vanity, and lust for other men, and on the part of the husband drunkenness, laziness, and not supporting his family.

28

praise. Stories and jestbooks poking fun at men were also popular, sold by street vendors and read aloud in taverns. Much of this humor was malicious and cruel, with vicious songs and jokes about wife beating and rape or about crippled men so weak they could not control their wives and children.

The debate about women also found visual expression in the early modern period, particularly in single-sheet prints that were hung in taverns or people's homes, again an indication that this was not simply a debate among intellectuals. Prints that juxtaposed female virtues and vices were popular, with the virtuous women depicted as those of the classical or biblical past and the vice-ridden dressed in contemporary clothes. The favorite metaphor for the virtuous wife was either the snail or the tortoise, both animals that never leave their "houses" and are totally silent, although such images were never as widespread as those depicting wives beating their husbands or hiding their lovers from them. Most of the prints, which people purchased to hang on their walls or were published as part of emblem books, portrayed the same negative stereotypes of women that the written attacks on women did; women are shown with their hands in men's purses, tempting men by displaying naked breasts, or neglecting their housework. Artists frequently portrayed misogynist stories involving classical figures, such as Socrates' wife Xantippe nagging him or Aristotle being so seduced by the beauty of Phyllis that he allowed her to ride him around a garden, so that these became part of popular culture as well as that of Europe's learned elite.

The debate about women's character and nature was not limited to pamphlets and prints that addressed it directly but was also contained in works that considered larger topics, such as mystical writings or discussions of civil and natural law. Paracelsus, for example, a Swiss physician and alchemist, wrote that women had a special place in the cosmos because they bore children and were thus the endpoint of God's creative process; marriage was essential for both women and men because it was not simply a physical but also a mystical union ordained by God. Mary, in his view, was more important than Christ because she was the heavenly wife of God, an idea taken up in the seventeenth century by German pietists. Legal scholars such as Jean Bodin included the standard list of female vices to prove that women were naturally inferior and so should never be allowed to rule or hold public office: "Gynecocracy [rule by a woman] is squarely against the laws of nature that give men the strength, the prudence, the arms, and the power to command and take [these things] away from woman."[6] As I discuss in Chapter 4, the

---

[6] Jean Bodin, *Six Books of a Commonweale* (London, 1606), p. 753.

debate about women also became part of the discussion of the merits of women's education, and, as shown in Chapter 8, it was the springboard for considerations of gender, that is, considerations of what was distinctive about male as well as female experience. Writers of poetry, drama, and fiction also expressed their position in the debate through the female characters they created and the relationships between women and men they portrayed, but the best authors, such as Shakespeare, Milton, or Cervantes, recognized the complexity of the issue and so did not unambiguously support one side or another. The analysis of female characters and gender relations in the literature of the early modern period is an enormous, booming, and highly contentious field of literary criticism, and one best explored separately from our investigation of the lives of actual women.

Religious Reformers of the Sixteenth and Seventeenth Centuries

If the ideas about women expressed by writers of literature are a matter of debate among literary scholars, those held by religious thinkers in the early modern period are even more hotly disputed by contemporary scholars. One of the key reasons for this may be seen in the two quotations from Martin Luther that open the chapter. Many of the most important religious leaders of the period were not consistent, expressing strongly negative opinions of women at some points and positive ones at others. Other leaders, such as John Calvin, expressed their view of women only obliquely while considering other issues, so that their opinions must be extrapolated and require a high degree of interpretation. Many contemporary scholars also have strong personal or religious convictions regarding certain religious leaders or the denominations they founded, so that it is sometimes difficult for them to accept the opinions they find. Despite the contradictions and ambiguities in the writings of religious thinkers and the differences of opinion among modern scholars, however, we can make some generalizations about the impact of religious change on ideas about women.

The sixteenth century saw a movement of religious reform, soon labeled the "Protestant Reformation," in which reformers denounced many of the theological ideas, institutions, and practices of the Catholic Church. Eventually, about half of western Europe separated from the Catholic Church, and new types of Christian churches were established. Although they challenged tradition on many things, Protestant reformers did not break sharply with the medieval Scholastic theologians in their ideas about women. For Protestant reformers such as Luther, Zwingli, and Calvin, as well as the leaders of the English Puritans, women were created by God and could be saved through faith; spiritually, women and men were equal. In every other respect, however, women were to be subordinate to men. Women's subjection was inherent in their very being and was present from creation – in this, the reformers agreed with Aristotle and the classical tradition, although Luther in particular denounced the ideas of Aristotle on other matters and saw the Scholastic attempt to reconcile Aristotle and the Bible as misguided. Most reformers accepted Eve's principal responsibility for the fall and thought this had made women's original natural inferiority and subjection to male authority even more pronounced. The Protestants supported the Pauline teaching that women should be silent in church, although Calvin noted that this was determined by tradition and custom rather than divine commandment and so might be open to change; he did not see this change as happening in the foreseeable future or make any practical attempts to bring it about, however.

The Protestants did break with official Catholic teachings on the relative merits of celibacy and marriage, though some fifteenth-century writers had also thought that God had set up marriage and families as the best way to provide spiritual and moral discipline, so Protestant opinions were not completely new. Protestant writers championed marriage with greater vigor, however, and wrote large numbers of tracts trying to convince men and women to marry or advising spouses (particularly husbands) how best to run their households and families. It is in this pro-marriage literature that we find the most positive statements about women, for the writers recognized that many of their readers were former priests or monks who had been trained to regard marriage, sexuality, and women in general as destroyers of their spiritual well-being; Johannes Mathesius, for example, a Lutheran pastor, writes: "A man without a wife is only half a person and has only half a body and is a needy and miserable man who lacks help and assistance."[7] Many of the writers included lists of virtuous women drawn from Boccaccio or Agrippa, although, not surprisingly, they often included only those women who had been model wives. They use the story of Eve being created out of Adam's rib as proof that God wanted women to stand by the side of men as their assistants and not be trampled on or trod underfoot (for then Eve would have been created out of Adam's foot); these directives always mention as well, however, that women should never claim authority over men, for Eve had not been created out of Adam's head.

Protestant writers generally cite the same three purposes of marriage, in the same order of importance, that pre-Reformation writers did – the procreation of children, the avoidance of sin, and mutual help and

---

[7] Johannes Mathesius, *Ehestand und Hauswesen* (Nuremberg, 1564), XIII, p. xx, 11. ii.

companionship – although Calvin did view the last purpose as the most important. Some of them did interpret "mutual help and companionship" to have a romantic and sensual side, so there tends to be less of an antipathy toward sexuality (as long as it was within marriage) among Protestants than Catholics.

The ideal of mutuality in marriage was not an ideal of equality, however, and Protestant marriage manuals, household guides, and marriage sermons all stress the importance of husbandly authority and wifely obedience. This obedience, for almost all Protestants, was to take precedence over women's spiritual equality; a woman's religious convictions were never grounds for leaving or even openly disagreeing with her husband, although she could pray for his conversion. The only exceptions to this were some of the radical reformers, who did allow women to leave their unbelieving spouses, but the women who did so were expected to remarry quickly and thus come under the control of a male believer. Women were continually advised to be cheerful rather than grudging in their obedience, for in doing so they demonstrated their willingness to follow God's plan. Men were also given specific advice about how to enforce their authority, which often included physical coercion; in both Continental and English marriage manuals, the authors use the metaphor of breaking a horse for teaching a wife obedience. Although the opinions of women who read such works were not often recorded, we can tell somewhat from private letters that women knew they were expected to be obedient and silent, for they often excused their actions when they did not conform to the ideal. Such letters also indicate, however, that women's view of the ideal wife was one in which competence and companionship were as important as submissiveness.

The Protestant exhortation to marry was directed to both sexes but particularly to women, for whom marriage and motherhood were a vocation as well as a living arrangement. Marriage was a woman's highest calling, even though it brought physical dangers and restraints on her freedom. Luther's words at the beginning of this chapter make this clear, as do those of the Tudor homily on marriage, which the crown required to be read out loud regularly in all English churches:

Truth it is, that they [women] must specially feel the griefs and pains of matrimony, in that they relinquish the liberty of their own rule, in the pain of their travailing [i.e., labor and delivery], in the bringing up of their own children, in which offices they be in great perils, and be grieved with many afflictions, which they might be without, if they lived out of matrimony.[8]

---

[8] Church of England, *The Two Books of Homilies* (Oxford, 1859), p. 505.

Despite their recognition of the disadvantages of marriage for women, however, most Protestants urged all women to marry, for they thought no woman had the special divine gift of freedom from sexual urges. Unmarried women were thus suspect, both because they were fighting their natural sex drive and because they were upsetting the divinely imposed order, which made woman subject to man. It is important to recognize, then, that the Protestant elevation of marriage is not the same as and may, in fact, directly contradict an elevation of women *as women*.

The opinions of Protestant leaders about marriage and women were not contained simply in written works but were communicated to their congregations through marriage sermons and homilies; because people in many parts of Europe were required to attend church, there was no way they could escape hearing them. Their opinions were also reflected in woodcuts and engravings that illustrated religious pamphlets, an important tool in the spread of Protestant ideas. The ideal woman appears frequently in both sermons and illustrations: sitting with her children, listening to a sermon or reading the Bible, dressed soberly and with her hair modestly covered. Negative depictions also appear: the nun who "parrots her psalter without understanding it . . . tortures her own body and creates her own cross, which God has not commanded"[9]; the priest's concubine; prostitutes or women dressed extravagantly buying indulgences or expensive rosaries; disobedient wives being beaten by their husbands.

The Catholic response to the challenge of the Protestant reformers, usually termed the "Catholic Reformation," included a response to the elevation of marriage. As with so many other issues, Catholic thinkers reaffirmed traditional doctrine and agreed that the most worthy type of Christian life was one both celibate and chaste. There was some disagreement about the relative importance of the three traditional purposes of marriage, with more liberal thinkers stressing the emotional bond between the couple more than procreation or the avoidance of sin, but in general there was a strong sense that all sexuality, including marital, was sinful and disruptive. The Catholic Church was much more vigorous in enforcing clerical celibacy after the middle of the sixteenth century but accomplished this through stronger instilling of the virtues of celibacy in the seminaries and weeding out of unsuitable candidates for the priesthood rather than simply stressing the evils of women. Catholic leaders from the late sixteenth century on often recognized that women were useful allies in the fight to reconvert or hold areas to the Catholic faith and so did not openly express the type of harshly misogynist ideas that were common in early Christian thinkers or medieval theologians.

[9] Georg Albrecht, *Der Hausstand* (Nuremberg, 1657), p. 1074.

Catholic authors also realized that despite exhortations to celibacy, most women in Europe would marry and so wrote marriage manuals to counteract those written by Protestants. The ideal wife they described was exactly the same as that proposed by Protestant authors – obedient, silent, pious – and their words give clear indication that they still regarded women as totally inferior. Fray Luis de Leon, for example, in the late-sixteenth-century treatise *La perfecta casada (The Perfect Wife)*, comments:

When a woman succeeds in distinguishing herself in something praiseworthy, she wins a victory over any number of men who have given themselves over to the same endeavor. For so insignificant a thing as this which we call woman never undertakes or succeeds in carrying out anything essentially worthwhile unless she be drawn to it, and stimulated, and encouraged by some force of incredible resoluteness which either God, or some singular gift of God, has placed within her soul.[10]

Thus, the opinions of learned Catholic authors about women, as well as marriage, tended to reaffirm traditional negative ideas, although the harshest criticisms were generally reserved for specific women who challenged male authority in some way rather than simply being addressed to women in general in the style of Tertullian or Jerome.

In Jewish opinion, like Protestant, all women should marry, and the qualities of the ideal wife had changed little since Old Testament times. According to Isaac ben Eliakim, the author of a Yiddish ethical manual written in the early seventeenth century and frequently reprinted, the ideal wife was thrifty, cheerful, obedient, never jealous, and always responsive to her husband's physical and emotional needs. Although this differs little from contemporary Christian opinion, the tone of the manual is a bit less dreary, commenting practically, "If you treat him like a king, then he, in turn, will treat you like a queen," rather than dwelling on obedience as a religious duty.[11]

The Scientific Revolution

The phrase "Scientific Revolution" was invented in the nineteenth century to label a group of changes in the way learned individuals approached, conceptualized, and studied the natural world, stretching from work in anatomy and astronomy that began in the middle of the sixteenth century through work in physics, mathematics, and chemistry

---

[10] Luis de Leon, *The Perfect Wife*, trans. Alice Philena Hubbard (Denton, TX: The College Press, 1943), p. 14.
[11] Reprinted in Jacob R. Marcus (ed.), *The Jew in the Medieval World* (New York, Meridian, 1960, c. 1938), pp. 443–44.

that began in the seventeenth century. As with religious reformers, most of the leading figures of the Scientific Revolution did not challenge inherited ideas about women, although they did dispute ancient and medieval authorities in many other fields. During the last half of the sixteenth century, female anatomy and physiology became a popular topic for medical authorities, who based their opinions somewhat on the recent actual anatomical experiments of Andreas Vesalius and Gabriele Fallopia, but more on the works of Aristotle, Hippocrates, and Galen that had just been reedited and reprinted, although the newest of these was 1,300 years old. The major dispute became one between Aristotelians and Galenists over the existence and function of female semen. Aristotelians generally held that women produce no semen or anything comparable and so contribute nothing to the form, intellect, or spirit of a fetus; their menstrual blood simply produces the matter out of which the fetus is formed. Galenists believed that women also produce semen that contributed to the form of the fetus, although they thought this was colder and less active than that of the male and that the father was still the more important parent. This female semen, in their opinion, also played a role in determining the sex of a child, whereas Aristotelians held that the father's semen alone determined this, although it was influenced by conditions at the time of intercourse; optimum conditions would always produce male offspring.

The Galenic view gradually gained more adherents, particularly because it made it much easier to explain why some children looked like their mothers, but some of Europe's leading scientists began to view the male semen as even more important than Aristotle had. The English anatomist and royal physician William Harvey (1578–1657) was in many ways a Galenist, for he thought that female humans, like chickens, produced eggs that did contribute materially to the child, but he thought the male sperm so powerful that it did not even need to touch this egg to fertilize it. He dissected large numbers of does just after coition and could see no sperm in their uteri and so determined that sperm could act at a distance, just like a magnet. Male semen not only fertilized the egg but also "has such prodigious power of fecundation, that the whole woman both in mind and body undergoes a change."[12] The Dutch lens maker and scientist Anton von Leeuwenhoek (1632–1723) supported the Aristotelian position with what he viewed as physical evidence. Using the newly developed microscope, he thought he could see preformed humans (what he called "animalcules") in sperm and wrote that God had placed enough there to allow for the eternal perpetuation of the human species.

[12] William Harvey, *Works*, trans. Robert Willis (London, Sydenham Society, 1847), p. 576.

He argued that each sperm was the seed of an individual and that sperm contained the full formative structure of the embryo, including its sex. This "spermatic" view of embryology was countered by "ovists" such as the Swiss physiologist Albrecht von Haller (1708–77), who thought that the embryo-in-miniature existed preformed in the female egg (*ovum* in Latin). The "ovist" position was threatening to the male scientific community, which reacted generally with ridicule, speculating on how many humans must have been within Eve's eggs to last until the end of time, particularly because each of these that was female had to contain all her future progeny ad infinitum. This is a problem in spermatic preformationism too, of course, and contributed to the slow recognition that somehow both parents must be essential. This understanding was limited by the fact that the mammalian ovum had not been definitively identified, which would not happen until 1827 – a remarkably late date considering its size relative to that of spermatazoa, which Leeuwenhoek had identified correctly in the 1670s.

Although they disagreed about the mechanism of conception, Galenists and Aristotelians agreed about many other aspects of human anatomy and physiology. All believed in the existence of bodily humors, four fluids – blood, phlegm, black bile, and yellow bile – which were contained in the body. Although the humors were distinct, under certain conditions they could also transform themselves into a different humor or into any other fluid that the body also produced, such as milk or semen. These humors were thought to correspond with the four elements – earth, air, fire, and water – and with the qualities of hot, cold, wet, and dry. These qualities varied from person to person but were sex-related, with men generally believed to be hotter and drier and women colder and wetter.

Learned physicians, medical writers, and ordinary people viewed illness as caused by an imbalance in these humors, which was why the most common form of medical treatment was drawing blood, the only one of these humors for which the amount could be adjusted easily. (Black bile and yellow bile were never clearly identified, and the amount of phlegm the body produces is limited.) Emotions and mental states were also linked to imbalances in the four bodily humors: too much blood made one bold, courageous, and *sanguine* (from the Latin word for blood, *sanguis*); too much phlegm made one sluggish, apathetic, and *phlegmatic*; too much yellow bile (choler) made one angry, irritated, and *choleric*; too much black bile made one sad, depressed, and *melancholic*.

Melancholic was the most worrisome of these states. A certain amount of melancholy could be a source of genius, inspiring music and poetry, but too much could lead to madness and both physical and mental illness. Physicians prescribed physical and spiritual treatments for their melancholic patients: a change in diet or sleeping patterns, vomits, bleeding, travel to a different climate, sex, music, astrology, wearing amulets, magic, prayer. Melancholy was linked to love, and for many physicians, love itself caused a range of illnesses. Too intense love could lead to lovesickness, which in the Middle Ages was generally viewed as an ailment afflicting aristocratic men but in the early modern era became more associated with young women. Love might lead women to hysteria – a word that comes from the Latin word for womb – in which passion took over their ability to control their bodies or their minds. Repressing or refusing love was also dangerous, however, for this could lead to "green-sickness," an ailment in young unmarried women that caused the stoppage of menstruation and turned the skin pale or greenish. In *Romeo and Juliet*, Juliet's father shrieks, "out you green-sickness carrion," when she refuses to marry the man he has chosen for her. Doctors treated green-sickness with warming remedies that would heat the body and cause the thickened blood to flow again, of which the best was sexual intercourse (in marriage, of course). This would release both the young woman's blood and her pent-up sexual desire. (In the nineteenth century, the same set of symptoms were deemed "chlorosis," – a Latinized translation of "green-sickness" – and judged to be the result of iron-deficiency anemia. The recommended treatment was still marriage, although now this was seen as a way to protect women's frail and weak condition from the harshness of industrialization, which was viewed as the cause of chlorosis.)

Of the various qualities associated with the humors, heat was viewed as the most positive. It was the force within the body that could most easily change one kind of fluid into another, and it rose naturally toward the heavens and toward the brain, which explained why men, being hot and dry, were more rational and creative; women, being cold and wet, were more like the earth. Women's lack of heat was seen as the reason they menstruated (men "burned up" unneeded blood internally), did not go bald (men "burned up" their hair), and had wider hips and narrower shoulders (women did not have enough heat to drive matter toward their heads). Men's greater heat also meant they more often possessed qualities associated with heat – courage, honesty, reason, and physical and moral strength. Early modern anatomists such as Andreas Vesalius and William Harvey often quietly ignored the humoral theory because they could not discover any anatomical proofs of its existence but still spoke about women's character and temperament being determined by their cold and moist nature. Not until the late eighteenth century would the idea of the psychological effects of the humors die out among learned Europeans, and not until the nineteenth did bloodletting completely lose favor as a medical procedure.

Galenists and Aristotelians thus agreed that men were superior, but Aristotelians tended to view human anatomy and physiology on a single scale, describing women as imperfect or misbegotten males, whose lack of body heat had kept their sex organs inside rather than pushing them out as they were in the more perfect male. Galenists generally viewed men and women as equally perfect in their sex, a view that became more common after 1600. They thus stressed that males and females complemented one another and held that each sex desired the other mutually, whereas Aristotelians asserted that women desired men more because imperfect things always strive after perfection. The idea that women had a greater sexual drive than men did not die out in popular understanding with the triumph of Galenic ideas among learned writers, however, but remained constant until very late in the eighteenth century.

Another topic of great concern for scientists and medical writers was the nature and power of the uterus. Illness in women was often attributed to the power of the uterus, particularly mental illnesses such as depression or irrational behavior; the word "hysteria" is, in fact, derived from the Greek word for uterus. Plato had proposed that the uterus was an independent animal that could smell and move on its own, an idea hotly debated in the sixteenth century; the ability to smell was generally rejected but the notion of a "wandering womb" retained. Wombs were most likely to wander when they were not filled regularly through sexual intercourse and reproduction, and both male and female authors suggested various alternative remedies for single women and nuns. The uterus was also thought to be influenced by the moon and the maternal imagination, so that pregnant women in particular were advised to be aware of the stages of the moon and to avoid certain thoughts. Anger was regarded as particularly dangerous, for its "heat" could cause the woman's blood that normally nourished the fetus to destroy it instead.

The Scientific Revolution, which created a new view of the universe for educated Europeans, therefore did little to challenge existing ideas of the inferiority of women. In fact, some historians, most prominently Carolyn Merchant and David Noble, have argued that it deepened that inferiority by championing reason, order, control, and mechanical processes, all associated with men or defined as somehow masculine, and continued to link women with irrationality, disorder, and nature. All of the members in the new scientific societies that developed in the seventeenth century were men, other than a very few women in Italy, many of whom were "honorary" members. The purpose of the English Royal Society established in 1660 was expressly stated as the advancement of "Masculine Philosophy." Londa Schiebinger has pointed out that the acceptance of Galenic ideas of the complementarity of the two sexes, far from leading to greater egalitarianism, led instead by the end of the eighteenth century to the idea that gender differences pervaded every aspect of human experience, biological, intellectual, and moral; even the bones of the body demonstrated to most observers that women were destined to stay home and raise children.

Ideas about gender differences based in the body were interwoven with those about racial differences as European countries developed colonial empires: white women were viewed as most likely to incorporate female qualities viewed as positive, such as piety and purity, whereas nonwhite (especially black) women were seen as incorporating negative female traits, such as disobedience and sensuality. White men, in this view, were more rational because of their sex *and* their race, and nonwhite men were more likely to demonstrate negative or ambiguous male qualities such as anger or physical prowess. Exactly how these two hierarchies intersected was a matter of dispute for European thinkers, who also debated the ways in which class distinctions further complicated the picture. (We return to this topic again in Chapter 9.) In general, however, science provided much more "evidence" for differences among people than for their similarities in the early modern period. Not until the twentieth century was science used as often to argue for the equality of men and women of all racial and ethnic groups as for their essential inequality.

The Enlightenment

Eighteenth-century writers and thinkers looked to the development of science as a source of inspiration and began to advocate using the "light of reason" to examine human society as well as the natural world. They described their enterprise as "Enlightenment," a self-conscious intellectual movement that advocated using reason and knowledge against the darkness of prejudice, superstition, blind belief, ignorance, tyranny, and injustice. Thinkers in the Enlightenment – those in France called themselves *philosophes* – looked to principles the German philosopher Immanuel Kant (1724–1804) summarized in 1784 in the phrase: "*Sapere aude!* [dare to know] Have the courage to use your *own* understanding!"[13] Enlightenment ideas were exchanged in new social and cultural institutions, including scientific and literary societies, journals and newspapers, clubs or lodges that one paid to join, coffeehouses, and taverns. In some

---

[13] Immanuel Kant, "An Answer to the Question: What Is Enlightenment?" (1784), trans. James Schmidt, in James Schmidt (ed.), *What Is Enlightenment? Eighteenth-Century Answers and Twentieth-Century Questions* (Berkeley, University of California Press, 1996), p. 58.

OPIS SATVRNI CONIVNX
maternue Deorum.

Die erd ist fruchtbar mit aller krafft   Vnd wie auch ein weib das schwanger ist
Gibt öl wein milch most vnd gute safft.   Auch also die erd zu aller frut
Item koal fische gewechs früchte vnd thier   Sehr gut vnd fein alles geberet
kriechendts vnd alles fleisch speit von ir   Von irm leyb vnd reichlich erneret
Ein mutter erneret ir kinder klein   Die gantze natur. Merck mit allm fleis
Auß iarem weiblichen brüstlein rein.   Gott zu ewigem lob ehr vnd preis.

parts of Europe, they were also exchanged in salons, gatherings of men and women in the drawing rooms of well-to-do hostesses, which we discuss in Chapter 4.

In these new institutions, men (and a few women) discussed many topics, one of which was the nature of women and men and the reasons for differences between the sexes, what was often termed the "woman question." In a continuation of the earlier debate about women, they argued about women's intellectual capacities, moral virtues, and proper social role. Some, such as Madame de Châtelet (1706–40), who translated Isaac Newton's major work, the *Principia*, into French, held that women's unequal and limited education was responsible for women's lesser contributions in science and philosophy. Louise d'Epinay (1726–83), who held a salon in her home in Paris, agreed, asserting that "Men and women have the same nature and the same constitution ... [woman's] physical constitution has become weaker than man's as a result of education."[14] The marquis of Condorcet (1743–94), a mathematician and philosopher, similarly emphasized men's and women's equal capacities: "Among the progress of the human mind that is most important for human happiness, we must count the entire destruction of the prejudices that have established inequality between the sexes, fatal even to the sex it favors."[15] Others were less sure, arguing that women's lack of achievement was the result of a smaller

[14] Louise d'Epinay's Letter to Abbé Ferdinando Galiani, translated and reprinted in Lisa DiCaprio and Merry E. Wiesner, *Lives and Voices: Sources in European Women's History* (Boston, Houghton Mifflin, 2001), p. 247.
[15] Condorcet, *Sketch for a Historical Picture of the Progress of the Human Mind*, from Paul Halsall (ed.), "Modern History Sourcebook," http://www.fordham.edu/halsall/mod/condorcet-progress.html.

←——

Figure 2. Melchior Lorch, *Allegory of Nature*, 1565. The poem beneath the image reads:

> The earth is fruitful with all power
> Gives wine, milk, cider, and good juice
> Birds, fish, plants, fruit and animals
> Crawling or walking, all eat from her.
> A mother nourishes her small children
> With tender and fine feminine breasts
> And like a woman who is pregnant
> The earth also lets all
> Who are born fine and good from her body
> Eat from her and nourishes them all richly.
> The whole earth does its best
> To praise and honor God.

capacity for reason and that men and women were fundamentally different in their basic natures. Women might have moral superiority to balance their intellectual inferiority, but the proper sphere for demonstrating that morality was the private sphere of the family, not the public world of politics. Even Condorcet sees the primary benefit of treating men and women equally as the "greater happiness of families, and ... the spread of the domestic virtues, the first foundation of all other virtues."[16]

The most influential voice arguing for women's and men's radically different natures was the philosopher Jean-Jacques Rousseau (1712–78), who commented that "a perfect woman and a perfect man ought not to resemble each other in mind any more than in looks."[17] Rousseau was born in Geneva, in French-speaking Switzerland, and came to Paris intent on making his intellectual mark. Success eluded him as a young man, and although he was financially supported for a while by Louise d'Epinay, he grew suspicious of salon hostesses and his *philosophe* friends. He also began to doubt Enlightenment belief in reason and progress, attacking rationality and culture for destroying human freedom and corrupting humanity. In his treatise *Emile: Or, On Education* (1762), Rousseau calls for education that removes children from the corrupting influences of cities and places the boys under a wise tutor who will understand them and guide their interests. Most of the book – which became one of the most widely read books on education throughout the world – discusses the education of Emile, the boy at its center, but the last chapter turns to the education of Sophie, the girl destined to be Emile's wife. "Woman," Rousseau declares, "is made specially to please man ... and to be subjugated." Her education was to focus on purity, virtue, and "the cares of her household," although she should gain some knowledge, for "how [else] will she incline her children toward virtues she does not know?" Rousseau did not use his own children to test his ideas; he had five, by the illiterate seamstress who lived with him and whom he eventually married, but he sent them to orphanages. For Rousseau, nature had created distinct and permanent differences between the sexes, just as God had created such differences for Luther two centuries earlier.

Laws Regarding Women

Ideas about women and "woman" in the abstract based on religion, biology, intellectual notions, or tradition directly influenced the legal systems

---

[16] Ibid.
[17] Jean-Jacques Rosseau, *Emile*, trans. Allan Bloom (New York, Basic Books, 1979), p. 358.

and law codes in early modern Europe. It is important to recognize that laws are yet another type of theory; like sermons and domestic guides, they describe an ideal situation that their authors are trying to create and do not describe reality. To some degree, laws may be used as evidence that the actions they attempt to prohibit or regulate are in fact going on, for, as legal historians have pointed out, lawmakers only feel it necessary to restrict actions that people are actually doing or which the lawmakers think they might contemplate doing. When surveying laws regarding women, however, we cannot carry this too far, because all lawmakers in early modern Europe, except for a few queens, were male; laws thus reflect male notions and worries more than real female actions.

Law itself changed significantly in the early modern period. Beginning in the thirteenth century in Italy and most of southern Europe, and in the sixteenth century in Germany and most of northern Europe (although not England), legal scholars encouraged governments to change their law codes to bring them into conformity with Roman law, a legal system based on the collection of laws and commentaries made by the Roman emperor Justinian in the sixth century. Roman law was viewed as systematic and comprehensive, perfect for rulers who were attempting to bring political and judicial unity to their territories and get rid of the highly localized and often contradictory and conflicting law codes that had grown up in medieval Europe. Legal scholars who taught at universities and advised rulers came to regard law as an important tool for shaping society and advised rulers to expand their law codes and prosecute those who broke these codes more vigorously. In areas of Europe that became Protestant, secular rulers took over the control of matters such as marriage and morals from Catholic church courts, thus further expanding and centralizing their legal systems. The drive for comprehensiveness and uniformity also affected Catholic church courts, for the Council of Trent in the mid-sixteenth century cleared up many ambiguities in canon law, particularly in regard to marriage.

All of these changes had an impact on the legal position of women. Traditional medieval law codes in Europe had accorded women a secondary legal status, based generally on their inability to perform feudal military service; the oldest legal codes required every woman who was not married to have a male legal guardian who could undergo such procedures as trial by combat or trial by ordeal for her. This gender-based guardianship gradually died out in the later Middle Ages as court proceedings replaced physical trials, and unmarried women and widows generally gained the right to hold land on their own and appear in court on their own behalf. In most parts of Europe, unmarried women and widows could make wills, serve as executors for the wills of others, and serve as witnesses in civil and criminal cases, although they could not serve as witnesses to a will.

Thus, limitations on women's legal rights because of feudal obligations lessened in the late Middle Ages, but marriage provided another reason for restricting women's legal role. Marriage was cited as the key reason for excluding women from public offices and duties, for their duty to obey their husbands prevented them from acting as independent persons; the fact that an unmarried woman or widow might possibly get married meant that they, too, were included in this exclusion. A married woman was legally subject to her husband in all things; she could not sue, make contracts, or go to court for any reason without his approval, and in many areas of Europe, she could not be sued or charged with any civil crime on her own. In many parts of Europe, all goods or property that a wife brought into a marriage and all wages she earned during the marriage were considered the property of her husband, a situation that did not change legally until the nineteenth century. This was not true in Spain, where married women were freer to own and manage their own property than they were elsewhere in Europe.

Roman law was not adopted in England, which maintained the system of common law that had gradually developed over centuries. In common law, legal precedent (which means previous decisions of judges and courts) is an important factor in any case, along with actual statutes and regulations. This emphasis on precedent and tradition extended to definitions of marriage, with a "common-law marriage" one in which the spouses were understood to be married "by habit and repute," that is, by living together and presenting themselves to the world as husband and wife. Although people were supposed to marry in their own parish church after obtaining a license, common-law marriages and other sorts of "irregular" marriages were legal in the British Isles throughout most of the early modern period. In fact, Fleet Prison in London, which primarily housed debtors, became a popular site for irregular and secret marriages, with thousands performed every year. This ended in 1753, when Parliament passed a Marriage Act nullifying any marriage not performed publicly in church with a license and putting teeth in its act by forbidding children born in secret or common-law marriages to inherit. (The law only applied to England, so people seeking a "quickie" wedding traveled to villages right across the border in Scotland.)

Under common law, a married woman was not considered a legal person but was totally subsumed within the legal identity of her husband; she could not accept a gift from her husband or make a will separate from him because they were "one person." Two special courts, the Court of Chancery and the Court of Requests, were established specifically to make decisions case by case on the basis of principles of equity, rather than a strict interpretation of common law. These courts heard all types of cases but became particularly popular with married women in the sixteenth century, for they allowed them to bring cases independently, even against their husbands.

The husband's control of his wife's property could be modified somewhat by a marriage contract, which gave her legal ownership of the dowry she brought into the marriage. The husband then had the use of this money, goods, or property as long as both spouses were alive, but she or her heirs were to receive the actual property or something of comparable value at his death. In many parts of Europe, widows were also assured of a certain portion of their husbands' estate, termed a dower, after his death, usually fixed by law or custom at one-third to one-half; this was hers to use for the remainder of her life, although it reverted to his heirs after her death, so was not legally regarded as belonging to her. Widows were generally free to manage this property as they wished, although the heirs could take them to court if they felt the widow was harming the value of the property.

Along with marriage contracts, late medieval and early modern cities and states began to offer other ways for wives to gain some legal and economic independence from their husbands, for political and legal authorities recognized that a wife's totally dependent legal position often did not fit with economic needs or social realities. In almost all city law codes beginning in the fourteenth or fifteenth centuries, married women who carried out business on their own, or alongside their husbands, were allowed to declare themselves unmarried (*feme* [sic] *sole*) for legal purposes. This meant they could borrow and loan money and make contracts on their own, although sometimes the amounts were still limited. They could also be jailed for debt or for violating civil laws. Wives were also gradually allowed to retain control over some family property if they could prove that their husbands were squandering everything through drink, gambling, or bad investments; such laws were described as protection for women and children, but they were also motivated by lawmakers' concerns to keep such families from needing public charity.

In addition to these exceptions provided through law codes, it is clear from court records that women often actively managed their dowry property and carried out legal transactions without getting special approval. Judges and officials were often willing to let women act against the letter of the law if the alternative would be financial problems for the family or if they thought the law itself was harmful or unfair. Other women simply acted and risked the consequences rather than seeking approval beforehand; it is clear that the legal provisions for exceptions in no way encompass all of women's actual legal and financial activities.

The proliferation of exceptions and the fact that women were often able to slip through the cracks of urban law codes began to bother jurists in many parts of Europe who were becoming educated in Roman law with its goals of comprehensiveness and uniformity. Roman law also gave them additional grounds for women's secondary legal status, for it based this not on feudal obligations or a wife's duty to obey her husband but rather on women's alleged physical and mental weaknesses, their "fragility, imbecility, irresponsibility, and ignorance," in the words of Justinian's code. Along with peasants and the simpleminded, women were regarded as not legally responsible for all of their own actions, and they could not be compelled to appear before a court; in all cases, their testimony was regarded as less credible than a man's. These ideas led jurists in many parts of Europe to recommend, and in some cases implement, the reintroduction of gender-based guardianship; unmarried adult women and widows were again given male guardians and prohibited from making any financial decisions, even donations to religious institutions, without their approval.

Ironically, Roman law itself had not required unmarried adult women to have guardians but had only known guardianship for children. Early modern jurists were thus selective in what they took from Roman law in regard to women, in general adopting clauses that placed women in a dependent or secondary position and neglecting those that gave women specific independent rights. This can be seen in changes in a mother's rights to her own children. Early medieval law codes had known only fatherly authority, but the concept of joint parental authority over children had grown gradually in the Middle Ages. This died out again with the reception of Roman law, for its concept of the absolute rights of the father (*patria potestas*) was cited frequently, and the control it gave mothers over their children was not. In many parts of Europe, women lost the right of guardianship over their own children if they remarried or were only granted guardianship in the first place if they renounced remarriage at the death of the children's father.

Increasing restrictions on unmarried and married women continued throughout the early modern period. In 1731, for example, the Paris Parliament passed the *Ordonnance des donations*, which reemphasized the power of the husband over the wife; its provisions limiting women's legal rights later became part of the Napoleonic Code. In 1776, the Spanish monarchy issued the Royal Pragmatic, which required a parent's or guardian's consent to all marriages. This was extended to Spanish America in 1778, and fathers in particular used it to prevent marriages they thought were socially unequal or otherwise objectionable.

Court records indicate that male guardianship was enforced because fewer and fewer women appeared on their own behalf. Governments generally became less willing to make exceptions in the case of women because they felt any laxness might disrupt public order. Customs of inheritance, although not specified by law, were also affected by notions of women's incapacity and ignorance, for in many parts of Europe, daughters increasingly received only goods (movables) and no land (immovables) when they had brothers, whether land was normally divided between brothers (partible inheritance) or inherited as a block by the eldest brother (primogeniture). Daughters were required to renounce all claims to family land when they received their dowry, thus keeping land more closely within the patrilineage and taking away what had often been a source of great economic and legal power for upper-class women.

The spread of Roman law thus had a largely negative effect on women's civil legal status in the early modern period because of both the views of women that jurists chose to adopt from it and the stricter enforcement of existing laws to which it gave rise. Its impact on criminal law was less gender-specific, just as criminal law itself was. In general, women throughout Europe were responsible for their own criminal actions and could be tortured and executed just like men. Some mildness was recommended in the case of pregnant women, although generally this meant simply waiting until after delivery to proceed with torture. Women were often executed in a manner different from men, buried alive or drowned instead of being beheaded, largely because city executioners thought women would faint at the sight of the sword or ax and make their job more difficult. The wifely duty of obedience did enter into criminal law in a few instances, with both positive and negative effects for women. In England, a woman's marital status could affect her independent culpability for criminal actions because women who were unmarried sometimes said they were in order to claim husbandly coercion in capital cases, which could keep them from being executed. On the other hand, women who killed their husbands were judged guilty of petty treason as well as murder, which would assure them of the death penalty. (Husband-murder does not appear to have been regarded as petty treason on the Continent, although it was still judged as the most detestable type of murder.) In Spain, only in the sixteenth century did the state take over from the husband the right to punish his wife for adultery, and husbandly revenge was still allowed as long as he killed both his wife and her lover. In Germany, a wife was often included in her husband's banishment for criminal actions – including banishment for adultery! – but the opposite was not the case.

Along with concepts of feudal obligation, wifely obedience, and Roman law, one additional idea was essential in shaping women's legal rights in early modern Europe – the notion of honor. Honor in this period was highly gender-specific and, in the case of men, class-specific. For upper-class men, honor still revolved around notions of physical bravery and loyalty, a link that was also accepted by journeymen and marginal groups such as professional criminals. For bourgeois and most working men, honor was primarily related to honesty, good craftsmanship, and integrity. For all women, honor was a sexual matter. In most parts of Europe, women of all classes were allowed to bring defamation suits to court for insults to their honor, and it is clear from court records that they did this frequently; such records also indicate that the worst thing a man could be called was "thief" or "coward," whereas for women, it was "whore." Because of ideas of female sinfulness, irrationality, and weakness drawn from tradition, religion, and science, however, women, particularly those in the middle and upper classes, were never regarded as able to defend their own honor completely without male assistance. Lower-class women might trade insults or physically fight one another, but middle- and upper-class women were expected to internalize notions of honor and shame and shape their behavior accordingly, depending on male relatives to carry out any public defense of their honor. Male defense of female honor often took the form of laws and customs that might appear to protect women but actually safeguarded their male family members. In Spain, for example, a woman whose fiancé had died after the engagement but before the marriage was granted one-half of the goods promised for the marriage, for a kiss was part of the betrothal ceremony, which made it extremely difficult for her to find another spouse. The property would allow her either to support herself in an unmarried state or perhaps find a partner who would not mind the fact that she "remained shamed" and would also free her father and brothers from having to support her. Similar motivations are behind laws that required rapists to compensate their victims, or the fathers of their victims, which are found throughout Europe. In Muscovy until the reforms of Peter the Great, elite women were totally secluded in separate quarters and did not mix socially with men at all; they rode in closed carriages even when going to church and were veiled whenever they appeared in public. This was done in the name of family honor but also kept family property in male hands because the women often did not marry and so did not receive a dowry.

As I discuss more fully in Chapter 8, honor, along with order and the public good, were all concepts that in both theory and reality were closely linked not only to ideas about women but also to ideas about men. The educated men whose notions we have concentrated on in this chapter were much less willing to generalize about their own sex than about the opposite one, but underlying all their ideas about women, and the laws that resulted from those ideas, were concepts about their own nature as men.

For Further Reading

A good place to start for studying negative attitudes about women from the ancient period to the modern is Katherine Rodgers, *The Trouble-some Helpmate: A History of Misogyny in Literature* (Seattle, University of Washington Press, 1966), although there is no comparable long-term survey of positive attitudes. Several of the chapters in Judith Baskin (ed.), *Jewish Women in Historical Perspective* (Detroit, Wayne State University Press, 1991), discuss ideas about women. For ideas about women in early Christianity, see Joyce Salisbury, *Church Fathers, Independent Virgins* (New York, Verso, 1991). Lisa M. Bitel, *Women in Early Medieval Europe, 400–1100* (Cambridge, Cambridge University Press, 2005), has good information, as does Christopher N. L. Brooke, *The Medieval Idea of Marriage* (Oxford, Clarendon Press, 1994). On courtly love, see the new books by ffiona Swabey, *Eleanor of Aquitaine, Courtly Love and the Troubadours* (London, Greenwood, 2004); and James A. Schultz, *Courtly Love, the Love of Courtliness, and the History of Sexuality* (Chicago, University of Chicago Press, 2006).

On the debate about women, see Thelma Fenster and Clare A. Lees (eds.), *Gender in Debate from the Early Middle Ages to the Renaissance* (New York, Palgrave, 2002); Aluin Blamires, *Woman Defamed and Defended: An Anthology of Medieval Texts* (New York, Oxford University Press, 1992); and Glenda McLeod, *Virtue and Venom: Catalogs of Women from Antiquity to the Renaissance* (Ann Arbor, University of Michigan Press, 1991). Ian Maclean, *The Renaissance Notion of Woman* (Cambridge, Cambridge University Press, 1980), analyzes the debate in philosophical, theological, medical, and legal writings and provides the best overview of ideas about women through the sixteenth century; there is, unfortunately, nothing like it for the seventeenth or eighteenth centuries. Many of the female-authored defenses of women written by Continental Europeans have been translated and published by the University of Chicago Press in the series "The Other Voice in Early Modern Europe"; full details of the ever-growing number of books in this series may be found on the series Web site: http://www.press.uchicago.edu/Complete/Series/OVIEME.html. Works that focus on the debate in England include Joan Larsen Klein (ed.), *Daughters, Wives and Widows: Writings by Men about Women and Marriage in England, 1500–1640* (Urbana, University of Chicago Press, 1992); and Cristina Malcolmson and Mihoko Suzuki (eds.), *Debating Gender in Early Modern England, 1500–1700* (New York,

Palgrave, 2002). For an analysis of visual material, see Cindy McCreery, *The Satirical Gaze: Prints of Women in Late Eighteenth-Century England* (New York, Oxford University Press, 2004).

Christine de Pizan has been the focus of a number of studies in the last few years, including Rosalind Brown-Grant, *Christine de Pizan and the Moral Defence of Women: Reading beyond Gender* (Cambridge, Cambridge University Press, 1999); and Kate Langdon Forhan, *The Political Theory of Christine de Pizan (Burlington, VT, Ashgate, 2002). An excellent selection of her writings can be found in The Selected Writings of Christine de Pizan, ed. and trans. Renate Blumenfeld-Kosinski and Kevin Brownlee (New York, Norton, 1997).* There is no overview of Reformation ideas about women. *Luther on Women: A Sourcebook*, ed. and trans. Susan C. Karant-Nunn and Merry E. Wiesner-Hanks (Cambridge, Cambridge University Press, 2003), contains translations and analysis of Luther's main writings on women, the family, and sexuality. Jane Dempsey Douglass, *Women, Freedom and Calvin* (Philadelphia, Westminster Press, 1985), analyzes Calvin's ideas. See the list of readings following Chapter 6 and the Web site for more suggestions.

Joan Cadden, *Meanings of Sex Differences in the Middle Ages: Medicine, Science, and Culture* (Cambridge, Cambridge University Press, 1993), analyzes medieval scientific ideas about gender; and David Noble, *A World without Women: The Clerical Cultural of Western Science* (New York, Knopf, 1992), points out ways in which medieval misogyny carried over into modern science. Ideas about women that developed in the Scientific Revolution have been surveyed from a critical feminist perspective by Carolyn Merchant, *The Death of Nature: Women, Ecology and the Scientific Revolution* (New York, Harper & Row, 1980); and Londa Schiebinger, *Nature's Body: Gender in the Making of Modern Science* (New Brunswick, NJ, Rutgers University Press, 2nd ed., 2004). Clara Pinto-Correia, *The Ovary of Eve: Egg and Sperm and Preformation* (Chicago, University of Chicago Press, 1998), is a witty look at the preformationist debate. Katharine Park, *Secrets of Women: Gender, Generation and the Origins of Human Dissection* (San Francisco, Zone Books, 2006), notes the centrality of the dissection of women's bodies to the development of knowledge about human anatomy.

For women in Enlightenment thought, see Samia I. Spencer, *French Women and the Age of Enlightenment* (Bloomington, Indiana University Press, 1984); Lieselotte Steinbrugge, *The Moral Sex: Woman's Nature in the French Enlightenment*, trans. Pamela E. Selwyn (New York, Oxford University Press, 1995); Hans Erich Böedeker and Lieselotte Steinbrugge, (eds.), *Conceptualizing Women in Enlightenment Thought* (Berlin,

Berlin Verlag Arno Spitz, 2001); Sarah Knott and Barbara Taylor, (eds.,) *Women, Gender, and Enlightenment* (London, Palgrave, 2005); and Judith Zinsser, *La Dame d'Esprit: A Biography of the Marquise du Châtelet* (New York: Viking, 2006).

Information about laws regarding women may be found in most surveys of the development of law, particularly those that focus on private law, and in general surveys of women's lives. The most important study of church law on these issues is James A. Brundage, *Law, Sex, and Christian Society in Medieval Europe* (Chicago, University of Chicago Press, 1987), which extends its scope into the sixteenth century. Works that look at actual legal cases as well as legal theory include Thomas Kuehn, *Law, Family, and Women: Toward a Legal Anthropology of Renaissance Italy* (Chicago, University of Chicago Press, 1992); and Tim Stretton, *Women Waging Law in Elizabethan England* (Cambridge, Cambridge University Press, 1998). Lawrence Stone, *Uncertain Unions: Marriage in England 1660–1753* (New York, Oxford University Press, 1992), examines common-law and irregular marriages. Ulinka Rublack, *The Crimes of Women in Early Modern Germany* (New York, Oxford University Press, 1999), and Garthine Walker, *Crime, Gender, and Social Order in Early Modern England* (New York, Cambridge University Press, 2003), examine women's criminal actions and their consequences. Renato Barahona, *Sex Crimes, Honour, and the Law in Early Modern Spain: Vizcaya, 1528–1735* (Toronto, University of Toronto Press, 2003), uses legal cases to study issues of honor.

For more suggestions and links, see the companion Web site www.cambridge.org/womenandgender

Part I

Body

2   The Female Life Cycle

> All the world's a stage,
> And all the men and women merely players;
> They have their exits and their entrances;
> And one man in his time plays many parts,
> His acts being seven ages . . .
>> Jacques in William Shakespeare, *As You Like It*, Act II, Scene 7

> All women are thought of as either married or to be married.
>> Anonymous, *The lawes resolution of women's rights* (London, 1632), fol. 6

Beginning with the ancient Greeks, and perhaps earlier, Western scholars debated about how many stages made up a man's life. Some argued for four, corresponding to the four seasons; some twelve, corresponding to the months and the signs of the zodiac; and some three, five, six, eight, or ten. The number that was increasingly accepted was seven, corresponding to the seven known planets (the planets out to Saturn plus the moon) and identified by St. Ambrose in the fourth century as infancy, boyhood, adolescence, young manhood, mature manhood, older manhood, and old age. Discussions of the "ages of man" abounded in the Middle Ages and early modern period, and the stages were depicted in manuscript illuminations, stained-glass windows, wall paintings, and cathedral floors so that people who did not read were also familiar with them.

The seven ages of man began with stages of physical and emotional maturing and then were differentiated by increasing and decreasing involvement in the world of work and public affairs. As men moved from one stage to another, they were shown with different objects symbolizing changing occupations or responsibilities. For men, in only the third stage, adolescence, was sexuality a factor, and marriage or fatherhood were almost never viewed as significant.

Most written discussions of the ages of man never mention women at all; even Jacques, who begins by talking about men and women on the stage of life, goes on to describe a male life cycle. People did talk less formally about the stages of a woman's life, however, and when they did, it was her sexual status and relationship to a man that mattered most, as the second quotation at the beginning of the chapter makes clear. A woman was a virgin, wife, or widow or, alternately, a daughter, wife, or mother. The visual depictions of the ages of man that show couples demonstrate the difficulties artists faced in trying to show stages in an adult woman's life, for although men are depicted as gaining status and authority in their occupations until old age, adult women of all ages are simply portrayed with spindles.

This difference in conceptualization both reflected and shaped social reality. For the vast majority of women in early modern Europe, the most important change in their lives was marriage. The choice of a spouse, whether made by themselves or their parents or a larger kin group, determined their social and economic status and place of residence. Although an early modern woman did not generally look to her husband for the same level of emotional intimacy and support that a contemporary Western woman does, she certainly hoped that day-to-day life with him would be pleasant and that he would not physically or emotionally abuse her. Because divorce was either impossible or difficult for women to obtain, and even living apart from an abusive spouse was illegal without court approval, the only possible relief from an unpleasant marriage was the death of a spouse, over which a woman, of course, had no control. It was the death of her husband, rather than any development in her own life, that moved a woman from one stage of life to another. Because this might happen at any age, and because remarriage meant a woman returned to the status of wife, the "ages of woman" correspond much less to her chronological age than the "ages of man" do to a man's. Although we might regard the early modern conceptualization of the female life cycle as overly physical and marriage-oriented, lending too little credence to women's intellects or decisions, I follow that conceptualization in this chapter because corporeal accidents such as births and deaths not only shaped a woman's physical state but also her emotional health, economic position, opportunities for education, and status in the community.

Childhood and Adolescence

The earliest studies of childhood in the early modern period, undertaken in the 1960s and 1970s, argued that childhood was not recognized as a distinct stage in life and that children were raised harshly or regarded with indifference. These views were derived largely from child-raising manuals that advocated strict discipline and warned against coddling or showing too much affection and portraits of children that showed them dressed as little adults. This bleak view has been relieved somewhat in the last several decades by scholars using archival sources about the way children were actually treated; they have discovered that many parents showed great affection for their children and were very disturbed when they died young. Parents tried to protect their children with religious amulets and pilgrimages to special shrines, made toys for them, and sang them lullabies. Even practices that to us may seem cruel, such as tight swaddling, were motivated by a concern for the child's safety and health at a time when most households had open fires, domestic animals wandered freely, and mothers and older siblings engaged in productive work that prevented them from continually watching a toddler.

The attitudes about the relative value of men and women and the inheritance laws described in the last chapter led early modern parents to favor the birth of sons over daughters. Jewish women prayed for sons, and German midwives were often rewarded with a higher payment for assisting in the birth of a boy. English women's letters sometimes apologize for the birth of daughters. Girls significantly outnumbered boys in most orphanages or foundling homes because poor parents decided their sons would ultimately be more useful; infants had a much poorer chance of survival in such institutions than among the population at large. An interesting exception to this is London, where more boys were abandoned than girls. Study of the London records from 1550 to 1800 indicates that infants were generally abandoned when they were more than a month old, rather than the several days that was common elsewhere in Europe, so that mothers may have become much more attached to them than they were at birth and chose to abandon those children – the boys – who would be likely to receive better care and have a greater chance of survival. Infanticide statistics do not allow us to assess whether girls were more likely to be killed than boys because court records generally simply refer to "child" or "infant," and the number of infanticides by the early modern period was not high enough to have affected the sex ratio among the population at large even if there was a greater likelihood for girls to be victims.

It is also difficult to know how much differentiation by gender there was in the treatment of most infants and small children. Although society had sharply defined gender roles for adults, children were all dressed alike for the first several years of their lives (there is no early modern equivalent of the pink and blue dichotomy), and comments by parents about their small children show less gender stereotyping than is evident among many contemporary parents. It was when children began their training for adult life, at the age of four or five, that clear distinctions became evident. Girls of all classes were taught skills that they would use in running a household – spinning, sewing, cooking, care of domestic animals; peasant girls were also taught some types of agricultural tasks. As we see in Chapter 4, they were much less likely than their brothers to be taught to read or to receive any formal schooling; the depictions of the ages of man that show both sexes portray the female in the second age spinning and the male reading.

The onset of menstruation, termed "menarche" in modern English and "the flowers" in the sixteenth century, provided a girl with the clearest signal of bodily changes leading to adulthood. We know that the average age at menarche has declined in the Western world for the last century, from about 15.5 in the 1890s to less than 13 today, but it is not clear that the average age in the early modern period was significantly higher than that in the nineteenth century. In fact, it may even have been lower because age at menarche is affected by nutrition and other environmental factors, and many girls in the nineteenth century had a poorer diet and performed more physically debilitating work than those of earlier centuries. Somewhere around fourteen was probably about average, with poorer girls starting later than wealthier ones.

Because the actual biological function of menstruation had not yet been discovered, menstruation was viewed medically as either a process that purified women's blood or that removed excess blood from their bodies. As we saw in the last chapter, the humoral theory regarded all bodily fluids as related, and doctors recommended bloodletting as a treatment for disease in both men and women. Because of this, menstruation was not clearly separated from other types of bleeding in people's minds and was often compared to male nosebleeds, hemorrhoids, or other examples of spontaneous bleeding. Menstrual blood was thought to nourish the fetus during pregnancy and, because the body was regarded as capable of transforming one sort of fluid into another, to become milk during lactation. (In the same way, male blood was held to become semen during intercourse.) Semen and milk were not viewed as gender-specific fluids, however, for "virile" women who had more bodily heat than normal were seen as capable of producing semen, and effeminate men who lacked normal masculine heat were thought to lactate.

The cessation of menstruation (amenorrhea) was regarded as extremely dangerous for a woman, either because it left impure blood in her that might harden into an abnormal growth or because it would allow excess blood to run to her brain, which would become overheated. (The opposite idea would be cited as a reason for barring women from higher education in the nineteenth century; education would cause all their blood to remain in their brains, which would halt menstruation and eventually cause the uterus to shrivel away.) Thus, doctors recommended hot baths, medicines, pessaries placed in the vagina, and, for married women, frequent intercourse, to bring on a late menstrual period.

Menstruation was not simply a medical matter, however, but carried a great many religious and popular taboos, for although all bodily fluids were seen as related, menstrual blood was still generally viewed as somehow different and dangerous. Hebrew Scripture held that menstruation made a woman ritually impure so that everything she touched was unclean, and her presence was to be avoided by all. By the early modern period in Jewish communities, this taboo was limited to sexual relations and a few other contacts between wife and husband for the seven days of her period and seven days afterward. At the end of this time, a woman was expected to take a ritual bath (*mikvah*) before beginning sexual relations again. Among the Orthodox Slavs in eastern Europe, menstruating women could not enter churches or take communion. Western Christian churches were a bit milder, but canon lawyers and other Catholic and Protestant commentators advised against sexual relations during menstruation. This was originally based strictly on the religious notion that women were unclean during this period, although during the sixteenth century, the idea spread that this was medically unwise because it would result in deformed or leprous children. Menstruation was used to symbolize religious practices with which one did not agree, with English Protestants, for example, calling the soul of the pope a "menstruous rag." According to popular beliefs, menstruating women could by their touch, glance, or mere presence rust iron, turn wine sour, spoil meat, or dull knives. Although these ideas declined among educated Europeans during the seventeenth century, they are recorded well into the twentieth century among many population groups.

What women themselves thought of menstruation is more difficult to ascertain than male religious or medical opinion. One of the few direct comments by a woman comes from the autobiography of Isabella de Moerloose, published in Amsterdam in 1695, in which she writes that she asked her husband to sleep separately while she was menstruating because "the stink will cause thee to feel aversion for me." He would not allow it because he feared people might think they were Jews, although he, too, commented that he was "so terribly disgusted" by the smell.[1] Women's handwritten personal medical guides, small books in which they recorded recipes for cures and other household hints, include recipes for mixtures to bring on a late menses and to stop overly strong flow. Women turned to midwives and other women for help with a variety of menstrual ailments

---

[1] Isabella de Moerloose, *Gegeven van den Hemel door Vrouuwen Zaet...* (Amsterdam, 1695), quoted in Herman W. Roodenbuerg, "The Autobiography of Isabella de Moerloose: Sex, Childrearing and Popular Beliefs in Seventeenth-Century Holland," *Journal of Social History* 18 (1985), 529.

and, by the eighteenth century, they also consulted male physicians. Physicians' case books from the early eighteenth century indicate that women worried most when menstruation ceased unexpectedly, especially if they thought something other than pregnancy was the cause. They requested the physician prescribe something to get the "flow" started again because regular menstruation was a sign that all the fluids in the body were flowing as they should. Most women seemed to view menstruation not as an illness or a sign of divine displeasure but as a normal part of life; only in the nineteenth century would normal menstruation come to be regarded as pathological. Although calling someone a "menstrual rag" was a serious insult, washing out one's own (or, if one was a servant, one's employers') menstrual rags was as much a part of women's lives as washing soiled infant clothing.

Sexuality

Learned opinion about menstruation was closely related with attitudes toward female sexuality in general, which were also a mixture of medical and religious opinion. In medical terms, male sexuality was the baseline for any perception of human sexuality, and the female sex organs were viewed as the male turned inside out or simply not pushed out. The great sixteenth-century anatomist Andreas Vesalius depicted the uterus looking exactly like an inverted penis, and his student Baldasar Heseler commented: "The organs of procreation are the same in the male and the female. . . . For if you turn the scrotum, the testicles and the penis inside out you will have all the genital organs of the female."[2] This view of the correspondence between male and female sexual organs survived the Renaissance discovery of the clitoris, with scientists simply deciding that women had two structures that were like a penis. This idea meant that there was no precise nomenclature for many female anatomical parts until the eighteenth century because they were always thought to be congruent with some male part and so were simply called by the same name. In the minds of some learned authors, the parallels between the two could lead to unusual sex changes. The prominent French doctor Ambrose Paré solemnly reported the case of a young woman whose sex organs suddenly emerged during vigorous physical activity, transforming her into a man. After 1600, physicians generally discounted stories of such gender transmutations of women into men, and at no time did they describe the opposite process of a man becoming a woman.

---

[2] Baldasar Heseler, *Andreas Vesalius' First Public Anatomy at Bologna 1540: An Eyewitness Report*, ed. Ruben Eriksson (Uppsala: Almqvist and Wiksells, 1959), p. 181.

Because female sex organs were hidden, they seemed more mysterious than male organs to early modern physicians and anatomists, and anatomical guidebooks use illustrations of autopsies on women's lower bodies as symbols of modern science uncovering the unknown. Early modern sex manuals spread this idea to a wider public. The best seller among these was the anonymous *Aristotle's Masterpiece*, first published in 1684 and reprinted in many different versions, often with a subtitle such as "The Secrets of Generation Displayed." Attributing the work to Aristotle gives it a claim to respectability, authority, and ancient pedigree; the real Aristotle, although he had nothing to do with it, would have probably agreed with many of its assumptions. One of these was the notion that both men and women needed to experience orgasm for procreation; only through orgasm would the female "seed" be released, an idea that was yet another example of female experience being simply extrapolated from male. This supposed connection between female orgasm and procreation allowed the manuals to go into great detail about ways to heighten sexual pleasure, while still claiming moralistically to be guides for happy marital life.

Sexuality was also a key issue in religious texts. Those written by Orthodox Slavic writers in eastern Europe saw all sexuality as an evil inclination originating with the devil and not part of God's original creation. Even marital sex was regarded as a sin, with the best marriage an unconsummated one; this led to a large number of miraculous virgin births among Russian saints and to the popular idea that Jesus was born out of Mary's ear, not polluting himself with passage through the birth canal.

Western Catholic opinion did not go this far but displayed an ambivalent attitude toward sexuality. Sex was seen as polluting and defiling, with virginity regarded as the most desirable state; members of the clergy and religious orders were expected, at least in theory, to remain chaste. Their chastity and celibacy made them different from, and superior to, lay Christians who married. On the other hand, the body and its sexual urges could not be completely evil because they were created by God; to claim otherwise was heresy. Writers vacillated between these two opinions or held both at once, and the laws that were developed in the Middle Ages regulating sexual behavior were based on both of them. In general, early modern Catholic doctrine held that sexual relations were acceptable as long as they were within marriage, not done on Sundays or other church holidays, done in a way that would allow procreation, and did not upset the proper sexual order, which meant the man had to be on top (what has since been termed the "missionary position"). Spouses were held to enjoy a mutual right to sexual intercourse (the "marital debt"), which would even excuse intercourse when procreation was not possible. It was better, for example, for a pregnant or menstruating woman to allow her husband to have intercourse with her if refusing this would cause him to turn to a prostitute. Sixteenth- and seventeenth-century Catholic authors adopted a more positive view of marital sex than their medieval predecessors, regarding sexual pleasure, even fantasies and variant positions, as acceptable as a prelude to procreative intercourse.

The Protestant reformers broke clearly with Catholicism in their view that marriage was a spiritually preferable state to celibacy and saw the most important function of marital sex not as procreation but rather as increasing spousal affection. Based on his own experience, Martin Luther stressed the power of sexual feelings for both men and women and thought women in particular needed intercourse to stay healthy.

Western Christian authors and officials thus generally agreed that sexual relations were permissible as long as they were marital and "natural," although interpretations of the latter varied. Jewish authorities agreed, seeing procreation as a commandment of God, although marital sex still made one ritually impure. Islam regarded sex within marriage or other approved relationships as a positive good. Sexual relations did not have to be justified by reproduction, so that contraception was acceptable, although having children, and particularly having sons, was also seen as essential to a good life for Muslims.

Sexuality was also an important theme in popular literature. Many historians have viewed traditional popular culture in Europe as unrestrained, celebrating male sexuality with bawdy stories, obscene songs, and, after the development of the printing press, a range of pornographic literature. These songs and stories express a fear of rampant female sexuality and often advocate beating as the proper way to treat women who showed too much independence. One mid-sixteenth-century German song titled "Song of how one should beat bad women" included the following verses:

> Now will I sing so gaily
> Hit thy wife on the head
> With cudgels smear her daily
> And drink away her dress . . .
> Her body be sure well pound
> With a strong hazel rod;
> Strike her head till it turns round,
> And kick her in the gut.[3]

Such sentiments were extreme, but many surviving ballads and other forms of popular literature present polarized and stereotyped views of

---

[3] "Ein Tagweyss/wie man die bösen weyber schlahen sol" quoted and translated in Joy Wiltenburg, *Disorderly Women and Female Power in the Street Literature of Early Modern England and Germany* (Charlottesville, University Press of Virginia, 1992), p. 121.

women: they are shrewish wives, saintly virgins, betraying sweethearts. A few songs, however, may have been more appreciated by female hearers. The seventeenth-century English ballad "Well Met, Neighbour" presents a conversation between two women:

> Heard you not lately of Hugh,
> How soundly his wife he bang'd?
> He beat her black and blue
> *O such a rogue would be hang'd!* . .
> If my husband should
> Not use me so wells he ought,
> My hands I should hardly hold,
> For I'd give him as good as he brought.[4]

Pornography reflects a different type of fantasy than do popular songs. Authors and printers produced sexually explicit materials, often illustrated, beginning in the late fifteenth century. Some of these were bawdy jokes, puns, poems, and epigrams; others showed various sexual positions or described in lurid detail the range of services offered by prostitutes. Many included stories of sexual scandal and deviance involving contemporary political figures. Protestants told scurrilous stories of lusty monks and debauched nuns, and Catholics answered that the Protestant Reformation was solely the result of Martin Luther's inability to control his sexual voraciousness. In France, King Henry III (ruled 1574–89) was ridiculed for surrounding himself with male favorites and Louis XV (ruled 1715–74) for his inability to satisfy any of his mistresses. Scurrilous anonymous pamphlets about the sexual exploits of the royal couple were particularly common during the reign of Louis XVI (ruled 1774–89), the most graphic of which focused on his queen, Marie Antoinette, who was accused of every type of sexual perversion. Such pamphlets were part of the opposition to the monarchy that led to the French Revolution. Most sexually explicit material was not as politically explosive, but much of it cast women as especially deviant.

Sexual Crimes and Deviance

Women's deviation from accepted norms of behavior was not simply a subject of pornography in early modern Europe but also the regular business of law courts. All early modern societies attempted to control sexual behavior through a variety of means, from secular and church courts to

---

[4] *Roxburghe Ballads* 3:98–103, quoted in Pamela Allen Brown, *Better a Shrew than a Sheep: Women and the Culture of Jest in Early Modern England* (Ithaca: Cornell University Press, 2003), p. 147.

popular rituals designed to humiliate those perceived as deviant. Court records can give us an idea of at least which types of acts communities felt it most important to control. Because the consequences of sexual misconduct became visible within the bodies of women, they appeared more frequently than men in the courts that handled moral behavior, which confirmed people's notions that women were more sexual.

The vast majority of cases involving sexual conduct were for premarital intercourse, termed "fornication." This has been best studied for England, where researchers in various counties have found that between one-fifth and one-third of brides were pregnant upon marriage in the sixteenth and seventeenth centuries, and up to one-half in the eighteenth. Much of this was because by the sixteenth century, the marriage ceremony involved several stages, a contract between the two parties agreeing to get married, and then, often much later, a formal ceremony in the church. Although officially the couple was not married until after the church ceremony, if they had agreed to marry or were regarded simply as seriously courting, sexual relations between them were not condemned in the popular mind, and they might never be prosecuted for fornication. The same was also true in Norway, where 40 to 50 percent of first children were born within eight months of marriage, but it was not true in Scotland, where people never regarded sex as a normal part of courting. The contract was supposed to be somewhat formal, with witnesses and a clear understanding on the part of both parties about what they were doing, but breach-of-promise cases indicate that the two parties often had a very different understanding of what had been agreed upon.

It was often difficult for unmarried women to avoid sexual contacts. Many of them worked as domestic servants, where their employers or employers' sons or male relatives could easily coerce them. Or they worked as unpaid labor at home, where they were vulnerable to stepfathers and brothers-in-law. Charges of incest came to light most often through cases involving premarital pregnancy. Women worked in close proximity to men (a large number of cases involved two servants in the same house) and were rarely supervised or chaperoned. Female servants were sent on errands alone or with men, or worked by themselves in fields far from other people; although notions of female honor might keep upper-class women secluded in their homes, in most parts of Europe there was little attempt to shield female servants or day laborers from the risk of seduction or rape.

Once an unmarried woman suspected she was pregnant, she had several options. In some parts of Europe, if she was a minor, her father could go to court and sue the man involved for "trespass and damages" to his property. The woman herself could go to her local court and attempt to prove there had been a promise of marriage to coerce the man to marry her. This might also happen once her employer or acquaintances suspected pregnancy. Marriage was the favored official solution and was agreed upon in a surprising number of cases, indicating that perhaps there had been an informal agreement or at least that the man was now willing to take responsibility for his actions. In cases in which marriage was impossible, such as those involving married men, the courts might order the man to maintain the child for a set period of years.

The woman might also charge the man concerned with rape. Rape was a capital crime in many parts of Europe, but the actual sentences handed out were more likely to be fines and brief imprisonments, with the severity of sentence dependent on the social status of the victim and perpetrator. The victim had to prove that she had cried out and made attempts to repel the attacker and had to bring the charge within a short period of time after the attack had happened. As noted earlier, her pregnancy might be used as disproof that a rape had occurred, but not all jurists accepted the notion that conception proved consent. Charges of rape were fairly rare, which suggests that it was underreported, but examinations of trial records indicate that rape charges were taken seriously. Women bringing rape charges were often more interested in getting their own honorable reputations back than in punishing the perpetrator and for this reason sometimes requested that the judge force their rapists to marry them. We may have difficulty understanding why any woman would do this, but it was often the easiest way for a woman who was no longer a virgin to establish an honorable social identity as a married woman.

Many women attempted to deny the pregnancy as long as possible. Early modern clothing styles, with full skirts and aprons, allowed most women to go until late in the pregnancy without showing clear visible signs. A woman might attempt to induce an abortion, either by physical means such as tying her waist very tight or carrying heavy objects, or by herbal concoctions that she brewed herself or purchased from a local person reputed to know about such things. Recipes for what we would term "abortificients" were readily available in popular medical guides, cookbooks, and herbals, generally labeled as medicine that would bring on a late menstrual flow or "provoke the monthlies." As noted earlier, both doctors and everyday people regarded regular menstruation as essential to maintaining a woman's health, so anything that stopped her periods was dangerous. Pregnancy was only one possible reason, and a woman could not be absolutely sure she was pregnant until she quickened – that is, felt the child move within her. This was the point at which the child was regarded as gaining a soul to become fully alive – that is what "quickening" originally meant – so that a woman taking medicine to start her period before quickening was generally not regarded as attempting an abortion. Whether any of these medicines would have been effective is another matter, however. Some of them did contain ingredients that do strengthen uterine contractions, such as ergot, rue, or savin, but these can also be poisonous in large doses. It was difficult for women to know exactly what dosage they were taking, for the raw ingredients contain widely varying amounts of active ingredients and their strength depends on how one prepares them, so that it was very likely a woman would take too little to have any effect or too much and become violently ill or die.

Penalties for attempting or performing an abortion after the child had quickened grew increasingly harsh during the early modern period. In the Holy Roman Empire, aborting a "living" child was made a capital offense in 1532, with death to be by decapitation for men and by drowning for women. Midwives were ordered "when they come upon a young girl or someone else who is pregnant outside of marriage, they should speak to them of their own accord and warn them with threats of punishment not to harm the fetus in any way or take any bad advice, as such foolish people are very likely to do."[5] Abortion was very difficult to detect, however, and most accusations of abortion emerged in trials for infanticide, in which a mother's attempts to end her pregnancy before the birth became evidence of her intent. (Contraception was even harder to detect, and although religious and secular authorities all opposed it, there were almost no cases in which it was an issue.)

In most cases, women resigned themselves to having the baby even if they could not get married, often leaving their normal place of residence to have it with friends or relatives, although it was illegal in many parts of Europe to harbor an unmarried pregnant woman. The consequences of unwed motherhood varied throughout Europe, with rural areas that suffered labor shortages being the most tolerant. In Scotland, for example, unmarried mothers had to do a public penance that could be very humiliating, but then they were officially regarded as "purged" of their sin and apparently were able to gain employment even with their child. In rural Norway, about one-quarter of the unwed mothers married men other than the father of their child one to six years after giving birth, and the others managed fairly well. Even in areas where the stigma attached to giving birth out of wedlock was strong, such as England, some women gave birth to two or three children without marrying. Certain families

---

[5] Prussian court record from 1746, quoted in Ulrike Gleixner, *"Das Mensch" und "der Kerl": Die Konstruktion von Geschlecht in Unzuchtsverfahren der Frühen Neuzeit* (Frankfurt, Campus, 1994), p. 158. My translation.

were particularly prone to unwed parenthood among both their female and male members.

For many unmarried women, however, pregnancy meant disaster, and this was particularly the case for pregnancies in which the father was the woman's married employer or was related by blood or marriage to her, for this was adultery or incest rather than simple fornication and could bring great shame on the household. Women in such situations were urged to lie about the father's identity or were simply fired; they received no support from the wife of the father, whose honor and reputation were tightly bound to her husband's. Even when the man was accused of rape, his wife would stoutly defend him, asserting, as one village woman did, that "he always acted honorably during the 23 years that they have been married, so this person [the pregnant maid] must have seduced him into doing this."[6] A pregnant woman fired by her employer was often in a desperate situation because many authorities prohibited people from hiring or taking in unmarried pregnant women, charging them with aiding in a sexual offense if they did.

Women in such a situation might decide to hide the birth. They gave birth in outhouses, cowstalls, hay mounds, and dung heaps, hoping that they would be able to avoid public notice, and took the infant to one of the new foundling homes that had opened during the fifteenth or sixteenth centuries in many cities, or they killed it. Before the sixteenth century, church and secular courts heard few cases of infanticide because jurists recognized that physicians could not make an infallible distinction among a stillbirth, a newborn who had died of natural causes, and one who had been murdered. This leniency changed in the sixteenth century, when infanticide became legally equated with murder in most areas of Europe and so carried the death penalty, often specified as death by drowning. A French royal edict promulgated in 1556 carried this even further, requiring all unmarried women to make an official declaration of their pregnancy and decreeing the death penalty for any woman whose infant died before baptism after a concealed pregnancy or delivery, whether or not there was evidence of actual infanticide. A similar statute was passed in England in 1624, in Scotland in 1690, and in various German states throughout the seventeenth century.

These stringent statutes were quite rigorously enforced. More women were executed for infanticide in early modern Europe than any other crime except witchcraft. In the Spanish Netherlands (modern-day

[6] 1578 Memmingen ordinance, quoted in Merry E. Wiesner, *Working Women in Renaissance Germany* (New Brunswick, NJ, Rutgers University Press, 1986) p. 62.

Belgium), women found guilty of infanticide were generally also accused of witchcraft – the reasoning being that only the devil could lead a mother to kill her child – and executed in gruesome ways, such as being impaled on a stake and then buried alive, or having the offending hand cut off before being drowned. In England, the conviction rate went down after 1680 when women successfully argued that they had not intended to kill the child because they had prepared linen for it or had killed it accidentally or through ignorance. Women were still executed for presumed infanticide in Scotland until 1776, however.

Midwives were enlisted to help enforce the statutes. They were to report all births and attempt to find out the name of the father by asking the mother "during the pains of birth." If an accused woman denied giving birth, midwives or a group of women from the village examined her to see if she had milk or showed other signs of recent delivery; in the case of foundlings, they might be asked to examine the breasts of all unmarried women in a parish for signs of childbirth. Although always justified with comments about a rising tide of infanticide, sometimes this surveillance of unmarried women bordered on the pornographic; an eighteenth-century German physician suggested, for example, that all unmarried women between the ages of fourteen and forty-eight should be viewed monthly at a public bath to see if their bodies showed any signs of pregnancy. Midwives also examined the bodies of infants for signs that they had drawn breath. Courts were intent on gaining confessions, occasionally even bringing in the child's corpse. Records from a 1549 trial in Nuremburg report: "And then the midwife said, 'Oh, you innocent little child, if one of us here is guilty, give us a sign!' and immediately the body raised its left arm and pointed at its mother."[7] The unfortunate mother was later executed by drowning.

Execution for infanticide was the most extreme result of premarital sexual activity for women, but women also suffered for much less serious actions. In many southern European cities, women charged with fornication or even unseemly behavior such as flirting or physically demonstrative conduct might be locked up in institutions established by church or city authorities for repentant prostitutes and other "fallen women." Such houses, often dedicated to Mary Magdalene, also began to admit women who were regarded as in danger of becoming prostitutes, generally poor women with no male relatives; the ordinances stated explicitly that the women admitted had to be pretty or at least acceptable looking, for ugly women did not have to worry about their honor. Many of these asylums were started by reforming bishops or leaders of religious orders, and some

[7] Nuremberg State archives, quoted in ibid., p. 71.

began to admit a variety of other types of women along with prostitutes, such as girls who had been raped, women whose husbands threatened them, attractive daughters of prostitutes, poor young widows, or young women regarded as in danger of losing their sexual honor. These various types of residents were supposed to be separated, and those still "honorable" were taught a trade and given the opportunity to earn a dowry; in practice, the residents were often housed together. The founders of such asylums also supported the establishment of orphanages and foundling homes (termed *ospizi* in Italy), in which unwed mothers were required to leave their children (and in which they might be required to work as wet nurses for other infants along with nursing their own). All of these institutions were attractive charities for those interested in moral reform and were sometimes also supported by taxes on registered prostitutes and courtesans.

In such asylums, the women did not take vows and could leave to marry, but otherwise they were much like convents, with the women following a daily regimen of work and prayer. Some of them stressed penitence and moral reform; others were more purely punitive, closer to prisons than convents. The latter were seen as particularly appropriate for women who refused to change their ways, who – in the words of the reforming nun Madre Magdalena de San Gerónimo – "insult the honesty and virtue of the good ones with their corruption and evil" and as "wild beasts who leave their caves to look for prey" spread "family dishonor and scandal among all the people." Madre Magdalena recommended the establishment of a special women's prison to King Philip II of Spain in 1608 "where in particular the rebellious incorrigible ones will be punished."[8]

This mixture of punishment and penitence may be seen clearly in the Parisian women's prison of the Salpêtrière. In 1658, Louis XIV ordered the imprisonment there of all women found guilty of prostitution, fornication, or adultery, with release only coming once the priests and sisters in charge had determined the inmate was truly penitent and had changed her ways. Imprisoning women for sexual crimes marks the first time that prison was used as a punishment in Europe rather than simply as a place to hold people until their trial or before deportation. Such prisons later became the model for similar institutions for men and young people – often specifically called "reformatories" – in which the inmate's level of repentance determined to a great degree the length of incarceration.

[8] Madre Magdalena de San Gerónimo, *Razón,y forma...* (1608) translated and quoted in Mary Elizabeth Perry, "Magdalens and Jezebels in Counter-Reformation Spain," in Anne J. Cruz and Mary Elizabeth Perry (eds.), *Culture and Control in Counter-Reformation Spain* (Minneapolis, University of Minnesota Press, 1992), pp. 135–36.

(This, of course, is still true for prisons and "reform schools" today.) Once men and boys as well as women and girls were locked up, however, sexual crimes were no longer the basis of the majority of incarcerations the way they were in the earliest women's prisons.

Premarital sexuality was also controlled through less formal means, such as the discussions among a woman's neighbors and acquaintances about her reputation and honor. Such discussions show up in court records when they led to charges of slander, in which, as we saw in the last chapter, the most serious accusation for a woman was to be termed a "whore," and most sexual slander directed at men – terms such as "cuckold," "whoremaster," or "pimp" – actually involved the sexual activities of the women ostensibly under their control. Concern for their sexual honor combined with a clear recognition of the consequences of premarital pregnancy made women themselves the most effective controllers of their sexual conduct. Courts were only successful in imposing standards that most members of the community already accepted, as witnessed by their largely unsuccessful campaign against intercourse between engaged persons. Many women took a more pragmatic view of their honor than church and state authorities did, however, recognizing that it could often be redeemed for a price (such as a dowry) and thus had material as well as moral aspects.

Same-Sex Relations

Most sexual relations that have left traces in legal sources were heterosexual because an out-of-wedlock pregnancy was the most common ground for charges of sexual misconduct. What about same-sex relations? Since the 1980s, in part because of the gay rights and more recently LGBTQ (Lesbian, Gay, Bisexual, Transgendered, Queer) movements, historians have turned their attention to the history of same-sex relations. They emphasize that such relations vary greatly over time and from place to place, both in terms of the relationships themselves and in attitudes toward them. In some societies, same-sex relations among men were culturally acceptable and primarily age-based, involving an older man and a younger man, who both eventually married. In some societies, there were special same-sex subcultures, with distinctive styles of dress, behavior, and meeting places. In many societies, sexuality was conceptualized in terms of the actions that one did, but in the late nineteenth century, medical professionals in Europe began to assert that people had a permanent "sexual identity." Those who felt desire toward members of their own sex were "homosexual," a word invented in 1869, and those who desired people of the opposite sex were "heterosexual," a word that acquired its current usage in the early twentieth century. Because the notion of a "sexual identity" and the words to describe it are relatively recent developments, some historians choose not to use them for earlier eras; there were same-sex acts, they argue, but not homosexuals. In the early modern period, the most common word for same-sex relations was sodomy, although sodomy also included other types of sexual acts viewed as aberrant, including bestiality and heterosexual anal intercourse.

Although same-sex relations have varied enormously, one thing has remained the same: those involving men show up far more often in all types of sources than those involving women. Jewish tradition from biblical times through the early modern period prohibited female same-sex relations, but the punishment was much less than that for male same-sex relations. The New Testament makes no clear mention of female homosexuality, although medieval Christian commentators including Augustine and Aquinas interpreted a vague reference in Paul's Letter to the Romans to refer to it. Guides to priests and monks about what penances to set for various sins specifically refer to female homosexuality, generally setting lower penances than for male, although higher if the women involved were nuns or used dildos. Among the Orthodox Slavs in eastern Europe, women who had sex with women were accused of praying to female spirits and charged with paganism as well as deviant sexual behavior; female homosexuality therefore carried with it an anti-Christian component that male homosexuality did not. In western Europe, some authors commented that witches engaged in female-female sex, although this was not a standard charge against women accused of witchcraft. In 1532, same-sex relations between women were explicitly listed as a capital crime in Germany, although two years later, an English statute prohibiting same-sex sexual relations made no mention of women at all. In fact, same-sex relations between women were never outlawed in England.

These somewhat contradictory attitudes toward female-female sex stemmed in large part from misunderstandings about female anatomy combined with the male perspective of commentators and lawmakers. Although the more enlightened sex manuals such as *Aristotle's Masterpiece* mentioned the role of the clitoris in female orgasm, most male authors could not imagine satisfying sex without penetration. For many of them, there was simply no sex without penetration, so that they regarded female homosexuality as a kind of masturbation. It is, in fact, classed with masturbation as a lesser sin by many clerical commentators, for whom only male-male sex, bestiality, and heterosexual anal intercourse are major sins. Scientific writers such as Ambroise Paré interested in biological anomalies began to report in the sixteenth century about women in other parts of the world, usually the Near East or Africa, with clitorises so enlarged they could penetrate and included these women in their discussions of monsters and prodigies. (These reports may have been motivated by learning that women in these areas underwent clitoridectomies, which led European men to assume the women's clitorises must have been overly large.) European women charged with female-female sex began to be examined for signs of enlarged clitorises and were termed "tribades" or "fricatrices," words of Greek and French origin that meant women who enjoyed rubbing.

Although there may have been some women whose clitorises were as large as those imagined in travel literature and anatomical texts, a more realistic way for women to effect penetration was to use a dildo or similar device. Early modern pornography portrayed women using dildos in both text and illustrations, as did "whore's biographies," books that purportedly traced the life of a woman from debauched to respectable. Such books, such as *The Wandering Whore* (1642) or *Fanny Hill: Memoirs of a Woman of Pleasure* (1749), contain many titillating scenes of sex between women, although in the end the women usually end up in a heterosexual relationship. Dildos also show up in a few actual cases of female-female sex, and their use was uniformly condemned as far worse than female-female sex without one. A woman using a dildo was, of course, taking the male role, and most authorities regarded such gender inversion as much more serious than female homoeroticism. (In the same way, many punishments for male homosexual activity were more severe for the man who took the passive role because he was perceived as letting himself become feminized.)

Trials involving female-female sex were extremely rare and generally involved transvestite dress or women who had otherwise usurped male prerogatives, such as the abbess Benedetta Carlini in Italy who took on the persona of a male angel to engage in sexual relations with another nun. Many of the women who were discovered dressed in men's clothing were serving as soldiers and sailors and reported that they dressed as men primarily to gain the greater opportunities and mobility available to men, rather than for sexual reasons. Catalina de Erauso, for example, fled as a teenager from the Spanish convent where she had lived since she was four, reworked her habit into a shirt and breeches, and took off for South America. She described her various adventures in her memoirs, and, at least in her own writings, drinking, gambling, and brawling were the most significant aspects of her male identity. A few cross-dressing women actually married other women, however, including Maria of Antwerp (1719–81), who was arrested twice for marrying a woman. In her trial, she described herself not as a woman who was sexually attracted to women but as a man in a woman's body, indicating perhaps that, like those who arrested her, she had difficulty figuring out how to describe sexual love between two women. Maria of Antwerp was exiled, and in several other cases in which cross-dressing women married other women, the judges, recommended that the transvestite partner be executed. In all of these cases, the "wife," that is, the woman who remained in women's clothing, received a milder punishment. Literary evidence suggests that female-female desire itself was increasingly demonized by the eighteenth century, but in legal cases, gender inversion continued to be viewed as more threatening than female-female sex alone.

Some historians note that searching for evidence of same-sex relations among women in trial records, pornography, and religious texts is the wrong way to approach the topic because it privileges male-authored sources and puts undue emphasis on genital sex as the defining characteristic of a relationship. They are thus exploring a wide range of relationships among women, which may or may not have involved genital sex. Given the all-female milieus in which many early modern women lived, worked, and slept, and, as we will see later, the late age of marriage and high percentage of women who never married in some parts of Europe, close relationships among women were probably far more common than legal records would indicate. Because they did not produce children who would need to be supported, they occasioned little comment from male authorities, which means it is difficult to find sources about such relationships among the vast majority of women who could not read or write.

Historians studying relationships among women argue about whether to use the word "lesbian" to describe them. "Lesbian" was first used in English in the 1730s to refer to same-sex love between women and was used even earlier in other languages, so it is a much older term than "homosexual." Some historians assert, however, that because today "lesbian" has a distinctly sexual connotation, describing women who had close relations to other women in earlier eras as lesbian transforms relationships that may have been primarily or exclusively emotional into sexual ones. It also carries modern notions of sexual identity back into a period in which people did not understand themselves in this way. Others argue that "lesbian" *should* be used for women whose primary attachments were with other women, for to avoid it denies that such women existed. Others suggest a middle ground, such as "lesbian-like," a phrase that includes the word but highlights its changing meaning.

Whether one chooses to describe close relationships among early modern women as lesbian or not, evidence from women who could read and write gives clear evidence that these were not unusual. Letters, poetry, diaries, and drama written by women reveal passionate attachments and close friendships to other women, both among the female characters they create and between themselves and other actual individuals. Such

Figure 3. Anne Bonney as a pirate. Book illustration from *Historie der Englesche zeerovers*, 1725. Bonney was one of the women who chose to dress in men's clothing to live a more independent life and became an almost mythic figure. Besides highly romanticized portrayals such as this, there were also songs and stories written about her life and adventures.

"romantic friendships," as they came to be termed in the eighteenth century, were expressed physically through kissing and caressing; they did not necessarily include genital sex, although they might have. In poetic expressions of such attachments, the author sometimes adopted a male persona or cast the relationship within the Platonic ideal of spiritual love. Other authors expressed their feelings more openly, as in Lady Mary Chudleigh's poem "*To Clorissa*" (1703):

> O'let our Thoughts, our Interests be but one,
> Our Griefs and Joys, be to each other known;
> In all Concerns we'll have an equal share,
> Enlarge each Pleasure, lessen ev'ry Care;
> Thus, of a thousand Sweets possest,
> We'll live in one another's Breast:
> When present, talk the flying Hours away,
> When absent, thus, our tender Thoughts convey:
> And, when by the decrees of Fate
> We're summoned to a higher State,
> We'll meet again in the blest Realms of Light,
> And in each other there eternally delight.[9]

Marriage

For the majority of women in early modern Europe, sexual desires and relations did not lead to charges of fornication, infanticide, or deviancy or to romantic poetry but were simply one part of the institution that most shaped their lives – marriage. Marital patterns and customs varied widely throughout Europe, but in all places and at all times the vast majority of women and men married at least once, and society was conceived of as a collection of households, with a marital couple, or a person who had once been half of a marital couple, as the core of most households.

The choice of a spouse often determined one's social and financial situation, as well as one's personal well-being and happiness, so that this decision was far too important to leave up to the young people themselves. Family, friends, and neighbors played a role in finding an appropriate spouse and bringing the marriage to realization. Particularly among the upper classes, there were often complicated marriage strategies to cement family alliances and expand family holdings. On the other end of the economic spectrum, communities and cities in some parts of Europe refused to give marriage permits to people who were poor. They

---

[9] Lady Mary Chudleigh, "*To Clorissa*," in Robert W. Uphaus and Gretchen M. Foster (eds.), *The "Other" Eighteenth Century: English Women of Letters 1660–1800* (East Lansing, MI, Colleagues Press, 1991), p. 148.

worried that poor households would need public support and saw marriage as a privilege open only to those who could afford it. This local restriction of marriage permits became state law in the early nineteenth century in many parts of central Europe and lasted until after World War I.

There are numerous examples of children and parents who fought bitterly over the choice of a spouse, but in the vast majority of marriages, the aims of the people involved and their parents, kin, and community were largely the same: the best husband was the one who could provide security, honor, and status, and the best wife one who was capable of running a household and assisting her husband in his work. Therefore, even people who were the most free to choose their own spouses, such as widows and widowers or people whose parents had died, were motivated more by what we would regard as pragmatic concerns than romantic love. This is not to say that their choice was unemotional but that the need for economic security, the desire for social prestige, and the hope for children were as important emotions as sexual passion. The love and attraction a person felt for a possible spouse could be based on any combination of these, with intense romantic desire often viewed as more likely to be disruptive than supportive of a marriage. Marriage manuals, which became a common genre in the sixteenth century, reinforced these ideas; Catholic, Protestant, and Jewish authors agreed that the ideal wife was obedient, chaste, cheerful, thrifty, pious, and largely silent, and the ideal husband was responsible, firm, and honorable.

Spouses did not live up to the ideals set for them all the time, of course, and people regarded it as important to stipulate many legal and financial arrangements with a marriage contract. Marriage contracts were not limited to the wealthy, but by the sixteenth century in some parts of Europe, quite ordinary people, including servants and artisans, had marriage contracts drawn up before they wed. Contracts were especially important in second and third marriages because they had to stipulate how any inheritance might be divided among all of the children. Only after all parties had signed the contract (often including the parents of both spouses, if they were still living) could the actual marriage ceremony proceed. Ceremonies varied throughout Europe, but they generally involved some sort of religious ceremony, followed by as expensive a feast as the family could afford.

Just as marriage ceremonies varied according to region, so did marriage patterns. The most dramatic difference was between the area of northern and western Europe, including the British Isles, Scandinavia, France, Germany, and much of Italy and Spain, as well as eastern and southern Europe. In most of northwestern Europe, historians have identified

a marriage pattern unique in the world, with couples waiting until their mid- or late twenties to marry, long beyond the age of sexual maturity, and then immediately setting up an independent household. (Demographers term this a "nuclear, neolocal" household structure.) Husbands were likely to be only two or three years older than their wives at first marriage, and although households often contained servants, they rarely contained more than one family member who was not a part of the nuclear family. In most of the rest of the world, including southern Europe, most of eastern Europe, and a few parts of northwestern Europe, such as Ireland, marriage was between teenagers who lived with one set of parents for a long time, or between a man in his late twenties or thirties and a much younger woman, with households again containing several generations. (Demographers term this a "complex" family household and make further distinctions between "extended" family households with one conjugal unit plus one or more other kin, and "multiple" family households with two or more kin-related family units.) There were regional and class variations from these patterns – in southern Italy and southern Spain, nuclear families were more common than complex, which was also true among agricultural wage laborers in Hungary and Romania – but, in general, these two family patterns marked two large regions.

Historians are not sure exactly why northwestern Europe developed such a distinctive marriage pattern, but its consequences are easier to trace than its causes: fewer total pregnancies per woman, although not necessarily fewer surviving children; a greater level of economic independence for newlyweds, who had often spent long periods as servants or workers in other households saving money and learning skills; more people who never married at all. The most unusual feature of this pattern was the late age of marriage for women. Women entered marriage as adults and took charge of running a household immediately. They were thus not as dependent on their husbands as were, for example, upper-class women in early modern Italian cities, where the average age of marriage for men was over thirty and for women fifteen. They were not under the authority of their mothers-in-law the way women were in eastern European households where younger couples lived with the husbands' parents. Visitors from southern and eastern Europe frequently commented on what they regarded as the "freedom" of women in northern European cities, although such remarks were occasioned primarily by the large number of adult unmarried women who worked and socialized in public places. Marriage law throughout Europe placed wives in a clearly dependent relationship no matter how old they were when they married, so that it is difficult to assess whether the late age of marriage in and of itself worked to women's advantage.

One of the key ideas of the Protestant Reformation was the denial of the value of celibacy and championing of married life as a spiritually preferable state. One might thus expect religion to have had a major effect on marriage patterns, but this is difficult to document, in large part because all the areas of Europe that became Protestant lie within northwestern Europe. There were a number of theoretical differences. Protestant marriage regulations stressed the importance of parental consent more than Catholic ones and allowed the possibility of divorce with remarriage for adultery or impotence and, in some areas, also for refusal to have sexual relations, deadly abuse, abandonment, or incurable diseases such as leprosy. Orthodox law in eastern Europe allowed divorce for adultery or the taking of religious vows. The numbers of people of any Christian denomination who actually used the courts to escape an unpleasant marriage were small, however, and apparently everywhere smaller than the number of couples who informally divorced by simply moving apart from one another. In parts of Europe where this has been studied, women more often used the courts to attempt to form a marriage, that is, in breach of promise cases or to renew a marriage in which their spouse had deserted them, than to end one. The impossibility of divorce in Catholic areas was mitigated somewhat by the possibility of annulment and by institutions that took in abused or deserted wives; similar institutions were not found in Protestant areas.

Jewish law allowed divorce (termed *get*) for a number of reasons, including incompatibility; in theory, the agreement of both spouses was needed, and the economic division of the assets was to be based on each spouse's behavior. Muslim law allowed a man to divorce his wife at any time, although he was required to continue supporting her; wives seeking divorce – which emerge more in actual court records than in theoretical law codes – gave up their right to this support. Muslim law also allowed a man to have up to four wives, but polygamy was relatively uncommon in the Ottoman Empire.

Place of residence and social class had a larger impact than religion on marital patterns. Throughout Europe, rural residents married earlier than urban ones and were more likely to live in complex households of several generations or married brothers and their families living together. They also remarried faster and more often. Women from the upper classes married earlier than those from the lower, and the age difference between spouses was greater for upper-class women. Women who had migrated in search of employment married later than those who had remained at home and married someone closer to their own age.

Along with significant differences, there were also similarities in marriage patterns throughout Europe. Somewhere around one-fifth of all

marriages were remarriages for at least one of the partners, with widowers much more likely to remarry than widows and to remarry faster. The
reasons for this differ according to social class; wealthy or comfortable
widows may have seen no advantage in remarrying, for this would put
them under the legal control of a man again, and poor widows, particularly elderly ones, found it difficult to find marriage partners. Women
of all classes and religions were expected to bring a dowry to their marriage, which might consist of some clothing and household items (usually
including the marriage bed and bedding) for poor women or vast amounts
of cash, goods, or property for wealthy ones; in eastern Europe, the dowry
might even include serfs or slaves. The size of the dowry varied by geographic area and across time as well as by social class. In fifteenth- and
sixteenth-century Florence, for example, dowries required for a middle-
or upper-class woman to marry grew staggeringly large, and families
placed many of their daughters in convents instead of trying to find husbands for them because convent entrance fees were much lower than
dowries. The dowry substituted in most parts of Europe for a daughter's
share of the family inheritance and increasingly did not include any land,
which kept land within the patrilineal lineage. Laws regarding a woman's
control of her dowry varied throughout Europe but, in general, a husband had the use, but not the ownership, of it during his wife's lifetime –
although, of course, if he invested it unwisely, this distinction did not make
much difference. Women could sue their own husbands if they thought
they were wasting their dowries, however, and courts in many areas sided
with the women, taking control of the dowry out of the husbands' hands.
This was clearly something done only as a last resort because it meant a
woman had to admit publicly her husband was a wastrel or spendthrift.
During the late medieval period, women appear to have been able freely
to bequeath their dowries to whomever they chose, but in many parts of
Europe, this right was restricted during the sixteenth century to prevent
them from deeding property to persons other than the male heirs.

This increasing legal emphasis on the male lineage paralleled an
increasing concern among male religious, literary, and political writers
with the authority and role of the male head of household, as we have seen
in Chapter 1. At the same time, Puritans and some other Protestant writers also stressed the wife's authority over children and servants and the
importance of mutual affection between spouses. Yet what about actual
marital relations? Did husbands and wives show more or less affection for
one another than modern couples? Which injunction was followed more
in practice, that of husbandly authority or that of mutual respect? Some
historians have seen the early modern family as unfailingly patriarchal
and authoritative, whereas others have found that people, particularly

women, expected a marriage to include affection and companionship and were distressed when it did not. Examples of both tyrannical husbands and of mutually caring relationships abound, with the safest generalization that which also seems the most obvious: marriages appear to have been most egalitarian when husband and wife were close in age, of the same or relatively the same social class, when the woman had brought some property or cash to the marriage as her dowry, and when her birth family supported her in disputes with her husband.

Marriage brought a woman into a relationship not only with her husband but also with her husband's family and often a new neighborhood and community; it also transformed her relationship with her birth family. Despite the increased emphasis on patrilineality, women in most parts of Europe continued to think of themselves as still belonging to their birth families or as belonging to two families at once. Women's wills often bequeathed items and cash to their sisters or nieces and provided for masses to be said for members of their birth as well as marital family; women sometimes chose to be buried with their birth families rather than their husbands.

Marriage was the clearest mark of social adulthood for both women and men. For men, marriage often meant that they could now be part of the governing body of their village or town, a role from which unmarried men were excluded; for women, it meant that they would have authority over dependent members of the household. Middle-class urban women also began during the early modern period to redefine what it meant to be a "housewife." In part, this was a response to their exclusion from productive labor outside of the household, which I discuss in the next chapter, and in part a response to the increased emphasis on the family and marriage, particularly in Protestant areas. In fact, it was the wives of Protestant pastors who were often the leaders in a town in the creation of this expanded domestic role. Medieval urban "housewives" had had little time for purely domestic labor; cooking was simple, cleaning tasks were few, and many domestic tasks such as baking and laundry were hired out. This began to change in the sixteenth and even more in the seventeenth centuries, when foodstuffs were more likely to come into households in a less finished state and middle-class households contained more consumer goods that needed cleaning and care. Of necessity, the time spent by middle-class women on domestic tasks expanded, particularly as things that had been unavailable or unimportant in the Middle Ages – glass windows, a stone floor instead of a dirt one, several courses at dinner – became important signs of middle-class status. Now the ideal wife was not simply one who showed religious virtues such as piety and modesty but also economic ones such as order, industriousness, and thrift. We are used to thinking about the early modern period as a time of growing prosperity among the middle classes; the fruits of that prosperity, what we would term the "bourgeois lifestyle," were determined and to a large degree created by middle-class married women.

Singlewomen

What about women who could not or chose not to get married? In eastern Europe, with a much earlier average age at first marriage, the number of women who never married was small, and most of these women were in convents. In southern Europe, wealthy or middle-class women who chose not to marry or whose parents could not raise a dowry large enough to obtain an appropriate husband also ended up in convents, the standards about austerity of which were often not very high so that the women lived the same comfortable lifestyle they would have on the outside. In 1552 in Florence, for example, there were 441 male friars and 2,786 nuns out of a population of 59,000; the difference between the two numbers results not from women's great religious fervor but from a staggering increase in the size of the dowry required for a middle- or upper-class woman to marry. Historians are currently debating the cause of this dowry inflation, and it was decried at the time by moralists who rightly saw it as preventing people from marrying. Families were unable to control it, however, and so placed their daughters in convents instead of trying to find husbands for them because, as noted earlier, convent entrance fees were much lower than dowries.

Entrance fees for convents were too high for poor women, however, and, as described earlier, special institutions were opened in Italian cities by the Catholic Church and municipal governments for young, attractive unmarried women to allow them to earn a dowry and thus perhaps a husband. Women whose marriage chances were seen as unlikely in any case were also often sent to convent-like religious institutions, where they did not take formal vows and worked at spinning or sewing to support themselves. Unmarried poor women also worked as domestic servants for their entire lives, living in the household of their employer and so under his control.

In the cities of northwestern Europe, the number of unmarried women – which English sources refer to as "singlewomen" – had been significant since the Middle Ages and did not decrease in the early modern period. Demographers estimate that between 10 and 15 percent of the northwestern European population never married in the early modern period and that in some places in some eras, this figure may have been as high as 25 percent, making this more important than late marriage as a check on population growth. Cities attracted singlewomen with the possibility of employment as domestic servants or in cloth production; their dominance in spinning is reflected in the gradual transformation of the word "spinster" during the seventeenth century from a label of occupation to one of marital status. The types of employment open to singlewomen or widows left without resources were generally poorly paid, which we can see from the fact that households headed by widows and unmarried women were always the poorest in any city; unattached women often had to live together to survive.

In the late Middle Ages, city governments worried about how to keep unmarried women and widows from needing public support, and in the sixteenth century, cities began to view women living independently as both a moral and an economic problem. They were "masterless," that is, not members of a male-headed household, at a time when greater stress was being laid on the authority of the husband and father, and so were perceived as a possible threat to the social order. Laws were passed forbidding singlewomen to move into cities and ordering unmarried female servants who had left one domestic position to leave the city should they refuse to take another one. In some cases grown, unmarried daughters were ordered to leave the household of their widowed mothers to find a position in a male-headed household if their mothers could not prove need for them at home. Suspicion of unmarried women was not completely new in the sixteenth century, for medieval religious groups such as the Beguines had also experienced it, but this was the first time actual laws had been enacted against secular singlewomen. Both Protestant and Catholic authorities increasingly viewed marriage as the "natural" vocation for women – for all women in Protestant areas and for most women in Catholic areas – so that women who did not marry were somehow "unnatural" and therefore suspect.

Women themselves sometimes internalized the stigma attached to never being married. This was particularly true for middle- and upper-class Protestant women, who in only a few parts of Europe had convents as an alternative. The funeral sermons of unmarried women, for which the women themselves often chose their own biblical texts and wrote the biographical segment, explain that the deceased was not simply a person who had lost out in the marriage market but one who had fulfilled her Christian duties in other ways than being a wife or mother, such as taking care of elderly parents or serving the needy. Middle-class unmarried women in England took part in philanthropy and in the eighteenth century began to teach in schools that were slowly opening for poor children, a field they would come to dominate in the nineteenth century.

Not all women agreed that marriage was preferable, however. The opposite opinion was expressed most eloquently by Anna Bijns, a sixteenth-century Antwerp poet:

> How good to be a woman, how much better to be a man!
> Maidens and wenches, remember the lesson you're about to hear
> Don't hurtle yourself into marriage far too soon.
> The saying goes: "Where's your spouse? Where's your honor?"
> But one who earns her board and clothes
> Shouldn't scurry to suffer a man's rod.
> So much for my advice, because I suspect
> Nay, see it sadly proven day by day –
> 'T happens all the time!
> However rich in goods a girl might be,
> Her marriage ring will shackle her for life.
> If however she stays single
> With purity and spotlessness foremost,
> Then she is lord as well as lady. Fantastic, not?
> Though wedlock I do not decry:
> Unyoked is best! Happy the woman without a man.[10]

Pregnancy and Childbirth

Very shortly after marriage (and, in many cases, before marriage, as we have seen) most women in early modern Europe were pregnant. In all religious traditions, the procreation of children was viewed as one of the most important functions of marriage – or the most – and childless couples were viewed with pity. Childlessness hit women particularly hard, because despite the fact that many people regarded the man as the source of all the active forces in the creation of a child and the woman simply the vessel, childlessness was invariably seen as the woman's fault. This is one of the reasons that suggestions about how to promote fertility through diet, exercise, potions, and charms were extremely common in midwives' manuals and advice books for women. Childless men could test their fertility outside of marriage with little public condemnation (although not officially condoned, adultery if one's wife was barren was rarely punished), but childless wives did not have this opportunity.

Determining whether one was pregnant was not an easy matter, however. The cessation of menses opened up the possibility, but midwives' manuals and women's private medical guides cautioned women against

---

[10] Anna Bijns, "Unyoked is best! Happy the woman without a man," trans. Kristiaan P. G. Aercke, reprinted in Katharina M. Wilson (ed.), *Women Writers of the Renaissance and Reformation* (Athens, University of Georgia Press, 1987), p. 382.

regarding this as a clear sign because it may also have been due to other medical conditions. Nausea, breast enlargement, and thickening around the middle also pointed toward pregnancy, but only at quickening – that is, when the mother could feel the child move within her body, which usually happens during the fourth or fifth month – was the mother regarded as verifiably pregnant. Until the late eighteenth century on the Continent and the nineteenth century in England, quickening was also viewed as the point at which a child gained a soul, so that charges of abortion could not be brought against a woman who had not yet quickened. This legal definition affected the way that women thought about their own pregnancies, for they did not describe a miscarriage before quickening as the end of a pregnancy or the death of a child but as the expulsion of blood curds or leathery stuff or wrong growths. Pregnancy was not a condition affirmed externally and visually the way it is today with home pregnancy tests and ultrasound screenings, but internally and tactilely, with only the mother able to confirm that quickening had happened.

Once a woman suspected or knew she was pregnant, she received a great amount of advice. The sixteenth century saw the publication of the first midwives' manuals in most European languages, which contained advice for prenatal care for the mother as well as the handling of deliveries. These manuals were reprinted and pirated for centuries, and new ones were published in the seventeenth century, but their advice for expectant mothers changed little. Much of what they advise is still recommended today: pregnant women should eat moderately of nourishing foods, including a good amount of protein, and avoid foods that make them nauseous or that are highly spiced; they should moderate their drinking and avoid strong liquors; they should get regular exercise but avoid strenuous lifting; they should wear low-heeled shoes and loosen their lacing or corsets. The advisability of sexual intercourse during pregnancy was debated, as was the practice of letting blood from pregnant women. Many of their suggestions have to do with the mental rather than strictly physical well-being of the expectant mother and stem from a strong belief in the power of the maternal imagination. Both learned and uneducated people in early modern Europe believed that what a woman saw or experienced during pregnancy could affect the child. The desire to drink red wine or eat strawberries might lead to children with red birthmarks; being frightened by a hare or longing to eat hare caused harelip; sudden frights might cause a miscarriage or deform the fetus in some way. Birth defects were regularly attributed to bad experiences during pregnancy or to a woman's frequent contact with animals.

As the time of the birth approached, a woman began to make preparations. She decided which friends and neighbors she would invite to

assist her, a matter taken very seriously; witchcraft accusations occasionally stemmed from the curses and anger of a neighbor who had not been
invited. If she lived in a town where the services of professional midwives
were available, the mother chose which midwife would direct the birth.
If she lived in a rural area, she would generally contact a woman known
to be experienced in handling childbirths, for midwives who had undergone some theoretical training in childbirth procedure were rare in the
countryside. In rural areas where church approval was needed to practice
midwifery, village women simply chose one of their number as the most
experienced and then gave her name to the church authorities.

Until the mid-seventeenth century, and until the twentieth in many
parts of Europe for most women, childbirth was strictly a female affair.
The husband was not present unless his wife was dying, and male medical
practitioners took little interest in delivery. Male physicians were only
called in if the child, mother, or both were dead or dying, so their presence
was dreaded.

This began to change in France in the mid-seventeenth century, where
some male barber-surgeons began to advertise their services for childbirth
as well, and the use of "man-midwives" came to be fashionable among
the wealthy. At first, the techniques of these men differed little from those
of educated urban female midwives, for both read the same books and
had the same concepts of anatomy and the birth process, but gradually
the training of male midwives improved as they took part in dissections
and anatomical classes, from which women were excluded.

Male midwifery spread to England, where sometime in the seventeenth
century the forceps was invented by the Chamberlen brothers, who kept
its design a family secret for nearly a century and then revealed it only
to other male midwives. The forceps allows a midwife to grasp the head
of a child who has become lodged in the birth passage and pull it out, a
procedure that is not usually possible with the hands alone and had been
accomplished earlier only on dead children with hooks stuck in their
mouths or eyes. A higher level of training and more use of instruments
made male midwives appear more scientific and "modern" to middle-
and upper-class English and French women, although there was still a
strong sense of the impropriety of male practitioners touching women
in childbirth among rural residents and lower-class urban dwellers, who
could not pay the fees demanded by male midwives in any case. Male
midwives were not common in the early modern period in Germany and
were not found at all in eastern and southern Europe, where female urban
midwives were much more likely to be granted access to formal training
in female anatomy and physiology than they were in France or England.
In northern Italy in particular, midwifery schools were founded in the

Figure 4. Albrecht Dürer, *The Birth of Mary*. Though ostensibly the depiction of the birth of the Virgin Mary, in reality Dürer's engraving portrays a typical sixteenth-century birth scene, with a number of women bustling about, the baby being bathed, and the tired midwife asleep by the bed.

mid-eighteenth century to teach women anatomy, although most midwives continued to be educated through apprenticeship.

Once labor had begun, the women assisting transformed the room, or in small houses the bed, into a "lying-in chamber," according to local traditions of what was proper. In many parts of Europe, air was viewed as harmful to the mother, so doors and windows were shut and candles lit. Special objects felt to be efficacious in speeding delivery were brought in, such as amulets, relics of saints, or certain herbs. Special prayers were offered, prayers that were often the most resistant to change when the religious allegiance of an area changed. The women prepared broth or mulled wine (termed "caudle" in England) to nourish the mother through the delivery and arranged the swaddling clothes for the infant.

Midwives varied in their techniques of delivery. Some midwives and mothers preferred to use a birthing stool, a special padded stool with handles that tipped the mother back slightly; other mothers lay in bed, kneeled, stood, or sat in another woman's lap. Midwives tended to intervene only if something was going wrong, which was usually a case of abnormal presentation. If the child was emerging feet or knees first (breech), it could usually be delivered, but if it emerged arm- or face-first it generally needed to be turned. Until the invention of the forceps, the best way to do this was to reach inside the uterus and grasp the feet, turning the child by the feet to effect a feet-first birth (this technique is termed "podalic version"). Midwives' manuals beginning in the sixteenth century recommend this, and records of births handled by professional midwives throughout the early modern period indicate they handled this technique successfully.

Childbirth was an event with many meanings, at once a source of joy and the cause of deep foreboding. Most women experienced multiple childbirths successfully, but all knew someone who had died in childbed, and many had watched this happen. Using English statistics, it has been estimated that the maternal mortality rate in the past was about 1 percent for each birth, which would make a lifetime risk of 5 to 7 percent. Women knew these risks, which is why they attempted to obtain the services of the midwife they regarded as the most skilled.

Although we have few records from midwives themselves, those that exist can give us a glimpse of both their activities and their self-concept. Catharina Schrader (1656–1746) was a professional midwife in the Netherlands who kept notebooks of all of her cases between the years 1693 and 1745, more than 3,000 in all. When she was in her eighties, she decided to pull all of her most complicated cases into a single book,

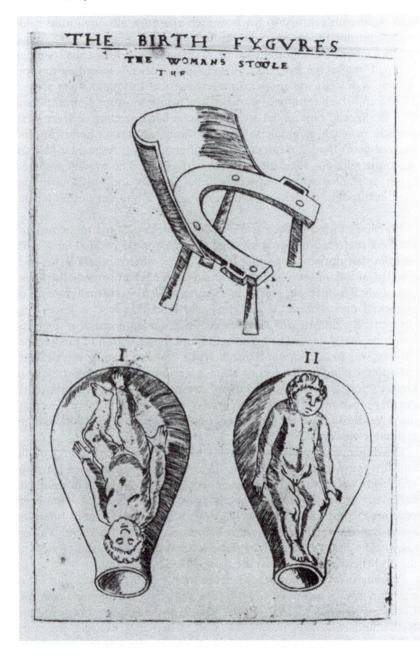

dedicating it to the women she had delivered. Her discussion of one difficult delivery reads:

1711 on 10 February I was fetched to Nijkerk to Wattse Jennema, whose wife was called Alltie Jouwkes. She wanted me to attend to her, but didn't call for me. And fetched a midwife from Morra, who tortured her for three days. She turned it over to the man-midwife, doctor Van der Berrg. He said, he must cut off the child's arms and legs. He took her [the mother] for dead. And he said, the child is already dead. Then I was fetched in secret. When I came there her husband and friends were weeping a great deal. I examined the case, suspected that I had a chance to deliver [her]. The woman was very worn out. I laid her in a warm bed, gave her a cup of caudle, also gave her something in it; sent the neighbors home, so that they would let her rest a bit. An hour after her strength awakened again somewhat. And I had the neighbors fetched again. And after I had positioned the woman in labour, [I] heard that the doctor came then to sit by my side. I pulled the child to the birth canal and in half of a quarter hour I got a living daughter. And I said to the doctor, here is your dead child, to his shame. He expected to earn a hundred guilders there [about 10–20 times what Schrader usually earned]. The friends and neighbors were very surprised. The mother and the child were in a very good state.[11]

Midwives were responsible for the spiritual as well as the physical well-being of the children they delivered. In both Catholic and Protestant areas, they were allowed to perform emergency baptisms on children they thought might die, and midwifery ordinances contain careful instructions on how to do this properly. By the middle of the eighteenth century in Catholic areas, they were also instructed to baptize a fetus that had miscarried and to perform a Caesarean section on any pregnant woman who had died to baptize the fetus within her.

Mothers of all religions in Europe recognized that the dangers of child-birth might be intensified when children were born too close together and attempted to space births through a variety of means. Many nursed their children until they were more than two years old, which acted as a con-traceptive, for suckling encourages the release of the hormone prolactin, which promotes the production of milk and inhibits the function of the

[11] Hilary Marland, *Mother and Child Were Saved: The Memoirs (1693–1745) of the Frisian Midwife Catharina Schrader* (Amsterdam, Rodopi, 1987), pp. 62–64.

Figure 5. Illustrations from Thomas Raynalde, *The Byrth of Mankynde*, London, 1545. These illustrations from a popular English midwives' manual depict a standard birthing stool, with handles at the sides for the mother to grasp, and early modern ideas of a baby in utero. They had originally appeared in a German midwives' manual and were frequently reprinted in manuals in other languages throughout Europe.

ovaries. They sought to abstain from sexual relations during the time of their monthly cycle regarded as most fertile, although this "rhythm method," based on an incorrect view of the menstrual cycle, was even less effective than that practiced in the twentieth century. Judging by the frequency with which such practices were condemned, couples regularly attempted to restrict fertility through coitus interruptus, magical charms, and herbal potions; the first of these was the most effective. Condoms made from animal intestines or bladders were available to those who could afford them by the mid-sixteenth century, but they were originally designed to protect men from venereal disease carried by prostitutes and were only slowly seen as a possible means of fertility control for married couples. All of the methods that could be effective – abstinence, coitus interruptus, condoms – required the cooperation of the woman's husband, of course.

The experience of childbirth did not end with actual birth. In most parts of Europe, mothers were advised to undergo a period of "lying-in" after the birth, in which they sharply restricted their activities and contacts with the outside world. Although this was difficult for many rural and poor women, religious taboos that made a recently delivered mother impure meant that such restrictions were often followed even when they were economically disadvantageous. Early modern Russia had perhaps the strongest taboos, for Orthodoxy taught that everything associated with childbirth, including the midwife, attendants, place, and even the child, was defiled. Not until her ritual of purification, which occurred forty days after birth, was anyone supposed to eat in the woman's company; baptism was often delayed until the same day so that the newborn remained impure and could nurse from its impure mother. Judaism and Catholicism had a similar ritual of purification, although contacts with the mother were not so sharply restricted. Her movements outside the home were restricted, however, which meant a Catholic woman could not attend her child's baptism; in Italy, the midwife who carried the child was the only woman normally present at a baptism. In some parts of Catholic Europe, this purification ceremony was seen as so important that it was performed over the coffin of a woman who had died in childbirth.

Protestants rejected the idea that women needed to be purified after giving birth, but Anglicans and some Continental Protestants retained the ceremony, commonly called "churching," terming it instead a service of thanksgiving. In some Lutheran areas, churching was required of all married mothers and forbidden to those who gave birth out of wedlock, another mark of the distinction between honorable and dishonorable women. In England, unmarried women who had given birth were only to be churched if they named the father and wore a white sheet signifying their penitence during the service. Churching was violently opposed by English Puritan men in the seventeenth century as a Catholic holdover, but many Puritan women continued to demand it, as did other English women into the twentieth century even if they never attended other church services. We may view churching and similar ceremonies as stemming from clerical hostility toward the female body and childbirth, but there is evidence that early modern women rejected this interpretation and instead regarded churching as a necessary final act of closure to a period of childbirth. A woman attended her churching in the presence of the women who had been with her during the birth, including the midwife, and many of the rituals that were part of churching were of popular, rather than ecclesiastical, origin. Women objected when pastors sought to change the ritual in any way; one 1668 report from Abingdon in England noted that "women refuse to be churched because they have not their right place, and midwives are excluded ... from their women, who always used to sit together."[12] Churching is, in fact, only one of many popular rituals and beliefs surrounding birth that did not die out in the eighteenth century. Evidence gathered in the mid-twentieth century indicates that people continued to regard a woman who had recently given birth as unlucky and prohibited her from touching wells or stalls or visiting her neighbors.

Motherhood

The vast majority of women during the early modern period nursed their own children, often until they were more than two years old and on demand rather than on a set schedule. Women who could not produce their own milk and middle- and upper-class women in many parts of Europe relied on wet nurses, the very wealthy hiring the nurse to come into their own homes, and the rest sending the child to the home of the wet nurse, often for two or three years. Although by the eighteenth century this practice came to be viewed by moralists such as Rousseau as a sign of the heartlessness and decadence of wealthy women, it actually stemmed from the fact that nursing was incompatible with many of their familial and social duties. Wealthy women were pressured to produce many heirs, and people seem to have been aware of the contraceptive effects of lactation; they were advised that nursing would ruin their physical attractiveness; they were taught that sexual intercourse would corrupt their milk and that their first duty was to their husbands. The decision

---

[12] Quoted in David Cressy, *Birth, Marriage and Death: Ritual, Religion, and the Life Cycle in Tudor and Stuart England* (London, Oxford, 1997), p. 227.

to hire a wet nurse was often made not by the woman herself but by her husband, who made a contract with the wet nurse's husband for her services.

Wet nurses were chosen with great care, with those from rural areas who had borne many healthy children favored. Psychological and moral qualities were also taken into consideration, for it was thought that an infant gained these through the nurse's milk; after the Reformation, for example, parents inquired about the religious affiliation of any prospective nurse, for Catholic parents feared the corruption caused by Protestant milk and vice versa. The wet nurse and her husband had to agree to refrain from sexual relations during the period of the contract, for it was thought that pregnancy tainted a woman's milk.

Along with the children of the wealthy, wet nurses also cared for the children of the poor; communities hired wet nurses to suckle foundlings and orphans, and by the eighteenth century working women in some parts of Europe hired wet nurses so that they could work longer hours without stopping. Many of these poor children died, as did many of the wealthy, some no doubt because of neglect or carelessness but also because the wet nurses themselves were generally poor and took on more children than they had milk; in many cases, these women had sent their own infant to an even poorer woman to take on children to nurse in the first place. These deaths led wet nurses to be called "angel-killers" by eighteenth-century writers advocating maternal nursing, but it is difficult to document whether infant mortality rates were actually higher for the children in their care than they would have been otherwise; for orphans or foundlings, there was no other option anyway, and evidence clearly indicates that mortality among children put to nurse went up when dry nursing (feeding infants with flour gruel or pap sucked off a rag) was substituted for wet nursing.

Wet nurses often became fond of the children they suckled and were reluctant to return them to their parents, sometimes remaining with the children as servants or companions into adulthood. Some historians have speculated that children in early modern Europe also suffered emotional distress because of the wet-nursing system; frequent changes in wet nurses, the absence of their biological mother, and permanent separation from the wet nurse at weaning could prevent small children from forming good relationships with women. Because infant feelings affect later psychological development, wet nursing has been seen as contributing to negative ideas about women, particularly their fickleness and changeability. The irony of these possible consequences is the fact that, until the mid-eighteenth century, it was husbands who made the decision about how a child would be nursed. Only at that point did some middle- and upper-class women begin to assert their right to nurse their own children, and the rate of maternal nursing among these social groups increased.

Motherhood is, of course, an emotional and intellectual experience as well as a physical one. Although historians used to argue that premodern parents were cold and unfeeling, in fact, early modern mothers generally became deeply attached to their children. Even those forced to abandon them for economic reasons could be torn apart by the decision, as this note pinned to a foundling left in 1709 indicates:

This child was born the 11th of June 1708 of unhappy parents which is not able to provide for it; therefore I humbly beg of you gentlemen whosoever hands this unfortunate child shall fall into that you will take that care that will become a fellow creature and if God makes me able I will repay the charge and redeem the child with thanks to you for her care . . . pray believe that it is extreme necessity that makes me do this.[13]

The deaths or illnesses of their children often led women into depression or even suicidal despair, and those who showed no attachment to their children were viewed as mentally disturbed.

Women's concern over their children became particularly acute during their own illnesses, leading a number of middle- and upper-class women to write advice books for their children in case they should die. Dorothy Leigh in *The Mother's Blessing* (London, 1616) commented that "motherly affection" led her to risk public censure by writing, and Elizabeth Grymeston opened *Miscelanea, Meditations, Memoratives* (London, 1604) with the comment:

My dearest son, there is nothing so strong as the force of love; there is no love so forcible as the love of an affectionate mother to her natural child: there is no mother can either more affectionately show her nature, or more naturally manifest her affection, than in advising her children out of her own experience, to eschew evil, and incline them to do that which is good.[14]

These books include much more advice about personal and family matters such as the choice of a spouse than do similar books written by men; a guide for her son written by Elisabeth, the widowed ruler of Braunschweig in Germany, includes long discussions of his role as a father as well as a

---

[13] St. Martin in the Fields parish examination book, quoted in Valerie Fildes, "Maternal Feelings Re-assessed: Child Abandonment and Neglect in London and Westminster, 1550–1800," in her *Women as Mothers in Pre-industrial England* (London, Routledge, 1990), p. 153 (spelling modernized).

[14] Elizabeth Grymeston, *Miscelanae, Meditations, Memoratives* (London, 1604), quoted in Betty Travitsky, *The Paradise of Women: Writings by Englishwomen of the Renaissance* (New York, Columbia University Press, 1989), p. 52 (spelling modernized).

ruler, a concern not found in similar "mirrors of princes" written by male rulers.

Widowhood and Old Age

The loss of a spouse was a common feature of married life throughout Europe; people became widowed at all ages and might easily be widowed several times during their lives. The death of a spouse brought a more dramatic change in status for women than it did for men. Women's link to the world of work often depended on their husband's professional identity, so that his death affected his widow's opportunities for making a living, whereas the death of a wife did not. We can see this distinction in the fact that the word for "widower" in most European languages derives from the word for "widow," whereas the more common pattern is for the female designation to derive from the male – princess from prince, actress from actor. The word "widower," in fact, does not enter common usage until the eighteenth century, when people began to think about the loss of a spouse more as an emotional than an economic issue; sources from before that time indicate clearly when women are widows, but only rarely that men have lost their wives.

Images of widows in this period are generally negative, with widows portrayed as ugly old crones or as greedy and sexually rapacious women looking for their next husbands (or sometimes as both). The reality was more complex. The death of a husband often brought financial hardship, and widows were more likely to be dependent on public or religious charity than married women. The poorest households in towns and villages were those headed by elderly widows; because the death of his wife did not mean a man had to change occupations, widowers did not become significantly poorer. On the other hand, widowhood provided social and financial opportunities for some women. Widows who had inherited money or property from their husbands or who received their dowry back at his death were often relatively free to invest it or dispose of it as they wished. Aristocratic widows were often active managing their families' business affairs and identified the rights and privileges attached to their position as *theirs*, not simply belonging to them in trust for their sons. Widowhood could also place a woman in a position of great power over her children, deciding the amount of dowry for her daughters and assisting her sons in gaining positions of political influence.

This social and economic independence was disturbing to many commentators, who thought the best solution might be remarriage. Remarriage was also troubling, however, for this lessened a woman's allegiance to the family of her first husband, could have serious economic consequences for the children of her first marriage, and, if she was wealthy, might also give her what was seen as an inappropriate amount of power over her spouse. Thus, both advice books and laws regarding widows reflect an ambivalence, although in actual practice whether a widow remarried was determined more by her economic and personal situation than by laws or theoretical concerns. Younger widows remarried much more readily than older ones and widows with few children more readily than those with many. The opposite is true in the case of widowers; those with many children were most likely to remarry, and to remarry quickly. In general, widowers were far more likely to remarry than widows; French statistics indicate that 50 percent of widowers in the sixteenth and seventeenth centuries remarried, whereas only 20 percent of widows did so. For very poor widows or those with many children, this low rate of remarriage stemmed from the fact that they were less attractive on the marriage market than singlewomen, but for middle- and upper-class women, it was often the result of their choice. The "lusty widow" who wants to remarry as quickly as possible is a common figure in early modern literature, but studies indicate that women who could afford to resisted all pressure to remarry and so retained their independence.

Widowhood was a clear legal status, but "old age" in the early modern period is harder to define. For women, the best marker might be menopause, which usually occurred somewhere in a woman's forties; the mean age at which women in northwestern Europe bore their last child was forty. Generally, a woman's fertility lessened as she grew older, and attempts at contraception appear to have increased in England and France by the late seventeenth century among older couples. Because life expectancy was less than it is today, however, even if a woman stopped having children before forty, she still had children in her household for most of her later years of life. Older women (and men) whose children had all left home generally continued to live on their own as long as possible. Evidence from England indicates that middle-class children were more likely to assist their elderly parents by providing them with servants so that they could stay in their own households rather than taking them in; the elderly lived with their married children only among the poor. Although we often romanticize earlier periods as a time when the elderly were cherished for their wisdom and experience, this was not necessarily so. In many parts of Europe, parents made formal contracts with their children to assure themselves of a certain level of material support (e.g., "twelve bushels of rye and a place by the fire"), and public welfare rolls included many elderly whose children were still in the area but were not supporting them.

Older women were generally more in need of public support than older men, in part because their spouses were less likely or able to care for them than were the wives of older men, who were generally younger or had no way to leave an ailing spouse. Younger relatives were also more willing to take in elderly men than women; older women often formed joint households with other older female relatives or simply acquaintances to pool their resources and expenses, a practice almost unknown among men. The higher percentage of elderly female welfare recipients may have also been partly because there were simply more older women than men around. Despite the dangers of childbirth, female life expectancy seems to have been gradually growing longer than male throughout the early modern period; by the eighteenth century in France, female life expectancy at birth was about thirty-four and male about thirty-one.

Aging brought physical as well as economic changes, and there is evidence that these were viewed as more of a problem for women than men already in the sixteenth century. Postmenopausal women were widely believed to experience increased sex drive, which might even lead them to seek demonic lovers to satisfy themselves. They were held to emit vapors from their mouths that could cause nursing women's milk to dry up or animals and children to sicken. They were thought to be especially concerned with the lessening of their physical attractiveness, for a Spanish physician's remedies to combat wrinkles were all directed to women.

Women themselves do not discuss wrinkles or sexual frustration, but complain about more serious types of age-related infirmities. Though she lived to be sixty-five, Alessandra Strozzi, a wealthy Florentine, described herself as old at forty-two because of her frequent pregnancies and many illnesses. Poorer women, of course, shared these problems and added to them the effects of hard physical labor, which often continued through pregnancies and illnesses. Shakespeare has Jacques in *As You Like It* describe the seventh (and last) age of man as "second childishness and mere oblivion"; old women, often caring for both an even older spouse and children who were not yet grown, did not have the luxury of being able to lapse into such a state.

As we investigate the female life cycle in early modern Europe, it may appear at first glance that little had changed since ancient times and that, in fact, little has changed since. Hasn't women's experience always been more influenced by the condition of their bodies – menstruating, pregnant, lactating, menopausal – than men's? Haven't most women married and had children, with those who did neither or only one without the other regarded as somehow deviant? Haven't men always tried to control female sexuality and regarded the female body as inferior because it lacked a penis? The answer to all these questions is yes, which is why it remains extremely important in analyzing the history of women in any period to pay attention to the physical and social life cycle. The new scholarship on men as men and on masculinity, which I explore in Chapter 8, has begun to take these issues into account as well, although most studies of famous men continue to focus on their public words and actions and ignore their personal and familial life cycle.

Although many aspects of the female life cycle appear to be true across time, our investigation has also demonstrated ways in which early modern women's experience differed dramatically from that of contemporary Western women. Bodily processes – menstruation, sexual arousal, fertility cycles, pregnancy, menopause – are now regarded almost solely as physical matters, to be controlled and affected by hormones, drugs, and other medical treatments; to a large degree, they have lost their religious or magical meaning. Through this medicalization, women have achieved greater control of these processes – they can now prevent conception or achieve it outside the womb, establish regular menstrual periods, and limit the discomfort of menopause – yet they have also lost connections with what these processes used to mean to women. Women have also achieved greater control of their social life cycle; they can often choose to accept or reject men as sexual partners or husbands, choose how many children to have, choose to remain unmarried or widowed without sinking into poverty. This greater range of choice is threatening to many people, however, including many women, who long for what they perceive as the "traditional" female roles of the period we have been discussing and attempt to restrict contemporary women's choices through legislation or social pressure. One of the key elements in this view of women's traditional role is the idea that paid employment and economic activities outside of the family were largely the province of men, an idea I test in the next chapter.

For Further Reading

Works on the family provide important information on many of the topics covered in this chapter. These include the following: Christiane Klapisch-Zuber, *Women, Family, and Ritual in Renaissance Italy* (Chicago, University of Chicago, 1985); Sherrin Marshall, *The Dutch Gentry, 1500–1650: Family, Faith and Fortune* (New York, Greenwood, 1987); Mary Abbott, *Family Ties: English Families 1540–1920* (London, Routledge, 1993); Michael Anderson, *Approaches to the History of the Western Family 1500–1914* (New York, Cambridge University Press, 1995); Margaret Hunt, *The Middling Sort: Commerce, Gender, and the Family in England, 1680–1780* (Berkeley, University of California Press, 1996); and Martha C. Howell, *The Marriage Exchange: Property, Social Place, and Gender in the Cities of the Low Countries, 1300–1500* (Chicago: University of Chicago Press, 1998). Naomi J. Miller and Naomi Yavneh (eds.), *Sibling Relations and Gender in the Early Modern World: Sisters, Brothers and Others* (Burlington, VT, Ashgate, 2006), is one of the few books that looks at sibling relations.

Katherine Crawford, *European Sexualities, 1400–1800* (Cambridge, Cambridge University Press, 2007), provides an excellent introduction to the topic of sexuality, as does Ruth Mazo Karras, *Sexuality in Medieval Europe: Doing unto Others* (New York, Routledge, 2005), for an earlier period. Jacqueline Murray and Konrad Eisenbichler (eds.), *Desire and Discipline: Sex and Sexuality in the Premodern West* (Toronto, University of Toronto Press, 1996), and Louise Fradenburg and Carla Freccero (eds.), *Premodern Sexualities* (New York, Routledge, 1996), are important collections of articles. Lloyd Davis (ed.), *Sexuality and Gender in the English Renaissance* (New York, Garland, 1998), provides selections from original sources. For the impact of European ideas about sexuality outside of Europe in the period, see Merry Wiesner-Hanks, *Christianity and the Regulation of Sexuality in the Early Modern World: Regulating Desire, Reforming Practice* (London, Routledge, 2000).

Laura Gowing, *Domestic Dangers: Women, Words and Sex in Early Modern London* (Oxford, Clarendon Press, 1996), pays particular attention to the way women and men portray themselves or are portrayed in cases involving sex and gender relations. Two studies that focus on popular literature are Joy Wiltenburg, *Disorderly Women and Female Power in the Street Literature of Early Modern England and Germany* (Charlottesville, University Press of Virginia, 1992), and Pamela Allen Brown, *Better a Shrew than a Sheep: Women, Drama, and the Culture of Jest in Early Modern England* (Ithaca, Cornell University Press, 2003). Dena Goodman, *Marie Antoinette: Writings on the Body of a Queen* (London, Routledge, 2003), includes essays on the sexual slander involving that queen; and Karen Harvey, *Reading Sex in the Eighteenth Century: Bodies and Gender in English Erotic Culture* (New York, Cambridge University Press, 2004), examines erotica.

Valerie Traub, *The Renaissance of Lesbianism in Early Modern England* (Cambridge, Cambridge University Press, 2002), explores female same-sex desire in many types of texts, as does Emma Donoghue, *Passions between Women: British Lesbian Culture 1668–1801* (London, Scarlet Press, 1993), and Francesca Canadé Sautman and Pamela Sheingorn (eds.), *Same Sex Love and Desire among Women in the Middle Ages* (New York, Palgrave Macmillan, 2001). Rudolf M. Dekker and Lotte C. van de Pol, *The Tradition of Female Transvestism in Early Modern Europe* (New York, St. Martin's, 1989), examine several hundred Dutch cases of women accused of dressing in men's clothing, some of whom were sexually attracted to other women, and Catalina de Erauso, *Lieutenant Nun: Memoir of a Basque*

Transvestite in the New World, Michele and Gabriel Stepto (ed. and trans.), (Boston, Beacon/Press, 1995), presents a fascinating autobiographical text of the Spanish nun who purportedly went to the New World dressed as a soldier.

The essays in Susan Frye and Karen Robertson (eds.), *Maids and Mistresses, Cousins and Queens: Women's Alliances in Early Modern England* (New York, Oxford University Press, 1999), look at many types of relationships among women, as does Bernard Capp, *When Gossips Meet: Women, Family, and Neighbourhood in Early Modern England* (Oxford, Oxford University Press, 2003).

Two excellent studies of how women themselves understood and experienced their bodies are Barbara Duden, *The Woman beneath the Skin: A Doctor's Patients in Eighteenth-century Germany* (Cambridge, MA, Harvard University Press, 1991), and Laura Gowing, *Common Bodies: Women, Touch and Power in Seventeenth-Century England* (New Haven, CT, Yale University Press, 2003).

Engagement and wedding ceremonies have been explored most fully in Susan C. Karant-Nunn, *The Reformation of Ritual: An Interpretation of Early Modern Germany* (London, Routledge, 1997), and David Cressy, *Birth, Marriage and Death: Ritual, Religion, and the Life-Cycle in Tudor and Stuart England* (Oxford, Oxford University Press, 1997).

Women who remained unmarried have been a significant topic of historical research. See Judith M. Bennett and Amy M. Froide (eds.), *Singlewomen in the European Past* (Philadelphia, University of Pennsylvania Press, 1998); Bridget Hill, *Women Alone: Spinsters in England, 1660–1850* (New Haven, CT, Yale University Press, 2001); and Amy M. Froide, *Never Married: Singlewomen in Early Modern England* (New York, Oxford, 2005).

Motherhood has been explored from many angles in the essays collected in Valerie Fildes (ed.), *Women as Mothers in Pre-industrial England* (London, Routledge, 1990), and Naomi Miller and Naomi Yavneh (eds.), *Mothers and Others: Female Caregivers in the Early Modern Period* (London, Ashgate, 2000). Jacqueline Marie Musacchio, *The Art and Ritual of Childbirth in Renaissance Italy* (New Haven, CT, Yale University Press, 1999), looks at visual representations of childbirth. Peter C. Hoffer and N. E. H. Hull, *Murdering Mothers: Infanticide in England and New England 1558–1803* (New York, New York University Press, 1981), investigate women accused of killing their own children.

The physical side of giving birth and the role of the midwife who assisted is discussed in the essays in Hilary Marland (ed.), *The Art of Midwifery: Early Modern Midwives in Europe and North America* (London, Routledge, 1993), and in Audrey Eccles, *Obstetrics and Gynaecology in*

Tudor and Stuart England (London, Croom Helm, 1982). Caroline Bicks, *Midwiving Subjects in Shakespeare's England* (Burlington, VT, Ashgate, 2003), examines the broader legal and cultural roles of midwives, and Lianne McTavish, *Childbirth and the Display of Authority in Early Modern France* (Burlington, VT, Ashgate, 2005), analyzes obstetrical treatises and other texts during the period in which men-midwives first began practicing in France.

Sandra Cavallo and Lyndan Warner (eds.), *Widowhood in Medieval and Early Modern Europe* (London, Longman, 1999), and Allison Levy (ed.), *Widowhood and Visual Culture in Early Modern Europe* (Burlington, VT, Ashgate, 2003), include essays that look at widowhood and representations of widows in many countries. Lucinda M. Becker, *Death and the Early Modern Englishwoman* (Burlington, VT, Ashgate, 2003), explores the female experience of death.

For more suggestions and links see the companion Web site www.cambridge.org/womenandgender.

3 Women's Economic Role

Alas! Our labors never know no end,
On brass and irons we our strength must spend;
Our tender hands and fingers scratch and tear:
All this, and more, with patience we must bear.

The Poems of Mary Collier, The Washerwoman of Petersfield (Petersfield:
W. Minchin, 1739), p. 10

God in Heaven, who gave me soul and body, reason and understanding, for which I have to thank him daily, gave me my skill at healing. I heal out of charity for the poor and needy . . . [as is] done by honorable women not only here but also in other cities just as large and important as Memmingen. Such are fine things for women to do.

Elisabeth Heyssin, a medical practitoner in Memmingen, Germany, 1598,
quoted in Merry E. Wiesner, *Working Women in Renaissance Germany*
(New Brunswick, NJ, Rutgers University Press, 1986), pp. 51–52

At that time I was busied in the merchandise trade, selling every month to the amount of five or six hundred Reichsthalers. . . . My business prospered, I procured my wares from Holland, I bought nicely in Hamburg as well, and disposed of the goods in a store of my own. I never spared myself, summer and winter I was out on my travels, and I ran about the city the livelong day.

Glickl bas Judah Leib, *The Memoirs of Glückel of Hameln*, trans. Marvin
Lowenthal (New York, Schocken, 1977), p. 179

Including a separate chapter on women's economic role in some ways contradicts recent feminist scholarship and other revisions of both traditional and Marxist economic history, which persuasively argue that work and other economic activities cannot be detached from the family and political and social institutions. This revisionist scholarship reminds us that, to be accurate and inclusive, an analysis of economic life in any period must include reproductive as well as productive activities; reproduction is defined not simply as childbearing but as the care and nurturing of all family members, which allowed them to take part in productive labor. This is especially true for preindustrial societies in which production often went on in the household, for all family members took part

101

in both productive and reproductive labor. Thus, women's childbearing, discussed in the last chapter, may properly be considered an economic activity. It is also important to recognize that in early modern Europe, a family's economic status might be more dependent on its access to royal or noble favors than on anything we would recognize as labor. The training of upper-class girls and young women in decorum and dancing that I examine in the next chapter was carried out by families not for the girls' own enjoyment but to allow them to catch a royal eye and perhaps gain a lucrative post for a family member; service at court was therefore also an economic activity.

Thus, we need to keep in mind a broad understanding of "economic," but we can also distinguish certain activities as *primarily* economic without misrepresenting how early modern society operated or how people thought it operated. These activities fall under two basic categories: work and the control of property. This chapter examines women's activities in each of these areas, exploring their labor in the countryside and cities, and their management and administration of property through business activities, investments, bequests, and the purchase of consumer goods.

Work Identity and Concepts of Work

Although the actual work that men and women performed in the early modern economy was often similar or the same, their relationship to work and work identities were different. Male work rhythms and a man's position in the economy were to a large degree determined by age, class, and training, with boys and men often moving as a group from one level of employment to the next. Female work rhythms were also determined by age and class but even more so by individual biological and social events such as marriage, motherhood, and widowhood, all of which were experienced by women individually and over which they might have little control. Women often changed occupations several times during their lives or performed many types of jobs at once, so that their identification with any one occupation was generally not strong. As we saw in the last chapter, a man's stages of life were often differentiated by his place in an occupational or professional hierarchy, whereas a woman's depended on her marital status. Popular rituals such as festivals and processions strengthened men's identification with their profession, with men and boys celebrating or marching as an occupational group, often wearing distinctive clothing. Women had no similar rituals to mark their solidarity with other women performing the same types of work; their rituals revolved around family or neighborhood events such as births and funerals, further encouraging them to identify with the family rather than with an occupation. The only exceptions to this appear to be midwives in some cities, who required new midwives to provide a celebratory meal for the entire group, and female members of the few all-female guilds in a handful of cities, who bequeathed tools and property to other members of their all-female guild.

Women rarely received formal training in a trade, but even when they did, they were not as closely identified with the trade as men were. Apprenticeship contracts from sixteenth-century Paris, for example, include a small proportion of women as teachers as well as apprentices, some of whom taught trades that were different from those of their husbands. Even in such documents, however, women are identified primarily by their familial situation, and described as *teaching* such-and-such a trade, not as *being* such-and-such an occupation. These women, and the parents who wanted their children's apprenticeship formally recorded, may have had a sense of themselves as linen makers, fish sellers, hosiers, or sewers, but the notaries who recorded the contracts certainly did not.

During the early modern period, many occupations professionalized, setting up required amounts of formal training and a licensing procedure before one could claim an occupational title. Thus, in the Middle Ages, although only men could attend universities for professional medical training, women who had learned to heal through less formal means were sometimes called "physician" (*medica*) in various records. By the sixteenth century, male physicians stopped this. This professionalism trickled down to occupations that did not require university training; women might brew herbal remedies, but only men could use the title "apothecary." Professionalization affected not simply titles but also the fees people could charge for their services; a university-trained physician, for example, could easily make ten times the annual salary of a female medical practitioner.

Religious opinion and the language of laws and records also made it difficult for women to see themselves as members of a certain occupation. In their desire to remove the distinction between clergy and laity, Protestant writers described all occupations as "vocations" for men, that is, activities to which a man could be called by God and be blessed through his labor; for a woman, however, the only possible vocation was wife and mother. Advice manuals and sermons by Protestant clergy, and later in the sixteenth century by Catholic clergy as well, all viewed whatever productive labor a woman did as simply part of her domestic role of being a helpmate to her husband and an example for her children. This idea also permeates secular laws, tax records, and the ordinances passed by guilds and other occupational groups beginning in the fifteenth century. When a woman performed an activity, such as sewing clothes, it was defined as "domestic work" or as "housekeeping," even if those clothes were not for her own family's use; tax records note that the woman had an income but neglect to mention how she received it. When men did the same activity, also in their own homes, it was regarded as "production"; only very rarely do tax records fail to mention explicitly what this production was. Thus, the gender of the worker, not the work itself or its location, marked the difference between what were considered domestic tasks and what was considered production.

City and state governments often suggested that guilds and other occupational groups overlook the production of a small number of items by widows and other poor women because this was not really "work" but simply "support," and the women would otherwise need public assistance. Guilds generally agreed to accept this fiction unless the woman was so successful that her products were favored over those of guild members; they then argued that she had overstepped the boundary into production and should be prohibited in the same way any male nonguild member would be. Women themselves also used this language, rarely asking for the right to work or produce but simply to "earn my meager piece of bread . . . as a lonely widow . . . so that I and the poor infant mouths I have to feed may be supported."[1]

Gender also became an important factor in separating what was considered skilled from what was considered unskilled work. Women were judged to be unfit for certain tasks, such as glass cutting, because they were too clumsy and "unskilled," yet those same women made lace or silk thread, jobs that required an even higher level of dexterity than glass cutting. Historians of the industrial period have pointed to the de-skilling of certain occupations, in which jobs that had traditionally been done by men were made more monotonous with the addition of machinery and so were redefined as unskilled and given to women, with a dramatic drop in status and pay. The opposite process can be seen in the early modern period in the transformation of stocking knitting in some parts of Europe into a male-dominated occupation. During the sixteenth century, wherever the knitting frame was introduced, men began to argue that using it was so complicated, only men could possibly learn; the frame actually made knitting easier and much faster, but women were prohibited from using it anyway with the excuse that they were unskilled. They were relegated to knitting by hand and had to sell their products more cheaply to compete with stockings made much more quickly by male frame knitters.

---

[1] Frankfurt guild records, 1663, quoted in Merry E. Wiesner, *Working Women in Renaissance Germany* (New Brunswick, NJ, Rutgers University Press, 1986), p. 160.

Economic historians have viewed the early modern period as a time when the meaning of work changed because of the rise of capitalism from a medieval notion of work as all tasks that contributed to a family's sustenance to work as participation in the market economy and particularly in production. Economic explanations alone do not fully explain why the newer meaning of work was so gender-biased; however, why tasks for which women were paid, such as taking in sewing or boarders, came to be defined as housekeeping and therefore not work. To explain this fully, the process of professionalization, ideological changes brought by the Protestant Reformation, guild notions of honor (discussed later), and continuities in gender ideology all have to be taken into account. Whatever its sources, the gendered notion of work meant that women's work was always valued less and generally paid less than men's. Because, as we saw in the last chapter, all women were thought of as "married or to be married," women were usually paid about half of what men were paid, even for the same tasks, with the reasoning that they were either single and had only themselves to support or married and so were simply helping their husbands support the family. The large number of widows with dependent children, or women whose husbands had deserted them or could not work, did not affect the thinking of employers or the officials who set wage rates. All economies need both structure and flexibility, and during the early modern period, these qualities became increasingly gender-identified: male labor provided the structure, so that it was regulated, tied to a training process, and lifelong; female labor provided the flexibility, so that it was discontinuous, alternately encouraged or suppressed, not linked to formal training, and generally badly paid. Women's work was thus both marginal and irreplaceable.

Women's Work in the Countryside

Despite enormous economic changes during the early modern period, the vast majority of people in almost all parts of Europe continued to live in the countryside, producing agricultural products for their own use and for the use of their landlords. Agricultural tasks were highly, although not completely, gender-specific, though exactly which tasks were regarded as female and which as male varied widely throughout Europe. These gender divisions were partly the result of physical differences, with men generally doing tasks that required a great deal of upper-body strength, such as cutting grain with a scythe. They were partly the result of women's greater responsibility for child care, so that women carried out tasks closer to the house that could be more easily interrupted for nursing or tending children. They were partly the result of cultural beliefs, so that women in parts of Norway, for example, sowed all grain because people felt this would ensure a bigger harvest. Whatever their source, gender divisions meant that the proper functioning of a rural household required at least one adult male and one adult female; remarriage after the death of a spouse was much faster in the countryside than in the cities, and the number of rural women who remained permanently widowed was much smaller than it was in the city. Those who could not find a husband were often forced into the city for work because the opportunities for wage labor for women in the countryside were generally fewer than those in the cities, except at harvest time.

Rural women were largely responsible for tasks within or close to the house: they took care of poultry and small animals; prepared dairy products, beer, and bread; grew flax; made linen and wool cloth; and did all cooking for the household's own consumption, generally over an open fire with perhaps a bread oven along its side. They also worked in the fields during harvest time, particularly in areas where grain harvesting was done with a sickle; a recent study of harvesting in seventeenth-centuries York-shire finds that women put in 38 percent of the time needed to bring in the grain. In areas where the harvesting was done with a scythe, women gathered and bound the grain and gleaned the fields, jobs that were actually physically more taxing than cutting because they involved constant stooping and bending. Women also transported rural products to market, particularly if this was done on foot, for driving teams was generally regarded as men's work. In parts of Europe where the adult men were away during the summer months, such as western Norway where the men fished or worked in shipping, agricultural production was completely the women's responsibility.

Women's labor changed as new types of crops and agricultural products were introduced and as agriculture became more specialized. During the seventeenth century, turnips and other root crops were increasingly grown in many parts of Europe, crops that were labor-intensive and seen as women's responsibility because they were generally fed to animals. Raw materials for manufactured products, such as flax, hemp, and plants for dye, became important commodities in many parts of Europe and were also cared for by women. As certain areas intensified stock raising, animals were fed all year in stables instead of being allowed to range freely in the summer – again creating more work for women. In fact, some historians would even see the late seventeenth and early eighteenth centuries as a period of the feminization of agriculture especially in central Europe, when the demand for female agricultural workers grew faster than that for male and when the wives of artisans in many smaller towns were forced to raise food in nearby gardens or fields because the family's income from production was no longer able to support it. Demographic statistics support this view, with the significant increase in female life expectancy that began in the early nineteenth century attributed largely to the mechanization of agriculture, which somewhat lessened the physical demands on rural women.

In only a few parts of Europe were rural households still solely subsistence producers by the early modern period; most participated to some degree in a market economy, and some, such as serf households on the vast estates of eastern Europe, produced almost completely for an export market. Serf men and women in eastern Europe produced grain that was exported to western Europe, although they did not control or profit from this trade. In western Europe, serfdom steadily declined in the early modern period, and rural women could make some choices as to what they would produce and sell. They made butter, cheese, and soap and sold these along with eggs, manure, small animals, and fruit in market towns, using the proceeds to buy manufactured products increasingly available from peddlers or to fulfill the household's rent and tax obligations. They traveled farther away to cities to sell nuts or herbs they had gathered or made deals with urban middlemen (or middlewomen) to transport the produce to market for them. Unlike the sale of grain, which their husbands controlled, women's products were sold year-round, making such goods a particularly important part of the household economy. Women also peddled pins and needles, ribbons, candles, and other small items that they had obtained from other rural women or merchants in the cities. Women thus served as an important human link between the rural and urban economies, with rural women traveling to town to sell their products or their labor and urban women going out to rural areas to buy products to sell or to work on parcels of land that were still owned by their families.

Besides selling products, rural women also sold their labor. Both women and men in poorer families hired themselves out to richer ones for agricultural tasks, with some landless families surviving solely by the labor of their members. Husbands and wives sometimes hired themselves out as a team, he cutting grain with a scythe while she bound it; they were generally paid according to how many bundles of grain they produced, one of the earliest examples of piecework. The sixteenth century was a period of inflation in most of Europe, and governments responded by attempting to limit wages and prices. From their maximum wage regulations, we can see that female agricultural laborers were to be paid about half of what men were and were also to be given less and poorer quality food, which often formed the most important part of an agricultural worker's income. An ordinance from south Germany in 1550, for example, notes that male laborers were to be fed soup and wine for breakfast; beer, vegetables, and meat at midday; and vegetables and wine at night, whereas women were to receive only soup and vegetables in the morning, milk and bread at midday, and nothing in the evening; they thus received less food, decidedly less protein, and no alcohol. Despite these disparities, women were better off than in areas of Europe where payment for agricultural labor was completely in cash, for wages did not keep up with prices, and women's wages would often not have paid for enough food to keep them alive. Women's cash wages appear to have been determined more by custom than by the market, for they fluctuated much less than men's both over the life cycle and with shifts in the economy; even during periods of rising wages, women's wages rose more slowly. In some parts of England, married women's wages were also less than those of widows for the same task, a wage structure based on the idea that married women needed less because they had a husband to support them, not on an evaluation of the quality of their work.

The inflation of the sixteenth century, which hit food prices particularly hard, and agricultural innovations in some parts of Europe that reduced the need for rural labor led large numbers of landless agricultural workers of both sexes to drift continually in search of employment or better working conditions, in addition to those who migrated seasonally. It appeared to many contemporaries that poverty was increasing at an alarming rate and that more of the poor were what they termed "sturdy beggars" – that is, able-bodied people who could work if they chose rather than those who were poor through no fault of their own such as orphans, infirm elderly people, or handicapped people. Most cities in Europe began to pass laws forbidding healthy people to beg, ordering them to go back to their home area or forcing them into workhouses. These laws were motivated by both increases in the actual numbers of the poor and changes in attitudes toward them, as Protestant and Catholic authorities came to regard beggars not as opportunities to show one's Christian charity but rather as dangerous vagrants to be expelled or locked up.

Rural women who migrated to cities in search of employment were particularly suspect, for any woman traveling on her own without a clear destination was thought to be dishonorable. In 1659, for example, the city of Dublin ordered that "a large cage [be] set up in the corn market to imprison all beggars, idle women and maids selling apples and oranges."[2] In many cities, female migrants were placed in special women's workhouses along with orphans, prostitutes, and poor urban women, where

[2] J. T. Gilbert and Lady Gilbert (eds.), *Calendar of the Ancient Records of Dublin* (Dublin, 1889), vol. 4, p. 157.

they were supposed to be taught a trade such as lace making or glove making so that they could escape poverty. In many of these institutions, the opportunities for actual training were minimal, although there were a few, such as the Presentation hospice in Grenoble, France, which did give women enough skills to allow them to at least support themselves. In Ireland, impoverished women were sometimes captured by press gangs and sent against their will to the English colonies of the New World, for English authorities saw this as a way to rid themselves of "dangerous rogues" and explicitly discussed the women's procreative role in increasing colonial populations.

The difference between male and female wages meant that in families with just a small plot of land, women often did all of the agricultural work on the family plot, while men worked for wages on other people's land or in fishing or forestry. Such families had little money to invest in new tools, so women continued to use old hand tools like the spade and hoe rather than horse-drawn plows; women also favored such tools because they could start and stop work with them easily, and so combine field work with care for children or animals.

Along with hiring women for specific agricultural tasks, rural households also hired them as permanent domestic servants. Ann Kussmaul has discovered that in England, the proportion of women among farm servants was much higher than among full-time agricultural laborers; 66 percent of rural women between the ages of twenty and twenty-four were servants. Their period of service was rarely determined by a written contract but instead by a verbal one sealed by a small sum of money. Servants were hired annually, often at local hiring fairs, and were supposed to stay with their employer for at least one year. Their tasks were similar to those of their mistresses – care of animals and production of animal products, particularly dairying, fieldwork, and cooking. They received room, board, and some clothing from their employers, and, except for very young girls, also an annual salary. This salary was paid only at the end of the year or even held until the servant left the household, so that servants actually lent their employers the use of their salary during their term of service. Young women generally regarded service as a time to save a dowry for later marriage, although they were also occasionally forced into service to pay off their parents' feudal dues, a practice that continued in Germany, Sweden, and Finland into the eighteenth century. In Muscovy (present-day Russia), where there was little wage labor, poor rural women sold themselves and occasionally their families (if they were heads of household) into slavery until the eighteenth century; about one-third of the slaves in Muscovy were women, with slaves making up about 10 percent of the population. Female slaves brought lower prices than male slaves, for male slaves were prized both for their managerial skills (i.e., running estates for absentee landlords) and for their physical strength. Female slaves generally worked at a variety of household tasks, and it appears that the Russian Orthodox prohibition of their being used for sexual purposes was generally effective.

Many parts of Europe began to specialize in certain crops as early as the fourteenth century, which often created greater opportunities for wage labor. In wine-growing areas, vast numbers of workers were needed during the harvest and at certain other times of the year, with workers frequently migrating seasonally from the cities. There was no clear division of labor along gender lines, though women were usually paid less for the same tasks, so that vineyard owners preferred them for all tasks other than those for which they regarded great physical strength as important. Silk growing also created paid employment because women or, more accurately, girls were viewed as having greater dexterity and ability to concentrate than men, both necessary for the tedious task of unwinding silk cocoons. Girls were also probably the only ones willing to accept the extremely low wages paid for this task, although the lifelong damage to their eyes that could result from unwinding fine thread in low light made even poor girls think twice about steady work in silk winding. Silk producers were often forced to hire whole orphanages (without the assent of the residents, of course) to have enough labor.

Mining and Domestic Industry

Women also found work in rural areas in nonagricultural tasks, particularly in mining. Although printed sources give little information about the division of labor in mining, starting in the fifteenth century, pictures and engravings show women carrying ore, wood, and salt; sorting and washing ore; and preparing charcoal briquettes for use in smelting. Most of the work underground was carried out by adult men in the preindustrial period, although the belief that women working underground brought bad luck was a consequence and not a cause of this division of labor, for it does not appear in any early modern sources. The development of large-scale capitalist mining operations that began in the late Middle Ages in some parts of Europe brought deeper tunnels, more use of machinery, and more complex smelting processes, all of which led to a professionalization of mining as an occupation. Although women were not always specifically prohibited from beginning an apprenticeship in mining, almost all those who learned and practiced mining as a lifelong career were men. This did not mean that women disappeared from mining operations but rather that their labor was more clearly identified as ancillary and assisting and, consequently, badly paid. Their labor might, in fact, be completely invisible because large firms hired adult men for certain tasks that could really only be performed through the work of a whole family; for example, men might be paid per basket for ore, but it was expected that this ore would be broken apart and washed, jobs that their wives, sisters, and children did. The records often do not indicate this, however, which led some middle-class officials in the eighteenth century to assume that women living in mining districts could easily improve their family's income by spinning during their otherwise "idle" days.

Large-scale capitalist investment was not limited to mining areas but gradually began to have an impact on the economy in grain-growing areas as well beginning in the fifteenth century. Urban investors began to hire rural individuals or households to produce wool, linen, and later cotton thread or cloth (or cloth that was a mixture of these materials), paying the household or individual only for the labor and retaining ownership of the raw materials and, in some cases, the tools and machinery used. This is often termed "domestic" or "cottage" industry because production went on in a household rather than a factory, or the "putting-out" system, as work was put out by capitalist investors, or proto-industrialization, because it was the earliest form of mass production. It is difficult to make generalizations about the impact of domestic industry on the labor of women that apply to all of Europe because this impact varied depending on whether whole households or only individuals were hired.

In areas of Europe where whole households were hired, domestic industry often broke down gender divisions, for men, women, and children who were old enough all worked at the same tasks. This upset some observers, such as the German religious reformer Sebastian Franck, who commented after visiting the villages around Augsburg and Ulm in the early sixteenth century: "Not only women and maids, but also men and boys, spin. One sees contradictions; they work and gossip like women, yet are still vigorous, active, strong and quarrelsome people, the kind any area would want to have."[3] Domestic industry might also lead to role reversal, with women producing thread and, in the words of an eighteenth-century German observer, "men . . . cook, sweep and milk the cows, in order never to disturb the good, diligent wife in her work."[4] In other areas, men did not spin, for this was the occupation most clearly identified as female in

---

[3] Gustav Schmoller, *Die Strassburger Tucher und Weberzünft: Urkunden und Darstellung* 2 vols. (Strasbourg, Karl J. Trübner, 1879), p. 519.

[4] Hans Medick, "The proto-industrial family economy: The structural function of household and family during the transition from peasant society to industrial capitalism," *Social History* 1 (1976), 312.

the preindustrial world, but they performed what were generally female household tasks so their wives and daughters could spin.

Whole households were generally hired in parts of Europe where the land was poorest and the agriculture was more or less subsistence. Some analysts find that in such areas the growth of proto-industrialization caused labor to become a more important economic commodity than property, which led to earlier marriage and weaker parental control over children. A woman's labor, rather than her father's occupation or wealth, determined her value as a marriage partner, giving her more power within the family and in the community at large. In other parts of Europe, however, proto-industrialization began in areas where there was a high level of seasonal unemployment, especially among women. In these areas, including parts of France, individual women, rather than whole households, were hired, with men continuing to work at agricultural tasks. In these areas, there was no sharing of domestic duties or reversal of roles, for the men's tasks were more highly paid and generally away from the household, so the women continued to do most domestic labor. Proto-industrialization in these areas did not lead to great improvements in women's status, for, although the wages women earned gave the family some disposable income, it was the men of the family who decided when and how that income could be spent, and they often gathered in taverns and, by the eighteenth century, in cafes to spend it.

Women's Work in Towns and Cities

Domestic industry was just one of the ways in which the economies of city and countryside were linked in early modern Europe. As we have seen, in parts of Europe where serfdom did not restrict people's movements, rural residents traveled to urban areas to sell their products or to search for employment; poorer urban residents worked in the countryside during harvest and planting, and urban women in smaller cities and towns often tended family gardens and fields beyond the city walls. The work carried out by women was also more similar in urban and rural areas than that carried out by men; in both town and countryside, women's work was generally low status, frequently changing, dependent on family circumstances, and badly paid. We therefore look first at the urban occupations that most closely paralleled those in the countryside and then examine the opportunities for women in distinctly urban trades.

As in the countryside, domestic service was probably the largest employer of women in most cities throughout the period. Between 15 and 30 percent of the population of most cities was made up of domestic servants; the larger commercial and manufacturing centers had a higher percentage of servants than the smaller cities, whose economies were more dependent on agriculture. One of every twelve people in Old Regime France were servants, two-thirds of them female; two-thirds of the servants identified in a 1631 census from Florence were female. Girls might begin service as young as seven or eight, traveling from their home village to a nearby town. They often depended on friends and relatives to find positions for them or, in some cities of Germany and France, used the services of an employment agent. These employment agents were usually older women, the wives or widows of craftsmen, or city officials who possessed a good knowledge of the households in their neighborhood. They were paid both by the servant and by the employer and were licensed and regulated by the city. In other cities, those in search of work simply gathered at certain spots or talked to the people they met in hopes of a lead. A young woman had to be particularly careful, for the wrong employer could not only mean unpleasant duties or nonpayment of wages but, as we saw in the last chapter, also sexual advances that could result in an out-of-wedlock child and ruin her hopes of marriage. Some servants in Europe were, in fact, slaves, purchased from eastern Europe in Italian households or from northern and western Africa in Spanish and Portuguese ones. Occasionally, such women accompanied their owners to the New World, for Spanish records mention both European and African slave women in the American colonies.

Most households that had servants could afford only one, a woman whose tasks were thus highly varied. She assisted in all aspects of running the household and rarely received any official time off, as the poem by Mary Collier quoted at the beginning of this chapter so clearly expresses. In artisan homes, the majority of her time was often spent in production, so that to call her a "domestic" is in some ways a misnomer. She generally ate and slept with the family, for there was rarely enough space for her to have separate quarters. Even in middle- or upper-class households that did have many rooms, servants were rarely separated from their employers the way they would be in the nineteenth century but rather lived on quite intimate terms with them. Although they usually came from poor families, they identified in many ways with their employers and tended to wear fancier clothing than other lower-class women. This upset bourgeois notions of the proper social order and, beginning in the sixteenth century, many cities passed sumptuary laws – in essence urban dress codes – that forbade servants to wear fine materials or jewels. Such laws were never very effective, for finer clothing was one of the ways in which servants tried to attract better marriage partners, a key aim of their deciding to go into service.

Sumptuary laws were only a small part of the regulations governing servants. No matter what their age, servants were legally considered dependents of their employers and could be punished or dismissed by them with little recourse. Male heads of household in particular were expected to oversee the conduct of their servants at all times; employers in Frankfurt whose maids became pregnant were required to pay the costs of the delivery and care for the maid and her infant for three months no matter who the father was because this would not have happened had they been fulfilling their duty. This dependent position meant that by law or custom, servants were generally prohibited from marrying, and most women regarded service as a stage in life rather than a lifelong career. They hoped that the wages they earned would form a dowry large enough to attract a better husband than they could otherwise have done and that their skills at running a household or experience in production would enable their new family to prosper. In Italian and German cities, being a servant was often seen as not entirely honorable because it left a woman open to her master's sexual advances. City governments in some areas attempted to change this attitude once they realized domestic service was one way in which poor women could earn dowries and so marry rather than require public support, but in others they heightened such disdain by using negative language in their regulations.

Servants were generally hired for a year at a time and could regard their employment as somewhat stable. For unmarried women unable to find a position, or married women at all times, cities also offered other types of service employment on a daily or short-term basis. Many of these jobs were viewed as extensions of a woman's functions and tasks in the home – cleaning, cooking, laundering, caring for children and old people, nursing the sick, preparing bodies for burial, mourning the dead. They usually required no training beyond what a girl learned from her mother and were poorly paid, with low status and no job security. Private account books tell us that households frequently hired women by the day for the heavy laundering and special cooking for weddings and funerals, and city expenditure records list women among those hired for heavy manual labor such as repairing city walls. What we don't know is exactly how these hirings were carried out or whether such women received enough employment to support themselves and their families; the preponderance of women among those receiving public or religious charity in every city indicates that they probably did not.

Women not only received charity in early modern cities, they also dispensed it. The hospitals, orphanages, and infirmaries run by the Catholic Church were largely staffed by women, as were similar secular institutions that many cities set up beginning in the fifteenth century. These were not hospitals in the modern sense but rather places where those with chronic, noncontagious diseases, poor expectant mothers, handicapped people, poor people recovering from injuries, foundling children, and mentally retarded or psychologically disturbed children or adults went for care. Those whose families could afford treatment or care in their own homes would not be found in such places and conditions were often horrendous. There was never any attempt to shelter women from the danger or drudgery of working in these hospitals, however, and women cooked, cleaned, and cared for the patients and also did administrative work and bookkeeping, led the patients in prayer, and carried out examinations for admission. In the Netherlands, for example, widows or married women often served as regentesses of almshouses, inspecting them daily, overseeing their operations, and contributing to the success of Dutch charity. In many cities throughout Europe, women distributed poor relief to families in their own homes, with the city governments relying on the women's knowledge of their own neighborhoods to prevent fraud.

Although no one raised objections to women working in church or city hospitals, the early modern period saw increasing opposition to women caring for the sick outside of an institution. Women could not attend university medical schools so could not call themselves "physicians" and were usually prohibited from performing diagnoses or prescribing treatment as a physician would. University medical training in the early modern period still largely depended on the teachings of Galen, however, so that most diagnoses were made by examining a patient's urine or eyes, and the most common treatment for any illness was bloodletting. Although because of this the treatments prescribed by physicians were at worst deadly and at best useless, their university training still gave physicians high social status and allowed them to charge high fees. Fortunately for their own health, most people in Europe could not afford the services of a physician but instead relied on barber-surgeons for bloodletting and the treatment of external ailments and on apothecaries for medications. Both barber-surgeons and apothecaries were trained through apprenticeship systems, with women increasingly forbidden to begin an apprenticeship or carry on a practice in which they had been serving as their husband's assistant after his death. Women who continued to practice medicine were often required to take no fees at all or only to treat children and women, despite their eloquent pleas, such as that of Elisabeth Heyssin at the beginning of this chapter, that care of the ill had been part of women's traditional role throughout European history. Because those who practiced medicine for a fee were increasingly required to be licensed, women were lumped automatically with unlicensed "quacks and charlatans," no matter what the effectiveness of their treatments. Because most treatment of illness was still handled with home remedies, however, women continued to be the main practitioners of medical care, and all cookbooks, herbals, and household guides contained huge numbers of recipes for the treatment of everything from colds to the plague. As we saw in the last chapter, women also continued to dominate midwifery in most parts of Europe, the one female occupation for which practitioners developed a sense of work identity nearly as strong as that of men.

Domestic and other types of service occupations thus provided employment for both rural and urban women, and city women also joined those of the countryside in retail sales. The city marketplace, the economic as well as geographic center of most cities, was filled with women; more than three-quarters of the traders in the markets of early modern Polish cities were women. Along with rural women with their agricultural and animal products were city women with sausage, pretzels, meat pies, cookies, candles, soap, and wooden implements that they had made. Women sold fresh and salted fish that their husbands had caught or that they had purchased from fishermen, game and fowl they had bought from hunters, imported food items such as oranges, and, in the eighteenth century, tea and coffee bought from international merchants. Pawnbrokers sold used clothing and household articles, and female money-changers exchanged travelers' money for the type of coinage that was accepted in the city. Because there was no way to preserve food easily, women or their female servants had to shop every day, and the marketplace was where they met their neighbors, exchanged information, and talked over recent events. Municipal market regulations were often strict in terms of product purity, honest weights and measures, and fair prices, but they generally made no distinction between male and female traders, as long as the women were from the local area and not migrants. As we saw in Chapter 1, cities recognized that married women who carried out retail business needed to be able to buy and sell without their husbands' permission and so had the special category of *femme sole*, which allowed them much greater freedom. Records from many cities indicate that far more women were simply carrying on business anyway without any special legal approval.

Along with selling at the marketplace, women also ran small retail establishments throughout the city. They made beer, mead, and hard cider and ran taverns and inns to dispense their beverages and provide sleeping quarters for those too poor to stay in the more established inns. These taverns also provided employment for serving-women, although there were perils with such a job; inn servants in France were the one group of women denied the right to sue their seducer if they became pregnant. Women's work as producers and distributors of alcohol changed somewhat during the period, for they often left or were pushed out of certain occupations, such as brewing beer, once these became larger scale, requiring more capital investment but also producing more profit. Women pickled and smoked meat, made sauerkraut, and prepared tripe in their own kitchens and sold it directly from their houses. Although economic historians discussing the rise of the market economy in this period primarily focus on male capitalist investors, bankers, and wholesale merchants, these female retail traders were just as market-oriented. The market they served was largely one of women and poor people, for they provided goods of generally lower quality at a lower cost than those sold by guild masters and major merchants. Despite the small scale of their businesses, female retail traders were quick to defend them against interlopers, calling people names in the street or hauling them into court; such market women often played a significant role in urban disturbances, from the iconoclastic riots associated with the Protestant Reformation to the political protests of the French Revolution.

Because retail trade was so clearly dominated by women, city governments in 1500 sometimes appointed women to official positions as inspectors and overseers. Women served as grain inspectors, cloth measurers, toll collectors, weighers of merchandise at the city scales, and gatekeepers. Over the sixteenth and seventeenth centuries, women's names gradually disappeared from the records as the men who generally served in these positions tried to emulate higher officials like judges, city physicians, and lawyers. These higher positions all required university training and so were closed to women; gradually, the lower positions were closed to women as well, even though special training was still not required. Wives of male officials might still do most of the actual work – male gatekeepers, for example, often had another trade and so depended on their wives to "man" the gate many hours of the day – but they were not considered officials in their own right and no longer had to swear an oath of office.

Domestic industry provided employment for increasing numbers of urban, as well as rural, women, particularly in spinning. Early modern techniques of cloth production necessitated up to twenty carders and spinners per weaver, so that cloth centers such as Florence, Augsburg, and Antwerp could keep many people employed. As we have seen, in the rural areas, both men and women might spin, but in the cities, economic need appeared never to be strong enough to break down the association of spinning with women, and men beyond adolescence simply did not spin. The identification of women and spinning became stronger in the early modern period for several reasons. In many parts of Europe, bureaucrats and officials began to advise rulers to encourage cloth production to increase exports and provide jobs for the poor so that they would marry earlier and by so doing increase the population size. A healthy export trade and a growing population were prime aims of the most widespread school of economic theory in the early modern period, mercantalism. To mercantilists, the best way to achieve these goals was to have as much of the population as possible engaged in what they viewed as productive labor. Along with the rest of their contemporaries, mercantalists did not recognize much of what women did as productive so saw them and children as a vast labor pool waiting to be tapped. They did recognize that spinning was the bottleneck in the production of cloth and so suggested and implemented countless schemes to encourage more spinning. They attached spinning rooms to orphanages, awarded prizes to women who spun the most, made loans easier for those who agreed to spin, and set up spinning schools for poor children. Poor law authorities in England opened spinstries for poor women, providing women too poor to own their wheels with the needed equipment. Women who were in the hospital or jail were expected to spin to defray part of the costs of their upkeep, and prostitutes in some cities were expected to produce a certain number of bobbins of yarn in their off hours.

Along with schemes or regulations that pulled women into spinning, there were also economic factors that pushed them into it. As the range of occupations open to women narrowed, spinning was often the only possible way for them to earn a living; in the seventeenth century, so many women turned to spinning that unmarried women in England all came to be called "spinsters." This crowded labor market kept wages low, certainly too low to support a family and often too low to support the woman herself, which is why prizes and loans may have been necessary inducements. Women identified as spinners often appealed to city councils for support, noting "what little I make at spinning will not provide enough even for my own bread."[5]

Spinners' wages were also kept low for noneconomic reasons. The idea that all women were either "married or to be married" meant that both city authorities and the investors who set up domestic cloth production could choose to view spinning as simply a stopgap employment until women attained or returned to their "natural" married state, even though they knew that in reality many women supported themselves with spinning for decades. They also hoped that low wages would encourage women to live in the households of master-weavers or other male artisans rather than live on their own. As we noted in Chapter 2, the early modern period was a time of increasing suspicion of masterless persons, and unmarried women working and living on their own were the most mistrusted. Authorities at times even tried to prevent grown daughters from continuing to live with their parents, arguing that parents gave them too much freedom, which caused "nothing but shame, immodesty, wantonness, and immorality," with their idleness leading to "tearing

[5] Frankfurt guild records, 1615, quoted in Wiesner, *Working Women*, p. 184.

hedges, robbing orchards, beggaring their fathers."[6] Low wages alone did not always succeed in forcing women into male-headed households, however. Spinners in Augsburg chose to pool their wages and live together, commenting in 1597 that they were not so dumb as to live with master-weavers who would deduct room and board from their wages at a rate higher than these were worth and so leave them with less than if they lived in rented rooms; the city responded by flatly forbidding all unmarried women to have their own households.

Religious and civic authorities also worried about what went on in both town and countryside at spinning bees, evening gatherings where young women brought their wheels or distaffs and spindles; they recognized that young men also gravitated to them and that the spinning was accompanied by songs, jokes, and drinking. They often tried to prohibit spinning bees, although the mercantalists countered that such gatherings actually promoted marriage by allowing young men to compare the skill and industriousness of various marriage partners and also promoted higher production levels because the young spinners competed with one another. Most authorities were more at ease when spinning bees were gradually replaced in urban areas by centralized locations at which women spun and wove under the direction of male overseers. Such centers, sometimes termed "manufactories" to distinguish them from the factories of the later Industrial Revolution, which used steam- or water-powered equipment, began to employ large numbers of young women in the early eighteenth century, paying them by the piece with frequent quality checks. Women were favored as workers because they would work for lower wages and were thought to have more delicate and nimble hands; the investors did not realize that these women also did rough housework and seasonal agricultural labor, so that their hands were swollen and scarred, which made their work uneven and led them to be fined for poor quality work. Conditions in these manufactories were often unpleasant and unhealthy, with cloth fibers filling the air and boiling vats causing them to be continually damp. Women's wages were much lower than those of men who worked in the same establishment, and they rarely achieved supervisory status, but young women sometimes preferred work in a manufactory over domestic service because it did allow a small amount of free time and a greater sense of independence.

---

[6] The first quotation is from a 1665 ordinance in Strasbourg, France, quoted in Wiesner, *Working Women*, p. 89; the second from an anonymous 1715 Scottish pamphlet, quoted in Jane Schneider, "Rumpelstiltskin's Bargain: Folklore and the Merchant Capitalist Intensification of Linen Manufacture in Early Modern Europe," in Annette B. Weiner and Jane Schneider (eds.), *Cloth and Human Experience* (Washington, Smithsonian Institution Press, 1989), 191.

Figure 6. Geertruydt Roghman, *Woman Spinning*, before 1650. Roghman was one of the few women engravers active during the "golden age"
of art in the seventeenth-century Netherlands. Her father and brothers were also engravers, but she concentrated more on the daily life of
women; this is from a series of engravings of women's occupations.

Moral as well as economic considerations shaped urban women's
employment in other types of domestic industry along with spinning.
In Florence, for example, women made up about 40 percent of those
employed in wool production, not counting spinners, and 84 percent of

workers in the silk industry. They were concentrated in low-skill jobs and only in those such as weaving that could be carried out in the home and did not require them to go out in public. This was not only because women were primarily responsible for domestic duties and child care along with their paid labor, but also because in Italy, more than in northern Europe, women were seen as the moral guardians of family honor whose reputations needed to be kept from any hint of scandal. Respectable women, even among the poor, were to avoid any jobs that put them in contact with men other than family members, so the range of paid employment open to them was even smaller than it was in northern Europe.

Along with occupations that paralleled those in the countryside, early modern cities also offered several distinctive types of employment for women. One of these was selling sex for money, or what later came to be called prostitution. During the late Middle Ages, most major cities in Europe and many of the smaller ones had an official brothel or an area of the city in which selling sex was permitted. Many cities in the fifteenth century set down rules for the women and their customers and justified the existence of municipal brothels with the comment that such women protected honorable girls and women from the uncontrollable lust of young men, an argument at least as old as Augustine. In a few cities, such as Florence, authorities also noted that brothels might keep young men from homosexual relations, another far worse alternative in their eyes. Visiting brothels was associated with achieving manhood in the eyes of young men, although for the women themselves their activities were work. Indeed, in some cases the women had no choice, for they had been traded to the brothel manager by their parents or other people in payment for debt or had quickly become indebted to him (or, more rarely, her) for the clothes and other finery regarded as essential to their occupation. Poor women – and men – also sold sex illegally outside of city brothels, combining this with other sorts of part-time work such as laundering or sewing.

Although selling sex for money was legal in the Middle Ages, the position of women who did so was always marginal, and in the late fifteenth century cities began to limit brothel residents' freedom of movement and choice of clothing, requiring them to wear distinctive head coverings or bands on their clothing so that they would not be mistaken for "honorable" women. They also began to impose harsher penalties on women who did not live in the designated house or section of town. Such restrictions increased dramatically after the Protestant Reformation, with most Protestant and then Catholic cities closing their municipal brothels, arguing that the possible benefits they provided did not outweigh their moral detriments. Selling sex was couched in moral rather than economic terms as simply one type of "whoredom," a term that also included premarital sex, adultery, and other unacceptable sexual activities. As we have seen, religious reformers such as Luther described women who sold sex in very negative terms and also regarded "whore" as the worst epithet they could hurl at their theological opponents. Closing the official brothels did not end the exchange of sex for money, of course, but simply reshaped it: smaller, illegal brothels were established; women moved to areas right outside city walls; police and other authorities were influenced or bribed to overlook it.

Government policy toward selling sex for money from the sixteenth century through the eighteenth varied throughout Europe and in many places was typified by alternating periods of tolerance and suppression. In general, major Italian cities such as Florence and Venice were the most tolerant, favoring regulation over suppression and often viewing prostitutes as significant sources of municipal income. From 1559 until the mid-eighteenth century in Florence, for example, all women registered as prostitutes were required to contribute an annual tax based on their income, which went to support a convent for those women who wished to give up prostitution; payment of extra taxes would allow a woman to live where she wished in the city and wear whatever type of clothes she chose. In Amsterdam, houses termed *speelhuizen*, which combined dancing, nightlife, and the sale of sex, were opened during the seventeenth century; although officially prohibited and subject to prosecution, they were favorite haunts of the thousands of sailors from the East and West India Companies who came to Amsterdam every summer. (In the nineteenth century, most of Continental Europe except for Spain permitted prostitution again, as long as the women registered and submitted themselves to weekly examinations for venereal disease.)

The official contempt of "whoredom" was not always internalized by women themselves, however, particularly in large cities such as Rome where their number remained high despite all attempts at prohibition. Roman prostitutes often offered their customers music and poetry along with sexual services and worked independently, living with other women or with their mothers or children; they often described their occupation in terms of the quality of their clients instead of simply monetary terms. Their neighbors did not shun them but socialized with them and defended them against verbal and physical attacks. The clear distinction in the minds of Italian authorities between respectable and unrespectable women may have kept most women out of jobs that required regular contact with men, but it did not separate prostitutes and their neighbors on the streets of Florence or Rome.

In both Italian cities and the capitals of northern Europe such as Paris
or London, there were always a few women who achieved great promi-
nence, wealth, and near-respectability through their sexual connections
with nobles, intellectuals, and officials, such as Ninon de Lenclos, who
was a friend of the playwright Molière, and Madame de Maintenon, the
future wife of King Louis XIV. Such courtesans were often glamorized
in plays and poetry, but it is important to remember that the lives of most
women who sold sex were filled with violence, imprisonment, disease,
and, by the seventeenth century, deportation. Their numbers went up,
as one would expect, during times of war, famine, and economic depression, when many women could not find other types of work. Although
authorities viewed such activities in moral terms, what few comments we
have from women indicate they saw it as the only way not to "suffer from
poverty, hunger, and need."[7]

Because many women who sold sex spent some time imprisoned, they
generally came into contact with and sometimes became part of the criminal world that operated in all early modern cities. Women might also
intentionally seek imprisonment during times of famine or economic
depression, for prisoners often worked for pay, which could then be sent
to their families outside. For a few women, crime became an occupation.
As in contemporary societies, early modern women were far less likely
to be involved in crimes of violence than men, but they were frequently
arrested for theft or receiving stolen goods. Records from the west coast
of Ireland, for example, mention a number of women arrested for plundering stranded ships or receiving goods from pirates but only a few who
actually sailed on pirate ships. Women were more likely to steal from
households or shops than directly from persons and often did so when
short-term employment or domestic service gave them an opportunity.
The number of women accused of theft increased during times of shortage, and city courts often gave women lighter sentences than men when
they pleaded that they had stolen solely because of "unimaginable and
incontestable poverty."[8] Simply being female did not lead to leniency,
however, for women were regularly banished, mutilated by branding or
having their nose or ears cut off, punished corporally, or executed for
theft or other criminal activities. In fact, being female made one *more*
likely to be accused of certain crimes, especially infanticide, witchcraft,

---

[7] Woman's testimony from Stralsund, Germany in 1560, quoted in Beata Schuster, *Die
freien Frauen: Dirnen und Frauenhäuser im 15. und 16. Jahrhundert* (Frankfurt, Campus,
1995), p. 200. My translation.

[8] Munich city council minutes, 1544, quoted in Wiesner, *Working Women*, p. 109.

and prostitution; far more women were punished for these three than for any other type of illegal activity.

Craft Guilds

If prostitution and crime represented the low end of the spectrum of urban female occupations in terms of respectability, honor, and what we might call status, the high end was represented by women who participated in craft guilds. Craft guilds, which were first organized in the twelfth and thirteenth centuries, were the most important way that production was organized in European cities throughout the early modern period and continued to dominate the production and distribution of many products into the nineteenth or even twentieth century. There were a few all-female guilds in cities with highly specialized economies such as Cologne, Paris, and Rouen and female apprentices in some guilds but, in general, the guilds were male organizations and followed the male life cycle. One became an apprentice at puberty; became a journeyman four to ten years later; traveled around learning from a number of masters; then settled down, married, opened one's own shop, and worked at the same craft full time until one died or got too old to work any longer. This process presupposed that one would be free to travel (something that was more difficult for women than men); that on marriage one would acquire a wife as an assistant; and that pregnancy, childbirth, and child rearing would never interfere with one's labor. Transitions between these stages were marked by ceremonies, and master craftsmen were formally inscribed in guild registers and took part in governing the guild.

Women fit into guilds much more informally. When guilds were first established, the master's wife, daughters, and female servants sometimes worked alongside him and the journeymen and apprentices. If the demand for products was especially great, master craftsmen sometimes hired female pieceworkers to assist, and in some cities girls entered formal apprenticeships. Women and girls thus served as a labor reservoir, to be utilized when guild needs required. Masters' widows ran shops after the death of their husbands and were expected to pay all guild fees, although they could not participate in running the guild. Other than masters' widows and a small number of female apprentices, however, women's ability to work was never officially recognized and usually depended not on their own training but rather on their relationship with a guild master.

Even this informal participation began to change in the fifteenth century, when some guilds in Continental Europe began to pass explicit restrictions on women's work. First, masters' widows were limited in the amount of time they could keep operating a shop or prohibited from hiring journeymen, then female domestic servants were excluded from any productive tasks, then the number of his daughters a master craftsman could employ was limited. In extreme cases, such as watchmaking in Geneva, masters were flatly prohibited from teaching any daughters or even their wives the essential part of their craft. The timing of these restrictions varied from craft to craft, town to town, and country to country; they did not begin until the sixteenth century in Scandinavia. Girls in England were formally apprenticed and then practiced independently in some trades well into the eighteenth century; by the early nineteenth century, however, female apprenticeship in England had also become limited to certain needlework trades only. Because women's participation in guild shops was generally not guaranteed by guild regulations and because widows had no political voice in running the guilds, women as a group were not able to protect their right to work. Individual women, especially widows, often requested that they be allowed to work despite the restrictions, appealing to the city council or other municipal or state authorities by stressing their poverty, old age, or number of dependent children and praising the mercy and "Christian charity" of the authorities. In a few cases, such as weavers in the Bologna area, women appealed to authorities in the name of a group of women, giving evidence of some type of organization, and emphasized their abilities rather than their need. Whatever the language of the women involved, however, the authorities to whom they appealed saw women's work as a substitute for charity, noting that it was "always better that one supports oneself than comes to the council for public charity," whereas men's work was their right.[9] They never allowed women as a group to continue working, however, but limited their permission to the woman or women making the request.

A number of reasons have been suggested as to why women were excluded from craft guilds: the competition of rural and urban proto-industrial production; real or fabricated concerns over the quality of products; the increasingly political nature of guilds in some cities after the guild revolutions of the fourteenth century. These economic and political reasons played a part, but the most significant factor was an ideological one – guild honor. As proto-industrial domestic production increased and threatened the guilds' monopoly on market production, craft guilds devalued all occupations that were carried out in a household rather than a workshop. Although the line between household and workshop was sometimes hard to establish clearly because small workshops might be simply part of one large room on the first floor of a house, guilds attempted to make a distinction and claimed that all domestic work was

---

[9] Strasbourg city council minutes, 1617, quoted in Wiesner, *Working Women*, p. 192.

inferior. Because women were identified with both the household and with proto-industrial production, guilds saw women's work as invariably domestic and workshops that still employed women as tainted and dishonorable. This attitude among the guilds became reflected in official policy when women who spun or washed in their own homes were not considered workers (and thus, by the nineteenth century in some parts of Europe eligible for pensions), whereas male shoemakers and tailors were, although these crafts were not regarded as highly as those that had separate workshops.

The guilds' nature as groups was another reason that guild work was increasingly seen as a "learned art and given to men alone."[10] Guild ceremonies and celebrations that did not include women grew more numerous and elaborate, increasing the opportunity for the male members to come together as a group. Guild regulations emphasized group cohesion among male members; in the words of an ordinance from the bakers of Linz, in Austria, in 1742: "This ordinance is proclaimed for the preservation of unity and honorable male decorum among masters, journeymen and apprentices."[11] Economists and other social scientists have recently pointed to the ways in which groups and networks create "social capital" by creating a sense of group cohesion, collective norms, and the sharing of information among members. Social capital is generally viewed as having beneficial effects and is linked, in the contemporary world, with such things as the spread of democracy and the expansion of technological expertise through the Web. Social networks require exclusion as well as inclusion, however. As Sheilagh Ogilvie has pointed out, guilds used social capital to exclude women (and other sorts of outsiders, including foreigners and Jews), narrowing their range of employment options, pushing them into low-paying work, and limiting the flexibility of the economy as a whole.

Ironically, this championing of male unity came at a time when craft guilds were actually becoming more splintered, when journeymen were increasingly forming separate guilds as they came to define their interests as distinct from and often antithetical to those of the masters. In the Middle Ages, journeymen had generally simply been part of the craft guild and looked forward to the day when they, too, could marry, become masters, and open a shop. In a few trades, they formed separate journeymen's associations, but these were generally only for religious and social purposes.

[10] Munich city council minutes, 1599, quoted in Wiesner, *Working Women*, p. 129.
[11] Quoted in Gerhard Danningen, *Das Linzer Handwerk und Gewerbe vom Verfall der Zunftfhoheit über die Gewerbefreiheit bis zum Innungszwang*, Linzer Schriften zur Sozial und Wirtschaftsgeschichte, vol. IV (Linz, Rudolf Trauner, 1981), p. 75.

This began to change in the late fifteenth century as craft guilds became more restrictive and limited membership to masters' sons or those who married a master's widow or daughter; many journeymen then began to work for a master all their lives, becoming essentially wage laborers. Their associations began to make economic demands, and new organizations were formed in trades that had previously not seen them. Often these organizations were secret, for public authorities and guild masters feared they would provoke social and political unrest and so prohibited them, but their secrecy made them even stronger. They met in taverns and inns, holding elaborate initiation ceremonies for new members and developing ever more complex rituals. Because journeymen traveled, they carried their organizations from town to town and enforced their economic demands by boycotting a master and sometimes an entire town that refused to comply.

These journeymen's guilds were totally masculine in membership and even more male in their orientation than craft guilds; journeywomen in the guilds that remained open to women in France and England did not form similar associations. Journeymen's guilds came to be the most vocal opponents of women's work in guild shops, refusing to work not only in shops that still allowed women but also next to any journeyman who had once worked in such a shop. They also opposed women working in the new manufactories, smashing the looms in one instance in Berlin in 1794 and driving the women from the building. States such as Prussia and Austria attempted to break their power in the eighteenth century to promote the free movement of labor, but their efforts often led to riots and strikes or simply to total noncompliance. As their own working conditions became more like those of women (i.e., dependent on wages with little hope of advancement and under the control of someone else), journeymen viewed the maintenance of an all-male workplace as a key part of their honor.

Along with craft and journeymen's honor, another type of status consideration also increasingly kept women out of guild shops, what we might term "bourgeois respectability." During the seventeenth and eighteenth centuries, the number of officials and professionals in most cities grew rapidly, men whose wives did not share in their occupation but concentrated on domestic tasks. Successful master craftsmen and capitalist entrepreneurs often wanted to emulate these professionals and increasingly regarded wives and daughters who did not engage in productive labor as a requisite of bourgeois status; the more elaborate meals, clothing, and household furnishings viewed as part of being bourgeois also meant that female household members would have little time for production anyway. Although guild masters were still required to be married, this was no longer based on the notion that the wife's work was essential in running a shop but rather on the idea that married men were more stable members of the community and more suitable heads of household. Occupations in which the married couple was still regarded as the unit of production and "wife" was still regarded as an occupational label, such as "fishwife," were found only at the bottom of the social scale. In 1500, by contrast, even "furrier's wife" would have been considered an occupational label as well as a designation of marital status.

The exclusion of women from guilds was not absolute. Because men were paid more for agricultural labor than women, more young women than men migrated to cities from the countryside. As we have seen, authorities worried about unmarried women and in some cases decided to adapt guild structures to provide employment for them. In Paris, Louis XIV and his economic adviser Jean-Baptiste Colbert set up an all-female guild of dressmakers in 1675, noting that "this work was the only means that they had to earn their livelihood decently."[12] Nearly twenty other French cities set up similar guilds over the next century. In the late seventeenth century, one-piece gowns called mantuas became more fashionable for women than the two-part bodice and skirt, and women also began to use bone, iron, or wooden stays to pull in their waistlines. Because mantuas were a new type of garment, they were not restricted by tailors' guild ordinances, and women began to make them and also to make and fit women's corsets with stays. In England, male tailors petitioned Parliament in 1702 to prohibit women from mantua making, but this national campaign failed. Most towns continued to try to prohibit women's work, but in York the tailors' guild instead decided to admit women, and by 1750 a third of all its members were female. Because mantua makers worked only with female customers, the trade was considered respectable and "genteel," so parents were willing to apprentice their daughters to it.

The new women's and mixed-sex guilds did not break with existing patterns, however. Clare Crowston has found that the women in the Parisian dressmakers guild were generally single and did not head a household filled with apprentices the way male guild masters did. In York, although some of the women in the tailors' guild operated shops with many apprentices, none held positions of power within the guild. By the early nineteenth century, most spinning had moved to manufactories or factories, with machines largely tended by women and children. Whether they were factory workers or dressmakers, however, women received low wages and were a large proportion of the urban poor.

---

[12] French royal statutes, 1675, quoted in Cynthia M. Truant, "The Guildswomen of Paris: Gender, Power, and Sociability in the Old Regime," *Proceedings of the Annual Meeting of the Western Society for French History* 15 (1988), p. 131.

Investment, Management, and Purchasing

Labor is certainly the most important of women's economic activities but not the only one. The early modern period saw the expansion of capitalism in Europe, which, as we have seen, had both positive and negative effects on women's work: providing them with jobs that allowed them to contribute to a family income or to earn wages on their own but also lessening the value of their unpaid domestic tasks and only rarely offering jobs that provided more than subsistence wages. What about women's other economic activities? Did capitalism expand or shrink their opportunities for active investment and management of property? How did capitalism shape their purchasing, and how, conversely, did gender differences in consumption shape trade and production?

The great merchant trading companies of Italy usually seen as the founders of commercial capitalism such as the Datini and the Medici were family firms, and female family members often invested money that they had inherited or acquired through marriage in business ventures. Widows were generally the most active in terms of independent investment because they tried to increase the capital that they would hand on to their sons and daughters or at least prevent its loss. As these and similar companies engaged in long-distance trade, banking, and large-scale money-lending opened themselves up to investment by nonfamily members, women generally formed at least a small share of the stockholders. Thirty-nine of the nearly 300 members of the Merchants' Society of Ravensberg, Germany, in the early sixteenth century were women. In the seventeenth and eighteenth centuries, women – especially single women and widows – invested in the great overseas trading companies of northern Europe such as the Dutch and British East India Companies. Some of these women inherited their shares and probably had little say in managing them, although others bought and sold shares on their own, moving capital from one investment to another. Women did not act as representatives for these firms or carry out long-distance trade themselves, however, for their freedom to travel was generally limited by family responsibilities and by the lack of places for female travelers to stay. Unaccompanied female travelers were often suspected of being prostitutes or thieves, and some cities specifically forbade inns to take them in.

We do find women actively directing commercial companies within individual cities, and a few were able to amass huge fortunes. These were almost all widows who did not have adult sons to compete with them, such as Elizabeth Baulacre of Geneva, widowed at twenty-eight in 1641, who transformed her husband's small dry-goods firm into the largest producer of gold thread and decorations in the city, employing hundreds of workers and leaving the second largest personal fortune in the city when she died. Widows in England ran coal mines, traded foodstuffs and wool wholesale, and made shipping contracts with the army and navy. Glickl bas Judah Leib (also known as Glückel of Hameln), a Jewish merchant's widow, inherited a business deep in debt, and through her own business acumen and constant work transformed it into a sizable fortune. She is one of the few women who traveled to fairs and markets herself, for in this her Judaism proved an advantage. Because Jews were prohibited from staying in most inns run by Christians, they often had networks of friends with whom women could stay safely; because Judaism prized the life of a scholar more than that of a merchant, Jewish women were often freer to run businesses than their Christian counterparts, as long as they did not have any connections with religious requirements such as butchering.

Glickl is particularly unusual because she wrote her own memoirs, which describe her family as well as business life. As we can see from the quotation at the beginning of this chapter, she was proud of her achievements, but the memoirs also reveal the limitations placed on women entrepreneurs. Despite her success while a widow, when she remarried at fifty-four, she turned her entire fortune over to her second husband, who promptly went bankrupt; Glickl ended her life, widowed again, living in the household of her daughter. During the period before her second marriage, she gave large amounts of money to one of her sons for his own business ventures, which all came to nothing and ended up costing her more when she paid off his creditors. Women's participation in trade and commerce was not only dependent on their own energy and skill but also on the abilities of male family members.

Women's participation in commerce was also restricted by their more limited access to capital than that available to men of their class. The capital available to female investors generally came to them through inheritance or dowries, and in many parts of Europe, there were increasing restrictions on women's ability to invest that capital in any way that might threaten their children's inheritance. As we saw in Chapter 1, married women were usually prohibited from borrowing money without the assent of their husbands, and the women who were able to escape these restrictions and have themselves declared *femme sole* were not borrowing at the level of a major investor. Such women, both rural and urban, often served as small-scale moneylenders as well as borrowers; more than half the loans made in Danzig and Warsaw in the seventeenth century were made by women. Thus, women did facilitate the movement of capital at the lowest level but were generally unable to borrow money for major investments.

Women were also increasingly limited in their access to the other major form of wealth in the early modern economy – land. From the thirteenth century on, most areas of Europe passed laws that either established primogeniture (an inheritance system in which all landed estates passed undivided to the eldest son, with younger sons and daughters inheriting much smaller portions of movable property and liquid capital) or favored sons over daughters. Motives for this varied. In western Europe, aristocrats hoped this would maintain family power by allowing them to retain an estate large enough to serve as a base of power against growing centralized state authority. In Muscovy, the state itself supported legislation in 1627 that prohibited childless widows from inheriting family lands and limited daughters' access to land so that all land would go to those capable of providing military service. Women were most likely to engage in the active management of landed property when they were widows with young sons, and records from many areas indicate that women's decline in access to land was not matched by a decline in their interest in or ability to administer that land for a profit. Women who were sole heirs also gained dispensations that enabled them to inherit land otherwise restricted to male heirs, but such cases often involved protracted legal battles and required the support of the woman's family in order to succeed.

Although land and liquid capital were the most important forms of wealth, most people had access to neither of these, and the property that they held or handed down to the next generation was solely in the form of movable goods; women from landed families might also have access only to movables once systems of primogeniture were established. Thus, women's most important function in the transfer of property, and the function over which they had most independent control, was probably their disposal of movables through wills, marriage contracts arranged for their children, and grants made while living to the church or other individuals. An individual's ability to bequeath property as he or she wished was limited in many parts of Europe by laws that required heirs to be granted a minimum amount, although in England both women and men had relative testamentary freedom. Most legal systems limited a wife's ability to bequeath property without the express approval of her husband, although sometimes marriage contracts and other sorts of premarital legal agreements allowed women to sidestep such laws. Widows and unmarried women were not restricted in their disposition of movables, and women's wills include bequests not only of clothing and household goods but also books, art objects, and, in parts of Europe that still had slavery, slaves. (Women slaveholders were less common than women slaves, but they bought, sold, traded, inherited, and bequeathed slaves just as they did other forms of movable property.) Women were more likely than men to pass property to other women and tended to specify a wider circle of relatives and friends for specific bequests than did men. They also generally included members of both their birth and marital families in their wills and often contributed to the dowries of nieces from both birth and marital families with grants of property or cash while they were still alive.

Women made more and larger donations for religious purposes than did the men of their families, leading in at least one instance to laws that restricted their testamentary freedom. In 1501, the Strasbourg city council limited the amount of money a woman could donate to a convent or deed to a convent when she entered, claiming that this unfairly disinherited her relatives and decreased the city tax base. The preacher and moralist Geiler of Kaisersberg, normally no great friend of women, opposed this move, commenting that "widows who are responsible and sensible persons" should be able to handle their own financial affairs, and that "it is a mockery of God, a haughty service of the devil to forbid a pious person to give everything that she owns for the will of God."[13] Geiler's arguments were unsuccessful, the law stood, and the city council further declared that all widows and unmarried women should be assigned guardians for their financial affairs, a move that occurred in many other European cities later in the sixteenth or seventeenth centuries as well.

Women's access to capital in this period was thus more limited than men's, although it was not as limited in actual practice as it was in legal codes. Women ignored, evaded, or contractually negated restrictions to become investors, entrepreneurs, and property owners. They also shaped the economy through the purchase and use of consumer goods. Traditionally, economic historians did not pay much attention to consumption, but as the purchase of goods and services plays such an important role in today's postindustrial economy, they are now paying greater attention to the role of the consumer in times past.

The increases in production and trade of the early modern period provided Europeans, including many with moderate incomes, with cheaper and more diverse consumer goods of all types. From Europe's overseas colonies came new foodstuffs such as sugar, chocolate, tea, and coffee; new types of fabrics such as calico; and new types of household goods such as lacquerware and the porcelain that came to be known as "china." The fashionable drank coffee and hot chocolate in coffeehouses and cafes, of which there were about 600 in Paris by 1750. Brewing and drinking tea became part of the lives of urban women in some countries, especially England, and even domestic servants bought their own teapots.

---

[13] Johannes Geiler von Kaisersberg, *Die aeltesten Schriften* (Freiberg in Breisgau, Herder'sche, 1877), p. 73.

Servants and other relatively poor women chose to spend their income on consumer goods such as parasols, fans, hats, hand mirrors, and lace. Middle-class women bought more and fancier clothing and home furnishings, paying attention not only to quality and price but also to changing styles, which they learned about through printed works and shop displays. In the eighteenth century, increasingly elaborate powdered wigs became an important part of the dress of fashionable men and women, crafted from human hair for the wealthy and animal hair for those with less money to spend.

Moralists often denounced these new consumer goods as "frivolous" in sermons and pamphlets, and some cities expanded their codes of sumptuary law to forbid servants and poor people from wearing new types of luxuries as well as older kinds of fine material and decorations. Such measures were ineffective, however, particularly because, as Maxine Berg has shown, more and more people regarded luxury as a virtue rather than a vice. They made distinctions between old-style luxuries that had been limited to wealthy aristocrats and new-style luxuries available to middle-class people. Especially in cities, women and men shopped eagerly for new commodities, and certain items, such as lace-trimmed handkerchiefs, collars, curtains, and tablecloths, became a mark of bourgeois status.

A dramatic increase in the importation of sugar – and its production in tropical colonies – was perhaps the most obvious result of women's changing tastes, but their demands for certain types of decorative objects, garments, and foodstuffs – feathers, small tea tables, flowers, curtains, lace collars and cuffs, Chinese tea sets, lighter undergarments and clothing, sugared cakes – also shaped the development of trade within Europe itself and between Europe and the rest of the world. This "consumer revolution" fueled Europe's economic growth. The demand for consumer goods in Europe was one of the major causes of the Industrial Revolution, which eventually allowed European countries to dominate much of the world.

The early modern period has been viewed as a time of tremendous economic change, with the expansion of commercial capitalism, the beginning of proto-industrial production, and the creation of a world market system because of European colonization. When we evaluate women's economic role during this period, however, we find that continuities outweigh the changes. Women were increasingly pushed out of craft guilds, but they had only rarely been full members in the first place. They took over new types of agricultural tasks but continued to be paid half of what men were paid no matter what types of work they did. They dominated the urban marketplace but only rarely were able to amass much profit.

Women's economic activities were increasingly restricted during the early modern period, but their legal dependence on father or husband, unequal access to family resources, and inability to receive formally acknowledged training had adversely affected their economic position in the Middle Ages and would continue to do so into the twenty-first century. The vast majority of women's work continued for centuries to be low status, badly paid or unpaid, frequently shifting, and perceived as marginal but essential to the operation of all rural and urban economies. These were also qualities that may be used to describe the work of many men in the early modern period, but they had the comfort of knowing that, however dismal their actual working conditions, their labor was valued higher than that of the women who worked beside them.

It is clear from the records, however, that restrictions did not mean women left the labor force entirely or had no impact on economic development. One recent study of the London labor market found that 72 percent of women in 1700 were doing full- or part-time paid work outside the home. Historians have suggested many reasons for the dramatic growth of the European economy and for European expansion around the world, including not only the Industrial Revolution but also an "Industrious Revolution" in which Europeans reduced their leisure time and worked more to have money to purchase consumer goods. This Industrious Revolution not only involved women, it also required their labor. It is also clear from the records that at least a few midwives, merchants, market women, and medical practitioners took great pride in their work, seeing it as a vocation the way many men did their occupations. This same sense of a calling, of being destined to carry out certain tasks, also motivated some women and girls to learn to read and write and to produce or support art, literature, music, and science, topics we take up in the following section.

For Further Reading

In many ways, all studies of women's economic role during this period look back to the pioneering work of Alice Clark, *Working Life of Women in the Seventeenth Century* (London, Routledge & Kegan Paul, 1919), which has seen three modern reprints (in 1968, 1982, and 1992). Clark found women's participation in the economy steadily decreasing and attributed that decrease to the advent of capitalism and the resulting end of domestic production. Much research on women's work over the last twenty years has tested Clark's ideas in many parts of Europe and has also examined noneconomic determinants of women's work. Such studies include Merry E. Wiesner, *Working Women in Renaissance Germany* (New Brunswick, NJ, Rutgers University Press, 1986); Martha Howell, *Women,*

Production and Patriarchy in Late Medieval Cities (Chicago, University of Chicago Press, 1986); Pamela Sharpe, *Adapting to Capitalism: Working Women in the English Economy 1700–1850* (New York, St. Martin's, 1996); E. C. Sanderson, *Women and Work in Eighteenth-Century Edinburgh* (Basingstoke, Macmillan, 1996); Deborah Simonton, *A History of European Women's Work, 1700 to the Present* (London, Routledge, 1998); Monica Chojnacka, *Working Women in Early Modern Venice* (Baltimore, Johns Hopkins University Press, 2001); and Marjorie Keniston McIntosh, *Working Women in English Society, 1300–1620* (New York, Cambridge University Press, 2005). Collections of articles include Lindsey Charles and Lorna Duffin (eds.), *Women and Work in Pre-Industrial England* (London, Croom Helm, 1985); Barbara Hanawalt (ed.), *Women and Work in Preindustrial Europe* (Bloomington, Indiana University Press, 1986); Daryl Hafter (ed.), *European Women and Preindustrial Craft* (Bloomington, Indiana University Press, 1995); Pamela Sharpe (ed.), *Women's Work: The English Experience 1600–1914* (Oxford, Oxford University Press, 1998); and Isabelle Baudino, Jacques Carré, and Cécile Révauger (eds.), *The Invisible Woman: Aspects of Women's Work in 18th Century Britain* (Burlington, VT, Ashgate, 2005).

Recent scholarship has complicated Clark's conclusions, viewing the precapitalist economy as less positive for women than she did and the changes brought by capitalism as less dramatic and more uneven in their impact. Judith Bennett in particular has argued that continuities in women's work created by patriarchal ideas and structures were more important determinants than any economic changes and that "in important ways women's work stood still." See her *Ale, Beer and Brewsters in England: Women's Work in a Changing World, 1300–1600* (New York: Oxford University Press, 1996), and *History Matters: Patriarchy and the Challenge of Feminism* (Philadelphia: University of Pennsylvania Press, 2006); the quotation is from p. 85 of the latter. Sheilagh Ogilvie notes that guilds, communities, and other traditional networks were not as beneficial to women as both Clark and contemporary "social network" theorists have asserted and that commercial capitalism may have offered better opportunities. See her *A Bitter Living: Women, Markets, and Social Capital in Early Modern Germany* (New York, Oxford University Press, 2003).

Two recent works on the production of textiles and clothing, which employed many women, are Gay L. Gullickson, *Spinners and Weavers of Auffay: Rural Industries and the Sexual Division of Labor in a French Village, 1750–1850* (Cambridge, Cambridge University Press, 1986); and Clare Haru Crowston, *Fabricating Women: The Seamstresses of Old Regime France, 1675–1791* (Durham, NC, Duke University Press, 2001). On servants, see Ann Kussmaul, *Servants in Husbandry in Early Modern*

England (Cambridge, Cambridge University Press, 1981); Sara Maza, *Servants and Masters in Eighteenth-Century France* (Princeton, NJ, Princeton; University Press, 1983); Cissie Fairchilds, *Domestic Enemies: Servants and their Masters in Old Regime France* (Baltimore, Johns Hopkins University Press, 1984); and Tim Meldrum, *Domestic Service and Gender, 1660–1750: Life and Work in the London Household* (Harlow, Longman, 2000).

The interplay between women's work patterns and opportunities and the structure of the family has received a great deal of attention. Two of the most important studies in this area are Louise A. Tilly and Joan W. Scott, *Women, Work, and Family* (New York and London, Methuen, 1978, rpt. 1987); and Bridget Hill, *Women, Work and Sexual Politics in Eighteenth-Century England* (Oxford, Basil Blackwell, 1989). The continuing importance of the family and kin network to economic stability and growth has been stressed in Richard Grassby, *Kinship and Capitalism: Marriage, Family, and Business in the English-Speaking World, 1580–1740* (Cambridge, Cambridge University Press, 2000); and Maria Ågren and Amy Louise Erickson (eds.), *The Marital Economy in Scandinavia and Britain 1400–1900* (Burlington, VT, Ashgate, 2005). For one of the few studies that looks at rural women, see Allyson M. Poska, *Women and Authority in Early Modern Spain: The Peasants of Galicia* (New York, Oxford University Press, 2005).

Women's property ownership and activities as entrepreneurs and merchants have been studied in Susan Staves, *Married Women's Separate Property in England, 1660–1833* (Cambridge, MA, Harvard University Press, 1990); Amy Louise Erickson, *Women and Property in Early Modern England* (London, Routledge, 1995); Rosemary Sweet and Penelope Lane (eds.), *Women and Urban Life in Eighteenth-Century England* (Burlington, VT, Ashgate, 2003); and Nancy E. Wright, Margaret W. Ferguson, and A. R. Buck (eds.), *Women, Property, and the Letters of the Law in Early Modern England* (Toronto, University of Toronto Press, 2004). Natalie Davis provides an in-depth look at the activities of Glickl bas Judah Leib in *Women on the Margins: Three Seventeenth-Century Lives* (Cambridge, MA, Harvard University Press, 1995), pp. 5–62.

Many historians are currently studying economic and cultural changes in the production, trade, purchase, and use of consumer goods. Marcia Pointon, *Strategies for Showing: Women, Possession, and Representation in English Visual Culture 1665–1800* (Oxford, Oxford University Press, 1998), analyzes relations between ideas of gender and "luxury"; Carole Collier Frick, *Dressing Renaissance Florence: Families, Fortunes, and Fine Clothing* (Baltimore, Johns Hopkins University Press, 2002), focuses on the ways expensive cloth was displayed on male and female bodies; and Maxine Berg, *Luxury and Pleasure in Eighteenth-Century Britain* (New York, Oxford University Press, 2005), explores the new, semiluxury, and fashionable consumer goods, both those brought from the East as part of global trade networks and those made at home.

For more suggestion and links, see the companion Web site www. cambridge.org/womenandgender.

Part II

Mind

4   Literacy and Learning

And if any woman reaches the stage at which she is able to put her thoughts into writing, she should do it with much thought and should not scorn the glory, but adorn herself with this rather than with chains, rings, and sumptuous clothes, which we are not really able to regard as ours except by custom. But the honor which knowledge will bring us cannot be taken from us ... in addition to the recognition our sex will gain by this, we will have furnished the public with a reason for men to devote more labor to virtuous studies lest they might be ashamed to see us surpass them when they have always pretended to be superior in nearly everything ...

> Louise Labé, 1555, quoted and translated by Jeanne Prine, in Katharina
> Wilson (ed.), *Women Writers of the Renaissance and Reformation* (Athens:
> University of Georgia Press, 1987), p. 149

My deep regard for learning, my conviction that equal justice is the right of all, impel me to protest against the theory which would allow only a minority of my sex to attain to what is, in the opinion of all men, most worth having. For since wisdom is admitted to be the crown of human achievement, and is within every man's right to aim at in proportion to his opportunities, I cannot see why a young girl in whom we admit a desire for self-improvement should not be encouraged to acquire the best that life affords.

> Anna Maria van Schurman, *The Learned Maid or Whether a Maid May Be
> Called a Scholar?* (London, 1659), p. 55

For since GOD has given Women as well as Men intelligent Souls, why should they be forbidden to improve them? Since he has not denied to us the faculty of Thinking, why shou'd we not (at least in gratitude to him) employ our Thoughts on himself their noblest Object, and not unworthily bestow them on Trifles and Gaieties and secular Affairs?

> Mary Astell, *A Serious Proposal to the Ladies* (London, 1694)

Since the nineteenth century, advocates of women's rights have made equal access for women to educational institutions one of their key demands. Only through education, they have argued, could women become knowledgeable citizens or enter careers in which they would be economically independent; they have seen education as inseparable from political and economic rights. Nineteenth-century feminists called for the opening of universities and professional schools to middle-class women who could afford to attend them. Twentieth-century feminists demanded an end to quotas that limited the number of women in advanced education and advocated greater public funding of higher education to make it more accessible to lower-class women and men. These efforts have been very successful. In the early twenty-first century, the majority of college students in many countries (including the United States) are female, and women outnumber men in some professional schools.

Calls for the improvement of women's education did not begin in the nineteenth century but rather much earlier. Women's education was an important theme in the debate about women we traced in Chapter 1, with women (and some men) arguing passionately that women were capable of learning at the same level that men were. Their lines of argument were different than those of more recent supporters of education for women, however. Learning, by which its advocates meant training in classical languages, philosophy, the sciences, theology, and history, was primarily for a woman's individual fulfillment or to make her a better Christian; it was not linked with political or vocational aims. Anna Maria van Schurman, quoted at the start of the chapter and widely regarded as the most highly educated woman in Europe in the seventeenth century, stated plainly that "the pursuit of letters does not involve any interference with public affairs."[1] Only rarely was the suggestion made that formal educational institutions, such as humanist academies, universities, or professional schools, be opened to women, but simply that women should be able to hire private tutors and learn on their own or perhaps that separate academies for women should be established.

Early modern supporters of women's learning felt it necessary to stress that their demands would not lead to social or political upheaval because what they were advocating, although it seems modest to us, was regarded as radical by most of society. For a number of reasons, formal educational opportunities for boys and men grew steadily during the early modern period. With the development of the printing press, written instructional manuals could supplement personal training by a master craftsman, so that artisan parents felt it important that their sons learn to read; by the end of the sixteenth century, nearly all male workers in certain trades, such as printing and goldsmithing, could read. Protestant reformers in many areas supported the opening of vernacular-language schools to

---

[1] Anna Maria van Schurman, "Letter to Dr. Rivet," quoted in Una Birch, *Anna van Schurman: Artist, Scholar, Saint* (London, Longman, 1909), p. 70.

allow individuals to read the Bible and other religious literature, and the vast majority of these were for boys only. For middle- and upper-class boys, training in Latin began at seven or eight, preparing them for later attendance at a university and an eventual professional career as a physician, lawyer, university professor, or government or church official. The suggestion that women should share in these advances was viewed by most people as at best impractical and at worst dangerous. Why should parents forgo the help of their daughters in the household while they learned things they would never use in later life? Why should women learn Latin, when they could not attend universities and none of the professions that required it were open to them? Why did women need to read the Bible themselves when they could listen to their fathers, brothers, or husbands read from it? Why couldn't women be content with education that was primarily training in the type of domestic skills they would use as married women, whether milking cows or hiring servants? Wouldn't a woman's reading or writing distract her from caring for her children and household? The supporters of female education continually had to answer questions such as these. Although they chose to downplay the connections between learning and social change, their opponents recognized that learning to read and write could radically alter a woman's view of the world and her place in it.

In this chapter, we investigate the ways in which, despite opposition and hostility, early modern women became literate and note what reading material was available to them once they had learned to read. We then examine the small group of women who went beyond basic literacy to gain a humanist education and discuss several women's plans for formal institutions of learning. The chapter ends with a look at two sites of political and social, as well as intellectual, training for women – the court and the salon – and the ways in which learned women in these milieus supported the careers of learned and talented men through social and financial patronage.

Basic Training in Reading and Writing

Before we go any farther in this chapter, it is important to remind ourselves that even basic literacy was never achieved by the vast majority of women (or men) in Europe during the early modern period. They were not necessarily uneducated, for they may have been highly skilled in a trade and astute about the world around them, but this education came through oral tradition and training in a workshop, not through books. As we saw in the last chapter, even their oral training was generally less formal than that of men, learned from their fathers and mothers or when an employer chose to teach them, rather than through a structured apprenticeship program.

A girl's parents were often her first teachers in reading as well. The words of Thomas Aquinas were frequently cited by Catholic authorities to urge fathers to take a greater interest in their young children's education: "For this the activity of the wife alone is not sufficient, but the intervention of the husband is better suited, whose reason is better suited for intellectual instruction and whose strength for the necessary discipline."[2] Protestant reformers urged both fathers and mothers who could themselves read to pass this knowledge on to their children or to send their small children to friends or neighbors who could. Older women in many towns and cities ran small "cranny schools" that combined child care with teaching young children their letters and the recitation of Bible verses or psalms. Often, these women were barely literate themselves, only being able to read but not write, so that they escaped the attention of authorities who were responsible for licensing and regulating teachers. If a woman became too successful, however, the official city schoolmasters often complained to the city council that she was drawing pupils away from them, and the council responded by ordering her to limit herself to basic reading only and only to take in girls. Jewish women in Italy taught children the Hebrew letters and the correct reading of Scripture in Hebrew, although translation and commentary were reserved for male teachers.

First in Protestant areas and then in Catholic, learning to read was viewed as a part of religious instruction, and political and religious authorities encouraged the opening of girls' elementary schools to teach girls who could not learn at home. In the sixteenth century, about forty Protestant church ordinances in Germany called for the establishment of girls' schools, although it is difficult to tell how many schools were actually opened, for many areas do not have good records. One that does is the province of Electoral Saxony in central Germany, the records of which indicate that by 1580, 50 percent of the parishes had licensed German-language schools for boys and 10 percent for girls; by 1675, those numbers had increased to 94 and 40 percent. By 1600, there were also a number of girls' schools in southwestern Germany and in the province of Brandenburg, alalthough many of these disappeared in the turmoil of the Thirty Years' War. Because of these girls' schools, it was long held that the Protestant Reformation increased opportunities for female education. More recently, historians have noted the continuation of a

---

[2] Thomas Aquinas, *Summa contra gentiles*, III, c. 123.

large gap between boys' and girls' opportunities for learning in even the most enlightened German states. A few girls' schools were opened, but in Protestant areas convent schools, which had served noble and upper middle-class girls, were generally closed.

Even where schools were established, the education they offered was meager. Girls attended for an hour or so a day, for one to two years, and were to learn "reading and writing, and if both of these can't be mastered, at least some writing, the catechism learned by heart, a little figuring, a few psalms to sing."[3] What did Protestant authorities see as the aim of girls' education? "To habituate girls to the catechism, to the psalms, to honorable behavior and Christian virtue, and especially to prayer, and make them memorize verses from Holy Scripture so that they may grow up to be Christian and praiseworthy matrons and housekeepers."[4] Whereas boys were engaged in competitions in Latin rhetoric, the best student in the Memmingen girls' school in 1587 was chosen on the basis of her "great diligence and application in learning her catechism, modesty, obedience, and excellent penmanship."[5] Along with reading, writing, and religion, sewing and other domestic skills were also often part of the curriculum at these schools, which worked to the advantage of female teachers, who were also hired in preference to male because they could be paid less. Scholarships set up for poor girls read: "To be sent to school, and especially to learn to sew."[6] A potential teacher's intellectual abilities often came third in the minds of city councils establishing girls' schools, after her "honorable lifestyle" and ability to teach domestic skills.

Along with urban schools specifically for girls, in some parts of Protestant Germany village schools for children of both sexes were established in the late sixteenth and seventeenth centuries. In these rural areas, the percentage of girls attending school was much closer to that of boys than in urban areas, although neither sex attended school as long nor as regularly as boys in the city. The curriculum for both sexes was identical, with no Latin or the advanced subjects offered to boys in the cities, so that rural girls' classroom experience was much closer to that of their brothers than that of urban girls, and the gender gap in education was not as pronounced.

[3] A 1533 ordinance of the girls' school in Wittenberg, Germany, translated and quoted in Gerald Strauss, "The Social Function of Schools in the Lutheran Reformation in Germany," *History of Education Quarterly* 28 (1988), p. 197.
[4] A 1552 school ordinance from Mecklenburg, Germany, quoted in ibid., p. 198.
[5] A 1587 ordinance of the girls' school in Memmingen, Germany, quoted in Merry E. Wiesner, *Working Women in Renaissance Germany* (New Brunswick, NJ, Rutgers University Press, 1987), p. 81.
[6] Ibid., p. 82.

Figure 7. Dirk Vellert, *The School Room*, 1526. In this woodcut, Vellert portrays not the reality of sixteenth-century schools but rather a scene that depicts the importance of education in bringing about order to the community, an ideal that Protestant reformers felt needed frequent repetition. Here, men and boys in secular dress study above and respectable women work, read, chat, and oversee the learning of children below. The vertical fold down the middle indicates that the woodcut may have originally been bound or pressed into a book, perhaps a Protestant pamphlet on education. Probably no actual early modern school ever looked like this, for boys and girls were separated except in their earliest years, and adult women in Protestant areas had no place to gather to read other than a private home.

During the sixteenth century, instruction for girls in Catholic areas, other than in convents, which were largely limited to the nobility and wealthy, lagged behind even the meager offerings of Protestant areas. A survey of schools in Venice in 1587–88 found about 4,600 male pupils, or about one-fourth of the school-age boys in the city, and only 30 girls. There were some informal catechism schools in Italy and Spain (those for boys taught by men and for girls by women) that did teach reading, but these only met for about two hours on Sundays and religious holidays so that the level of literacy achieved was not very high. Opportunities for girls increased in the seventeenth century in some parts of Catholic Europe with the spread of the female teaching orders such as the Ursulines, who opened more convent boarding schools for upper-class girls and day schools for poorer ones. Convent education emphasized piety and morals more than academic subjects, with everything taught by means of rote memorization. Even this limited curriculum was beyond the reach of most girls, however, for although religious orders and private individuals did open some charity day schools for girls, these were still far fewer than those opened for boys. A survey of school-age children in southern France in the late eighteenth century found about two-thirds of boys receiving some schooling, compared with only one girl in fifty.

Where girls' schools did exist, girls attended for a much briefer period than their brothers, which often meant they learned to read but not to write because the two were not taught simultaneously. Writing was also more expensive to learn because pupils had to have some material on which to write, which parents were often unwilling to provide for their daughters. Parish registers, marriage contracts, and wills throughout the early modern period generally reveal that about twice as many men as women from similar social classes could sign their names and that the women's signatures are more poorly written than the men's, so that their name might have been the only thing these women ever wrote. Women who were technically literate thus could not take jobs in which writing or figuring was required, which did not dramatically shape their employment opportunities in 1500 when few artisans could read but did by 1750 or even 1650 when in many cities of Europe the majority of male artisans could both read and write. Teaching women to read but not write was the result not only of an economic decision on the part of parents but also of contemporary notions about the ideal woman. Learning to read would allow a woman to discover classical and Christian examples of proper female behavior and to absorb the ideas of great (male) authors. Learning to write, on the other hand, would enable her to express her own ideas, an ability that few thinkers regarded as important and some saw as threatening.

The fact that women learned to read but not write makes measuring levels of female literacy difficult, for the ability to sign one's name is often taken as the basic indication of literacy. In East Anglia in eastern England, for example, 49 percent of male tradesmen and craftsmen and 6 percent of women in the decade of the 1580s could sign their names, proportions that had only risen to 56 percent and 16 percent in the 1680s. From other types of sources, however, such as wills and the inventories taken at death, we know that the proportion of people who could read was much higher, but there is no way of arriving at exact figures. The safest generalization is that literacy levels for women, as for men, were highest among the urban upper classes and lowest among the rural peasantry, and that they slowly increased from 1500 to 1750, although much more slowly than literacy levels for men.

Women's Reading

Once a girl or woman learned to read, what reading material was available? This, too, was highly class-specific. Although the development of the printing press in the fifteenth century had reduced the cost of books dramatically, not until the early eighteenth century had improvements in the printing process made books cheap enough so that most artisan households could afford more than a few small books. During the sixteenth century, the vast majority of reading material produced was religious, ranging from expensive illustrated Bibles to small collections of psalms or devotional verses to even less expensive pamphlets of religious controversy or saints' lives. From wills and inventories, it appears that women were slightly more likely than men to limit their book ownership to religious works in the sixteenth century and to works of a pious and devotional nature rather than those of religious controversy; when parents divided their books among their children, daughters usually received fewer and smaller books and only rarely any that were not religious. The proportion of nonreligious books produced increased steadily throughout the seventeenth and eighteenth centuries, so that women were reading a wider variety of materials in 1750 than they were in 1500. How-to manuals and household guides were popular, as were letter-writing manuals, travel reports, translations of classical Greek and Roman authors, and increasingly chivalric romances and books of stories, often produced as small chapbooks with paper covers that made them affordable. In the eighteenth century, journals and newspapers were increasingly important in the circulation of ideas. They were often set out at coffeehouses, taverns, and wine shops so that a single subscription was read by many people.

Most of the customers and readers at such shops were men, but a few women did visit them, and more read journals and newspapers at home.

Because male readers outnumbered female, most books were produced with both sexes in mind, but beginning as early as the sixteenth century, there were also books published specifically for girls and women. The first books written solely for girls were Protestant religious works, especially prayer books and books about virtuous young women in the Bible, whose authors often dedicated them to their daughters and envisioned the girls reading them aloud to their friends and servants who could not read. They differed from religious books for adults both in language and tone, with shorter, easier sentences and a milder tone, rarely mentioning hell and damnation. The prayer books often include special prayers for girls in special circumstances, such as orphans or the chronically ill, and reflections on the relative value of different types of suitors and on marriage in general. By the late seventeenth century, a few secular books were written specifically for girls, such as guides to conversation and manners, and even romances, although they continued to be strongly moral in tone and concentrated on chastity.

Books addressed to adult women readers in the sixteenth and seventeenth centuries were also largely devotional and published in small format so that they would be relatively cheap. There were books on marriage and general guides for how to be a Christian wife and mother written by men, although not nearly as many as similar guides directed to male heads of household. There were small books of devotions and consolation specifically designed for pregnant women, although it is doubtful how much solace a prayer thanking God for providing the opportunity of Christian service through dying in childbirth or gruesome stories about women who carried dead fetuses around for years would actually offer. Several cookbooks were addressed specifically to women and a few written by women, such as the nearly 1,000-page *The Excellent [Female] Cook Descended from Parnassus* published by Susanna Endter in 1691. Such works were designed primarily for the noble or upper-bourgeois household and also included recipes for home remedies, as the title of Anna Wecker's 1597 cookbook makes clear: *A delicious new Cookbook, not only for the healthy, but also and primarily for those sick with all types of illnesses and infirmities and also pregnant women, newly-delivered mothers and old weak people.* As literacy became more common among midwives, midwives' manuals were frequently reprinted and translated, for they provided printers with a steady market.

The vast majority of books for women, even midwives' guides and those discussing needlework, were written by men and probably purchased by men for their wives and daughters. The message they convey is, not surprisingly, not one promoting greater egalitarianism but one in which gender and class distinctions are paramount. Through all types of books, women were instructed to be chaste, silent, and obedient. Although we cannot know whether women received the message that was intended (or even that they actually read the books purchased for them), we do know that male authorities and authors worried about the possible effects of even the most pious material. The most extreme example of this was an act of Henry VIII of England in 1543 that forbade women to read the Bible except for "noblewomen and gentlewomen [who] might read it privately, but not to others."[7] Thomas Bentley simply altered the Bible to suit his purposes; in his *Monument of Matrones* (London, 1582), a guide for married women, he included all verses from Paul's letters to the Corinthians that stress female subservience but omitted without noting it those that suggest the interdependence of men and women. In the eighteenth century, German authors warned even upper-class women against letting their reading interfere with their household tasks; one designed a special reading platform for women so that they could spin, sew, or knit while they read. Such suggestions indicate that both female reading and female productive tasks were regarded as qualitatively different from male – neither required a woman's full attention, so that neither would be up to male standards.

In the eighteenth century, moralists were increasingly worried about women reading a new type of literature, the novel, which involves a long and complex plot that develops through the thoughts and actions of distinctive characters. Novels often incorporated exotic locales and sexuality, both seen as dangerous for women readers. As we will see in Chapter 5, female authors such as Aphra Behn in England and Madeleine de Scudéry and Marie-Madeleine de La Fayette in France were important in the development of the novel, but their gender did not make their works any more appropriate for young women in the eyes of many observers. Some writers addressed concerns about the impact on female readers by focusing on moral virtues in their novels. The heroine in Samuel Richardson's *Pamela: or, Virtue Rewarded* (1740–41), for example, is hired as a servant by a man who is her social superior; he tries to rape her – a scenario that, as we have seen, was common in real life – but she resists. Over the course of the very long novel, written in the form of letters, he is convinced by the virtuousness of the heroine that he should marry her instead. Richardson's novel became wildly popular, inspiring Pamela

---

[7] Quoted in Suzanne Hull, *Chaste, Silent and Obedient: English Books for Women 1475–1640* (San Marino, CA, Huntington Library, 1982), p. xii.

dolls and other merchandise, although it also led several novelists to write parodies that skewer its ideas about virtue, including Eliza Haywood's viciously satiric *Anti-Pamela* (1741) and Henry Fielding's pointed yet very funny *Shamela* (1741).

Humanist Education

The most important change in education during the early modern period is often seen as the spread of Renaissance humanism northward from its Italian birthplace. Humanism was an intellectual movement that admired the works of ancient Greeks and Romans for both their content and style and so advocated the study of classical literature as the best type of learning. Humanist teachers in Italian cities and courts established schools in which pupils began with Latin grammar and rhetoric, went on to study Roman history and political philosophy, and then learned Greek to study Greek literature and philosophy. Young men from other parts of Europe began to attend humanist schools in Italy and brought humanist ideas back to their own countries. By the sixteenth century, there were humanist academies in many cities in France, England, Germany, and elsewhere.

Humanists viewed an education in the classics as the best preparation for a political career as either a ruler or adviser, for it taught one how to argue persuasively, base decisions on historical examples, write effectively, and speak eloquently. Conversely, they taught that a public political career or the creation of a public reputation through writing should be the aim of all educated individuals, for the best life was not a contemplative one but a life of action. In this, they disagreed with medieval scholars, who had viewed the best use of an education to be the glorification of God through prayer, manuscript copying, writing, or teaching. Education, humanists taught, was not simply for individual or religious purposes but directly benefited the public good by providing knowledgeable public servants.

This emphasis on the public role and reputation of the educated individual led to questions about whether humanist education was appropriate for women. If the best models of moral behavior and clear thought were to be found in classical authors, why should women be denied access to these? But, was a program of study that emphasized eloquence and action ever proper for a woman, because women's speech, particularly in public, might indicate her unchastity? If simply learning to read drew women away from their family responsibilities, how were women to have the time for an extended education in the classics? Were women even capable of advanced learning, or was reason a masculine quality?

Male humanists answered these questions in several ways. Some, such as Juan Luis Vives, restricted the class of women for whom a humanist education was proper to those who might be forced into public service, such as Princess Mary Tudor, for whom he wrote *Instruction of a Christian Woman* in 1523. Vives also advocated omitting rhetoric from any program of study for girls and emphasized Christian reading material for women in preference to pagan classics. Such calls for a narrower education for women were common among male humanists, although there were also some who thought women's learning should not be limited.

Women were more bold in their claims that women were capable of higher education and that learning was compatible with virtue. Although humanist academies were not open to women, in the early fifteenth century some noble women in Italy were educated in the classics through their fathers or tutors. In the later fifteenth century, a few middle-class urban women also became excited by the new style of learning and through tutors or programs of self-study became extremely well educated. They argued in letters and then in published writings that women could indeed be both eloquent and chaste. Several put this assertion into practice, writing and reciting public orations in Latin and Greek and circulating their letters, both common practices for male humanists. Isotta Nogarola (1418–66), educated in Latin by a tutor, gave several public orations that combined biblical and classical allusions and circulated her correspondence. In one of her letters, she answers the standard complaint that women are far too talkative with a list of women who are "superior to men" not in verbosity but "eloquence and virtue."[8] Cassandra Fedele (1465–1558), the best-known female scholar of her time, gave an oration in Latin at the University of Padua in honor of her (male) cousin's graduation. She also gave several other orations before the ruler of Venice, where she lived, one of which specifically focused on the value of learning. Most of this oration praises the general merits of education, although she briefly highlights its benefits for women: "Even if the study of literature offers women no rewards or honors, I believe women must nonetheless pursue and embrace such studies alone for the pleasure and enjoyment they contain ... I myself intend to pursue immortality through such study."[9]

Fedele tended to set herself apart from other women (and men) as unusually gifted, but Laura Cereta (1469–99), another middle-class

[8] Isotta Nogarola, *Complete Writings*, ed. and trans. Margaret L. King and Diana Robin, (Chicago: University of Chicago Press, 2004), p. 100.

[9] Cassandra Fedele, *Letters and Orations*, ed. and trans. Diana Robin, (Chicago: University of Chicago Press, 2000), pp. 162, 159.

urban woman, forcefully argued that "all history is full of examples" of women who reached "the pinnacle of fame for their learning."[10] Nature, she argued, offered the gift of reason to all, although learning took work:

An education is neither bequeathed to us as a legacy, nor does some fate or other give it to us as a gift. Virtue is something that we ourselves acquire, nor can those women who become dull-witted through laziness and the sludge of low pleasures ascend to the understanding of difficult things. But for women who believe that study, hard work, and vigilance will bring them sure praise, the road to attaining knowledge is broad.[11]

During the sixteenth century, male scholars brought humanist ideas to England, and a small cluster of women gained a humanist education. These were almost all from high noble families, such as Lady Jane Grey and Mary and Elizabeth Tudor. The most celebrated of these was Thomas More's oldest daughter, Margaret Roper. Through his own teaching and that of tutors, More educated his children, their spouses, and other relatives in Latin and Greek, studying works of philosophy, poetry, science, and theology. His pupils prepared translations, gave oral disputations and dramatic performances, and came into contact with the leading humanist scholars of Europe. Margaret Roper also wrote a number of original Latin orations, poems, and treatises, although the only work of hers that was published, other than letters, is her English translation of Erasmus's *A devout treatise on the Pater Noster*, published in 1524. This is exactly the type of work by a learned woman that gained her praise instead of censure: it is a translation of a work written by a family friend, on a pious subject, and was originally published anonymously, although anyone with contacts with the More family would have known who the translator was. It therefore gained Roper a public reputation but one that demonstrated qualities regarded as admirable in women: piety, family loyalty, reticence. It is not simply derivative, however, but shows an independence of expression that places greater stress on human unworthiness and God's kindness than Erasmus's Latin original did; it is also written in a graceful, flowing, and straightforward style at a time when much English prose was awkward and stilted.

Roper was clearly very talented, although it is difficult to arrive at an objective assessment of her abilities because the contemporaries who described them generally saw them primarily as a reflection of Thomas More's own learning and moral character. Over the next two centuries,

---

[10] Laura Cereta, *Collected Letters of a Renaissance Feminist*, ed. and trans. Diana Robin, (Chicago: University of Chicago Press, 1997), p. 78.
[11] Ibid., p. 82.

her life was frequently used as an example by those who argued that education could augment rather than harm a woman's virtue. It is clear from More's own letters, however, particularly those relating to Roper's arguments with him over his defiance of King Henry VIII (which led to his execution), that she could also use her humanist education to oppose her father. She never used it to reflect on her own condition or that of women in general, however, for, in contrast to Italian humanist women, Roper made no public statements about women's education nor did she publish any of her own original works; this is also the case with the other women who received a humanist education in sixteenth-century England.

Sixteenth-century Italian and French humanist women were more willing to show their learning in public than were their English counterparts. In the 1530s, women in several Italian cities established informal groups for the presentation and discussion of written work – what would later be termed "salons." The poet Vittoria Colonna (1490–1547) was the center of several such groups and published a book of poetry under her own name in 1538, the first solo edition of a woman's poetry to appear in print. Several of these salons, including Colonna's, became associated with movements of religious reform, as did a group surrounding Marguerite of Navarre (1492–1549), the sister of the French king Francis I, with whom Colonna regularly corresponded. Marguerite supported religious reform in her own writings and protected reformers at her court. She also encouraged the education of the women at her court, including not only prominent French noblewomen but also Mary and Anne Boleyn, the future mistress and wife of Henry VIII of England, and Catherine de' Medici, the Italian future queen of France. Through the *Heptameron*, a group of seventy-three stories that she wrote and that were published shortly after her death, her influence extended far beyond her court. The book was extremely popular in France, was translated quickly into English, and many of the stories were lifted by other authors and published in their own story collections; English humanists complained that her stories were the favorite reading of literate women. Although they do not explicitly advocate women's education or improved social status, the stories do provide examples of assertive daughters and wives and criticize traditional views of marriage; they give female readers alternative models to the patient wives and daughters found in the Bible or early Christian writers.

Marguerite's willingness to break with both religious tradition and injunctions to female silence was due in part to her class position, as was also the case for other French noblewomen educated as humanists, such as Marguerite's daughter Jeanne d'Albret, her nieces Renée de France and Marguerite de France, and Jacqueline Longwy, the duchesse de Montpensier. A few middle-class urban women in France also began to

gain a classical education in the sixteenth century and explicitly asserted
that male restrictions rather than female inferiority were responsible for
women's lesser levels of learning. Louise Labé (1520?–66), quoted at the
beginning of this chapter, received a solid humanist education through
the efforts of her father and wrote sonnets and other types of poetry. She
urged women to show off their learning and not restrict themselves to a
domestic setting, writing to a supporter, "The time having come, Made-
moiselle, when the stern laws of men no longer bar women from devoting
themselves to the sciences and disciplines, it seems to me that those who
are able ought to employ this honorable liberty, which our sex formerly
desired so much, in studying these things and show men the wrong they
have done in depriving us of the benefit and honor which might have come
to us."[12] She took her own advice, publishing a collection of her writings
and sonnets written by men in her honor in Lyons in 1555; this work
received praise in some circles but was also severely criticized, particularly
because Labé primarily concerned herself with romantic love, which was
viewed as a highly inappropriate topic for women. Using the type of criticism frequently directed against eloquent women, John Calvin, the religious reformer of Geneva, accused her of gaining popularity by providing
sexual services to local nobles and clergy. Her work shows great familiarity with classical literature and skill at the conventions of classical rhetoric
and treats the issue of unrequited love both tragically and humorously.

Labé solved the problem of how to reconcile humanist demands for
public honor with restrictions on women's public actions and speech
by ignoring the restrictions and recommending all women who could
get an education do the same. Madeleine and Catherine des Roches, a
mother and daughter who were the center of a humanist group in the
French city of Poitiers, agreed, publishing several volumes of their own
poetry and letters. They shared with their male colleagues a new sense
of pride in French culture and devotion to the French monarchy and
perhaps because of this were widely praised for their writings. Madeleine
deplored the poverty of the education that most women received and
sharply criticized marriage laws, through which women lost the power
over their own property:

> Our parents have laudable customs,
> To deprive us of the use of our reason,
> They lock us up at home
> And hand us the spindle instead of the pen.

[12] Louise Labé, quoted and translated by Jeanne Prine, in Katharina Wilson (ed.), *Women Writers of the Renaissance and Reformation* (Athens: University of Georgia Press, 1987), p. 149.

> Conforming our steps to our [female] destiny,
> They promise us liberty and pleasure:
> But we reap continuous displeasure,
> When we lose our dowry to the laws of Marriage.[13]

Catherine decided to forgo her "female destiny" and never married, although she had many offers; she and her mother remained devoted to one another and died in the same outbreak of the plague, perhaps on the same day. Refusing marriage was highly unusual, and one of Catherine's most cited poems suggests her mixed feelings about balancing the domestic world of women and the public world of men. In this ode, she addresses her distaff (also called a spindle), the rod on which wool or flax is wound when spinning, and a primary symbol of women's household activities.

> To my distaff
>
> My distaff, my care, I promise you and swear,
> That I'll love you forever, and never exchange
> Your domestic honor for a good which is strange,
> And which, inconstant, wanders aimlessly and does not endure.
> With you at my side, I am far more secure
> Than with paper and ink arrayed all around me
> For, if I needed defending, you would be there,
> You are much better at repelling an assault.
> But distaff, my love, it is not really necessary,
> That in order to value you and love you so,
> I abandon entirely that honorable custom
> Of writing sometimes; for by writing as I do,
> I write of your worth, distaff, my care,
> As I hold in my hand my spindle and my pen.[14]

As literary scholars have pointed out, the final line could be interpreted in a number of different ways: as a reconciliation of writing (the pen) and domestic tasks (the spindle), as a recognition that balancing the two would always be awkward, as a subversion of the normal expectations for women's lives, or perhaps as all three. However it is interpreted, it captures issues still facing women today trying to balance work and family, which may account for the poem's continued popularity.

Male humanists sometimes praised individual women for their learning and achievements, using words such as "illustris" and "virtuousa." Some female humanists recognized the problems with this, particularly if the

---

[13] Quoted and translated in Madeleine and Catherine des Roches, *From Mother and Daughter*, ed. and trans. Anne R. Larsen, (Chicago: University of Chicago Press, 2006), p. 53.
[14] Ibid., p. 111.

highest form of praise was that the woman had "overcome her sex" and become like a man. They asserted, as we have seen, that women as a group had the capacity for learning, if only they were given the chance. That chance was slow in coming. Gradually, the classical learning advocated by humanists became the basis for intermediate and advanced education for a large share of the male middle- and upper-class population in Italy, France, England, and Germany, particularly when private, municipal, and princely schools adopted humanist curricula. These schools were not open to women. Men who attended such schools did not become celibate scholars, as had the most highly educated men in the Middle Ages, but rather were active in the world. This was particularly true in Protestant areas, where, as we saw Chapter 1, celibacy was rejected as an ideal; it was also true in Catholic areas, however, for humanists as well as Protestants argued that the best life for any man was that of an active citizen and head of household. Women still had to choose, and their choice of a life of learning often cut them off from the concerns of most women in a way that a similar choice no longer did for men.

Learned Women in the Seventeenth and Eighteenth Centuries

During the seventeenth and eighteenth centuries, calls for an expansion in women's education became louder and more frequent. Advocates of improved education for women built on the humanist idea that education was important for the public good but rejected the notion that the public good was only served by men in political careers. Women, too, they argued, could serve the public good through their influence on children and their management of households in their husband's absence or as widows. By being more interesting companions to their husbands through education, women could keep their husbands from prostitutes or other vices that harmed the public welfare. Some writers recognized that not only female rulers but other types of women might also be thrust into more "masculine" types of public service during times of war or revolt.

Advocates of serious learning for women were generally not pleased with the type of education offered by the few schools for girls that were beginning to be established in the seventeenth century. In English, French, and German cities, a few boarding schools for upper- and middle-class girls were opened that offered subjects judged to make their pupils more attractive marriage partners. These were usually termed "accomplishments" and included needlework, dancing, calligraphy, drawing and painting, moral instruction, domestic skills appropriate to their class such as planning meals, and in England, the Low Countries, and Germany, some instruction in French. Toward the end of the century, women also began to offer courses in similar subjects in their own homes to enterprising lower-class girls to make them more attractive not to prospective husbands but rather to prospective female employers, who wanted such "genteel" skills in their personal maids. Critics of such schools decried their shallowness, arguing that by not teaching Latin, they cut women off from classical culture and instead taught them frivolous ways to fill their time rather than things that were morally, spiritually, or socially useful.

Most supporters of more serious education for women, male or female, had themselves received classical training, in which the most effective way to argue was held to be by example. They built on the earlier lists of illustrious women such as that of Boccaccio to create huge books of learned and talented women with short biographies describing their achievements. The women included ranged from mythological figures such as the muses or the goddess Athena, through classical queens and writers, medieval abbesses and humanist women, to poets, translators, writers of hymns and prayers, and women simply reputed to be well learned who were their contemporaries. Such works include Gilles Ménage's *Historia Mulierum Philosopharum* (The History of Women Philosophers; Paris, 1690), C. F. Paullini's *Hoch- und Wohlgelahrtes Teutsches Frauenzimmer* (The Highly- and Well-educated German Lady; Frankfurt and Leipzig, 1712), and the two-volume *The Female Worthies* (London, 1766), all of which went through several editions and were frequently plagiarized by other writers. The authors generally regard quantity as a more effective argument than quality and so include any woman they have heard or read about, which is fortunate for modern scholars of women's learning and writing as they often mention women whose works are now lost or were never published. Although by terming such women "exceptional" or "extraordinarily accomplished," the authors appear to have accepted the argument that the capacity for learning in women is highly unusual, some viewed their lists instead as proof that large numbers of women could reach such heights if given the opportunity and that female learning was neither new nor dangerous.

Among the contemporary women included in such lists, Anna Maria van Schurman (1607–78) was often described as the ultimate learned woman; Paullini spends eight pages discussing her whereas most other women receive a paragraph or two. Born in Utrecht, the Netherlands, she was educated at her father's command alongside her two brothers. She first concentrated on painting, engraving, and other forms of art, then became friends with several well-educated noblewomen and male scholars and began to learn ancient languages, including Hebrew, Chaldean,

Figure 8. Anna Maria van Schurman, self-portrait, 1633, engraving on copper. Note her fashionably curled hair and very elegant dress, styles she later rejected when she became more interested in religion.

Arabic, and Syriac. She wrote an Ethiopian grammar and was granted the rare privilege of attending lectures at the University of Utrecht, although she had to stand behind a curtain. She became widely known for her learning throughout Europe and was visited by male scholars, but she also attracted criticism. In answer to her critics, she wrote a brief treatise in Latin debating the question "whether the study of letters is fitting to a Christian woman," which was first published, along with other of her letters on the topic, in Paris in 1638. This book was translated into English in 1659 as *The Learned Maid or Whether a Maid may be called a Scholar.* As the quotation that opens this chapter indicates, Schurman answered her own question with a clear "yes." That quotation, taken from a letter, suggests that she saw learning as a "right for all," although in her formal treatise she makes clear that her call was limited to women for whom "the circumstances of her time and fortune are such that it is possible sometimes to be free from any general or special calling ... and from the duties of the household."[15] For such women, education in subjects such as science and languages would lead to stronger faith, moral improvement, better guiding of their children, and "a more tranquil and free life." By stressing this last result and seeing education as an end in itself, Schurman argued that women's lack of opportunity for public careers was no reason to deny them classical learning. Schurman, in fact, goes further than this, commenting that educating women would not cause them to upset the political or social status quo but rather would lead them to support it: "Nor is there any reason why the Republic should fear such a change of this kind for itself, since the glory of the literary order in no way obstructs the light of the rulers. On the contrary, all agree that that state at length will flourish most which is inhabited by many subjects obedient not so much to laws as to wisdom."[16] Her call for women's education was thus a conservative one, and it is perhaps not surprising that during her later life, she rejected her earlier learning and argued that reading the Scriptures while guided by the Holy Spirit was all the education any Christian, male or female, needed.

Although she herself rejected them, Schurman's reasons for supporting serious education for women were picked up by other writers, particularly in England, where they led in the late seventeenth century to several specific proposals for women's academies. In 1673, Bathsua Makin, who had admired and corresponded with Schurman, published *An Essay to Revive the Antient Education of Gentlewomen, in Religion, Manners, Arts and Tongues,* to which was appended a prospectus for her school near London. She argues that education will give women "something to exercise their thoughts about," be a "Hedge against Heresies" and, in a more practical vein than Schurman, allow widows to "be able to understand and manage their own Affairs," wives to "be very useful to their Husbands in their Trades," and mothers to assist "their Children by timely instructing

---

[15] Anna Maria van Schurman, *Whether a Christian Woman Should be Educated,* ed. and trans. Joyce L. Irwin, (Chicago, University of Chicago Press, 1998), p. 26.

[16] Anna Maria van Schurman, *Opuscula,* trans. and quoted in Joyce Irwin, "Anna Maria van Schurman: From Feminism to Pietism," *Church History* 46 (1977), p. 55.

them."[17] She states clearly that educating women whose families are wealthy enough to allow it will benefit the public good but also that she does not see this as leading to greater calls for equality:

Women thus instructed will be beneficial to the Nation. Look into all History, those Nations ever were, now are, and always shall be, the worst of Nations, where Women are most undervalued; as in Russia, Ethiopia, and all the Barbarous Nations of the World. One great Reason why our Neighbors the Dutch have thriven to admiration, is the great care they take in the education of their Women, from whence they are to be accounted more vertuous, and to be sure more useful than any Women in the World. We cannot expect otherwise to prevail against the Ignorence, Atheism, Prophaneness, Superstition, Idolatry, Lust, that reigns in our Nation, than by a Prudent, Sober, Pious, Vertuous Education of our Daughters. Their Learning would stir up our Sons, whom God and Nature hath made superior, to a just emulation . . . My intention is not to Equalize Women to Men, much less to make them superior. They are the weaker Sex, yet capable to impressions of great things, something like to the best of Men.[18]

During the 1640s, Makin had been a tutor to the daughters of King Charles I, and although we have little specific evidence about her school, we know that several writers and other women later known for their learning are said to have been educated there.

If Makin emphasized the practical benefits to their families and society at large of women's education, Mary Astell (1666–1731) returned to Schurman's idea that at least some women could claim an education solely for their own benefit. In *A Serious Proposal to the Ladies . . . By a Lover of Her Sex* (London, 1694 and 1697), she called for the establishment of a spiritual and intellectual retreat for unmarried women and widows that would give them freedom to study away from male society. Her emphasis on the religious as well as educational purposes of such an institution and her sharp critiques of marriage and male treatment of women – for example, "the deceitful Flatteries of those who under pretence of loving and admiring you, really served their own base ends" – led her proposal to be ridiculed and attacked as a "Protestant nunnery."[19] Although she denies this by noting that there would be no vows, Astell was not alone among Protestant women, especially in England, who regretted the closing of the convents as an option for single women. Hostility to institutions that both looked Catholic and offered women a chance to be

---

[17] Bathsua Makin, *An Essay to Revive the Antient Education of Gentlewomen* (London, 1673), reprinted in Moira Ferguson, *First Feminists: British Women Writers 1578–1799* (Bloomington: Indiana University Press, 1985), pp. 136–38.

[18] Ibid., pp. 138–39.

[19] Mary Astell, *A serious Proposal to the Ladies . . . By a Lover of her Sex*, reprinted in Ferguson, *First Feminists*, p. 186.

independent from men was so strong in England that Astell's proposal was never followed until the nineteenth century when orders of Protestant deaconesses and women's colleges attached to Oxford and Cambridge began to offer serious spiritual and intellectual education for unmarried women.

The first woman to receive a university degree anywhere in Europe was not in Protestant England but in Catholic Italy. In 1678, Elena Cornaro Piscopia (1646–84) successfully defended her thesis in philosophy at the University of Padua before a crowd of more than twenty thousand people, although the following year, the university again forbade women, and it would be nearly fifty years before another woman received a degree. Women's education remained a hot issue in Padua and in 1723 was the topic of a formal debate sponsored by the city's leading scientific society. The debaters were both male, but female voices were included in a version of the debate published in 1729. One of these was a Latin oration by a nine-year-old child prodigy, Maria Gaetana Agnesi (1718–99), whose life was much like van Schurman's: early acclaim followed by a retreat into pious devotion. The other was a brief defense of women's education by the noblewoman and author Aretafila Savini de' Rossi (1687–). Savini de' Rossi shows an unusual egalitarianism in her assertions that all women should be given "access to a formal education, each according to her constitution, her circumstances, and, above all, her talent. . . . Let all women study on whom the heavens have bestowed a strong will and intellect." Not only should women be able to learn, she states, but also teach: talented "common women" should study "not for themselves alone, but in order to educate willing young women in the sciences."[20]

Arguments such as Savini de' Rossi's were apparently heard at the University of Bologna, which became the second university to grant a degree to a woman and the first to allow a woman to teach. Laura Bassi Veratti (1711–78) received her degree in 1732 and later lectured in physics and natural philosophy. Like Piscopia, she had been educated privately so that she was given a teaching appointment at a university without ever having attended classes at one. This was also true for several other women at the University of Bologna in the eighteenth century. A few Italian women, including Bassi, were also inducted as members into Italian scientific academies. Some of these inductions were as honorary members, so the women had no voice in governance, but they preceded by several

---

[20] Aretafila Savini de' Rossi, "Apology in Favor of Studies for Women," in Maria Gaetana Agnesi, et al., *The Contest for Knowledge: Debates over Women's Learning in Eighteenth-Century Italy*, trans. Rebecca Messbarger and Paula Findlen, (Chicago, University of Chicago Press, 2005), pp. 109, 110.

centuries the first inductions of women into the national learned academies of England and France.

Courts and Salons

The number of women who received a university education in early modern Europe can be counted on one hand, and most schools for girls in early modern Europe taught little besides basic literacy and genteel accomplishments. There were two other types of places where upper-class girls and women could gain training in practical politics and intellectual subjects, however, and where they could make the types of connections that would allow them to further their own interests and those of their families that men could in academies and universities. If we think of education as a lifelong process of acquiring skills and deepening one's understanding of the world, courts and salons were probably more important than schools in educating women from Europe's elite and allowing them to gain intellectual influence.

Upper-class families generally attempted to arrange a period of service for their daughters in the household of a family of higher status or at the court of their territorial ruler if their own status was high and the daughter physically attractive, especially intelligent, or unusually talented in things like music. During the period from the Reformation to the French Revolution, Europe's courts were not only sites of political and economic power but also cultural centers. Under the influence of humanists, who created a new ideal for rulers often termed the "Renaissance monarch," rulers began to support writers, artists, thinkers, and musicians to demonstrate their own learning and cultural interests. Thus, young women serving as ladies-in-waiting at a court could often come into contact with an area's leading intellectuals and expand their own learning through informal discussions or more formally arranged classes. At the English court, for example, young women from the most prominent noble families not only learned to play musical instruments, dance, and recite poetry but also joined the monarch's daughters and nieces for lessons in Latin, French, and history. Scottish noble daughters, by contrast, were rarely sent to London once Scotland had been joined to England, so that their level of education and sophistication lagged far behind that of their brothers who felt it important to spend time at court.

In France, Spain, and Portugal beginning in the sixteenth century, and then later in central and eastern Europe, territorial rulers claimed greater personal political power, gradually building up absolutist states. Noble families who had long held power independently became more dependent on the wishes and whims of the ruler and were forced to be more deferential if they wished to gain or hold political office or receive economic benefits. Noblemen had to learn their new roles as courtiers, for which the best guide was the Italian courtier Baldassar Castiglione's handbook, *The Book of the Courtier*. In many ways, Castiglione's advice to men was that they act more like women were supposed to – pay attention to their appearance, flatter those with power, never speak too forcefully, never appear too skilled at any one thing but show interest in whatever those with power are interested in, be discreet in all matters, and pay careful attention to their reputation.

Castiglione's advice to female courtiers was largely the same, and women who were able to learn the new role well could gain great influence over a ruler, which resulted in financial benefits and political offices for the male members of their families. In early modern monarchies, great attention was paid to ceremonies, rituals, and the physical and emotional needs of the monarch. Female and male courtiers spent long hours dressing and preparing their hair to take part in processions, play cards or games with the monarch (and lose if they were smart), observe or serve at royal meals, or simply, as the name "lady-in-waiting" implies, wait until the monarch called for them as well as wait on the monarch in whatever way he or she chose. The most prestigious tasks were those associated with the physical needs of the monarch – bringing in breakfast, handing napkins, emptying the royal chamber pot. Although we may view these activities as demeaning or disgusting, they offered great opportunities for personal access to the ruler. As with male royal "favorites," a woman who had learned her skills well, who was pleasant, charming, patient, and attentive, could gain a lucrative living allowance, high political positions for her father and brothers, and a prestigious marriage.

Although Castiglione emphasized the importance for court ladies of both chastity and the reputation for chastity, at many courts young women quickly learned that sexual favors were one of their most powerful tools, and the women who achieved the most personal and familial power were often royal mistresses. The presence of royal mistresses was accepted without question at most courts, with French kings such as Louis XIV even raising one woman at a time to the position of official mistress, *maîtresse-en-titre*. The most influential of these women was Madame de Pompadour (1721–64), *maîtresse-en-titre* for nearly twenty years to Louis XV, who read voraciously; patronized writers, composers, and architects; and reorganized several royal porcelain factories. Although Mme. de Pompadour was the antithesis of Mary Astell's learned woman, with an education geared almost completely to making her more appealing to the king, she fulfilled the humanist goal of education as training for public service in one of the few ways possible for early modern women.

Along with royal mistresses, the other type of woman who could demonstrate her knowledge and skills in a public forum without automatically inviting criticism was a queen. The early modern period saw a large number of queens and other types of female rulers throughout Europe, some ruling in their own names such as Mary and Elizabeth Tudor in England and Christina in Sweden, some as advisers to minor or incompetent sons such as Catherine de' Medici in France, and some as regents for part of a dynasty's holdings such as Margaret of Parma, a Hapsburg who ruled the Low Countries. Fortunately for their subjects, many of these women had not been limited to "accomplishments" in their education but had been given training in Latin and modern languages, which allowed them to communicate effectively with diplomats, courtiers, and other monarchs; lessons in history and the natural sciences, which aided them in military and economic decisions; and practical training in political skills, which strengthened their diplomacy and choice of advisers. Their sense of the privileges that came with rank made none of them strong advocates of better education for most women, although those with children generally took a keen interest in the education of their own offspring, and they appear to have been slightly more concerned about the training of their daughters than male monarchs were.

During the middle of the seventeenth century, women in Paris began to gather together men and women for weekly formal and informal discussions, holding these in the drawing rooms of their own homes. These were similar to those held in the sixteenth century in Italian cities and gave women access to the world of learning and "letters" (as literature and philosophy were often termed). The salon hostess (*salonnière*) selected the guests, determined whether the conversation on any particular night would be serious or light, and decided whether additional activities such as singing, poetry readings, or dramatic productions would be part of the evening's offerings. The first real salon in Paris is often regarded as that of Madame Rambouillet (1588–1666), and by the last quarter of the seventeenth century, a number of other Parisian women had followed her example.

The women who ran and attended salons in the seventeenth and early eighteenth centuries were generally from noble families but families who had been ennobled relatively recently. Often, these women married into families of higher standing and prestige, and the salons themselves mixed old and new nobles and wealthier nonnobles. They were not democratic institutions but did allow the old and new elite, as well as women and men, to mix. They focused on sociable conversation, not giving and listening to speeches, and often included consideration of gender differences among their topics for discussion. The women who founded and attended salons had generally been educated at convent schools, with their emphasis on piety and morals. The women recognized the deficiencies in their own education and explicitly viewed the salon as a place to improve their understanding of the world. They took what they did seriously, preparing themselves for their gatherings by reading and practicing letter-writing and conversational skills.

Women generally learned how to be salon hostesses by attending one of an older woman for years; running a salon may best be seen as a type of career for educated women, with a period of apprenticeship and mastership, although with no monetary income. Besides their protégées, *salonnières* often raised their own daughters to be highly educated, although the intellectual independence that resulted from this education often led daughters to open salons with pointedly different emphases than those of their mothers. In the late eighteenth century, English and German women also created salons on the French model; those in Germany were one of the few places where Christians and Jews could mix.

Salonnières were mocked by writers such as Moliére as intellectually pretentious and more interested in style than substance, but recent research has demonstrated that some were extremely powerful, which may be why Moliére chose to satirize them. They did not have any official public or academic role, but the approval of certain salon hostesses was often an unofficial requirement for a man to gain election to the Académie Française, the highest honor for a French intellectual or writer. (No woman was elected to the Académie Française until 1979.) The influential philosopher Jean-Jacques Rousseau worried about what he perceived as the great power of *salonnières*, warning that salons were "feminizing" French culture and weakening the country's military and work ethic.

Salons were one part of what historians label the "public sphere," a collection of new social and cultural institutions that developed in the seventeenth and eighteenth centuries through which ideas were exchanged. As we saw in Chapter 1, this "public sphere" included scientific and literary societies, newspapers, magazines, clubs and lodges that one paid to join, and coffeehouses and created what we now call "public opinion" on many issues. In the eighteenth century, the philosophical and political ideas associated with the Enlightenment were developed and disseminated through these new institutions, including salons. *Salonnières* such as Louise d'Epinay answered Rousseau, asserting that "Were you to attach, in the institutions and the education of women, the same prejudice to valor, you will find as many courageous women as men... since the number of courageous women is as great as the number of cowardly men."[21] In Italy, a few women spread Enlightenment ideas and argued for women's learning in journals as well as salons. Elisabetta Caminer Turra (1751–96), for example, oversaw a publishing house and founded several journals, which published reviews, opinion pieces, and summaries of important books. As had earlier learned women, such as Louise Labé in the quotation that opens this chapter, Turra advised women to pay more attention to their brains and less to their clothing. The new fashion magazines that Italian women were avidly reading – part of the growing "public sphere" – gave them tips on style, she asserted, but were not the educational reading material that their editors claimed they were.

Patronage

Women serving at royal courts in early modern Europe used their influence not only to further the careers of male family members but also to assist writers, composers, and artists. This was a period in which patronage was the most important factor in a literary or artistic career. Although some writers, composers, and artists simply produced works and then tried to sell them, more attempted to gain the attention of rulers, church officials, or wealthy individuals, who then paid them to write, compose, sculpt, or paint. Many patrons were very particular in their demands, suggesting themes and styles, ordering specific types of work, and requiring changes while a work was in progress. As certain artists, writers, and composers became popular and well known, they could assert their own artistic style and pay less attention to the wishes of a patron, although even major artists such as Raphael or Rubens generally worked according to a patron's specific guidelines.

The patronage system was not new in early modern Europe, nor were women's activities as patrons. Throughout the Middle Ages, queens, abbesses of convents, and noblewomen had supported artists, musicians, writers, and poets, for artistic and literary matters were considered part of women's sphere; their influence was certainly felt in the development of courtly love literature, and some art historians have argued that women's tastes shaped styles of painting and sculpture. The new ideal for rulers created by humanists in the sixteenth century made the arts and literature a male concern as well, for Renaissance monarchs were expected to support cultural activities as part of proving themselves well-rounded

---

[21] Louise d'Epinay's Letter to Abbé Ferdinando Galiani, translated and reprinted in Lisa DiCaprio and Merry E. Wiesner, *Lives and Voices: Sources in European Women's History* (Boston, Houghton Mifflin, 2001), p. 247.

individuals. Large public buildings, musical compositions, and literary works began to reflect more of the tastes and character of male patrons; Louis XIV's palace at Versailles, for example, captures his personality and concepts of society exquisitely.

Patronage by noblewomen, abbesses, and female rulers also remained important, however. Noblewomen hired architects and sculptors to transform castles designed for defense into châteaux and palaces where they could live comfortably and to construct elaborate tombs for themselves and their husbands. Abbesses arranged for the building and decoration of convents, churches, hospitals, and orphanages, choosing the architect and often approving the plans down to the smallest detail. Female rulers and the wives of rulers also established permanent positions at their courts, hiring court composers and musicians, official portrait artists, and, by the very late seventeenth century, scientists and philosophers. Sophie Charlotte of Prussia, for example, founded the Berlin Academy of Sciences, setting it up under the direction of Gottfried Leibniz, who had been her tutor from an early age. Noblewomen such as Anna Maria Luisa de' Medici, the last in the line of the grand dukes of Tuscany, recognized the importance of preserving as well as creating artistic products. She could not inherit the throne of her father because of her gender, and it passed to the royal house of Lorraine in 1737, but in the agreement arranging the transfer of power, called the Family Pact, she forbade the exportation out of Florence of any of the artistic works held by the de' Medici family, stating that these were for "the use of the Public and for the attraction of the curiosity of Foreigners."[22] The works that she held together form the core of the major art museums in Florence to this day.

Although a small commercial market in art and literature developed during the early modern period, most writers and artists still sought individuals who would provide them monetary support in return for being depicted as classical figures or pious onlookers in religious scenes or in return for having a book dedicated to them. Writers who felt that their work might not be acceptable for some reason took special care to find a powerful dedicatee, hoping that this individual would be flattered enough not only to provide a financial grant but also to push for the work's publication and sale. Women authors in particular, or those who wrote works directed to women or favorable works about women, often chose one or

---

[22] Translated and quoted in Elena Ciletti, "The Extinction and Survival of the Medici: Anna Maria Luisa de Medici and the Family Pact," in Cynthia Lawrence (ed.), *Women and Art in Early Modern Europe: Patrons, Collectors, and Connoisseurs* (University Park, Pennsylvania State University Press, 1997), p. 223.

more powerful upper-class women, hoping that this would forestall or lessen criticism.

With the expansion of literacy, wealthier middle-class women also became more significant as patrons of culture after 1500. They paid composers for their work and bought books of musical compositions, scientific treatises, and all types of literature. Women's reading often brought them into contact with the world of palaces and courtly life, and middle-class women responded by making their own homes more elaborate and their clothing more decorative. Although rulers and church officials (mostly male) set the style for large public buildings, women frequently decided how private homes were to be decorated, as we can tell from letters between husbands and wives and family account books. They ordered more furniture, small paintings of still life and domestic scenes, and silver table pieces. They also wore more jewelry, patronizing certain silversmiths and goldsmiths, and more lace and other costly fabrics.

We might wonder how much women's role as patrons or consumers actually influenced literary or cultural developments, however, particularly because today styles in clothing, home furnishings, and music are so often determined by a few designers and promoters and then marketed through mass advertising. Patrons in the early modern period were sometimes similarly passive but, as we have seen, were often very active; there is some evidence that middle-class women were just as specific in their orders for paintings or silverware as Louis XIV was in his for the decoration of Versailles.

Are there any significant differences between male and female patronage? This is a question that must be answered carefully. In realms other than culture, women's patronage does appear at times to be different from that of men. Because they were often not rulers themselves but rather the wives or female relatives of rulers, women were slightly freer than men to support religious thinkers who were regarded as questionable or suspect. Advocates of church reform in sixteenth-century France, for example, were protected and supported by a group of royal women, although discussion of reform was officially unacceptable. Evidence from Venice and Florence indicates that women's charitable patronage was generally directed toward poorer families in their own neighborhoods, whereas men's gifts went to support citywide projects such as the building of churches and hospitals.

In terms of literary and cultural patronage, it does appear that in the sixteenth century, women were more likely to support projects with religious themes and purposes than were the men of their families, a finding not terribly surprising. During the seventeenth century in the visual arts, class appears to be as important as gender, for queens such as Maria de' Medici favored large history pieces (in which they were prominently displayed), whereas middle-class Dutch women purchased still lifes. In terms of literature, philosophy, and music, however, there are a few tantalizing hints that some female patrons showed a consciousness of gender distinctions. As we have seen, the women who ran Parisian salons regarded themselves as better arbiters of grace and style in writing than the men they supported and specifically favored language they thought more refined, delicate, and "feminine." The subject of *La liberazione di Ruggiero*, a musical piece that retold a familiar story from a woman's point of view and that I discuss at greater length in Chapter 5, was suggested to its female composer by the female ruler of Florence, the Archduchess Maria Maddalena d'Austria. Elizabeth of Bohemia and Christina of Sweden, Descartes's noble patrons, were both especially concerned with the duality of matter and spirit, a philosophical issue generally connected to ideas about gender differences in the early modern period, when women were thought to be dominated more by matter and men by spirit. Because letters to and from patrons have often survived, this is an area of research that may yield many more examples in the future.

The early modern period has often been described as a time of one educational advance after another: humanism, with its emphasis on practical training in writing and speaking; the Protestant Reformation, with its emphasis on basic literacy; the beginnings of publicly funded schooling, with the goal of mass literacy. According to some commentators, it was during this period that Europe was transformed from an oral to a written culture. As we have seen in this chapter, however, women did not share equally in these educational advances. From basic literacy to advanced schooling, their educational opportunities were much more restricted than those of the boys and men of their social class, and even the most "exceptional woman," "learned lady," or sophisticated salon hostess recognized (and sometimes decried) the limits of her training. These unequal opportunities affected women's abilities not only to absorb information and provide patronage but also to use what they had learned to create literature, art, music, and science, a topic we explore in the next chapter.

For Further Reading

Jacqueline Pearson, *Women and Literature in Britain 1500–1700* (New York, Cambridge University Press, 1996); Heidi Brayman Hackel, *Reading Material in Early Modern England: Print, Gender and Literacy* (Cambridge, Cambridge University Press, 2005); and Edith Snook, *Women, Reading, and the Cultural Politics of Early Modern England* (Burlington,

VT, Ashgate, 2006), place women's reading practices into the story of the growth of literacy. The general survey that best integrates the experiences of girls and women is R. A. Houston, *Literacy in Early Modern England: Culture and Education 1500–1800* (London and New York, Longman, 1988; 2nd ed., 2001). Gerda Lerner, *The Creation of Feminist Consciousness: From the Middle Ages to Eighteen-seventy* (Oxford, Oxford University Press, 1993), includes discussion of literate women in the early modern period in several chapters. Kenneth Charlton, *Women, Religion and Education in Early Modern England* (London, Routledge, 1999), discusses both the opportunities for greater control and for greater freedom that Catholics and Protestants offered women through education.

Books that address the issue of reading material for girls and women include Margaret Spufford, *Small Books and Pleasant Histories: Popular Fiction and Its Readership in Seventeenth-Century England* (London, Methuen, 1981); Suzanne Hull, *Chaste, Silent and Obedient: English Books for Women 1475–1640* (San Marino, CA, Huntington Library, 1982); and Cornelia Niekus Moore, *The Maiden's Mirror: Reading Material for German Girls in the 16th and 17th Centuries*, Wolfenbütteler Forschungen, 36 (Wiesbaden, Harrasowitz, 1987). On novels, see Joan DeJean, *Tender Geographies: Women and the Origin of the Novel in France* (New York, Columbia University Press, 1991). On women in the printing industry, see Susan Broomhall, *Women and the Book Trade in Sixteenth-Century France* (Aldershot, Ashgate, 2002).

Margaret King has provided the most thought-provoking analyses of the position of Italian humanist women in *Women of the Renaissance* (Chicago, University of Chicago Press, 1991) and *Humanism, Venice, and Women: Essays on the Italian Renaissance* (Burlington, VT, Ashgate, 2005). King and Rabil are also the editors for the University of Chicago Press series, The Other Voice in Early Modern Europe, which has published translations of works by many of the women discussed in this chapter, including Laura Cereta, Cassandra Fedele, Isotta Nogarola, Louise Labé, the Mesdames des Roches, and Anna Maria van Schurman. The notes identify many of these, and for a complete list of the titles in this series, see http://www.press.uchicago.edu/Complete/Series/OVIEME.html. Diana Robin, *Publishing Women: Salons, the Presses, and the Counter-Reformation in Sixteenth-Century Italy* (Chicago: University of Chicago Press, 2007), analyzes the development and influence of groups of educated women in Italian cities. On French humanist women, see Patricia Francis Cholakian and Rouben Cholakian, *Marguerite de Navarre: Mother of the Reniassance* (New York: Columbia University Press, 2005); and Julie Campbell, *Literary Circles and Gender in Early Modern Europe* (Burlington, VT, Ashgate, 2006).

Jean R. Brink, *Female Scholars: A Tradition of Learned Women before 1800* (Montreal, Eden University Women's Publications, 1980), and Moira Ferguson, *First Feminists: British Women Writers 1578–1799* (Bloomington, Indiana University Press, 1985), include information about women scholars and women's proposals for institutions of higher education. The bibliography following Chapter 1 includes further sources about the debate about women, and that following Chapter 5 includes more about learned women, especially women writers.

Stephen Kolsky, *Courts and Courtiers in Renaissance Northern Italy* (Burlington, VT, Ashgate, 2003), explores gender in the world of the courts. French salons have been discussed in Caroline Lougee, *Les Paradis des Femmes: Women, Salons and Social Stratification in Seventeenth-Century France* (Princeton, NJ, Princeton University Press, 1976); Steven Kale, *French Salons: High Society and Political Sociability from the Old Regime to the Revolution of 1848* (Baltimore, Johns Hopkins University Press, 2004); and Faith E. Beasley, *Salons, History, and the Creation of Seventeenth-Century France* (Burlington, VT, Ashgate, 2006). Benedetta Craveri, *The Age of Conversation* (New York, New York Review Books, 2005), and Emily D. Bilski and Emily Braun (eds.), *Jewish Women and Their Salons: The Power of Conversation* (New Haven, CT, Yale University Press, 2005), consider salons in other parts of Europe. Dena Goodman, *The Republic of Letters: A Cultural History of the French Enlightenment* (Ithaca, NY, Cornell University Press, 1994); Carla Hesse, *The Other Enlightenment: How French Women Became Modern* (Princeton, NJ, Princeton University Press, 2001); and Elizabeth Eger et al. (eds.), *Women, Writing and the Public Sphere, 1700–1815* (Cambridge, Cambridge University Press, 2001), consider the issue of the women and the public sphere more broadly. Many of Elisabetta Caminer Turra's works are included in *Selected Writings of an Eighteenth-Century Venetian Woman of Letters*, ed. and trans. Catherine M. Sama, (Chicago, University of Chicago Press, 2003).

Women's artistic, literary, and musical patronage has recently received a great deal of attention, especially for Italy but increasingly for other parts of Europe as well. For Italy, see Catherine King, *Renaissance Women Patrons: Wives and Widows in Italy c. 1300–1550* (Manchester, Manchester University Press, 1998); Kelley Harness, *Echoes of Women's Voices: Music, Art, and Patronage in Early Modern Florence* (Chicago, University of Chicago Press, 2006); and Katherine A. McIver, *Women, Art and Architecture in Northern Italy, 1520–1580: Negotiating Power* (Burlington, VT, Ashgate, 2006). For one of the few studies that looks at eastern Europe, see Lucienne Thys-Senocak, *Ottoman Women Builders: The Architectural Patronage of Hadice Turhan Sultan* (Burlington, VT, Ashgate, 2007). Essay collections bring together many perspectives on women's patronage and creativity: Craig Monson (ed.), *The Crannied Wall: Women, Religion and the Arts in Early Modern Europe* (Ann Arbor, University of Michigan Press, 1992); Cynthia Lawrence (ed.), *Women and Art in Early Modern Europe: Patrons, Collectors, and Connoisseurs* (University Park, Pennsylvania State University Press, 1997); Ann Matter and John Coakley, *Creative Women in Medieval and Early Modern Italy* (Philadelphia, University of Pennsylvania Press, 1997); Sheryl E. Reiss and David G. Wilkins (eds.), *Beyond Isabella: Secular Women Patrons of Art in Renaissance Italy* (Kirksville, MO, Truman State University Press, 2001); Helen Hills (ed.), *Architecture and the Politics of Gender in Early Modern Europe* (Burlington, VT, Ashgate, 2003); and Konrad Eisenbichler (ed.), *The Cultural World of Eleonora di Toledo: Duchess of Florence and Siena* (Burlington, VT, Ashgate, 2004).

For more suggestions and links, see the companion Web site www.cambridge.org/womenandgender.

5   Women and the Creation of Culture

You will find the spirit of Caesar in the soul of this woman.

> Artemisia Gentileschi, describing herself in a letter to her patron
> Don Antonio Ruffo, 1649, quoted in Ann Sutherland Harris and
> Linda Nochlin. *Women Artists: 1550–1950* (New York,
> Alfred A. Knopf, 1976), p. 120

But I hope my readers will not think me vain for writing my life, since there have been many that have done the like, as Caesar, Ovid and many more, both men and women, and I know of no reason I may not do it as well as they. But I verily believe some censuring readers will scornfully say, why hath this lady writ her own life? Since none care to know whose daughter she was, or whose wife she is, or how she was bred, or what fortunes she had, or how she lived, or what humour or disposition she was of? I answer that it is true, that 'tis no purpose to the readers, but it is to the authoress, because I write it for my own sake, not theirs. Neither did I intend this piece for to delight, but to divulge; not to please the fancy, but to tell the truth. Lest after-ages should mistake, in not knowing I was daughter to one Master Lucas of St. John's near Colchester in Essex, second wife to the Lord Marquis of Newcastle; for, my lord having had two wives, I might easily have been mistaken, especially if I should die and my lord marry again.

> Margaret Cavendish, *A True Relation of My Birth, Breeding, and Life*
> (London, 1656), p. 391

During the Middle Ages, culture was largely the province of the Christian church. Most art, music, and drama had religious themes and was displayed or performed in church buildings, the majority of literature was written and copied by clerics and concerned religious topics, most philosophers and scientists were members of the clergy and viewed these topics as intimately related to theology, most musicians were clerics. This began to change in Italy during the fourteenth century with the Renaissance, when secular subjects and secular purposes also became acceptable. Although church officials remained important supporters of art, music, and literature, and religious themes continued, the bulk of cultural creation in the early modern period was no longer tied to the church. Scientists and philosophers in particular divorced themselves from

174

religious institutions and approached their subjects in a more secular manner.

A new attitude toward artists, writers, composers, and other creators of culture also developed during the Renaissance. During the Middle Ages, such individuals had been viewed as artisans, just like shoemakers or bakers, and their products the creation of a workshop, not an individual; this is the reason we know the names of so few medieval artists. During the Renaissance, the notion of the artist or writer as creative genius began to develop; artists started to sign their works, and certain branches of art – in particular painting, sculpture, and architecture – were deemed more significant than other types of art, such as needlework, porcelain manufacture, goldsmithing, and furniture making. This division hardened in the sixteenth century, particularly through the influence of Giorgio Vasari, who is often described as the first art historian. Painting, sculpture, and architecture were termed the "major" arts and everything else the "minor" or "decorative" arts. A similar split occurred in literature, with certain types of writing, such as poetry, history, and epics, now defined as "literature" and other types of writing, such as letters and diaries, excluded from this category.

New institutions for the creation of culture also developed during the early modern period. Many visual artists and musicians still trained through apprenticeships, but rulers also set up court-supported schools and hired large numbers of painters, sculptors, musicians, and composers. After the development of the printing press, journals that included and promoted the work of poets and other writers began to be published at regular intervals, and newspapers reported on current events. Regional and national academies and societies that rewarded and supported creativity in science, literature, and the visual arts were established, usually with a limited number of members. Individuals in larger cities established clubs in which people paid a fee to hear lectures, watch or perform scientific experiments, and participate in discussions. As we saw in the last chapter, women in Paris and other cities established salons for discussion of cultural and political matters. Although rulers and church leaders were still important shapers of culture, the institutions of what historians term the "public sphere" – learned societies, literary journals, discussion groups, newspapers, salons, and clubs – helped create what we now call "public opinion," a force that became more powerful as the eighteenth century progressed. Public opinion expressed through journals, academies, and societies increasingly determined which artistic and literary genres and styles and which scientific theories would be judged praiseworthy, and thus which artists, writers, and scientists would get commissions or support from patrons.

All of these developments shaped women's ability to participate in the creation of culture, particularly in those areas and genres judged most important. Women were often by regulation or practice excluded from schools and academies, and their writings were rarely accepted by literary journals. The self-promotion required by an artist, writer, composer, or thinker attempting to gain the support of a patron was judged unacceptable behavior when done by a woman. Europe's intellectuals debated whether women had the rational capacity for scientific or philosophical insights or were capable of true creative genius. This genius led great artists to lose themselves in their work but might also be taken too far, people thought, and lead to illness or death if it was not controlled by reason; those few women who might have such creative passion were thus susceptible to its negative consequences. The major arts, the most celebrated forms of music and literature, and the most noted philosophical ideas were all regarded as tied to characteristics deemed masculine – forcefulness, strength, power, logic, singularity of purpose. The work that women artists, writers, and scientists did produce was often judged to be the result not of genius but of nimble fingers, diligence in observation, skill at following the example of a male teacher, or beelike industriousness – in other words, "craft," not "art" or "science." If her work could not be dismissed in this way, the woman was said to have "overcome the limitations of her sex" and set herself apart from all other women, or she was judged a hermaphrodite, or the work was attributed to her male teacher or a male member of her family. These evaluations had a long life. Until 1986, the gigantic standard textbook in art history contained not one female artist, although it included 2,300 male artists; that year, nineteen women were added.

Thus, to assess women's artistic creations, musical compositions, and literary works, their participation in scientific and philosophical debates, and their theatrical and musical compositions and performances, we cannot ignore the social and intellectual setting. Restrictions on women's ability to participate in the creation of culture varied across time and from one geographic area to another and varied even more sharply from one artistic or literary genre and one scientific field to another, but at no time or place was women's access to cultural institutions the same as men's and at no time was the gender of the creator not a factor in how a work was judged.

Visual Artists

The gender bias inherent in the Renaissance division of the visual arts into "art" and "craft" and "major" and "minor" meant that new genres that women created would never achieve the status of major arts, and genres in which substantial numbers of women continued to work would decrease in status. Two examples of the former are miniature portraits painted on ivory, invented by Rosalba Carriera (1675–1757) and paper collage, invented by Mary Delany (1700–88). One example of the latter is flower painting, which in the seventeenth century was an important branch of still life in Holland but was later demoted. According to one commentator writing in the 1970s, flower painting "demands no genius of a mental and spiritual kind, but only the genius of taking pains and specific craftsmanship"; the best proof of this, in his eyes, is that of all known flower painters, "at least half of them are women."[1]

The best example of loss of status in an art form is embroidery, which in the Middle Ages was practiced by both women and men often organized into male-directed craft guilds and paid on a scale equivalent to painting but which throughout the early modern period became increasingly identified as feminine. Middle- and upper-class girls were taught to embroider because embroidered clothing and household objects became signs of class status and because embroidery was seen as the best way to inculcate the traits most admired in a woman – passivity, chastity, attention to detail, domesticity. As more embroidery was produced in the home for domestic consumption, it was increasingly considered an "accomplishment" rather than an art, and those who embroidered for pay received lower wages, except for the male designers of embroidery patterns and the few men employed as court embroiderers by Europe's monarchs.

Although most early modern women accepted the prevailing view of their needlework and would not have termed it "art," our recognition of the historically determined nature of artistic hierarchies allows us to view embroidery and other types of needlework as one of the visual arts, in the same way that quilts are now discussed as a standard part of American art history. In many ways, early modern embroidery parallels early modern painting. During the sixteenth century, the embroidery of plants, flowers, birds, and animals grew increasingly naturalistic, although embroiderers were also conscious of the symbolic meaning of these motifs. Both painted and embroidered emblems, designs that linked an image and a saying or motto, were very popular. Embroiderers experimented with perspective, paid greater attention to proportion and shadowing, and took their subjects from antiquity just as Renaissance painters did. In the seventeenth century, embroiderers dressed their subjects in elaborate clothing and

---

[1] Michael Grant, *Flower Painting through Four Centuries* (Leigh-on-Sea, Lewis, 1972), p. 21.

filled their work with details from the natural world, in the same way as baroque painters did, and in the eighteenth century, they portrayed Arcadian scenes of shepherdesses and milkmaids just as painters were doing. The lines of influence between painting and embroidery ran both ways, with embroiderers often copying paintings or taking their motifs from them and painters, in turn, attempting to portray embroidered brocades and laces or using scenes of women embroidering to represent domestic virtues.

Because embroidery was a visual art created primarily by women, however, it also differs from painting in major respects. Embroiderers were not trained to view their work as a product of individual genius, so they rarely included their names on their work, other than on samplers that were meant to demonstrate a girl's growing proficiency with a needle. The subjects embroiderers chose often reflected general cultural changes in women's role and position. Images of Mary and female saints became younger and gentler than they had been in the High Middle Ages, stressing their dependence on the power of God the Father rather than their independent authority. In Protestant areas, girls portrayed images of happily married couples from the Bible and stitched verses stressing daughterly and wifely obedience. Adult women in the seventeenth century, on the other hand, often chose to depict images of women who acted heroically, sometimes with men and sometimes against them, or who ruled virtuously. As we discussed in Chapter 1, this was the period of a great debate in many parts of Europe about the proper roles of men and women and the proper balance of power between them. Women's choosing such images in the very medium intended to teach passivity and obedience reflects this debate. By the eighteenth century, heroic women were replaced by domestic scenes and farmyards, as women's links with the home and natural world were accepted as givens rather than open to dispute.

Although architecture and sculpture remained male preserves in the early modern period – the sculptor Properzia de' Rossi (1490–1530) is the only exception that has been identified so far – and many more women produced art with the needle than the brush, there were women who did not accept the general view that only men could paint professionally. During the sixteenth century, several women became prominent painters in Italy, and a number of others are known to have painted regularly, although all or most of their works are now lost; during the seventeenth century, the best opportunities for women painters were in the Netherlands, and by the mid-eighteenth in France. Although stylistically their work is very different, the careers of female painters show many similarities. The majority of female painters were the daughters of painters;

one of the earliest identifiable female painters, Caterina van Hemessen (1528–after 1587), even signed her work "Caterina, daughter of Jan van Hemessen," indicating that she recognized the importance of this relationship. Those who were not the daughters of painters were often the daughters of intellectuals or minor noblemen with ties to intellectual or artistic circles. Many were eldest daughters or came from families in which there were no sons, so their fathers took unusual interest in their careers. A significant number came from aristocratic families, whereas most male painters had an artisanal background. Many women began their careers before they were twenty and produced far fewer paintings after they married, or stopped painting entirely; the cycle of their careers was thus similar to that of women humanists discussed in Chapter 4. Of those who married, many married painters.

Women were not allowed to study the male nude, which was viewed as essential if one wanted to paint large history paintings with many figures, so they generally painted portraits, smaller paintings with only a few subjects, or, by the seventeenth century, still lifes and interior scenes. We might consider such subjects more appealing than large history paintings, but the national academies of art from the seventeenth through the nineteenth centuries ranked them much lower in importance, which meant female painters could never gain the highest level of official recognition. Women could also not learn the technique of fresco, in which colors are applied directly to wet plaster walls, because such works had to be done out in public, which was judged inappropriate for women. They were thus limited in the media they could use as well as their subject matter.

The number of women recorded as active painters steadily increased throughout the early modern period, but this resulted more from better recording of the names of all painters than from continually expanding opportunities for women. Women's ability to gain recognition through painting followed a more circuitous path. They were generally more successful when there were only a few, for they could then be viewed as novelties. This was the case with Sofonisba Anguissola (1532/35–1625), the first Italian woman to gain international recognition for her art. Anguissola spent ten years as a court painter to Philip II of Spain and was extremely popular as a portrait painter throughout her long life. Lavinia Fontana (1552–1614) was trained by her painter father and also received a steady stream of commissions for portraits, including many from members of the papal court. One of her self-portraits – a common subject for both male and female painters – is on the cover of this book.

Seventeenth-century Italian women artists were fortunate in that they could gain commissions, unlike their French counterparts; the majority of commissions in seventeenth-century France came from the king, who

Figure 9. Sofonisba Anguissola, *Lucia, Minerva, and Europa Anguissola Playing Chess*, 1555. This painting of the artist's three younger sisters and their nurse shows each of the sisters looking at the sister immediately her elder, with the oldest (who has just won the game) looking directly at the painter herself. Chess playing became more popular with women and a wider group of people in general in the sixteenth century when the rules were changed to make the queen and several other pieces more powerful so that the game could go faster.

wanted only large-scale history paintings and hired only artists who were members of the Académie Royale, thus excluding all but a handful of women painters. In general, an open market for art, such as existed in the seventeenth-century Netherlands, was more favorable for women's work than one that was totally linked to commissions. Not only was it difficult for women to gain the type of training usually regarded as necessary for large public works, they also had difficulties traveling to establish a reputation with private patrons or determining a way to advertise their skills that would not jeopardize their reputation for respectability.

Women painters were also more successful when the genres in which they excelled were popular. The seventeenth-century Netherlands was advantageous in this regard as well, for wealthy middle-class families wanted still lifes, flower paintings, and small-scale portraits for the walls of their increasingly luxurious homes, paying for them with profits from the contemporary economic boom in their country. Clara Peeters (1594–c. 1657) and Rachel Ruysch (1666–1750) established many of the stylistic and iconographical conventions that later still-life and flower painters would follow, and their work is still widely appreciated for its compositional sophistication, treatment of differently textured surfaces, technical virtuosity, and sheer beauty. In the early eighteenth century, pastel portraits grew very popular, and Rosalba Carriera (1675–1757), who had earlier developed miniatures on ivory, became one of the most highly regarded artists in Europe in this medium. Pastel is worked with dry colored chalks rather than liquid paints, and Carriera used it brilliantly in portraits to capture the elegant fabrics and powdered hair prized by her wealthy contemporaries. Élisabeth-Louise Vigée-Le Brun (1755–1842) also became wildly popular as a portrait painter among the French nobility, including the royal household. Her portraits show people in graceful and naturalistic poses, often surrounded by the new consumer goods that marked a luxurious life. She painted numerous portraits of Queen Marie Antionette and her children, one of which was intentionally commissioned to counter the growing criticism of the queen noted in Chapter 2. Her connections with the monarchy and aristocracy led her to flee France with the French Revolution, but she found plenty of commissions from aristocrats and rulers throughout the rest of Europe.

The gender of early modern female painters thus affected the media and genres that they chose, but did it also shape their treatment of subject matter or their techniques? This is a difficult question, in part because art critics and historians since the sixteenth century have used "feminine" – by which they mean delicate, decorative, intimate, domestic – as a code word for "less worthy" and because it risks introducing biological essentialism into aesthetic judgments. It has been asked recently, however, by feminist art historians about the work of two of the most important early modern female painters, Artemisia Gentileschi (1593–1652/3) and Judith Leyster (1609–61), particularly because their work was judged in their own time and ours to be almost disturbingly "masculine" – vigorous and exuberant in the case of Leyster and violent and dramatic in the case of Gentileschi. Leyster's work is probably the best argument against seeing something distinctly "feminine" in the technique of female painters, for her existence was unknown from some time after her death until 1893, during which time all of her paintings were unquestioningly attributed to Franz Hals or his male followers. In terms of her treatment of subject matter, we can see a few differences. Many of her works show greater sympathy for the lives of women than those of her male contemporaries, especially those that depict women working at household tasks. Her most

Figure 10. Judith Leyster, *The Proposition*.

celebrated painting is *The Proposition* (1631), which shows a modestly dressed woman bent over her sewing while a man touches her arm and offers her a handful of coins. It contrasts dramatically with seduction and brothel scenes painted by her male contemporaries, in which the women are always clearly willing participants, and, as the art historians Ann Harris and Linda Nochlin have commented, "will instantly engage the sympathy of any woman who has ever been similarly approached by a man who stubbornly refused to believe that his attentions were unwelcome."[2]

Leyster's painting would have been well understood by Artemisia Gentileschi, who until recently gained greater notice from many art historians for the fact that she was raped by one of her teachers than for her paintings or her role in spreading the dramatic style of Caravaggio, which she learned from her father. The rape was viewed as the reason so many of her paintings depict strong women in acts of violence against men and conversely (often by the same author) as the reason for her allegedly numerous illegitimate children. Gentileschi does concentrate on women in most of her works, no doubt because she was so skilled at portraying the female nude and biblical and mythological heroines were extremely popular subjects. The art historian Mary Garrard's careful analysis of her paintings, especially her numerous depictions of the Old Testament heroine Judith, who cut off the head of the tyrant Holofernes during his war with the Israelites, shows that she does portray Judith as more powerful and the relationship between her and the maidservant who assists her as more personal and companionate than do male artists. Gentileschi appears to have recognized some of the ambiguities of her position as a female painter in a culture where women were more accepted as the inspiration for art than as artists. In a self-portrait, she depicts herself as an allegory of Painting itself, something that was impossible for male artists because Painting ("La Pittura") was always portrayed allegorically as female. In a letter to one of her patrons, she makes the comment that opens this chapter, a clear assertion that she recognized the limitations on female painters but chose to ignore them as much as possible.

Musicians, Composers, and Actresses

The same question posed by art historians, whether and how a woman's gender influenced her painting, has also been asked recently by historians of music as they uncover the role played by women in musical composition and performance. Many of the factors that shaped women's production of visual art also shaped their production of music. Although sixteenth-century writers worried about women using music to lure men into the dangers of love, by the seventeenth century, singing and playing an instrument became suitable "accomplishments" for middle- and upper-class young women. As the author of *The Young Ladies' Conduct*

[2] Ann Sutherland Harris and Linda Nochlin, *Women Artists: 1550–1950* (New York, Alfred A. Knopf, 1976), p. 140.

Figure 11. Artemesia Gentileschi, self-portrait.

wrote, "Music refines the Taste, polishes the Mind; and is an Entertain-
ment, without other views, that preserves them [young women] from the
Rust of Idleness, that most pernicious Enemy to Virtue."[3] Writers such
as Mary Astell who favored a serious education for women were critical of

[3] John Essex, *The Young Ladies' Conduct: Or Rules for Education* (London, 1722), p. 85.

the amount of time young women were expected to devote to their musical lessons, and other writers criticized or satirized lower-class families who tried to give their daughters "accomplishments" rather than training them in more marketable skills.

For most middle- and upper-class women, there was no acceptable public outlet for their years of musical training. They were to perform only for their own families and not even in the semipublic performances that typically brought together professionals and amateurs in the seventeenth and eighteenth centuries. One upper-class English father even had his daughter arrested for playing in public. Ironically, cartoonists and satirists frequently bemoaned the low level of skill of the amateur men who sang or played instruments – training in music was not a standard part of the education of an upper- or middle-class man – without recognizing that the female audience would have been much more competent had they been able to perform. Not surprisingly, many women gave up their music when they married, although music was often used as a symbol of marital bliss, its harmony a parallel to marital harmony. We have few comments on the reasons for this from women themselves, so we cannot judge whether they lost interest in an "accomplishment" that was specifically promoted as a way to win a husband or simply had no time for music because of domestic responsibilities.

We also have great difficulty in assessing precisely the involvement of women in the composition and performance of folk ballads, songs, lullabies, and other types of popular music. Many of these were never published or even written down, or else were published only long after they were composed. Most were published anonymously or attributed to a composer whose authorship was as much a matter of myth as the events they describe. There is no reason to assume that women did not write any of them – as one historian has put it, "anonymous was a woman" – especially because many of them were songs that accompanied traditionally women's work such as child care or weaving. Some scholars have identified certain attributes as typical in songs they suspect were written by women – women are described as whole persons rather than according to their physical attributes, relations between men and women are marked by mutuality rather than dominance, mother-child relationships involve both joy and sadness, or the song was traditionally sung only by women. Women were often the most well-known singers of all types of songs, adding verses, changing content, and altering tunes as they sang them. When folklorists began to be interested in these songs and ballads in the nineteenth century, first writing them down and then recording them, they turned to female singers.

The composition and performance of ballads and other songs relating heroic exploits were very much part of high culture during the

Middle Ages – the best-known medieval poets are the male and female troubadours who sang and played at noble courts – but during the Renaissance and early modern period, more elaborate forms of music developed that usually required years of training to compose or perform. Although amateur or mixed amateur and professional performances continued, church officials and nobles increasingly hired permanent professional composers and musicians. Until 1500, these were almost all men, but gradually singing became one of the duties expected of court ladies at many northern Italian courts. Women were taken on specifically for their singing abilities, more music was written that required trained women's voices, and in 1580, the duke of Ferrara established a separate group of singing women, the *concerto di donna*. This practice was copied by other Italian courts in the 1580s and 1590s, with female instrumentalists often added as well, and by the seventeenth century, some of these women composed much of their own music.

Like female painters, many female musicians were the daughters of musicians or came from musical families, and their fathers not only trained them but also helped them to get their music published. The best known of these singer-composers in seventeenth-century Italy, Francesca Caccini (1587–?), at one point the highest-paid performer at the Medici court in Florence, and Barbara Strozzi (1619–?), who wrote and sang arias and cantatas and ran a musical salon in Venice, both fit this pattern. Their careers also parallel those of female painters in other ways. Both disappeared from the records at midlife and composed in a more limited number of genres than their male contemporaries; Strozzi, for example, composed only small private pieces, most with the theme of unrequited love, at a time when opera was at its peak in Venice. Strozzi was accused of being a courtesan, a charge leveled at other female musicians as well, particularly those who had ties to the theater. Despite these limitations, Caccini and Strozzi set a pattern for other female composers both in Italy and the rest of Europe. By 1700, twenty-three women in Italy had had their music published, and during the early part of the next century, women began to compose larger pieces as well. Elisabeth-Claude Jacquet de la Guerre (1664?–1727) wrote an opera and major instrumental pieces, and Camilla di Rossi and several other women composed oratorios at the command of the emperor in Vienna.

Along with the courts, convents also provided opportunities for female musicians and composers; more than half of the women whose music was published before 1700 were nuns who wrote both secular and sacred music. In the early sixteenth century, convents began to perform polyphonic music, with nuns playing all types of instruments, and many nuns composed as well. In some places, this was encouraged, most notably

in Venice, where the city government even established special musical training schools for girls at four of the city's orphanages. The choirs these schools produced became so renowned that girls who were not orphans were taken on as day students, including some daughters of Venice's elite. These *Ospedali grandi* were not strictly convents, but the girls vowed to sing or play for ten years after they were trained and so could not leave until they were about thirty. They gave frequent public performances, which the city used as a source of income, and it also encouraged the girls and women to develop their talents by sending them to study with distinguished teachers and commissioning special works for them.

After the Council of Trent in 1563, the Venetian Ospedali and women's convents throughout Italy were ordered by the Catholic hierarchy to stop their performances of polyphonic music and the playing of any instrument except the organ. The Venetian city government was strong enough to ignore this order, and some convents were as well, especially those in Milan and Bologna, but in general the opportunities for convent residents to perform and create music began to decrease. In 1686, Pope Innocent XI extended this prohibition, forbidding all women – single, married, or widowed as well as nuns – to learn music for any reason from any man, including their fathers or husbands, or to play any musical instrument "because music is completely injurious to the modesty that is proper for the [female] sex."[4] This edict was renewed in 1703, and, although it was certainly not enforced everywhere, it does reflect a negative attitude toward women's musical creativity, which the women who did publish their compositions also noted by commenting that they expected to be criticized for their lack of modesty.

Many of the women who became noted as singers were also actresses, both in opera and spoken theater. From the middle of the seventeenth century, opera began to use women instead of castrati for female parts, and starting in the late sixteenth century, female actors began to appear in French and Italian court performances and in wandering troupes of players who performed comedy for popular audiences. Previously, all parts had been taken by men and boys, a tradition that continued in school and religious drama throughout the early modern period and in England until the restoration of the monarchy after the civil war in 1660. A few women took over the leadership of traveling companies, such as Madeleine Béjart (1618–72) in France and Caroline Neuber (1697–1760) in Germany; one of these actress-directors, Catherina Elisabeth Velten, also published

---

[4] Translated and quoted in Jane Bowers, "The Emergence of Women Composers in Italy, 1566–1700," in Jane Bowers and Judith Tick (eds.), *Women Making Music: The Western Art Tradition, 1150–1950* (Urbana, University of Illinois Press, 1986), p. 139.

a pamphlet defending the honor of popular comedy and the women involved in it. In general, however, actresses, opera singers, and ballerinas were not regarded as honorable women, and many were able to support themselves only by also being the mistress of an artistically inclined male patron.

As with female painters, a woman's sex thus shaped her opportunities for singing, playing music, or acting, and determined what genre of music she would be most likely to compose. It may have also shaped the content of her compositions to some degree. For example, Francesca Caccini's theatrical piece, *La liberazione di Ruggiero dall-isola d'Alcina* (1625), took a story familiar to Italian audiences, the liberation of the knight Ruggiero from the love magic of the wicked sorceress Alcina, but told it from Alcina's point of view and portrayed her sympathetically as abandoned and betrayed. Caccini composed this at a court that was, as we saw in Chapter 4, ruled by a woman and that was engaged in a debate about the merits and faults of women, where the writer Cristoforo Bronzini was in the middle of publishing an eight-volume work *On the Nobility and Dignity of Women* (Florence, 1622–30). Caccini's composition reflects this debate, conveying the ambiguous position of any powerful woman in a world where the rules of conduct are made by men.

Writers

When analyzing the art and music produced by women during the early modern period, it is fairly easy to make distinctions between that done for private use or enjoyment and that intended for public consumption. At first glance, women's writings seem similarly divided between unpublished works, such as letters, diaries, and personal collections of quotes and reflections, and works that were published. On closer analysis, it is difficult to draw a sharp line between the two. On one hand, writing that we regard as private, such as letters, was not regarded in the same way in the early modern period. Letters often contained political news as well as personal matters, and their writers knew that they would be circulated among a group of people, and perhaps even copied, for this was a period before regular newspapers. Most of the letters that have survived were written by members of Europe's elite, who tended to regard letter writing as more of a literary activity than we do today; they took great care with language and loaded their letters with classical allusions. Women in particular realized that letters might be the best or only place they could demonstrate their learning and creativity with language and so used letters to develop a personal literary style. Their addressees recognized this and saved them; for Madame de Sévigné (1626–96), for example, often described as the greatest letter writer in French literature, more than

1,300 letters survive. Many historians of literature view the letter as one of the ancestors of the novel, a literary form that was also developed to a great extent by women in the eighteenth century. Many early novels were, in fact, written in epistolary form – that is, as an exchange of letters. Handwritten journals, diaries, and collections of quotes were also often written to be handed down to future generations, with the writer careful about how she portrayed herself and intent on teaching a lesson to others through her writings. Women also circulated fiction, poetry, commentary, and other types of writing in manuscript long after the printed book became the standard form of publication, or presented such pieces to patrons.

"Private" writing thus often had a public audience in mind, yet the injunction to female silence was so strong that the majority of women who did publish felt the need to justify their boldness. Women's public speech was often linked with sexual dishonor in many people's minds; a "loose" tongue implied other sorts of loose behavior, and a woman who wanted her thoughts known by others was suspected of wanting to make her body available as well. Many women who did publish thus claimed that their works were really private but that some external force had compelled them to be published. For writers of religious works, it was divine inspiration; of advice manuals, their duty as mothers; of political pieces, the special gravity of the situation. Poets and playwrights stressed the pressures by male friends or the desire to stop pirated versions of their work that had been published without their knowledge. Katherine Philips (1632–62), one of the most widely acclaimed seventeenth-century female English poets, staunchly maintained:

[I] never writ any line in my life with an intention to have it printed . . . but only for my own amusement in a retir'd life . . . I am so innocent of that wretched Artifice of a secret consent (of which I am, I fear suspected) that whoever would have brought me those copies [of my poems] corrected and amended, and a thousand pounds to have bought my permission for their being printed, should not have obtained it.[5]

Even those who published women's works posthumously, often their husbands or other male relatives, included such justifications, noting that the author had been a paragon of female modesty whose writing had been done only out of duty to God or her children and had never interfered with her household or marital duties.

It is difficult to know exactly how to interpret these justifications. Did the authors include them to escape censure and the suspicion of immorality or to get their work published more easily? (Male authors, too, often

[5] Katherine Philips, *Poems* (London, 1667).

mention divine inspiration and their own unworthiness.) Or do they reflect the author's internalization of the command to silence? Or simply ambiguous feelings about letting other people read her work? Any interpretation is complicated by the fact that many authors also apologized for their lack of skill, noting that as women they could never meet the standards set by male authors; the tone of these explanations varies widely, from anger at not being accorded the same educational opportunities as men to subservient deference. Whatever the reasons for these justifications and apologies, and they probably vary with each author, even the most bitter and self-assertive ones reinforced the idea that women's writing was highly unusual and needed to be excused. By 1750, as more women began to publish, such explanations are slightly less frequent and less abject, but they are still there.

Along with directly apologizing, women writers also found other ways to conform to the cultural convention of silence and yet still publish. They published anonymously but then let their friends and acquaintances know the true author. They used male or female pseudonyms but did not completely hide their identity. They published translations or editions of male works but often subverted the text by their choice of words to insert personal and political statements. Mary Sidney (1561–1621), for example, only published works that were translations or revisions of works by male authors, although her alterations and revisions are so extensive that they are usually considered original pieces. She did not claim them as original, however; despite the fact that she was a member of the most prominent literary family in England and an important patron of humanists and writers, she still felt obliged to deflect criticism by calling her writing translations.

Because the line between public and private writing is fuzzy, then, it is best not to pay too much attention to whether a piece was published or not and simply examine the work of women writers by genre. (Nevertheless, we have to recognize that our analysis will be skewed by the fact that a much greater share of women's published writings survive than their unpublished ones, and that we have very few unpublished writings by nonelite women.) Throughout the period, publications by women represent a tiny share of the total amount of printed material; women's works comprise only 1.2 percent of the publications in England from 1640 to 1700, although even this figure represents a doubling of their pre–civil war rate. It is more difficult to make statistical comparisons for other countries, but publications by women probably accounted for less than 1 percent of the total, although their share elsewhere also increased during the early modern period.

In addition to the cultural admonitions advocating female silence and to women's relative lack of educational opportunities, economic factors also kept women from publishing. Authors who could not pay for a work to be published themselves had to find a patron who would or convince a publisher that a work would sell enough to earn back the investment. This was much more difficult for women than men, so that the most prolific female authors were those who paid for the publication themselves, such as Lady Eleanor Douglas, whose thirty-seven works of prophecy were all printed at her own expense. Almost all of the published works by women that appeared in seventeenth-century Germany were by members of the nobility, a result of both their ability to absorb the costs of printing and the fact that their class position at least partially deflected any criticism that resulted from their gender.

The majority of women's published works were religious, particularly in the sixteenth and early seventeenth centuries when the vast majority of all publications were religious. As we see in greater detail in Chapter 6, the Reformation inspired women to publish polemical works, the Puritan and Quaker movements led them to publish conversion narratives detailing their own religious convictions, and the wars of the seventeenth century provoked them to publish religious prophecies and warnings to repent. Most women authors did not write such dramatic or doctrinal works, however, but chose forms that were considered more acceptable for women – prayers, meditations, poems based on the psalms or epistles, spiritual and moral advice to children, reflections on death, or translations of works by men. Many of these express traditional pious sentiments or support existing religious institutions, but the mere fact that they were written by a woman made many male contemporaries uneasy. They also use female metaphors more often and in a different way than similar works by men; women use female metaphors for religious experiences in a way that stresses how faith and devotion can overcome differences between people and between the believer and God, whereas men use female metaphors more often to stress the distinction between the human and the divine. Women's religious writings occasionally reveal unusual aims. Anna von Medum, for example, published *Geistlicher Judischer Wunderbalsam* in 1646, trying to convince Jews to convert to Christianity and her fellow Christians to give up nonbiblical practices so that the Jews would convert. Like most women writers of religious works, she emphasizes God's command to take up this task but expresses this in very female terms; once she was a widow, she notes, God became her husband, impregnated her with spiritual seed, and then sustained her during the delivery as any good husband would.

Many women who wrote religious works, and the majority of women who wrote about nonreligious topics, chose poetry as their preferred mode of expression. Most female poets, in fact, wrote both religious and secular poetry, and even their secular poetry includes moral advice

or overtones of divine love; they were less likely than their male counterparts to use literary forms such as the pastoral, elegy, or love son-
net without in some way Christianizing or moralizing them, although
a few women did write purely secular love lyrics. Male poets in Italy
and Germany in the seventeenth century formed themselves into literary
societies and academies to provide themselves with a regular audience
for their poetry and to support its publication. These societies generally
accepted no women or only those with family connections to male members, leading a few women to found all-female literary societies, such as
the Academie des Loyales and the Tugendliche Gesellschaft. Like male
societies, these groups encouraged their members to correspond with one
another, study, and write, although they emphasized the importance of
moral virtues and religious conviction as well as poetic talents. The motto
of one of them was distinctly nonliterary: "Virtue Brings Honor."

As feminist literary critics have pointed out, female poets adapted
literary conventions that had been created by men to a female voice.
The French poet Louise Labé and the Italians Vittoria Colonna, Gaspara Stampa (1524–54), and Veronica Gambara (1485–1550) all worked
within the tradition of Petrarchan love poetry but modified it so that
women could be active lovers and not simply passive objects of male
desire. Their work was frequently included in printed poetry anthologies
published in Italy in the middle of the sixteenth century. Female poets
asserted that love could be a legitimate inspiration for their poetry, just
as it was for male poets. Gaspara Stampa wrote:

> Love, Having Elevated Her to Him, Inspires Her Verses
>
> If, being a woman so abject and vile,
> I nonetheless can bear so high a flame,
> Why should I not give to the world the same,
> At least in part, in proper wealth and style?
>
> If Love, with a new unprecedented spark,
> Could raise me to a place I could not reach,
> Why cannot pain and pen combine to teach
> Such arts as, never known, shall find their mark?[6]

Sibylle Schwarz (1621–38) went even further, describing the love of writing poetry as one that would enable women to rise above the need for
any mere physical love. Pernette du Guillet (1520–45), Catherine des
Roches, and Anna Owen Hoyer (1584–1655) all claimed the right to

---

[6] Translated and quoted in Frank J. Warnke, "Gaspara Stampa: Aphrodite's Priestess,
Love's Martyr," in Katherina M. Wilson (ed.), *Women Writers of the Renaissance and
Reformation* (Athens, University of Georgia Press, 1987), p. 12.

fame, although in more indirect ways than male poets. Katherine Philips wrote numerous poems celebrating her friendships with both women and men, asserting that women could be friends and not just lovers, seductresses, rivals, or accomplices.

Along with poetry, women also wrote long and short fictional pieces and plays, some of which were published during the author's lifetime. In Italy, Beatrice del Sera and other nuns wrote plays that were performed in convents, with nuns playing all parts; they were spiritual in message, but included profane themes in their serious and comic episodes and occasionally won their authors a reputation beyond the convent. As we will see in Chapter 6, nuns also wrote autobiographies, often at the request or demand of their male spiritual advisers but portraying their own personal and spiritual development. In France, Madeleine de Scudéry (1607– 1701) published *Grand Cyrus* in 1649, beginning a period of female dominance in the writing of romantic fiction; such works were generally set in a remote time and place and always included moral advice. In England, the most prolific writer was Aphra Behn (1640?–89), who is usually described as the first British woman (and sometimes as the first woman anywhere) to earn her living by selling her writing. She wrote almost sixty works, nearly one-tenth of the works published by women in England during her lifetime, including at least eighteen plays that appear to have been performed frequently. Her success resulted in vitriolic criticism, accusations of plagiarism, and charges of immodesty and lewdness, particularly because her plays were the bawdy comic romances popular with contemporary English audiences. Behn defended herself (often in her next play) against these charges, stating clearly that such criticism was largely the result of her sex:

The play had no other misfortune but that of coming out for [i.e., being written by] a woman: had it been owned by a man, though the most dull unthinking rascally scribbler in town, it had been an admirable play. [They said] *that it was bawdy*, the least and most excusable fault in the men writers, *but from a woman it was unnatural.*[7]

Like women painters, women writers who wished their works to be a commercial success followed popular styles, which Behn comments is no grounds for criticism; she describes herself as "[one] who is forced to write for bread and not ashamed to own it, and consequently ought to write to please (if she can)."[8] Women playwrights were more likely than their male counterparts to give more and larger parts to women, and

[7] Aphra Behn, *Sir Patient Fancy* (London, 1678), sig. A.
[8] Ibid.

there are some themes that female authors tend to emphasize more than male authors. Many women, including Behn and her fellow English playwrights Margaret Cavendish (1623–73), Frances Boothby (fl. 1670), and Elizabeth Polwhele (fl. 1670), all regard marriage, whether arranged or for love, as problematic for women. As one female character in Cavendish's *Love's Adventures*, refusing a public celebration of her wedding, states bluntly: "Do you call that a triumphant day, that enslaves a woman all her life after? No, I will make no triumph on that day."[9] In her collections of short stories published in Madrid, Maria de Zayas y Sotomayor (1590–1661 or 1669) describes husbands who lock up, starve, or beat their wives; many of her female characters decide to go into the convent, which she describes for one character as "not a tragic end, but the happiest that could be, since coveted and desired by many, she subjected herself to none."[10] Despite her harsh denunciation of marriage, Zayas y Sotomayor's works were frequently reprinted into the eighteenth century. Along with revealing a more negative view of the effects of marriage on women, women also create heroic female characters more often than do male authors. Their female heroes do not necessarily challenge convention, however, for the virtues for which they are most praised are those that are culturally approved: constancy, modesty, patience, chastity. Mariam in Elizabeth Cary's *The Tragedie of Mariam*, the Jewish queen executed by her tyrant husband through no fault of her own, all the while worrying whether she is guilty of wifely disobedience; Pamphilia in Lady Mary Wroth's *Urania*, who remains true to her beloved despite his inconstancy; and Mandane in Madeleine de Scudéry's *Grand Cyrus*, who survives a series of abductions with her honor intact, are prime examples of this conventional, although heroic, behavior.

Female authors were more likely than male to include moral advice in their poetry, drama, and fiction and also, like men, wrote and published pure advice books. These include cookbooks, almanacs, midwives' manuals, practical medical guides, and housekeeping manuals. The *Athenian Mercury* (1691–97), a journal of current events and commentary published in England, included a column providing advice for male and female readers on such matters as courtship and sex. In the early eighteenth century in England, several women's advice journals such as *The Female Tatler* (1709–10) and *The Female Spectator* (1744–46) contained articles by women as well as men. Advice manuals by women also include

[9] Margaret Cavendish, *Love's Adventures* (London, 1662), p. 66.
[10] Maria de Zayas y Sotomayor, *Desengaños amorosos*, translated and quoted in Sandra M. Fox, "Maria de Zayas y Sotomayor: Sibyl of Madrid (1590?–1661?)," in J. R. Brink (ed.), *Female Scholars: A Tradition of Learned Women before 1800* (Montreal: Edens Press, 1980), p. 59.

a number of books written by mothers for their children, often when the women were dying or suspected they were. Most advice books written in Germany were by reigning noblewomen instructing their sons on how to govern, but those written in England – more than ten in the seventeenth century – were largely by members of the gentry or middle class. One would think that a mother's duty to her children would alone provide enough justification for a woman to write, but many of the authors also included elaborate apologia describing their spiritual as well as maternal calling. Dorothy Leigh, the author of *The Mother's Blessing* (London, 1627), which went through fifteen editions in the seventeenth century, specifically says that through showing their religious devotion in writing, women could rid themselves of the sin of Eve: "because wee must needes confesse that sinne entred by us into our posterity; let us shew how carefull we are to seeke to Christ, to cast it out of us and our posterity" (p. 17).

Women also saw writing autobiographies and memoirs as a way of providing spiritual guidance and moral lessons to others, sometimes through the bad example of their own lives. Up to the middle of the seventeenth century, most autobiographies by both women and men were spiritual, detailing the author's religious conversion and spiritual progress; we discuss these more fully in Chapter 6. After that point, men began to write autobiographical works generally describing their public careers, and women ones that delved more deeply into emotional matters. These personal autobiographies are viewed, like letters, as a genre that contributed to the development of the novel, for they introduced the idea that one's emotions were appropriate subject matter for published works. Although women's autobiographical writings differ widely in form, style, and intent, and the authors emphasize their own uniqueness as they try to arrive at some kind of self-definition, the works do show certain common features. The authors all compare themselves with the accepted standards for female behavior and often discuss some kind of oppression they have experienced; they are very conscious of the actual writing process and frequently discuss their problems in achieving objectivity and "truth." All of these features appear in the quotation from Margaret Cavendish that opens this chapter; she also recognizes that women's individual identities were more easily lost than men's because they changed their names on marriage.

Women charged with criminal acts also often wrote their life histories, which were peddled as small pamphlets; sensational or scandalous cases could become best sellers. Such authors did not show the same level of introspection as those who wrote longer autobiographies, but they did hope to vindicate themselves by publishing their side of the story and make enough money to support themselves while in prison. They manipulated feminine stereotypes to make themselves appear less culpable, a tendency that also emerges in women's written requests to political authorities for pardons.

A concern for "truth" also emerges in memoirs written by female courtiers in the late seventeenth century. Especially at the French court, Madame de Lafayette (1634–93) and a number of other noblewomen wrote memoirs of court life explicitly to defend their names against gossip and rumor and tell the true stories of their actions; they had clearly internalized the concern with reputation that we saw in the last chapter was so important for female courtiers. Like letters, such memoirs can be seen as precursors to the novel, for their authors were much more concerned with relationships between people and with individual life stories than the male memoirists of the time who concentrated on military and political matters. These memoirs can also be seen as precursors to modern social history, which also explores personal stories and relationships and does not simply focus on public political events.

Women's writing of history in the early modern period was not limited to court memoirs, however, for the sense of self and of having something valuable to say that inspired some women to write autobiographies inspired others to write and publish other types of nonfiction. In the seventeenth century, Charlotte Arbaleste (1550–1606), Lucy Hutchinson (1620–81), and Margaret Cavendish all wrote biographies of their husbands that included analyses of political events. By the middle of the eighteenth century, several French women, such as Marguerite de Lussan (1682–1758), were writing local and national histories based on chronicles and manuscripts, and Catherine Macaulay (1731–91) published her widely respected eight-volume history of England. The English Civil War saw a dramatic upsurge in women's political writings – from six in the entire period 1600–40 to seventy-seven in the decade 1641–50 alone – ranging from political prophecy to women's petitions to Parliament to pamphlets arguing every political position from staunch royalist to radical Leveller. There was no similar expansion anywhere on the Continent, although the horrors of the Thirty Years' War did lead a few women, such as Martha Salome von Belta, to publish their own views of the war's causes and probable consequences.

Scientists

Scientific ideas and advances were among the topics discussed in the journals, societies, clubs, and coffeehouses that formed the growing "public sphere" of the seventeenth and eighteenth centuries. Public lectures and classes in anatomy, astronomy, physics, and chemistry drew large audiences, and books that explained complex scientific ideas to the layperson were published in England, France, Germany, and Italy. Science or, to use the terminology of the period, "natural philosophy" became a topic about which every educated person was expected to know at least a bit to be able to converse intelligently. To be regarded as modern and sophisticated, one's library should contain some scientific works, a requirement made easier by the decreasing price of books relative to other commodities in the seventeenth century.

Women formed a significant share of the audience for all of these activities, and some books and lectures were directed specifically to them. Many of the popular scientific works, such as Baron de Fontenelle's *The Plurality of Worlds*, which discusses the cosmology of the French philosopher Descartes, were written as dialogues between a woman and a man. Aphra Behn translated this from French to English, commenting in her preface that "I thought an English Woman might adventure to translate any thing a French Woman may be supposed to have spoken."[11] Isaac Newton's followers wrote popular works explaining Newtonian science in terms that educated people who were not mathematicians could understand, several (in various languages) titled "Newton for the Ladies" or something similar. We can tell that women read or at least purchased these books by the fact that they show up in women's personal libraries, and women's names appear on publishers' subscription lists. (Publishers often sold books in advance, by subscription, to be sure they would get an adequate return on their investment.) A popular imitator of the Royal Society of England, the Athenian Society, described its role specifically as the communication of the "Sciences to all men, as well as to both Sexes."[12] In 1704, the first women's almanac containing scientific information, *The Ladies Diary*, began to be published in England; John Tipper, the editor, originally included recipes and household hints, but his female readers requested that he stick to science and mathematics so that after 1709, the almanac devoted itself exclusively to science.

Women were not only an audience for the new science, however, but also active participants. A number of women contributed articles and brainteaser puzzles to *The Ladies Dairy* and translated both popular and learned scientific works; the most important and difficult of these was Madame du Châtelet's (1706–49) translation of Newton's *Principia* from Latin into French, which remains the sole French translation. She also published an original work explaining Newton and Leibniz to a French

---

[11] Aphra Behn, *A Discovery of New Worlds* (London, 1688), sig. A4r.
[12] Quoted in Hilda Smith, "'All men and both sexes': Concepts of Men's Development, Women's Education and Feminism in the Seventeenth Century," in Donald C. Mell, Jr., et al. (eds.), *Man, God, and Nature in the Enlightenment* (East Lansing, MI, Colleagues Press, 1988), p. 75.

audience and was probably the best-known woman scientist in the eighteenth century. Although unusual in her talents, du Châtelet was also typical of many women known to have scientific or philosophical interests in the early modern period: she was a member of the nobility who learned her science through personal contacts, created a scientific circle in her household that drew learned men to her, and published only translations or derivative works while keeping her original work unpublished. Anne Finch, the viscountess Conway (1631–79), who has recently been recognized as one of the sources of some of Leibniz's ideas, and Baroness Martine de Beausoleil (1602?–40), a geologist, both fit this pattern as well. The most prolific female scientific author of the period, Margaret Cavendish, the duchess of Newcastle, was also a noblewoman, but otherwise she was absolutely unique. Along with the plays and biographies we have already discussed, she wrote seven works of philosophy and science, giving her opinions on current topics of interest including matter and motion, the vacuum, atoms, sense perception, truth, perfection, and the mind. She based her first works solely on her own perceptions, arguing, like Thomas Hobbes, that one's own rational capacity was more valuable than outside authority, but by her later works she was also incorporating ideas from Descartes and John Locke.

Not all women scientists were members of the nobility, however. A few, particularly in Italy, were the daughters of university professors and went on to receive university degrees themselves. As we saw in Chapter 4, Laura Bassi lectured on physics at the University of Bologna in the eighteenth century. Several women in France and Germany, usually trained by their fathers, became well known for their botanical and anatomical illustrations or their mapmaking. Maria Sibylla Merian (1647–1717), for example, depicted plants and insects in *Wonderful Metamorphosis and Special Nourishment of Caterpillars* (1679) and later in life traveled to the Dutch colony of Surinam with her daughter where she gathered and drew insects and plants in preparation for her major scientific work, a study of the life cycle of Surinam insects. Astronomy was another science initially open to the work of women. Most astronomical observatories in seventeenth-century Germany, for example, were in private homes rather than public buildings or universities, and the daughters and wives of male astronomers peered through telescopes and calculated the movement of heavenly bodies along with their fathers and husbands. These women were not simply assistants, however, but rather made observations and sometimes published findings on their own.

In the nineteenth and twentieth centuries, science and mathematics had become fields of study clearly identified as masculine; but, in the early modern period, experimental science, especially on the Continent, was sometimes regarded as feminine. Those who had a negative view of women's intellectual capacities saw laboratory experiments as not too different from cooking, and observation of the natural world, especially botany, as likely to induce greater religious reverence. Science was also something women could do in their own homes, for even the most advanced scientific equipment, such as the microscope, was within the budgets of many upper-middle-class and noble households, and mathematics required no equipment at all. Classics, on the other hand, was regarded as masculine, for only the stronger male mind was up to the rigors of learning Latin and Greek, a requirement for all fields of university study until the late eighteenth century. Those who had a positive view of women's intellect also saw science and women as made for each other, for women's lack of a classical education would enable them to carry out more objective and original research, not influenced by the mistaken ideas of the past. Women, or better said, ladies, also had more time to speculate on scientific matters because they were unable to participate in politics and generally did not have to concern themselves with economic matters.

In some ways, then, an interest in science was yet another "accomplishment" welcomed in middle- and upper-class women but never to be used professionally. Like other accomplishments, it was satirized as amateurish dilettantism, as a feminine fad first by the French playwright Molière in *Les Femmes savantes (The Learned Ladies)* and then by other French and English playwrights who copied him. A more serious type of criticism came from Francis Bacon and other English scientists, who regarded continental scientists with their frequent ties to noblewomen as "effeminate," and called for a "masculine" science. The explicit goals of the Royal Society of London were "to raise a Masculine Philosophy" and to promote the "Masculine Arts of Knowledge."[13] What they meant by this was a science that was active, strong, and not tied to the past, all qualities that female scientists prized in their own work, but which the Royal Society viewed as intrinsically male as well as masculine. Other than a single visit to the Royal Society by the duchess of Newcastle in 1667, a visit described satirically in a ballad by one of the society's members, no women had any contact with England's leading scientific society throughout the period. Not until 1945, in fact, was a woman admitted as a full member.

This exclusion from the Royal Society was not peculiarly English, however, and points to what became more serious limitations on women's

---

[13] Francis Bacon, quoted in Londa Schiebinger, *The Mind Has No Sex? Women in the Origins of Modern Science* (Cambridge, MA, Harvard University Press, 1989), p. 138.

participation in science than satirical plays or Baconian ideas. Although women were part of the informal scientific circles that were the precursors to formal scientific and philosophical societies, and although popular societies like the Athenian Society in England saw part of their mission as communicating scientific information to women, no woman was ever admitted as a member to a scientific academy or society outside of Italy. No academy had formal statutes that barred women as a group, but when female scientists and philosophers applied, they were excluded explicitly on the basis of their sex. By the end of the eighteenth century, there were academies in every country of Europe, and much of the publication and communication of ideas was carried out at their meetings and through their journals; the exclusion of women meant female scientists and philosophers would always remain at the peripheries. The addition of courses in science to the university curricula at many European universities also created another avenue of scientific education that was blocked to women.

Anatomy and astronomy also became more closely tied to institutions that excluded women during the early modern period. Lectures and demonstrations in anatomy were added to university medical training for physicians and to the training of barber-surgeons and male midwives; proposals by female midwives for similar training, such as that of Elizabeth Cellier to James II of England in 1687, were never granted, except in Italy, where male midwives remained completely unacceptable to all social classes. Scientific academies opened astronomical observatories, where official positions were reserved for men. This was not because women had no access to training, for much astronomical training was still carried out privately, or because they were not skilled, but rather because such positions were public ones and therefore closed to women. Maria Winkelmann (1670–1720) was told this explicitly when she applied for an appointment as an assistant astronomer with the Academy of Sciences in Berlin. She had assisted her husband, the academy's official astronomer, for ten years and had published observations both with him and on her own; the two of them together prepared astronomical and astrological calendars, which the academy sold to support its projects. When her husband died, Winkelmann asked that she and her son be appointed assistant astronomers for the making of calendars because she clearly had the skills and because widows in many crafts often carried on their husbands' businesses. Her request was flatly rejected, not on the grounds of her lack of talent or training (she was later asked to assist the man who was appointed) but because, as the secretary of the academy wrote: "Already during her husband's lifetime the society was burdened with ridicule because its calendar was prepared by a woman. If she were now to be kept on in such a capacity, mouths would gape even wider."[14]

Thus, in science, as in art and music, gender shaped both women's access and the evaluation of their creative activities. Women might call their embroidery "art" (although usually downplaying it with the term "domestic arts") but did not call themselves artists. They played the harpsichord or sang but were not musicians, or only "lady musicians," a term that became popular in the eighteenth century. They studied the anatomy of plants and observed the stars but were not "scientists." Women's inability to become great artists, musicians, or scientists was then used as proof of male superiority in the realm of the mind. When they objected to their fewer opportunities, women were often consoled with the comment that at least in the realm of the spirit, they were men's equals, a statement we assess in the following section.

For Further Reading

Feminist art criticism led the way in understanding the gendered nature of the value placed on certain genres. The most important early theoretical essay is Linda Nochlin, "Why Are There No Great Women Artists?," in Elizabeth C. Baker and Thomas B. Hess (eds.), *Art and Sexual Politics: Women's Liberation, Women Artists and Art History* (New York, MacMillan, 1973), pp. 1–43, which analyzes why there have always been a smaller absolute number of women artists and why their work has been slighted; the book also contains replies to Nochlin by ten contemporary women artists. Fredrika H. Jacobs, *Defining the Renaissance Virtuosa: Women Artists and the Language of Art History and Criticism* (Cambridge, Cambridge University Press, 1997), and Paola Tinagli, *Women in Italian Renaissance Art: Gender, Representation and Identity* (Manchester, Manchester University Press, 1997), provide longer discussions of the ways in which ideas about gender shaped perceptions of art and the artist in Renaissance Italy. For northern Europe, see Jane L. Carroll and Alison G. Stewart (eds.), *Saints, Sinners, and Sisters: Gender and Northern Art in Medieval and Early Modern Europe* (Burlington, VT, Ashgate, 2003); and, for the eighteenth century, see Melissa Hyde and Jennifer Milam (eds.), *Women, Art and the Politics of Identity in Eighteenth-Century Europe* (Burlington, VT, Ashgate, 2003). Insightful analyses of the situation of women artists and gendered ideas of creativity can be found in Mary Sheriff, *The Exceptional Woman: Elisabeth Vigée-Lebrun and the Cultural Politics of Art* (Chicago, University of Chicago Press, 1996), and her

---

[14] Translated and quoted in ibid., p. 92.

Moved by Love: Inspired Artists and Deviant Women in Eighteenth-Century France (Chicago, University of Chicago Press, 2004).

Individual women artists are receiving increasing attention. On Judith Leyster, see Frima Fox Hofrichter, *Judith Leyster: A Woman Painter in Holland's Golden Age* (Doornspijk: Davaco Publishers, 1989); and James A. Welu and Pieter Biesboer (eds.), *Judith Leyster: A Dutch Master and Her World* (Zwolle, Netherlands, Waanders Publishers, and Worcester, MA, Worcester Art Museum, 1993). On Artemisia Gentileschi, see Mary Garrard, *Artemisia Gentileschi: The Image of the Female Hero in Italian Baroque Art* (Princeton, NJ, Princeton University Press, 1989); R. Ward Bissel, *Artemisia Gentileschi and the Authority of Art: Critical Reading and Catalogue Raisonne* (University Park, Pennsylvania State University Press, 1999); Mieke Bal (ed.), *The Artemisia Files: Artemisia Gentileschi for Feminists and Other Thinking People* (Chicago, University of Chicago Press, 2000). On Elisabeth Vigée Le Brun, see Gita May, *Elisabeth Vigée Le Brun: The Odyssey of an Artist in an Age of Revolution* (New Haven, CT, Yale University Press, 2005).

For information on female musicians, see Jane Bowers and Judith Tick (eds.), *Women Making Music: The Western Art Tradition, 1150–1950* (Urbana, University of Illinois Press, 1986); Jane Baldauf-Berdes, *Women Musicians of Venice: Musical Foundations, 1525–1855* (Oxford, Oxford University Press, 1993); and Thomasin LaMay (ed.), *Musical Voices of Early Modern Women: Many Headed Melodies* (Burlington, VT, Ashgate, 2005). The music of Italian nuns has been analyzed in Craig Monson, *Disembodied Voices: Music and Culture in an Early Modern Italian Convent* (Berkeley, University of California Press, 1995); and Robert Kendrick, *Celestial Sirens: Nuns and Their Music in Early Modern Italy* (Oxford, Clarendon, 1996). For actresses and women's stage roles, see Elizabeth Howe, *The First English Actresses: Women and Drama, 1660–1700* (Cambridge, Cambridge University Press, 1992); and Viviana Comensoli and Anne Russell (eds.), *Enacting Gender on the Renaissance Stage* (Champaign/Urbana, University of Illinois Press, 1999).

Early modern women writers have been the subject of hundreds of books and countless articles. The Web site for this book contains a large bibliography on this topic as does Betty S. Travitsky and Josephine A. Roberts, *English Women Writers, 1500–1640: A Reference Guide (1750–1996)* (New York, G. K. Hall, 1997), although the latter is limited to English women writers. For a broad overview of women's writings over the centuries, Katharina M. Wilson, *Medieval Women Writers, Women Writers of the Renaissance and Reformation, Women Writers of the Seventeenth Century* (Athens, University of Georgia Press, 1984, 1987, 1989), are good places to start; each contains selections from the work and discussions of the writings and lives of about twenty women from all over Europe. Along with critical scholarship, more printed and Web-based editions of the works of early modern women writers appear every year. An excellent selection of hundreds of fully searchable English texts, many with scholarly introductions, can be found at the Brown University Women Writers Project, www.wwp.brown.edu. The University of Chicago series, "The Other Voice in Early Modern Europe," edited by Margaret King and Albert Rabil, Jr., has published translations of continental writers in many genres (http://www.press.uchicago.edu/Complete/Series/ OVIEME.html).

Discussions of the interplay among gender, writing, and publishing include Elizabeth Goldsmith and Dena Goodman (eds.), *Going Public: Women and Publishing in Early Modern France* (Ithaca, NY, Cornell University Press, 1995); Paula McDowell, *The Women of Grub Street: Press, Politics, and Gender in the London Literary Marketplace 1678–1730* (Oxford, Clarendon Press, 1998); Axel Erdmann, *My Gracious Silence: Women in the Mirror of Sixteenth-Century Printing in Western Europe* (Luzerne, Gilhofer and Ranschberg, 1998); Susan Broomhall, *Women and the Book Trade in Sixteenth-Century France* (Burlington, VT, Ashgate, 2002); and Helen Berry, *Gender, Society and Print Culture in Late-Stuart England: The Cultural World of the Athenian Mercury* (Burlington, VT, Ashgate, 2003).

Women's activities as scientists and the gendered nature of science have been examined in Londa Schiebinger, *The Mind Has No Sex? Women in the Origins of Modern Science* (Cambridge, MA, Harvard University Press, 1989); Patricia Phillips, *The Scientific Lady: A Social History of Women's Scientific Interests, 1520–1918* (London, Weidenfeld and Nicolson, 1990); Lynette Hunter and Sarah Hutton (eds.), *Women, Medicine and Science 1500–1700: Mothers and Sisters of the Royal Society* (London, Sutton, 1998); and Judith P. Zinsser (ed.), *Men, Women, and the Birthing of Modern Science* (Dekalb, Northern Illinois University Press, 2005). A good survey of these issues designed for undergraduates is Patricia Fara, *Pandora's Breeches: Women, Science and Power in the Enlightenment* (London, Pimlico, 2004). The works of women scientists and philosophers have been reprinted in Margaret Atherton (ed.), *Women Philosophers of the Early Modern Period* (Indianapolis, Hackett, 1994). Studies of individual women scientists include Anna Battigelli, *Margaret Cavendish and the Exile of the Mind* (Lexington, University Press of Kentucky, 1998); Andrea Nye, *The Princess and the Philosopher* (on Princess Elizabeth of Bohemia) (London, Rowman and Littlefield, 1999); Stephen Clucas (ed.), *A Princely Brave Woman: Essays on Margaret Cavendish, Duchess of Newcastle* (Burlington, VT, Ashgate, 2003); Sarah Hutton, *Anne Conway: A Woman Philosopher* (New York, Cambridge University

Press, 2004); and Judith Zinsser, *La Dame d'Esprit: A Biography of Marquise Du Chatelet* (New York, Viking, 2006). Natalie Davis includes study of the illustrator Maria Sibylla Merian in *Women on the Margins: Three Seventeenth-Century Lives* (Cambridge, MA, Harvard University Press, 1995). Dava Sobel, *Galileo's Daughter: A Historical Memoir of Science, Faith, and Love* (New York, Penguin, 2000), centers on the translated letters of Galileo's eldest daughter, Marie Celeste, who became a nun; the letters themselves can be found online at Rice University Galileo Project: http://galileo.rice.edu/fam/daughter.html.

For more suggestions and links, see the companion Web site www.cambridge.org/womenandgender.

Part III

Spirit

6   Religion

Lord of my soul, you did not hate women when You walked in the world; rather you favored them always with much pity and found in them as much love and more faith than in men. Is it not enough, Lord, that the world has intimidated us ... so that we may not do anything worthwhile for You in public?

> St. Teresa of Avila, *The Way of Perfection* (1560s), quoted and translated in
> Alison Weber, *Teresa of Avila and the Rhetoric of Femininity* (Princeton, NJ,
> Princeton University Press, 1990), p. 41

Since it were very pernicious that the opinions of men, although good and holy, should be put in the place of the commandment of God, I desire that this matter [the decision by the Protestant consistory of her town, a disciplinary body made up of clergy, to excommunicate her and her entire household because she wore her hair in curls] may be cleared up for the well-being and the concord of the churches.

> Charlotte Arbaleste, 1584, quoted and translated in James Anderson, *Ladies
> of the Reformation: In Germany, France, and Spain* (London, Blackie and
> Sons, 1857), p. 466

The second opening quotation comes from a speech by Charlotte Arbaleste, a French noblewoman and Calvinist Protestant, to a group of religious leaders, known as the consistory, of her town. Matters such as the style of one's hair, Arbaleste continued, were no grounds for the exclusion of someone from church ceremonies and services, and she as a noblewoman was certainly not going to obey the middle-class pastors on an issue that had nothing to do with her or anyone else's salvation.

This conflict and Arbaleste's comments about it highlight many of the issues involving women's religious life in the early modern period. First, although we may view the arrangement of women's hair as trivial, it had tremendous social and symbolic importance. Immediately upon marriage, women covered their hair, for long flowing hair was the mark of someone who was sexually available, either as a virgin or prostitute. Both the New Testament and early Christian writers such as Tertullian had ordered women to cover their heads not simply as a gesture of respect but also specifically to lessen their sexual attractiveness. Thus, the pastors claimed biblical authority for their position, and at the heart of the issue was the control of female sexuality and the maintenance of a moral order in which women were subservient. These factors will emerge in nearly all the religious conflicts involving women in the early modern period, even when the participants did not articulate them.

Second, the key question for women was often the conflict between the authorities Arbaleste mentions: the opinions of men and the commandment of God. Women had to choose between what male political and religious authorities, and sometimes even their fathers and husbands, told them to do and what they perceived as God's plan for their lives. Third, Arbaleste and the pastors disagreed about the boundaries between public and private; early modern women frequently argued that their religious actions were private matters and that only God could be the true judge. Finally, Arbaleste's confidence in challenging the pastors, and the source of some of her irritation, came from her status as a noblewoman; the women whose religious choices had the most impact in early modern Europe were usually noblewomen or rulers, whose actions affected their subjects as well as themselves and their families. For women of all classes, however, religion provided the most powerful justification for independent action.

It may seem somewhat odd to think of Christianity, Judaism, or Islam as religions that empowered women, for all contain strong elements of misogyny and were in the early modern period totally controlled by male hierarchies with the highest (or all) levels of the clergy reserved for men. In all three, God is thought of as male, the account of creation appears to ascribe or ordain a secondary status for women, and women are instructed to be obedient and subservient; all three religious traditions were used by men as buttresses for male authority in all realms of life, not simply religion. Nevertheless, it was the language of religious texts and the examples of pious women who preceded them that were used most often by women to subvert or directly oppose male directives. Religion was even used as the reason women should study secular philosophy; Mary Astell, the English feminist and scholar writing in the first part of the eighteenth century, justified her call for women to learn Cartesian philosophy in part by stressing that this could help a woman not only to love God "with all her Heart and Strength" but also to "love Him with all her Mind and Soul."[1]

[1] Mary Astell, *The Christian Religion, As Profess'd by a Daughter of the Church of England* (1705), quoted in Hilda Smith, *Reason's Disciples: Seventeenth-Century English Feminists* (Urbana, University of Illinois Press, 1982), p. 119.

In exploring early modern women's religious ideas and actions, it will be useful to follow the standard religious chronology and divisions of the period because these determined the types of ideology and institutions within or against which women could operate. For Christianity, we start with a look at the late medieval Catholic and Orthodox churches, then at the Protestant and Catholic Reformations in western Europe, developments in Orthodoxy, and the changes in religious structures in the seventeenth and early eighteenth centuries. This is followed by a much briefer discussion of women in early modern Judaism and Islam, whose fate in most of Europe was shaped by the Christian authorities under whose control they lived.

The Role of Women in Late Medieval Christianity

We have already examined in some detail the ideas about women held by medieval theologians and clerics, but before we can assess the changes for women brought about by the Protestant and Catholic Reformations, and the role of women in both of these movements, we must have some idea of their role in the late medieval church. Here, we must distinguish, as would any of their contemporaries, between nuns and other women who had taken religious vows, the majority of laywomen who were married or lived with other family members, and women whose status was somewhere in between, who attempted to live a communal life of religious devotion without formal vows or rules.

The most powerful and, in many ways, independent women in the late medieval church were the abbesses of certain convents, who controlled large amounts of property and often had jurisdiction over many subjects. This was particularly true in Germany, where abbesses of free imperial convents had no secular overlord except the emperor, but was also true elsewhere in Europe where certain convents were aligned with powerful noble families. Although every convent had to have a priest available to say mass and hear confessions because the Catholic Church ruled these were functions that no woman could perform, all of the other administrative duties and much of the spiritual counseling of novices and residents were carried out by women. Since their foundings in the early and high Middle Ages, many convents had been open only to members of the nobility and were thus socially exclusive; lower-class women might be associated with a convent as lay sisters to do the harder physical labor or routine maintenance, but they could not become professed nuns.

The high points of many convents in terms of intellectual accomplishments and political power were the tenth and eleventh centuries.

Beginning in the late eleventh century, a reform movement usually termed the "Gregorian reform" after one of its most vocal proponents, Pope Gregory VII (pontificate 1073–85) attempted to cut the connections between the church and secular leaders and also to restrict all links between male clergy and women. Decrees were passed ordering clerical celibacy and declaring invalid priestly marriages that did exist. Reform-minded officials began a campaign against clerical families, driving women and children from their homes. Although there were protests against this change in policy, they were not effective, and clerical celibacy became the policy of the Western church from that point on. Women religious were to be cut off from the world, a practice known as enclosure, which became official policy in the papal decree *Periculoso* promulgated in 1298 by Pope Boniface VIII, although it was never successfully enforced until centuries later. These moves reduced the abbesses' power and visibility in the surrounding community and, at the same time, universities, which were closed to women, replaced monasteries as the main intellectual centers of Europe. In their writings and in their spiritual life, nuns in the late Middle Ages turned to mysticism and personal devotions rather than giving political advice or writing plays for public performance.

By the fifteenth century, it appeared to some church officials and the more rigorous nuns as if many convents had forgotten their spiritual focus. In many ways, this is not surprising because some convent residents were not there willingly but had been placed there by their parents because the cost of a dowry for marriage was too high; the entrance fees demanded by convents were generally lower than the dowry that a husband of one's own social class would expect. Such nuns often continued to live as they would outside the convent – they wore secular clothing and jewelry, entertained visitors, ate fancy food, retained servants, and frequently left the convent to visit family or friends. In many areas of Europe, leaders of the orders with which convents were affiliated or reform-minded abbesses attempted to halt such behavior and enforce strict rules of conduct and higher standards of spirituality. These fifteenth-century reforms had both positive and negative results for the nuns. On the negative side, they often put the convent more closely under the control of a local male bishop, taking away some of the abbess's independent power, and decreased the contact that the women had with the outside world, which also decreased their opportunities to get donations. On the positive side, they often built up a strong sense of group cohesion among the nuns and gave them a greater sense of the spiritual worth of their lives, particularly if an abbess herself had led the reform. This would lead, as we will see, to these reformed convents being the most vigorous opponents of the Protestant Reformation in the areas in which it was introduced.

In areas of Europe where Orthodox Christianity was dominant, such as eastern Europe and Russia, women's convents were rarely enclosed, and the women did not live communally but rather retained their own incomes, clothing, and food. Many of these convents were wealthy centers of pilgrimage, holding huge estates, and had close ties with noble and royal families. A larger share of the nuns in Orthodox convents were widows than was true in western Europe, for widows often entered convents for social and economic security, deeding their goods or property to the convent rather than fighting legal battles for it with other heirs. The abbesses of major convents, who were elected by the nuns, were often powerful, entertaining secular and ecclesiastical officials and handling relations with the tsar. Unlike Western convents, the women in Orthodox convents were not expected to have a strong religious vocation but rather simply to lead respectable lives. As the accounts of Russian saints' lives demonstrate, the ideal holy woman in Russia was not a nun as she was in the West but instead a devout mother who lived quietly at home and did her miracles and good deeds in private. Orthodoxy was not affected by the Protestant or Catholic Reformations so that women's convents in eastern Europe continued to operate into the eighteenth century just as they had in the Middle Ages.

In addition to living in convents, a number of women in the late Middle Ages lived in less structured religious communities. Because a dowry was required for either marriage or entrance into a convent, many poor women remained unmarried all their lives, and some chose to live communally in informal religious groups, supporting themselves by weaving, sewing, or caring for the sick. These women were often called Beguines and were initially ignored by the church but, in the fourteenth century, were increasingly regarded as suspect because they were not under male supervision nor did they take formal vows. They were also regarded as cheap competition in the labor market by the craft guilds that were establishing themselves in many cities, and so attempts were made to forbid women to live together unless they were cloistered in a convent. These attempts were sporadically successful, particularly in areas where Beguines were also charged with heresy, but groups of unmarried women and widows continued to live together in many cities because there was simply no other way they could survive.

Some women who felt a special religious calling remained with their families, devoting themselves to helping others, to fighting heresy, or to prayer, and perhaps attaching themselves to the Dominicans or Franciscans as lay followers called tertiaries. In the early Middle Ages, women who were regarded as particularly holy were almost all virgins, but by the late Middle Ages, there was even a number of saints who were wives and mothers. Some of these women convinced their husbands to live chastely within marriage, a few left their husbands, and others continued to have sexual relations and bear children. Given official church attitudes about the greater worth of virginity, motherhood often troubled women who felt they had a special religious calling, but they took heart in the example of Mary, the mother of Christ. Margery Kempe, a fifteenth-century English mystic who had fourteen children, despaired about being pregnant again but was relieved by a vision of Christ saying to her, "Forasmuch as thou art a maiden in thy soul, I shall take thee by the one hand, and my Mother by the other hand, and so shalt thou dance in Heaven with other maidens and virgins."[2]

The vast majority of women in late medieval Christianity were not nuns, Beguines, or mystics but rather laywomen – that is, daughters, wives, and mothers living in families or single women and widows living on their own. Late medieval Christianity offered lay believers a number of opportunities to improve their likelihood of going to Heaven or ask God to solve their problems here on earth. Women and men went on pilgrimages, bought and viewed relics, paid for memorial masses or special prayers, lit candles, founded lay confraternities dedicated to certain saints or devotional practices such as the rosary, and carried out a variety of other acts for religious reasons. Their lives were punctuated by ceremonies with religious meaning – baptisms, weddings, funerals – and the entire calendar was structured according to the church year, with feasts and fasts celebrated with family and community ceremonies. Both women and men frequently focused their piety on the figure of Christ, and Christocentric devotion became an important aspect of the lives of those held up as models of godly behavior.

Along with Christ, women and men venerated the Virgin Mary and the saints. Mary was depicted so often in the images and stories through which people learned about Christianity that many people felt she was one member of the Trinity. The saints served medieval Christians in the same way that minor gods and goddesses had served Greeks and Romans – as patrons of certain activities and individuals to turn to with supplications. Female saints were often regarded, not surprisingly, as having special powers over family and household matters, in the same way that goddesses had. Stories about holy women who had been martyrs or shown special qualities of piety and devotion circulated orally, as part of manuscripts, and later printed collections of saints' lives or were depicted in stained-glass windows, church statuary, and paintings. The popularity

---

[2] *The Book of Margery Kempe*, ed. William Butler-Bowdon (New York, Devin-Adair, 1944), p. 42.

of certain saints differed from region to region and changed over time. In the fifteenth century, Mary's mother Anne, a nonbiblical figure whose life was first discussed in written documents in the second century, became an increasingly important figure of devotion. Churches, shrines, and altars were dedicated to her, and many families named their daughters for her. Anne's life story was embellished with legends about her own mother, Emerentia, her three marriages, and her children other than Mary. Stories of her life, frequently reprinted in the fifteenth and sixteenth centuries in vernacular languages as small pamphlets, were popular with the urban middle classes because they portrayed family life in a positive way. Although we have no way of knowing exactly who purchased or read such stories, they were often illustrated with a female trinity – Mary, Anne, and Emerentia – and provided examples of normal human women, even older ones, acting in divinely approved ways.

Much of lay piety was shared by women and men, but careful sifting of visual and written sources has revealed several ways in which laywomen's religious life differed from men's. Other than a few noblewomen or queens who governed territories, no laywoman had any say in the financial or political affairs of the institutional church, although by 1500, city councils and other male lay officials played a large role in running the church in many parts of Europe. Men also oversaw municipal or church agencies for poor relief, whereas women tended to carry out less formal acts of charity, giving food to beggars or taking care of poorer women during illness or childbirth. Married and single women formed all-female parish guilds that raised funds, decorated the church, organized activities, and worshipped together. They participated in a few female-only religious rituals, such as the purification or churching of new mothers after childbirth (see Chapter 2). They gave daily acts, such as baking bread, religious significance by making the sign of the cross before kneading their dough.

Because all church services were in Latin, the vast majority of people could not comprehend the words but simply watched and listened to the music or chanting. Woodcuts and engravings of late medieval services show women more often than men carrying out an alternative religious action, such as saying a rosary or reading in a prayer book, while the priest is conducting the service. It is difficult to know, however, whether the artist was representing reality or implicitly criticizing women for not paying attention. Mary does not seem to have been a more popular figure of devotion among women than men, although Anne and other female saints may have been. Some of the evidence for this comes from later Protestant complaints about women's loyalty to nonbiblical figures and practices, but there is also a small amount of evidence from women themselves.

The Protestant Reformation

The Protestant Reformation was sparked by one of the many ways the late medieval church offered believers to affect their own salvation – giving money in return for indulgences, which substituted for earthly penance or shortened one's time in Purgatory. Martin Luther, Ulrich Zwingli, John Calvin, and most of the other prominent Protestant leaders, although they disagreed on a great many things, all thought that the Catholic Church placed too great an emphasis on good works; for them, an individual's access to salvation was determined by God alone and not by any human actions. The God of the Protestant reformers was a transcendent one, not influenced by pilgrimages or surrounded by a group of semidivine saints who could serve as intermediaries. In their opinion, the clergy were no better than anyone else – the standard phrase expressing this is "the priesthood of all believers" – and the Bible and all church services should be in the vernacular so that all Christians could have access to them.

Protestant teachings reinterpreted female figures who had been important in Christian beliefs. Mary's role changed; instead of an active intercessor with Christ for human salvation, she became a symbol of pious submission to God's will. Her obedience was held up in Protestant sermons, household guides, and other writings as a model for wives in regard to their husbands and also for all believers in their relations with God. Female as well as male saints were diminished in importance. The Protestant martyrs replaced the saints to some degree as models worthy of emulation, but they were not to be prayed to and did not give their names to any days of the year.

Like Christianity itself, the Protestant Reformation both expanded and diminished women's opportunities. The period in which women were the most active was the decade or so immediately following an area's decision to break with the Catholic Church or while this decision was being made. In Germany and many other parts of Europe, that decision was made by a political leader – a prince, duke, king, or city council – who then had to create an alternative religious structure. During this period, many groups and individuals tried to shape the new religious institutions. Sometimes this popular pressure took the form of religious riots, in which women and men destroyed paintings, statues, stained-glass windows, and other objects that symbolized the old religion or protected such objects from destruction at the hands of government officials. In 1536, at Exeter in England, for example, a group of women armed with shovels and pikes attacked workers who had been hired by the government to dismantle a monastery. Sometimes this popular pressure took the form of writing when women and men who did not have formal theological training took

Figure 12. Lucas Cranach d.A., *Women Assaulting Clergy*, after 1537. This is a detail from a much larger drawing in which women attack members of the clergy with agricultural implements; here, they are beating a bishop and a cardinal with a flail. This probably does not show an actual event, but women are reported to have participated in Protestant riots and actions against clergy in many parts of Europe.

the notion of the "priesthood of all believers" literally and preached or published polemical religious literature explaining their own ideas.

Women's preaching or publishing religious material stood in direct opposition to the words ascribed to St. Paul (1 Timothy 2: 11–15) which ordered women not to teach or preach, so that all women who published felt it necessary to justify their actions. The boldest, such as Argula von Grumbach, a German noblewoman who published eight works in 1523 and 1524, including a defense of a teacher accused of Lutheran leanings, commented that the situation was so serious that Paul's words should simply be disregarded: "I am not unfamiliar with Paul's words that women should be silent in church but when I see that no man will or can speak, I am driven by the word of God when he said, He who confesses me on earth, him will I confess and he who denies me, him will I deny."[3] Ursula Weyda, a middle-class German woman who attacked the abbot of Pegau in a 1524 pamphlet, agreed: "If all women were forbidden to speak, how could daughters prophesy as Joel predicted? Although St. Paul forbade women to preach in churches and instructed them to obey their husbands, what if the churches were full of liars?"[4] Marie Dentière, a former abbess who left her convent to help the cause of the Reformation in Geneva, published a letter to Queen Marguerite of Navarre in 1539 defending some of the reformers exiled from that city, in which she gives ringing support to this view:

I ask, didn't Jesus die just as much for the poor illiterates and the idiots as for the shaven, tonsured, and mighty lords? Did he only say, "Go, preach my Gospel to the wise lords and grand doctors?" Did he not say, "To all?" Do we have two Gospels, one for men and the other for women? . . . For we ought not, any more than men, hide and bury within the earth that which God has . . . revealed to us women?[5]

Katherine Zell, the wife of one of Strasbourg's reformers and a tireless worker for the Reformation, supported Dentière in this, asking that her writings be judged "not according to the standards of a woman, but according to the standards of one whom God has filled with the Holy Spirit."[6]

[3] Ludwig Rabus, *Historien der heyligen Außerwolten Gottes Zeugen, Bekennern und Martyrern* (n.p., 1557), fol. 41. My translation.
[4] Translated and quoted in Paul A. Russell, *Lay Theology in the Reformation: Popular Pamphleteers in Southwest Germany 1521–1525* (Cambridge, Cambridge University Press, 1986), p. 203.
[5] Translated and quoted in Thomas Head, "Marie Dentière: A Propagandist for the Reform," in Katharina M. Wilson (ed.), *Women Writers of the Renaissance and Reformation* (Athens, University of Georgia Press, 1987), p. 260.
[6] Quoted in Robert Stupperich, "Die Frau in der Publizistik der Reformation," *Archiv für Kulturgeschichte* 37 (1927), 226. My translation.

Zell's wish was never granted, and women's writings were always judged first on the basis of gender. Argula von Grumbach's husband was ordered to force her to stop writing, and Marie Dentière's pamphlets were confiscated by the very religious authorities she was defending. Once Protestant churches were institutionalized, polemical writings by women (and untrained men) largely stopped. Women continued to write hymns and devotional literature, but these were often published posthumously or were designed for private use.

Women's actions as well as their writings in the first years of the Reformation upset political and religious authorities. Many cities prohibited women from even getting together to discuss religious matters, and in 1543, an Act of Parliament in England banned all women except those of the gentry and nobility from reading the Bible; upper-class women were also prohibited from reading the Bible aloud to others. Class as well as gender hierarchies were to be maintained at all costs, although from women's diaries, we have learned that this restriction was rarely obeyed.

The ability of a woman to act out her religious convictions was largely dependent on class in reality as well as theory. Although none of the reformers differentiated between noblewomen and commoners in their public advice or writings, in private they recognized that noblewomen had a great deal of power and made special attempts to win them over. Luther corresponded regularly with a number of prominent noblewomen, and Calvin was even more assiduous at trying to win noblewomen to his cause. Their efforts met with results, for in a number of cases, female rulers converted their territories to Protestantism or influenced their male relatives to do so. In Germany, Elisabeth of Brunswick-Calenburg brought in Protestant preachers and established a new church structure; in France, Marguerite of Navarre and her daughter Jeanne d'Albert supported Calvinism through patronage and political influence; in Norway, Lady Inger of Austraat, a powerful and wealthy noblewoman, led the opposition to the Norwegian archbishop who remained loyal to Catholicism. The most dramatic example of the degree to which a woman's personal religious convictions could influence events occurred in England, of course, when Mary Tudor attempted to wrench the country back to Catholicism and Elizabeth created a moderately Protestant Church. In all of these cases, political and dynastic concerns mixed with religious convictions, in the same way they did for male rulers and nobles.

Most women expressed their religious convictions in a domestic rather than public setting. They prayed and recited the catechism with children and servants, attended sermons, read the Bible or other devotional literature if they were literate, served meals that no longer followed Catholic fast prescriptions, and provided religious instruction for their children.

Women's domestic religion often took them beyond the household, however, for they gave charitable donations to the needy and often assisted in caring for the ill and indigent. As it had been before the Reformation, most women's charity was on a case-by-case basis, but there are also examples from Protestant areas of women who established and supported almshouses, schools, orphanages, funds for poor widows, and dowry funds for poor girls. In a few places, such as Amsterdam, women who assisted widows and other poor women were given the title of female deacon *(deaconessen)*, but they did not participate in church governing bodies as male deacons did.

Such domestic and charitable activities were widely praised by Protestant reformers as long as husband and wife agreed in their religious opinions. If there was disagreement, however, Continental Protestants generally urged the wife to obey her husband rather than what she perceived as God's will. She could pray for his conversion but was not to leave him or actively oppose his wishes; in Calvin's words, a woman "should not desert the partner who is hostile."[7] English Puritans were less restrictive, urging their female followers to act as "domestic missionaries" and attempt to convert their children, servants, and husbands. During the first decades after the Reformation, marriages between spouses of different faiths were much more common than they would be later in the century, when the lines of religious confession hardened. Such mixed marriages occasioned less comment than one would assume given the violence of religious disagreements in general because for the nobility and gentry, dynastic concerns continued to override those of religion, and even among middle-class urban dwellers, neither spouse appeared to feel the need necessarily to convert the other. By the seventeenth century, official opinion had changed, with authorities in many areas prohibiting their citizens from marrying those of different denominations, or at least prohibiting female citizens from doing so. Sometimes they made other distinctions on the basis of gender. In 1697, for example, the Irish Parliament revived decrees that had first been issued as part of the Statutes of Kilkenney in 1366 – designed at that point to keep the Gaelic and Norman populations of Ireland apart – and ordered that any Protestant heiress who married a Catholic would lose her property to her Protestant next of kin. Her marriage would be considered treasonous if her husband had not signed the Oath of Succession in support of the English rulers of Ireland.

---

[7] Translated and quoted in John H. Bratt, "The Role and Status of Women in the Writings of John Calvin," in Peter de Klerk (ed.), *Renaissance, Reformation, Resurgence* (Grand Rapids, Calvin Theologial Seminary, 1976), p. 9.

The women whose domestic religious activities were most closely scrutinized in the first generation of the Protestant Reformation were the wives of the reformers. During the first few years of the Reformation, they were still likened to priests' concubines in the public mind and had to create a respectable role for themselves, a task made even more difficult by the fact that many were former nuns themselves. They did this largely – and quite successfully, within a generation or so – by being models of wifely obedience and Christian charity, living demonstrations of their husbands' convictions whose households were the type of orderly "little commonwealths" that their husbands were urging on their congregations in sermons. Whereas priests' concubines had generally been from a lower social class, by the second generation, Protestant pastors had little difficulty finding wives from among the same social class as themselves, a trend that further aided the acceptance of clerical marriage. Maintaining an orderly household was just as important for Protestant pastors as teaching and preaching correct doctrine; officials investigated charges of sexual improprieties or moral laxness just as thoroughly as charges of incorrect ideas. The women whose status was most tenuous were the wives of English bishops. Not only were many forced into exile or, worse yet, repudiated by their husbands during Mary's reign, but also their marriages were not formally approved by Elizabeth, so that their children could always be declared bastards. Bishops were expected to live like wealthy noblemen and were accorded high rank at all ceremonial occasions, but their wives had no rank whatever. Long after Continental pastors' wives had succeeded in making theirs a respectable position, bishops' wives in England still had not achieved even legal recognition despite all of their efforts at maintaining pious households.

No matter how much it was extolled in Protestant sermons and domestic conduct books, the vocation of mother and wife was not enough for some women, whose religious convictions led them to leave their husbands and continue to express their religious convictions publicly, even at the cost of their lives. One of the most famous of these was Anne Askew, an English woman who was tortured and then executed for her religious beliefs in 1546. Like Argula von Grumbach and Marie Dentière, she defended her actions, using the Bible against her inquisitors effectively throughout her trial; her standard response to their questioning was one that affirmed the right of every Christian to read and interpret the Bible on her own: "I beleue as the scripture doth teche me."[8] Askew was one

---

[8] Quoted in Diane Willen, "Women and Religion in Early Modern England," in Sherrin Marshall (ed.), *Women in Reformation and Counter-Reformation Europe: Public and Private Worlds* (Bloomington, Indiana University Press, 1989), p. 144.

of the few women martyrs to come from a gentry or middle-class background. Of the people martyred during the reign of Mary, one-fifth were women, and most of these were quite poor; wealthy people who opposed Mary fled to the Continent.

Most of the women executed for religious reasons in early modern Europe were religious radicals who were hated and hunted by Catholics and Protestants alike. Most radical groups were very small and they had widely divergent ideas, so it is difficult to make generalizations that apply to all. Many held that Christians should believe before they were baptized. They denied the validity of infant baptism and baptized adults; for this, they were often called "Anabaptists," a word meaning rebaptizer. Some groups emphasized divine revelation and spiritual experiences and took the visions of women prophets seriously. Others allowed believers to leave their unbelieving spouses, but women who did so were expected to remarry quickly and thus come under control of a male believer. In 1534, Anabaptists took over the northern German town of Münster and attempted to create their vision of a perfect community. Part of this vision was polygamy and enforced marriage for all women, for the male Anabaptist leaders took literally the statement in the Book of Revelations that the Last Judgment would come once 144,000 "saints" (true believers) were in the world. These radicals looked to the Old Testament, rather than the Gospels, for their models of gender relations.

The interrogations of Anabaptists are one of the few sources we have for the religious ideas of people who were illiterate; from these records, we learn that many women could argue complicated theological concepts and had memorized large parts of the Bible by heart. As Claesken Gaeledochter, who was drowned at Leeuwarden in 1559, put it, "Although I am a simple person before men, I am not unwise in the knowledge of the Lord."[9] Anabaptist women actively chose the path of martyrdom, often against the pressure of family members, and the records of their trials, which often appeared in print shortly after their executions, reveal a strong sense of determination. Their actions were praised after their deaths in special hymns that were later sung by fellow believers, full of the details about their martyrdoms and testimonies to women who were "in their faith strong, as men might be."[10] Although their strength of purpose may now appear heroic, in other ways the interrogations of

[9] T. J. van Braght, *The Bloody Theatre or Martyrs Mirror*, ed. Edward Bean Underhill (London, Hanserd Knollys Society, 1850), vol. II, p. 33.
[10] "Six Women of Antwerp" (written about six Anabaptist women executed in Antwerp in 1559), translated and quoted in Hermoine Joldersma and Louis Grijp (eds. and trans.), *"Elisabeth's Manly Courage": Testimonials and Songs by and about Martyred Anabaptist Women* (Milwaukee, Marquette University Press, 2001).

Anabaptists parallel later witchcraft interrogations. In both cases, young women were stripped naked before they were tortured and were asked not only to confess their beliefs but also to name accomplices; the beliefs they were accused of were viewed as so pernicious that normal rules of legal procedure did not apply; most of those accused were poor women.

So far, we have been examining new roles for women brought about by the Protestant Reformation: religious polemicist, pastor's wife, domestic missionary, philanthropist, martyr (which we may not view as positive, but which was viewed as such by most of the women who were). Protestant teachings also rejected many of the activities that had given women's lives religious meaning, however. Religious processions that had included both men and women, such as that of Corpus Christi, were prohibited, and sumptuary laws restricted the celebrations of baptism, weddings, and funerals, all ceremonies in which women had played a major role. Lay female confraternities, which had provided emotional and economic assistance for their members and charity for the needy, were also forbidden, and no all-female groups replaced them. The new charitable funds founded by women for women often had men as their overseers and, in any case, did not bring together women of different classes as comembers the way confraternities did but made sharp distinctions between the bestower and recipient of charity.

The Protestant rejection of celibacy had the greatest impact on female religious, both cloistered nuns and women who lived in less formal religious communities. One of the first moves of an area rejecting Catholicism was to close the monasteries and convents, either confiscating the buildings and land immediately or forbidding new novices and allowing the current residents to live out their lives on a portion of the convent's old income. In England and Ireland, where all monasteries and convents were taken over by the Crown, most nuns got very small pensions and were expected to return to their families, although not all did. Many Irish and English nuns fled to religious communities on the Continent or continued to fulfill their religious vows in hiding while they waited for the chance to emigrate. In many cities of the Dutch Republic, the convents were closed, their assets liquidated, and the women given their dowries and a pension. Some returned to their families, while others continued to live together in small, informal domestic groups. Because Catholic ceremonies and organizations were banned, it is difficult to find information about the religious life of these women, termed *kloppen* or *geestelijke maagden* (holy maidens). From land-ownership records and family genealogies, we do know that groups of them lived together or near one another long after areas became officially Protestant; one recent study estimates that *kloppen* comprised about 2 percent of the Catholic population of the Dutch

Republic in the seventeenth century. Many were members of wealthy and prominent upper-class families who had only slowly accepted the Reformation so were supported by their families in their decisions to remain unmarried and devote themselves to religious activities. *Kloppen* could also be found in the Catholic Spanish Netherlands, where their status as an intermediate group between nuns and laywomen made Catholic authorities increasingly uneasy.

Even when prominent families did become Protestant, they sometimes continued to support convents because of long-standing traditions. The convent at Vadstena in Sweden, for example, had long housed female members of the Swedish royal family, and when Swedish rulers became Protestant in the 1520s, they thought it inappropriate simply to close it down. Instead, they attempted to convince the nuns to accept Protestantism willingly, but the nuns resisted, stuffing wool and wax in their ears when they were forced to attend Lutheran services. The convent survived until the 1590s, when royal patience gave out; the nuns were then forcibly evicted and the convent's treasures and library confiscated.

This link between convents and prominent families was most pronounced in the Holy Roman Empire, where many convents had been established by regional ruling houses or by the wives and daughters of emperors. Many of them had been reformed in the fifteenth century, and long traditions of power, independence, and prestige combined with a reinvigorated spiritual life to make reformed convents the most vocal and resolute opponents of the Protestant Reformation. This was recognized by their contemporaries as, for example, a papal nuncio who reported that "the four women's convents [in Magdeburg] have remained truer to their beliefs and vows than the men's monasteries, who have almost all fallen away."[11] The nuns' determination had social and political as well as religious roots, however, for they recognized that as women they could have no office in any Protestant Church; the role of a pastor's wife was an unthinkable decrease in status for a woman of noble standing.

In some territories of central Germany, the nuns' firmness combined with other religious and political factors to allow many convents to survive for centuries as Catholic establishments within Protestant territories. In the bishoprics of Magdeburg and Halberstadt, which became Protestant, half of the female convents survived but only one-fifth of the monasteries.

[11] Quoted in Franz Schrader, *Ringen, Untergang und Überleben der katholischen Klöster in den Hochstiften Magdeburg und Halberstadt von der Reformation bis zum Westphälischen Frieden*, Katholisches Leben und Kirchenreform im Zeitalter der Glaubensspaltung, 37 (Münster, Aschendorff, 1977), p. 74. My translation.

Some of this was certainly due to the women's zeal noted by papal nuncio but also to the fact that religious and political authorities did not regard the women's institutions as being as great a threat as the men's. The marriage market for upper-class women also played a role. The cost of dowries was rising in early modern Germany, and even wealthy families could often not afford to marry off all their daughters to appropriate partners. As six noblemen who wrote to one of the dukes of Brunswick when he was contemplating closing the convents in his territory put it, "What would happen to our sisters' and relatives' honor and our reputation if they are forced to marry renegade monks, cobblers, and tailors?"[12] And these were Lutheran nobles!

Some convents also survived as religious institutions by accepting Lutheran theology except for its rejection of the monastic life. Anna von Stolberg, for example, was the abbess of the free imperial abbey of Quedlinburg and so governed a sizable territory including nine churches and two male monasteries. When she became Protestant in the 1540s, she made all priests swear to Luther's Augsburg Confession and turned her Franciscan monastery into an elementary school for both boys and girls, an interesting gender reversal of the usual pattern of male authorities transforming female convents into schools or using convent property to fund (male, of course) scholars at universities. She continued to receive both imperial and papal privileges, for Catholic authorities were unwilling to cut off support from what was, at any rate, still a *convent*. She was also not uniformly criticized by Lutheran leaders, however, who emphasized that she was, at any rate, *Lutheran*. Quedlinburg was not the only abbey in this situation. At least fourteen Lutheran convents in the relatively small territory of Brunswick/Lüneburg survived into the nineteenth century, most of which are still religious establishments for unmarried women today.

It is difficult to determine how many convents throughout the empire were able to survive as either Catholic or Protestant institutions because their existence was, in some ways, an embarrassment to secular and religious authorities attempting to enforce a policy of religious uniformity. Many of the urban convents in south Germany, such as those in Strasbourg and Nuremberg, fought disbanding as long as they could, despite being forced to listen to daily sermons, being denied confessors and Catholic ceremonies, and even having residents forcibly dragged out by their families. (The few male monasteries that actually opposed the

---

[12] Quoted in Johann Karl Seidemann, *Dr. Jacob Schenk, der vermeintlicher Antinomer, Freibergs Reformator* (Leipzig, C. Hinrichs'sche, 1875), Appendix 7, p. 193. My translation.

Reformation were simply ordered shut and their residents banished from the territory, an action that could not be used against convents because their residents were usually the daughters of local families and would have nowhere outside the territory to go.) Finally, urban authorities often gave up their direct attacks and simply forbade the taking in of new novices so that the convents slowly died out. A few also followed the central German pattern of becoming Protestant; one convent in Ulm, for example, survived as a Protestant institution until the nineteenth century.

The distinction between Protestant and Catholic that is so important in understanding the religious and intellectual history of sixteenth-century Europe may have ultimately been less important to the women who lived in convents or other communal groups than the distinction between their pattern of life and that of the majority of laywomen. Evidence from convents in Brunswick and Augsburg indicates that Protestant and Catholic women lived together quite peacefully for decades, protected by the walls of their convent from the religious conflicts surrounding them. Women in the Netherlands and England, denied the possibility of continuing in their convents, continued to live together, letting their formal religious affiliation remain a matter of speculation, both for contemporaries and for historians. The Protestant championing of marriage and family life, which some nuns accepted with great enthusiasm as a message of liberation from the convent, was viewed by others as a negation of the value of the life they had been living; they thus did all in their power to continue in their chosen path.

The Catholic Reformation

The response of the Catholic Church to the Protestant Reformation is often described as two interrelated movements: one, a Counter-Reformation, which attempted to win territory and people back to loyalty to Rome and prevent further spread of Protestant ideas, and the other a reform of abuses and problems within the Catholic Church that had been recognized as problems by many long before the Protestant Reformation. Thus, the Catholic Reformation was both a continuation of medieval reform movements and a new crusade. Women were actively involved in both movements, but their actions were generally judged more acceptable when they were part of a reform drive; even more than the medieval crusades, the fight against Protestants was to be a masculine affair.

The masculine nature of the Counter-Reformation was intimately related to one of the key aspects of church reform – an enforcement of cloistering for women. Reforms of the church beginning with the

Gregorian in the eleventh century had all emphasized the importance of the control of female sexuality and the inappropriateness of women religious being in contact with lay society; cloistering was a key part of the restrictions on Beguines in the fourteenth century and of the fifteenth-century reform of the convents. The problem became even more acute after the Protestant Reformation, for numerous women in Europe felt God had called them to oppose Protestants directly through missionary work or to carry out the type of active service to the world in schools and hospitals that the Franciscans, Dominicans, and the new orders like the Jesuits were making increasingly popular with men. For example, Angela Merici founded the Company of St. Ursula in Brescia, Italy. The Company was a group of lay single women and widows dedicated to serving the poor, the ill, orphans, and war victims, earning their own living through teaching or weaving. Merici received papal approval in 1535, for the pope saw this as a counterpart to the large number of men's lay confraternities and societies that were springing up in Italy as part of the movement to reform the church.

Similar groups of laywomen dedicated to charitable service began to spring up in other cities of Italy, Spain, and France, and in 1541, Isabel Roser decided to go one step further and ask for papal approval for an order of religious women with a similar mission. Roser had been an associate of Ignatius Loyola, the founder of the Jesuits, in Barcelona. She saw her group as a female order of Jesuits that, like the Jesuits, would not be cut off from the world but would devote itself to education, care of the sick, and assistance to the poor and, in so doing, win converts back to Catholicism. This was going too far, however. Loyola was horrified at the thought of religious women in constant contact with laypeople, and Pope Paul III refused to grant his approval. Despite this, her group continued to grow in Rome and in the Netherlands, where they spread Loyola's teaching through the use of the Jesuit catechism.

The Council of Trent, the church council that met between 1545 and 1563 to define what Catholic positions would be on matters of doctrine and discipline, reaffirmed the necessity of cloister for all women religious and called for an end to open monasteries and other uncloistered communities. Enforcement of this decree came slowly, however, for several reasons. First, women's communities themselves fought or ignored it. Followers of Isabel Roser, for example, were still active into the seventeenth century, for in 1630 Pope Urban VIII published a bull to suppress them and reported that they were building convents and choosing abbesses and rectors. The residents of some of Roser's communities and other convents that fought strict cloistering were often from wealthy urban families who could pressure church officials. Second, church officials themselves recognized the value of the services performed by such communities, particularly in the area of girls' education and care of the sick. Well after Trent, Charles Borromeo, a reforming archbishop in Milan, invited in members of the Company of St. Ursula and transformed the group from one of laywomen into one of religious who lived communally, although they still were not cloistered. From Milan, the Ursulines spread throughout the rest of Italy and into France and began to focus completely on the education of girls. They became so popular that noble families began to send their daughters to Ursuline houses for an education, and girls from wealthy families became Ursulines themselves.

The very success of the Ursulines led to the enforcement of cloistering, however, as well as other Tridentine decrees regulating women religious. Wealthy families were uncomfortable with the fact that because Ursulines did not take solemn vows, their daughters who had joined communities could theoretically leave at any time and make a claim on family inheritance. (Solemn vows bound one permanently to a religious establishment and made an individual legally dead in the secular world.) Gradually, the Ursuline houses in France and Italy were ordered to accept cloistering, take solemn vows, and put themselves under the authority of their local bishop, thus preventing any movement or cooperation between houses. They were still allowed to teach girls but now only within the confines of a convent. Some houses fought this as long as they could, although others accepted cloistering willingly, having fully internalized Church teachings that the life of a cloistered nun was the most worthy in the eyes of God.

Extraordinary circumstances occasionally led church leadership to relax its restrictions but only to a point. The situation of English Catholics under Protestant rulers was viewed as a special case, and a few women gained approval to go on their own as missionaries there. One of these was Luisa de Carvajal y Mendoza (1566–1614), a Spanish noblewoman who opposed her family's wishes and neither married nor entered a convent. She went to London and spoke openly about converting to the Catholic faith in shops and streets, writing later that people said, "I was some Roman Catholic priest dressed like a woman so as to better persuade people of my religion." For this she was jailed several times and "while in jail I spoke about religion much more than I had out of it."[13] Paul V, pope from 1605 to 1621, was relatively open to female initiatives and in 1616 granted Mary Ward, who had run a school for English Catholic girls in exile in the Spanish Netherlands, provisional approval for her Institute of the Blessed Virgin Mary. She wanted women in her Institute

---

[13] Elizabeth Rhodes, ed. and trans, *This Tight Embrace: Luisa de Carvajal y Mendoza (1566– 1614)* (Milwaukee: Marquette University Press, 2000), p. 29.

to return to England as missionaries, for "it seems that the female sex also in its own measure, should and can ... undertake something more than ordinary in this great common spiritual undertaking."[14] She openly modeled the Institute on the Jesuits and began to minister to the poor and sick in London, visiting Catholic prisoners and teaching in private homes.

The reports of Ward's successes proved too much for church leadership, and she was ordered to stop all missionary work, for "it was never heard in the Church that women should discharge the Apostolic Office."[15] Undaunted, Ward shifted her emphasis, and the Institute began to open houses in many cities throughout Europe in which women who took no formal vows operated free schools for both boys and girls, teaching them reading, writing, and a trade. The Institute needed constant donations, for which Ward and her associates traveled extensively and corresponded with secular and church authorities. Ward recognized that this public solicitation of funds was necessary for her schools to flourish and so asked that the Institute never be under the control of a bishop but report directly to the pope. She also realized that this sort of public role for women was something new in Catholicism, in her words, "a course never thought of before," but she stressed that there "is no such difference between men and women that women may not do great things as we have seen by the example of many saints."[16] Her popularity and independence proved too much for the Church hierarchy, however, and the year after the bull was published against Roser, Ward's schools and most of her houses were ordered closed; Ward herself was imprisoned by the Inquisition in Munich. "Jesuitesses," as Ward's Institute was termed by her enemies, were not to be tolerated, and similar other uncloistered communities of women, such as the Visitation, started to serve the poor by Jeanne de Chantal, a French laywoman, and Francis de Sales, a priest, were ordered to accept cloistering or be closed.

Thus, the only active apostolate left open to religious women was the instruction of girls and that only within the convent. No nuns were sent to the foreign missions for any public duties, although once colonies were established in the New World and Asia, cloistered convents quickly followed. The exclusion of women from what were judged the most exciting and important parts of the Catholic Reformation – countering Protestants and winning new converts – is reflected in the relative lack of women

[14] Quoted in Elizabeth Rapley, *The Dévotes: Women and Church in Seventeenth-Century France* (Montreal and Kingston, McGill-Queen's University Press, 1990), p. 29.

[15] Ibid., p. 31.

[16] Quoted in Marie B. Rowlands, "Recusant Women 1560–1640," in Mary Prior (ed.), *Women in English Society, 1500–1800* (London and New York, Methuen, 1985), p. 173.

from the sixteenth century who were made saints. Luisa de Carvajal was raised to the status of Venerable, the first rung on the ladder to sanctity, but only 18.1 percent of those who reached the top of the ladder from the sixteenth century were women, whereas 27.7 percent of those from the fifteenth century had been female. Most of the women who did achieve sainthood followed a very different path, one of mysticism or reforming existing orders, a path in some ways set by the most famous religious woman of the sixteenth century, Teresa of Avila.

Teresa was a Carmelite nun who took her vows at twenty and then spent the next twenty-five years in relative obscurity in her convent at Avila. During this time of external inaction, she went through great spiritual turmoil, similar to that experienced by Loyola and Luther, but came to feel the presence of God not through founding a new denomination or new order but by mystical union with the divine. She went through extremes of exaltation and melancholy, suffering physical effects such as illness, trances, and paralysis. Her mystical path was not one of extreme mortification of the flesh but rather of prayer, purification of the spirit, and assistance to the women of her convent. At other times or places, she might have spent her life unnoticed, but this was Spain during the sixteenth century, when the Spanish crown was using its own Inquisition to stamp out any sign of humanist, Lutheran, or other deviant ideas. Other nuns and *beatas* (laywomen who felt a sense of religious vocation) had been accused of heresy and questioned, so Teresa's confessors ordered her not only to describe her mystical experiences in writing but also to reflect on them and try to explain why she thought these were happening to her. Although Teresa complained about having to do this, she also clearly developed a sense of passion about her writing, for she edited and refined her work, transforming it into a full spiritual autobiography. Like many of the authors discussed in Chapter 5, she manipulated stereotypes of femininity, conceding women's weakness, powerlessness, and inferiority so often that it appears ironic, and using informal language both to appeal to a wider audience and deflect charges that she was teaching theology.

Like Angela Merici and Mary Ward, Teresa also yearned for some kind of active ministry and explicitly chafed at the restrictions on her because of her sex, as the quotation at the beginning of this chapter makes clear. In part, she solved this by interpreting her prayers and those of other nuns as public actions: "we shall be fighting for Him [God] even though we are very cloistered."[17] When she was fifty-two, she also

---

[17] *The Way of Perfection*, translated and quoted in Jodi Bilinkoff, *The Avila of St. Teresa: Religious Reform in a Sixteenth-Century City* (Ithaca, Cornell University Press, 1989), p. 136.

began to reform her Carmelite order, attempting to return it to its original standards of spirituality and poverty. To do this, she traveled all around Spain, founding new convents and writing meditations, instructions for monastic administrators, and hundreds of letters, provoking the wrath or annoyance of some church authorities; a papal nuncio called her a "restless gadabout, a disobedient and obstinate woman, who invented wicked doctrines and called them devotion . . . and taught others against the commands of St. Paul, who had forbidden women to teach."[18]

Teresa's success in reforming the Carmelites won her more supporters than critics within the church, however, for – unlike Angela Merici and Mary Ward – she did not advocate institutionalized roles for women outside of the convent. Her frustration at men's alterations of Christ's view of women did not lead her to break with the male Church hierarchy, and the words quoted at the beginning of this chapter expressing that frustration were expunged from her works by church censors. The version of Teresa that was presented for her canonization proceedings, held shortly after her death, was one that fit her into the acceptable model of woman mystic and reformer, assuming a public role only when ordered to do so by her confessor or superior. Only recently have we begun to understand that Teresa thought of herself as a Counter-Reformation fighter, viewing the new religious houses she established as answers to the Protestant takeover of Catholic churches elsewhere in Europe.

It is easy to view Teresa as a complete anomaly, but in many ways she fits into a pattern of women's religious experience that was quite common in Spain, the Spanish colonies, and Italy. Other nuns also composed spiritual autobiographies and shared them with others; other nuns and some *beatas* acted as reformers and social critics, combining mysticism and activism. Their visions and ecstatic trances sometimes led to their being investigated by the Inquisition, which was also concerned about their modesty and chastity. Diego Pérez de Valdivia, a professor at the University of Barcelona, complained that some *beatas* had "much freedom and little modesty" and were easily tempted by "the devil, the world, and their own flesh."[19] Women who were religiously scrupulous, whether nuns or laywomen, confessed often and developed intense emotional relationships with their confessor. By the seventeenth century, church authorities recognized that this emotional intimacy might lead to physical intimacy, especially as confession was to entail a detailed examination

---

[18] Translated and quoted in Alison Weber, *Teresa of Avila and the Rhetoric of Femininity* (Princeton, NJ, Princeton University Press, 1990), pp. 3–4.

[19] Diego Pérez de Valdivia, *Aviso de gente recogida* (1585), translated and quoted in Stephen Haliczer, *Sexuality in the Confessional: A Sacrament Profaned* (New York, Oxford University Press, 1996), p. 111.

of one's conscience and a minute accounting of sins, including sexual sins. Thus, they paid close attention to the relationship between women and their confessors and sometimes excluded nuns and women under forty from a priest's first license to hear confessions. These relationships led sometimes to charges of rape, seduction, or solicitation on the part of the priest or to charges of fraud and falsifying miracles on the part of the women. Despite examples of such "false saints," however, many women retained their reputations as, in the words of the time, "living saints." They resolved local conflicts and were sought for advice on personal, political, and religious matters, gaining power over political leaders, who in turn used the approval of such women as an endorsement of their policies and an enhancement of their prestige.

The respect accorded to Teresa and other "holy women" did not lead to any lessening of the call for the cloistering of religious women, however. Their separation from the world lessened the ability of women's communities to solicit funds, and the post-Tridentine emphasis on the sacraments meant that most benefactors preferred to give donations to a male house whose residents could say Mass. Thus, many female houses grew increasingly impoverished or more interested in the size of the dowry of a prospective entrant than the depth of her religious vocation. By the seventeenth century, convents in many parts of Europe were both shrinking and becoming increasingly aristocratic; in Venice, for example, nearly 60 percent of all women of the upper class joined convents. The long-range effect of cloistering was not an increase but a decrease in spiritual vigor.

The effects of the Catholic Reformation on religious women were thus to a great degree restrictive. What about laywomen in Catholic Europe? Here, the balance sheet is more mixed, in large part because of the ambivalent attitude of church leadership about marriage. Catholic authors did begin to publish manuals for husbands and wives to counteract those written by Protestants and emphasized their continued view of the sacramental nature of marriage. On the other hand, virginity continued to be valued over marriage, and spouses who took mutual vows of chastity within a marriage or left marriage to enter cloisters were praised. Catholic authors criticized the veneration of Anne, seeing the intercession of an older woman as no longer an appropriate avenue to God; the depiction of an all-female trinity disappeared from religious pamphlets, replaced by illustrations of Mary with both of her parents. Mary herself was also portrayed differently. Up to the early sixteenth century, she was generally shown as an adult woman, capably caring for the infant Jesus while an older Joseph hovered in the background or was not shown at all. By the late sixteenth century, she was depicted as an adolescent girl, clearly under the protection of a strong and vigorous Joseph, who was now a much more dominant figure. Joseph replaced Anne as the fully human individual most often held up for emulation, and his cult grew in popularity with the spread of the Catholic Reformation.

In Italian cities, Catholic reformers began to open institutional asylums for repentant prostitutes (*convertite*) and also asylums for women who were felt to be at risk of turning to prostitution or losing their honor, such as orphans, poor unmarried women, and widows, or those whose marriages had failed, called *malmaritate*. As we saw in Chapter 2, women in these institutions were taught basic skills with which to support themselves, usually weaving, and given large doses of religious and moral instruction. The drive to cloister all women's communities affected them as well, although some were able to remain uncloistered, with the residents even allowed to keep any wages earned because it was seen as so important to prevent the women from landing back on the streets. In Catholic theory, marriage was indissoluble, but in practice the *malmaritate* houses offered women who had been abandoned or victimized by their husbands a respectable place to live, an alternative that was unavailable in Protestant areas.

No Catholic author went so far as to recommend that Catholic wives leave Protestant husbands, but in practice Catholic authorities put fewer blocks in the path of a woman who did. Protestant city councils in Germany were suspicious of any woman who asked to be admitted to citizenship independently and questioned her intently about her marital status. Catholic cities such as Munich were more concerned about whether the woman who wanted to immigrate had always been a good Catholic than whether she was married, particularly if she wanted to enter a convent. Catholic writers were also more open in their support of women working to convert their Protestant or indifferent husbands than were Continental Protestant writers, or even of daughters converting or inspiring their parents. "Young girls will reform their families, their families will reform their provinces, their provinces will reform the world."[20] It was during this period that the confessional box was used more widely, for the Counter-Reformation church saw private confession as a way to combat heresy. Catholic women married to Protestant men could find in the priest hearing their confession a man who could give them a source of authority to overrule or disobey their husbands. The husbands recognized this, for court records in Venice indicate that men charged with heresy often beat their Catholic wives after they came home from confession.

England and Ireland provided the most dramatic example of the importance of Catholic women's domestic religious activities. In 1559, Queen

[20] Quoted in Rapley, *Dèvotes*, p. 157.

Elizabeth ordered that everyone attend services in the Anglican church or be penalized with fines or imprisonment. Many English and Irish Catholics outwardly conformed, but others did not, becoming what were termed "recusants." Among these were a large percentage of women, who posed a special problem for royal officials. A single woman or widow found guilty of recusancy could be fined, but a married women, according to common law, controlled no property; imprisoning her would disrupt her family life and harm her husband, who might not even share her religious convictions. The Crown tried a variety of tactics to solve the problem, but only the most adamant Protestant men were willing to back measures that would allow a wife to be legally responsible as an individual for her religious choices and put her husband's property at risk. Catholic husbands often outwardly conformed and attended services, leaving their wives to arrange for private masses held in the home or even to shelter illegal Catholic missionaries. A few women, such as Margaret Clitherow and Anne Line, were executed for their Catholic faith, but most recusant women were able to avoid strict punishment. Because of this, whereas Continental Catholicism was becoming increasingly parish-oriented after the Council of Trent, Catholicism in England and Ireland grew increasingly domestic. As stories were collected about the persecution of Catholics, a new type of Catholic heroine emerged – capable, benevolent, intelligent, and in many ways crafty in her dealings with authorities – an idealization but one modeled on real recusant women, for judges and the Privy Council frequently complained about the influence such women had on their husbands, children, and servants.

Eastern Orthodoxy

Orthodox Christianity in eastern Europe did not experience a permanent division in the sixteenth century as did Western Christianity, although during the seventeenth century, a number of reformers emerged in the Russian Orthodox Church. Like both Protestants and Catholics who were their inspiration, they wanted to strengthen the role of the clergy in parish life and rid popular piety of its – to their eyes – non-Christian elements and immoral excesses. Church ceremonies became an increasingly important part of weddings, and confession and penance were required. The consent of the spouses and their parents were required for a valid marriage, and divorce was allowed for incompatibility, drunkenness, and violence as well as adultery, although it was frowned on, as was remarriage. Modest reforms in church liturgy, prayers, and rituals advocated by some Orthodox leaders – which would make them more like those of Western Christianity – were violently opposed by those who wanted to stay with traditional practices, termed "Old Believers." Old Believers were convinced that the reforms were the work of the Antichrist and that the Apocalypse was at hand. Consequently, they saw little purpose in marriage and procreation, although they moderated this position when it became apparent that the end of the world was more distant than they had originally calculated. Because they cast the tsar and the government as the "spirit of the Antichrist" and rejected their authority, they were subjected to persecution, often severe. Some Old Believers chose the route of martyrdom, usually by self-immolation; others fled to the fringes of the enormous Russian Empire or even abroad; still others found ways of accommodation, politically and ideologically, with the Russian state.

The modest adoption of Western practices that so horrified Old Believers paled in comparison to those demanded in the late seventeenth century by Tsar Peter I (ruled 1682–1725), who became known as Peter the Great. Peter was intent on modernizing and Westernizing Russia to make it a larger and more powerful state. To this end, he engaged in nearly constant warfare and so favored anything that would increase the Russian population. Peter was convinced that unhappy marriages produced fewer children, so in 1722, he added his voice to that of the Orthodox Church forbidding forced marriages at all social levels. Landlords were not to force their serfs to marry against their wishes – a common practice despite church opposition – and elite women were to appear in public and have a voice in the choice of their spouse. The state established foundling homes and encouraged desperate mothers to bring their newborns there, instead of abandoning their babies or practicing infanticide, which was criminalized. Peter regarded marriages between social equals as preferable and so required spouses to be of the same social class. Religious differences, on the other hand, were not an issue; over the objections of the church, he allowed marriages between spouses of different Christian denominations, demanding only that the children be baptized into the Orthodox faith. Because Peter saw no purpose in wasting human resources on monastic life, he forbade physically capable men and women of childbearing years from taking vows.

Although the church and state of Peter's era issued many new regulations, it proved much more difficult to alter ingrained attitudes and behavior. Nobles successfully lobbied Peter's successors to undo some of his laws concerning parental consent to marriage and effectively prevented their serfs from marrying. Rules concerning entrance into monasteries were relaxed, and displaced middle-aged women in particular sought this alternative. Orthodox convents continued to house a wide range of women, as they had in the Middle Ages, and their abbesses were powerful individuals. The spiritual life in these convents is only beginning to be studied, and we will no doubt learn more in the future about their residents' religious aims and ideas.

Protestant Women in the Seventeenth and Eighteenth Centuries

In contrast to eastern Europe, we know a great deal about women's religious ideas in western Europe during the seventeenth and eighteenth centuries. From the late sixteenth century, religious and political leaders worked together in most countries of Europe to create state churches that were powerful institutions with rigid and complex theological systems. By the seventeenth century, however, large numbers of people thought the established churches, both Protestant and Catholic, had lost their spiritual vigor and encouraged empty conformism. *Spiritual Conversation between a Mother and Child about True Christianity* (1650) transforms a literary form normally supportive of traditional piety, the conversation between parent and child, into a bitter satirical poem. The mother first asks, "'What did you learn about salvation and the Bible in church today?' 'Nothing,' the child answers. 'About the prophets and Revelation?' 'Nothing.'" The mother then launches into a harsh critique of the clergy's monopoly of religious discussion despite their lack of spiritual understanding:

> No one is allowed to contradict him
> Even if he says that crooked is straight
> And black is white. He must be right.[21]

The author of this poem, Anna Owen Hoyer (1584–1655), attacked the clergy in an established state church for pride, greed, and empty formalism in many of her writings. She called on laypeople to develop practices that met their spiritual needs better than the state churches did. Many people agreed and turned to groups that emphasized personal conversion, direct communication with God, and moral regeneration. Some of these groups, such as the Levellers who advocated communal ownership of property during the English Civil War, survived only briefly and had little long-term impact. Others, such as the Quakers, became involved in social and political changes in both Europe and the European colonies.

---

[21] Gottfried Arnold, *Unpartheiische Kirchen und Ketzerhistorie* ... (Frankfurt, Fritschens sel. Erber, 1729), p. 106. My translation.

Others, such as Moravians in central Europe and Methodists in Britain, became institutionalized in separate denominations. Still others, such as Jansenists in the Netherlands and France and pietists in Germany and Scandinavia, shaped the existing Protestant and Catholic churches.

Many groups regarded personal religious devotion as more important than theological training or holding an official clerical position in determining who was properly called by God, so that women often played more important roles than they did in the official state churches. Although few of these groups explicitly broke with Christian traditions that privileged men, female followers sometimes used the language of religious texts and the examples of pious women who preceded them to subvert or directly challenge male directives. A few of these groups were inspired by or even founded by women. Antoinette Bourignon (1616–80), a French mystic, had a small group of followers, although she refused to form any official group, saying that the divisions within Christianity were signs of the coming end of the world. She believed spiritual rebirth to be more important than baptism so that Jews and Muslims might also be blessed and resurrected. Jane Leade (1623–1704) wrote that true religious knowledge came only through turning inward and finding one's own inner light. She formed a group of like-minded people called the Philadelphia ("love of wisdom") Society, urging them to seek the "virgin wisdom of God" and not go "whoring after Lord Reason."

To their adherents and supporters, the actions of female leaders were heroic signs of God operating through the least of his creatures. To their opponents, the women's actions were proof of a group's demonic or at least misguided nature. Among the "errors, heresies, blasphemies and pernicious practices of the sectaries," described by Thomas Edwards in *Gangraena* (London, 1646), a long tract against those who opposed state churches, was the fact that they allowed women to preach. Johann Feustking, a German theologian, turned his attention entirely to women in *Gynaeceum Haeretico Fanaticum* (Frankfurt and Leipzig, 1704), spending 700 pages describing, as his full title reads, the "false prophetesses, quacks, fanatics and other sectarian and frenzied female persons through whom God's church is disturbed." Individuals claiming to be divinely inspired, whether female or male, were "enthusiasts" whose practices, in the eyes of their more restrained critics, were both theologically suspect and politically dangerous. Many women and the groups they were associated with were driven from place to place seeking more tolerant political authorities. Anna Hoyer was forced to flee religious persecution, as was Antoinette Bourignon, who moved from France to Flanders to Germany and finally to the Netherlands, which provided a refuge for

Philadelphians as well. The Netherlands was the most tolerant part of Europe and so was also the most common place of publication for the works of these women and those of other radical religious thinkers.

Disagreements about the state church were one of the factors leading to the English Civil War (1640–60), during which the monarch was deposed and executed, an interim government established, and then the monarchy restored. England had become Protestant in the sixteenth century, but many people grew increasingly dissatisfied with the Church of England (called "Anglican") and wanted to "purify" it of what they saw as vestiges of Roman Catholicism, such as a hierarchical structure of bishops and elaborate ceremonies. These "Puritans," as they came to be known, were an important force in the opposition to the king. With the restoration of the monarchy and the reestablishment of the Anglican Church in 1660, many English Puritans immigrated, and they took their ideas about gender and sexuality as well as theology with them to Continental Europe and, ultimately, to North America.

Although most Puritan writers and preachers did not break with Anglicans or Continental Protestants on the need for wifely obedience or women's secondary status, certain aspects of Puritan theology and practice prepared women for a more active role. All believers, male and female, were to engage in spiritual introspection and, in particular, to focus on their experience of conversion. This experience was an indication that one was among the elect and, in more established Puritan communities such as those of New England, became a requirement for membership in a congregation. A particularly dramatic conversion could give one a certain amount of power, especially if it resulted in the healing of an illness or a continuing experience of divine revelation. Women's conversion narratives are often very personal and physical, such as that of Sarah Wight published as *The Exceeding Riches of Grace Advanced* (London, 1647): "Now I have my desire; I desired nothing but a crucified Christ and I have him; a crucified Christ, a naked Christ; I have him and nothing else . . . *I am so full of the Creator, that I now can take in none of the Creature. I am filled with heavenly Manna.*"[22] Although Wight appears in some ways as passive, she is discussing her own spiritual development publicly in a way that was new for Protestant women; nuns were the only other women whose spiritual growth and trials had been viewed as all important, and not even St. Teresa's autobiography made it into print during her lifetime.

Puritans shared something else with St. Teresa: the conviction that prayer was an active force that could influence state affairs. Puritan

---

[22] Quoted in Barbara Ritter Dailey, "The Visitation of Sarah Wight: Holy Carnival and the Revolution of the Saints in Civil War London," *Church History* 55 (1986), p. 447.

women (and men) privately and publicly prayed for certain political changes and were firmly convinced that prayer aided one's family, community, and political allies. For Puritans, who had rejected the efficacy of exorcism, group prayer was the most powerful weapon in cases of possession, and many tracts report on the efficacy of such prayers against that worst of enemies, Satan.

Women's prayers and conversion narratives often grew into more extended prophecies in seventeenth-century England, some of which were described by others (often hostile to the woman or the message) and some of which were published by the women themselves. Lady Eleanor Douglas, for example, published thirty-seven pamphlets during her life, despite frequent imprisonments for sedition. Female prophets were occasionally criticized for speaking out publicly on political and religious matters, but they had Old Testament and classical precedents for what they were doing and were usually viewed in the way they viewed themselves – as mouthpieces of God as, in the words of some, "impregnated with the Holy Spirit." Women who went beyond prophecy to actual preaching also emphasized the strength of their calling, but this was not enough in the eyes of most observers to justify such a clear break with the Deutero-Pauline injunction forbidding women to teach. It is difficult to know how common female preaching actually was during the civil war decades, for most reports of it come from extremely hostile observers such as Thomas Edwards, who were in turn criticized for making up some of their accounts. Women tended to preach spontaneously at informal or clandestine meetings, and their listeners never thought to record the content of their sermons, so it is unclear how much sustained influence they exerted.

Women clearly did have an impact on the spread of more radical religious ideas through two other activities: organizing what were known as "gathered" churches in their own homes and publishing pamphlets. Puritan women had often organized prayer meetings and Bible readings in their houses during the early part of the seventeenth century and after the Restoration (which restored the Anglican Church as the official religion of England when it restored the monarchy) continued to open their homes to Baptists, Presbyterians, Quakers, and other groups. Post-Restoration commentators belittled such groups by pointing out the large number of women they attracted, although again we have few objective records with which to judge the actual gender balance. Political and religious pamphlets authored by women appeared most frequently during the two decades (1641–60) when censorship was not rigorously enforced, as part of a more general explosion of pamphlet literature by a wide range of authors. Although most female authors deprecate their own abilities and describe themselves as "instruments of God's power," they clearly intended their works to be read by men and felt no limits as to subject matter, delving into complex theological and doctrinal matters and directly challenging the actions of the king or Parliament.

Such actions came to an abrupt end with the Restoration, and most of the radical groups in which women had participated died out. The most important exception to this was the Society of Friends, commonly known as the Quakers, who had been the most supportive of women's independent religious actions throughout the decades of the civil war. George Fox, the founder of the Quakers, did not advocate women's social or political equality. Separate women's meetings, first in England and then in British North America, oversaw the readiness of candidates for marriage, cared for the poor and orphans, upheld the maintenance of decorous standards of dress, and at times ruled on other moral issues. Quakers taught that the spirit of God did not differentiate between men and women and advocated qualities for all believers similar to those that most Protestants stressed for women: humility, self-denial, piety, devotion, modesty. These were not to make one weak in the face of persecution, however, and Quakers were the most viciously persecuted of all the radical groups, perhaps because they were the most adamant in proclaiming their beliefs. Quaker women preached throughout England and the English colonies in the New World and occasionally elsewhere. They were whipped and imprisoned for preaching, refusing to pay tithes or take oaths, or holding meetings in their houses; no special treatment was accorded women for age, illness, pregnancy, or the presence of young children. Quaker women also published a large number of pamphlets, most of them apocalyptic prophecies or "encouragements" for co-believers, and wrote spiritual autobiographies, which are one of the few sources we have from the seventeenth century written by middle- or lower-class women.

Margaret Fell Fox (1614–1702), who eventually married George Fox after years of organizing, preaching, visiting prisoners, and being imprisoned herself for her Quaker beliefs, published *Women's Speaking Justified* in 1669, which argued that Paul's prohibition of women's preaching had only been meant for the "busie-bodies and tatlers" of Corinth and provided a host of biblical examples of women who publicly taught others. Fell did not argue for women's equality in secular matters, but for Quakers spiritual matters were more important anyway. The women's meetings she organized gave many women the opportunity to speak in public and to engage in philanthropic activities for persons outside of their own families. Although Quakers as a group became increasingly apolitical in the eighteenth century, social action by Quaker women continued; many of the leaders of the abolitionist and women's rights movements in

nineteenth-century America were women who had been brought up as Quakers.

The Quakers were influential but never numerous. A much larger movement, and one that did not break totally with state churches, was pietism. Different pietists had different specific aims but, in general, pietists wanted to build a meaningful religious fellowship *within* the state church through devotion, Bible study, moral discipline, and personal religious experiences. The history of pietism is often written as the history of its male leaders, but in many ways it was a grassroots movement of laypeople who met in prayer circles and conventicles, among whom were many women. Johanna Eleonora Petersen (1644–1724) organized several pietist circles and wrote a huge number of tracts, including a commentary on the Book of Revelations. Erdmuthe von Zinzendorf (1700–56) was largely responsible for the financial security and day-to-day operations of her husband's colony of Moravian Brethren at Herrnhut in Germany. Count Nicholas von Zinzendorf had originally wanted the Herrnhutters to be simply a group within the Lutheran Church that encouraged deeper religious sensibilities, but they became instead a separate body. Zinzendorf was banished from Germany for more than ten years and traveled to America and England to set up Moravian congregations. During this time, Erdmuthe handled missionary work in Denmark and Livonia, established orphanages, and ran the home colony; her dowry and family money provided most of the support for all Herrnhutter activities.

The strong faith of Moravian missionaries made a deep impact on a young English pastor, John Wesley (1703–91), who later broke with the Anglican Church and founded Methodism, a form of pietism that eventually grew into the largest Protestant denomination in the English-speaking world. John Wesley's mother Susanna held unauthorized meetings with more than 200 in attendance at which she read sermons and discussed religious issues. Both men and women in Methodism were encouraged to give public testimony of their conversion experiences and spiritual life and to "exhort" others to faith and repentance. By the 1760s, Sarah Crosby (1729–1804) and Mary Bosanquet Fletcher (1739–1815) had, with John Wesley's reluctant approval, gone from less formal "exhorting" to being leaders of Methodist "classes," weekly meetings at which members were to give an account of their actions and discipleship. Methodism was ridiculed for allowing female preaching and often criticized in gendered language – as "silly women" – because of women's active role and because the testimony of all followers seemed overly emotional and sentimental. After John Wesley's death in 1791, Methodists became increasingly hostile toward a female preaching ministry and, from 1803, women were restricted to addressing other women and could do so only under strict conditions. Some women continued to preach anyway, however, particularly in rural, frontier, and mission areas.

Like the Methodists, the Moravians also became less open to women's activities. In 1764, they explicitly forbade women from all governing offices except the most minor, noting that this would help them control their "desire for [masculine] power [*Herrnsucht*]." Zinzendorf himself criticized Erdmuthe for her independence, which he called pride; his second wife was a much younger woman who had long been his traveling companion. Pietist and Methodist historians who did include women such as Johanna Petersen, Erdmuthe von Zinzendorf, and Susanna Wesley in their histories were careful to describe them as "helpmates."

Shakers – officially the United Society of Believers in Christ's Second Appearing – had no such reservations. They first began in the 1740s around Manchester in England and, in 1758, Ann Lee (1736–84) joined and became the leader. Lee was a visionary and mystic whose followers regarded her as the second coming of Christ; God, in their eyes, was both female and male, so Christ's second coming would have to be in a female body. Her visions also told her that sexuality was depraved, and her followers swore celibacy and chastity. She and her followers were severely persecuted and, in 1774, she led eight of them to the American Colonies; persecution continued, and she died as the result of beatings. Despite – or perhaps because of – their advocacy of celibacy, the Shakers continued to win followers; at their peak, about 1830, American Shakers may have numbered 6,000 people.

The Shakers were not the only radical or pietist group to develop unusual ideas about sexuality or distinctive systems of marriage. Such groups did not regard marriage as a sacrament – most rejected the idea of sacraments completely – but they placed more emphasis on its spiritual nature than did Lutherans or Calvinists. Marriage was a covenant – a contract – between a man and a woman based on their membership in the body of believers and thus was linked to their redemption. Because of this, the group as a whole – or at least its leaders – should have a say in marital choice, broadening the circle of consent far beyond the parental consent required by Luther, Calvin, and other less radical reformers. Quakers who wished to marry had to produce a certificate stating that both parties were Quaker or risk expulsion. Moravians in Pennsylvania were segregated by sex until marriage; when a man wished to marry, he came to the Elders' Conference, which proposed a possible spouse. Three colored ballots standing for "yes," "no," and "wait" were placed in a box, and one was drawn, which was regarded as the "Savior's decision."

Ideas such as this horrified most Protestant authorities (and Catholic, for that matter), who regarded male-headed households in which fathers controlled their wives, children, and servants as structures established by God and believed that church and state should act together to enforce morality and order. Unusual structures of marriage joined women's leadership as one more reason to ridicule and oppose such groups.

Catholic Women in the Seventeenth and Eighteenth Centuries

Catholic women as well as Protestant were active in the seventeenth and eighteenth centuries, and their contributions were similarly criticized, mocked, or minimized. As we saw earlier, enclosure was increasingly enforced in women's religious communities, and Isabel Roser in Italy and Mary Ward in England were blocked in their efforts.

Beginning in the later seventeenth century, however, laywomen in some parts of Europe were slowly able to create what had been so forcibly forbidden to religious women – a community of women with an active mission out in the world. The leader in this was the Daughters of Charity (now often called the Sisters of Charity) begun in 1633 by Vincent de Paul and Louise de Marillac. Although both founders privately thought of the group as a religious community, they realized that outwardly maintaining secular status was the only thing that would allow them to serve the poor and ill. The Daughters took no public vows, did not wear religious habits, and constantly stressed that they would work only where invited by a bishop or priest. This subversion of the rules was successful, for the Daughters of Charity received papal approval and served as the model for other women's communities that emphasized educating the poor or girls; by 1700, numerous teaching and charitable "congregations" were found throughout Catholic Europe. They explicitly used the Virgin Mary as their model, stressing that she, too, had served as a missionary when she had visited her cousin Elizabeth during Elizabeth's pregnancy with John the Baptist, revealing to Elizabeth that they would both give birth to extraordinary sons.

The Daughters of Charity and other congregations were often backed by larger women's religious confraternities, in which elite women supported a congregation financially or engaged in charitable works themselves. Such confraternities were patterned after the much more common men's confraternities that had been founded by Jesuits as a key part of both combating Protestantism and deepening Catholic spiritual life. Some of them were dedicated to spiritual practices with special meaning for women, such as saying the rosary. Congregations and confraternities provided women with companionship, devotional practices, and an outlet for their energies beyond the household. Huge numbers of women joined them in the seventeenth and eighteenth centuries, which certainly contributed to women's greater loyalty to the church in a period of growing secularism. During the French Revolution, women hid priests who refused to sign oaths of loyalty to the government, attended illegal worship services, and occasionally organized prayer meetings and processions.

Many Catholic women joined confraternities or engaged in charitable activities, but a few advocated a more interior form of devotion. Louise Françoise de la Vallière (1644–1710) was the mistress of Louis XIV during the 1660s, by whom she had four children. After she fell out of favor with the king and went through a near-fatal illness, she had a spiritual conversion and withdrew from Paris to a nearby Carmelite convent. She wrote a series of prayers to God repenting for her earlier life and presenting a model of redemption through direct mystical encounters, *Réflexions sur la miséricorde de Dieu.*

The best-known female mystic of this period was Jeanne-Marie Bouvier de la Mothe Guyon (1647–1717). Madame Guyon taught that one should try to lose one's individual soul in God, reaching inner peace through prayer and pure disinterested love of God, an idea generally termed "quietism." She felt herself called to spread this mystical method and, in 1685, she published *Moyen court et facile de faire oraison* ("Short and Easy Method of Prayer"). Her ideas attracted women and men, including high church officials such as Archbishop Fenelon, who wrote that he had learned more from her than any theologian. Madam Guyon was imprisoned several times on the orders of Bishop Bossuet, the most powerful conservative French cleric, who was particularly incensed that her quietism, detachment, and lack of concern for external religious structures took her in spiritual terms out of his power; if such ideas spread further, wrote Bossuet, they would lead to an intolerable lack of respect for authority. Her writings were placed on the Index of Forbidden Books, and although she always asserted she was submissive to the Catholic Church, after her death her ideas became better known among Protestants than Catholics. Her writings began to be published in Holland in the early eighteenth century, and in translation they became popular with Methodists in Britain and North America. They are available in paperback versions from many Christian publishers today, advertised for their guidance in prayer and spirituality, not as historical documents.

During the early seventeenth century, Angélique Arnauld (1591–1661), the abbess of Port-Royal convent, began a program of reforms in her convent that emphasized personal holiness and spiritual renewal. The abbey became the spiritual center of Jansenism in France, a movement based on the ideas of the Dutch theologian Cornelius Jansen, who advocated greater personal holiness, lay reading of and meditation on

Scripture, lay participation in church services, scrupulous attention to morality, and less frequent communion for the faithful. Such ideas lessened the role of the clergy, and two papal bulls in 1653 and 1656 condemned some of the ideas of Jansen. In 1661, King Louis XIV ordered all members of the French church to sign a statement indicating their adherence to the bulls. The nuns at Port-Royal refused, commenting that, as women, they were clearly not capable of making judgments about theological matters that learned men disagreed on; they pointed out that God's law (as stated in the letter of Timothy in the New Testament) ordered women to keep silent on matters of theology, and they were simply obeying this higher law rather than Louis's command. The nuns at Port-Royal may have learned how to use stereotypes about women's weakness and duty of obedience to their advantage from the writings of Teresa of Avila, whom Arnauld in particular greatly admired and who had been made a saint in 1622. The archbishop of Paris interrogated the women, exiled some to other convents, and put some under house arrest. A truce with the papacy quieted the debate for several decades, but in 1705, the Port-Royal nuns were ordered to accept another anti-Jansenist papal bull. They again refused and, in 1709, Louis XIV demolished the convent and banished the nuns to other houses.

The writings of the Port-Royal nuns became part of a body of Jansenist literature that continued to circulate, and the fight over Jansenism continued. Although some Jansenist priests fled France, Jansenist laity continued to hold underground prayer meetings. There is some evidence that women read and commented on Scripture at these meetings, and women were also imprisoned for distributing prohibited Jansenist literature. Jansenism continued to shape the religious life of many women in France, encouraging them not only to become literate but also to become frequent readers and to develop their children's spiritual lives through family devotions.

Jewish and Muslim Women's Religious Life

Judaism in the early modern period did not go through the same type of schism that Western Christianity did, but it did suffer from increasing repression, restriction, and, in some cases, outright prohibition. Jews thus gathered in cities that were less hostile, such as those of Italy and the Low Countries. In 1492, Ferdinand and Isabella of Spain ordered all Jews to leave Spain or convert, and during the next several centuries, those who converted and their descendants (termed "New Christians") were frequently targets of the Inquisition. Women as well as men were questioned, tortured, physically punished, and, in some cases, executed, leading Jews in other parts of Europe to make special efforts to help women of Jewish ancestry leave Spain and Portugal. Portuguese Jews in Amsterdam, for example, set up a special dowry fund in 1615 for poor women and girls from the Iberian peninsula who were willing to migrate to Amsterdam, readopt Judaism, and marry Jewish men, although women often had to wait ten years before enough money became available for them. Gracia Nasi (1510–69), who after fleeing Portugal ran her family business from Antwerp, Venice, Ferrara, and Constantinople, helped establish an "underground railway" to get Jews out of Portugal and Spain and organized a boycott against Ancona when that city began to persecute Jews. She supported rabbis and scholars and encouraged book publications; a number of Jewish scholarly works from the sixteenth century were dedicated to her.

Women were often particularly suspect in the eyes of Spanish authorities because they were responsible for religious rituals that took place in the home or that involved their own bodies, both more difficult to control than the public rituals that were the province of men. This was true not only in Spain but in all of Europe and in the Spanish New World. Like Christian women, Jewish women were excluded from public religious life; they rarely learned Hebrew, did not receive training in Jewish law (*halakhah*) or religious literature (the Torah and Talmud), and were excluded from rabbinical courts. They did have three very specific religious duties, however: separating a portion of dough each time they baked and burning it in the oven in memory of priestly tithes; lighting the Sabbath candles; and avoiding sexual relations with their spouses during menstruation and for seven days afterward.

This last duty, termed *niddah*, fostered an elaborate group of menstrual laws and practices. The woman herself was responsible to know when she was menstruating, count seven "clean" days after the last issue of blood, and if possible, take a ritual bath (*mikvah*) before beginning sexual relations again. *Niddah* stemmed from ideas of ritual impurity that had originally required a menstruating woman to avoid many other types of contacts along with sexual, but by the medieval and early modern periods, only sexual relations and a few other contacts between husband and wife were forbidden. Popular beliefs had also developed that interpreted *niddah* more positively; proper observance was thought to foster conception, easy childbirth, and male children. The first of these actually has biological basis, for most women ovulate roughly fourteen days after the beginning of their menstrual period, the day *niddah* allowed sexual relations again.

Women were not required to take part in public formal prayers and were in some cases excluded from them, but they did develop special voluntary prayers for events that had special meaning for them. These prayers, termed *thkines*, began to be published in the seventeenth century, and we can gain an insight into Jewish women's spiritual lives from them. They were written in Yiddish by a variety of authors, some of whom were probably female and who vary in their level of knowledge of Jewish tradition. They often concern biological and cultural events particularly important for women, such as menstruation, pregnancy, childbirth, baking bread, or visiting cemeteries. Although they were meant to be said in private, they exhibit a sense of community with generations of Jewish women who had done the same thing and often transform folk rituals not mentioned in Jewish law, such as making candles for Yom Kippur, into true religious duties. This dignified women's folk rituals and enabled women to compare themselves to priests in their carrying out of religious duties. Unlike much of the religious literature by Christian women during the seventeenth century, the *thkines* were not mystical, for women were excluded from most Jewish mysticism just as they were from official Hebrew prayer services. Jewish mysticism in the early modern period centered on the kabbalah, a group of writings from various ancient authors in which women were generally associated with the demonic; women occasionally took part in mass outbursts of mystical enthusiasm, such as that sparked by the pseudo-Messiah Sabbatai Zevi in the seventeenth century, but were not leaders or even regular participants in the secret meetings (conventicles) held by kabbalists.

Occasionally, individual Jewish women did step beyond their domestic religious roles. A few women learned Hebrew, generally from their fathers or brothers, and recited group prayers along with men. Sarra Copia Sullam (1592–1641), who had established a literary salon in Venice, published a pamphlet defending herself against charges that she did not believe in the immortality of the soul, an essential part of both Jewish and Christian teachings. She was accused of plagiarism, for her work was considered too learned to be that of a woman, although several years later some of her literary admirers also wrote in her defense. Women sometimes served as ritual slaughterers, which required a high level of training, although usually they were granted permission only in unusual circumstances such as periods of persecution or disruption when their families might otherwise go hungry. Jewish women in Italy were normally confined to a balcony during services, but they could and did enter the main floor if they had a specific grievance against one of the male members of the congregation. Women used this opportunity to charge men with abandonment, physical abuse, broken engagements, or the refusal to acknowledge children born out of wedlock, a practice that custom allowed as a sort of appeals court of last resort. Men could also use the service to air their grievances, however, particularly in cases in which their wives refused to have intercourse with them.

Public religious activities by Jewish women are even rarer than those of Christian women, however, and, because men were charged with overseeing the early religious training of their sons within the household, domestic religious activities were also not solely women's sphere. As in Christianity, women were responsible for the ultimate destination of their souls; some medieval and early modern popular spiritual works even describe a separate Paradise for women, where they will have the opportunity for prayer, study, and contemplation and not be burdened by domestic responsibilities. No suggestions were made for the establishment of such a place on earth, however, giving such ideas as little practical impact as the concept of spiritual equality had for most Christian women.

Jews lived in many parts of Europe during the early modern period, but Muslims lived primarily in the Iberian peninsula and southeastern Europe, where the Ottoman Turks were expanding their territory. At roughly the same time that they ordered Jews to leave or convert, Spanish and Portuguese authorities also outlawed the practice of Islam and gave the Inquisition jurisdiction over those suspected of Muslim practices as well as Jewish. Muslims – termed "Moriscos" – comprised a large share of the population in many parts of Spain, however, and many lived in rural areas, so that it was difficult for the Inquisition actually to exert control, although persecutions and forced conversions increased throughout the early modern period. Many Moriscos in the kingdoms of Valencia and Granada in southern Spain spoke only Arabic and had practically no contact with Christians, and Muslim clergy, teachers, and legal authorities continued to operate in these areas.

In places where Islam was more heavily persecuted, such as Aragon, women were extremely important in its survival. Like English recusants and Jews, Spanish Muslim women (termed "Moriscas") carried out religious rituals in their homes and taught them to their children. According to the records of the Inquisition, Moriscas observed the Muslim holy month of Ramadan; performed daily prayers; wore Muslim dress while Morisco men adopted Christian-style clothing; hid religious books and amulets written in Arabic in their clothing and furniture; taught Muslim ideas and practices to Christian women who married Muslim men; and organized funerals, weddings, and other ceremonies. Muslim midwives circumcised baby boys and failed to report births to Christian priests, as they were required to do. Although they generally stayed away from controversy, a few Moriscas publicly argued with their Christian neighbors about points of theology; through this, or other actions, they came to the attention of the Inquisition. Like Muslim men, they were whipped, imprisoned (often in convents), subjected to rituals of public humiliation, and occasionally executed at ceremonies termed *autos de fe*. In Saragossa, the Inquisitors complained that "the Moriscas of this kingdom are worse than the men, many of whom do not dare drink wine or eat bacon [both practices forbidden to Muslims] or do other Christian things from fear of their wives."[23]

The Inquisition paid special attention to marriages between Christians and Moriscos, which were generally allowed and at times even promoted, as long as the Muslim spouse converted; in 1548, for example, an edict of the Spanish Crown ordered converted Muslims to marry Old Christians. (Old Christians were those whose ancestors were not known to have been Jewish or Muslim.) At the same time, however, laws that favored "purely" Old Christian families (generally termed "purity of the blood" laws) worked against intermarriage and also led couples in which the husband was of Muslim background to adopt the wife's Christian surname to disguise his Muslim ancestry. In the Turkish areas of southeastern Europe, conversion went in the opposite direction, with women who had been Orthodox converting to Islam to marry Muslim men. In a few cases, Orthodox women who were already married divorced their husbands and married Muslim men, although to do this they had to swear in a Muslim court that they had converted of their own volition and that their husbands had refused conversion. Little is known about the religious practices of either Orthodox or Muslim women in these areas because the Turkish authorities were largely tolerant in matters of religion, and there were thus no investigations comparable to those of the Inquisition.

In Christianity, Judaism, and Islam, the sixteenth and seventeenth centuries were a time when the domestic nature of women's acceptable religious activities was reinforced. The proper sphere for the expression of women's religious ideas was a household, whether the secular household of a Jewish, Orthodox, Catholic, Protestant, or Muslim marriage, or the spiritual household of an enclosed Catholic convent. Even men who otherwise broke with tradition or questioned existing structures of power concurred that gender hierarchy was ordained by God. Women occasionally ignored their subservient status when their religious convictions were at stake, but only a handful directly challenged that status in the name of religion, and even fewer left any record of that challenge. Times of emergency and instability, such as the expulsion of the Jews and Muslims from Spain, the first years of the Protestant Reformation, and the English Civil War, offered women opportunities to play a public religious role.

---

[23] Translated and quoted in William Monter, *Frontiers of Heresy: The Spanish Inquisition from the Basque Lands to Sicily* (Cambridge, Cambridge University Press, 1990), p. 227.

However, both the times and the women were clearly regarded as extraordinary by most male religious thinkers, who expected such women to return to their households once things returned to normal. Women who were too assertive in expressing themselves during more stable times or who were too individualistic in their ideas risked being termed insane (as were Lady Eleanor Douglas and Antoinette Bourignon) or being imprisoned by religious or secular courts (as were Mary Ward and Madame Guyon).

"Extraordinary" women did not completely disappear, however, and they created new avenues of religious creativity and activism in the seventeenth and eighteenth centuries. Women bought many more devotional books than did men, joined confraternities and prayer groups in record numbers, and wrote religious books that were read by both women and men. Whether in sectarian groups or state churches, women rarely broke with religious traditions that privileged men and instructed women to be obedient and subservient, but their independent actions provided a more ambiguous message. This "feminization of religion," as it has been termed, continued into the nineteenth century, with religion increasingly viewed, along with the family, as part of the female sphere. This trend was noted at the time by hostile observers such as Thomas Edwards, although more of his contemporaries were worried about women's spiritual activities of a different sort – those in which they pledged themselves to the devil, as we see in the following chapter.

For Further Reading

The role of women in late medieval Christianity has been examined in Shannon McSheffrey, *Gender and Heresy: Women and Men in Lollard Communities, 1420–1530* (Philadelphia, University of Pennsylvania Press, 1995); Walter Simons, *Cities of Ladies: Beguine Communities in the Medieval Low Countries, 1200–1565* (Philadelphia, University of Pennsylvania Press, 2003); Anne Winston-Allen, *Convent Chronicles: Women Writing about Women and Reform in the Late Middle Ages* (University Park, Pennsylvania State University Press, 2004); and Virginia Nixon, *Mary's Mother: Saint Anne in Late Medieval Europe* (University Park, Pennsylvania State University Press, 2005).

Christine Peters, *Patterns of Piety: Women, Gender, and Religion in Late Medieval and Reformation England* (New York, Cambridge University Press, 2003), emphasizes continuities in religious ideas and devotional practices across the era of the Reformation, whereas Beth Kreitzer, *Reforming Mary: Changing Images of the Virgin Mary in Lutheran Sermons of the Sixteenth Century* (New York, Oxford University Press, 2004), explores one aspect of devotion that changed significantly. Nancy Bradley Warren, *Women of God and Arms: Female Spirituality and Political Conflict, 1380–1600* (Philadelphia, University of Pennsylvania Press, 2005), looks at the political dimensions of women's religious activities.

Sherrin Marshall (ed.), *Women in Reformation and Counter-Reformation Europe: Public and Private Worlds* (Bloomington, Indiana University Press, 1989), has articles about women in many countries and is a good place to begin for further information. For analysis of the effects of the Reformation on women's religious and family life, see Retha Warnicke, *Women of the English Renaissance and Reformation* (Westport, CT, Greenwood Press, 1983); Lyndal Roper, *The Holy Household: Women and Morals in Reformation Augsburg* (Oxford, Clarendon Press, 1989); and Patricia Crawford, *Women and Religion in England, 1500–1750* (London, Routledge, 1993). The writings of Protestant women are now appearing in editions and translations, including Peter Matheson (ed. and trans.), *Argula von Grumbach: A Woman's Voice in the Reformation* (Edinburgh, T. & T. Clark, 1995); Elaine V. Beilin (ed.), *The Examinations of Anne Askew* (New York, Oxford University Press, 1996); Marie Dentière, *Epistle to Marguerite de Navarre and Preface to a Sermon by John Calvin*, ed. and trans. Mary B. McKinley (Chicago, University of Chicago Press, 2004); and Katharina Schütz Zell, *Church Mother: The Writings of a Protestant Reformer in Sixteenth-Century Germany*, ed. and trans. Elsie McKee (Chicago, University of Chicago Press, 2006). Merry Wiesner-Hanks and Joan Skocir (ed. and trans.), *Convents Confront the Reformation: Catholic and Protestant Nuns in Germany* (Milwaukee, Marquette University Press, 1996), and Amy Leonard, *Nails in the Wall: Catholic Nuns in Reformation Germany* (Chicago, University of Chicago Press, 2005), focus on the effects of the Reformation on nuns. The role of women in the radical Reformation is becoming a focus of much research. Joyce Irwin (ed.), *Womanhood in Radical Protestantism* (New York, E. Mellen, 1979), provides extensive examples of (male) Anabaptist ideas; and C. Arnold Snyder and Linda A. Heubert Hecht (eds.), *Profiles of Anabaptist Women: Sixteenth-Century Reforming Pioneers* (Waterloo, Ontario, Wilfried Laurier University Press, 1996), discusses the lives and ideas of women.

Studies of the effects of the Protestant Reformation on marriage and the family include Jeffrey R. Watt, *The Making of Modern Marriage: Matrimonial Control and the Rise of Sentiment in Neuchâtel, 1550–1800* (Ithaca, Cornell University Press, 1992); Eric Josef Carlson, *Marriage and the English Reformation* (Oxford, Basil Blackwell, 1994); Joel F. Harrington, *Reordering Marriage and Society in Reformation Germany*

(Cambridge, Cambridge University Press, 1995); and Robert Kingdon, *Adultery and Divorce in Calvin's Geneva* (Cambridge, MA, Harvard University Press, 1995).

Many historians have recently examined changes in convents during the era of the Catholic Reformation: Patricia Ranft, *Women and the Religious Life in Premodern Europe* (New York, St. Martin's, 1996); Jutta Gisela Sperling, *Convents and the Body Politic in Renaissance Venice* (Chicago, University of Chicago Press, 2000); P. Renée Baernstein, *A Convent Tale: A Century of Sisterhood in Spanish Milan* (New York, Routledge, 2002); K. J. P. Lowe, *Nuns' Chronicles and Convent Culture in Renaissance and Counter-Reformation Italy* (New York, Cambridge University Press, 2003); Mary Laven, *Virgins of Venice: Broken Vows and Cloistered Lives in the Renaissance Convent* (New York, Penguin, 2004); and Elizabeth Lehfeldt, *Women and Religion in Golden-Age Spain: The Permeable Cloister* (Burlington, VT, Ashgate, 2006). Ulrike Strasser, *State of Virginity: Gender, Religion, and Politics in an Early Modern Catholic State* (Ann Arbor, University of Michigan Press, 2004), sets convents within a broad political and ideological framework. Barbara B. Diefendorf, *From Penitence to Charity: Pious Women and the Catholic Reformation in Paris* (New York, Oxford University Press, 2004), focuses on laywomen's active role as founders of religious congregations.

There are several excellent studies of various aspects of the life of St. Teresa, including Jodi Bilinkoff, *The Avila of St. Theresa* (Ithaca, Cornell University Press, 1989); Alison Weber, *Teresa of Avila and the Rhetoric of Femininity* (Princeton, Princeton University Press, 1990); and Gillian T. W. Ahlgren, *Teresa of Avila and the Politics of Sanctity* (Ithaca, Cornell University Press, 1996). Recent studies of *beatas* and "living saints" in southern Europe include Richard Kagan, *Lucrecia's Dreams: Politics and Prophecy in Sixteenth Century Spain* (Berkeley, University of California Press, 1990); Fulvio Tomizzio, *Heavenly Supper: The Story of Mary Janis*, trans. Anne Jacobson Schutte (Chicago, University of Chicago Press, 1991); Anne Jacobson Schutte, *Aspiring Saints: Pretense of Holiness, Inquisition, and Gender in the Republic of Venice, 1618–1750* (Baltimore, MD, Johns Hopkins University Press, 2001); and Francisca de los Apóstoles, *The Inquisition of Francisca: A Sixteenth-Century Visionary on Trial*, ed. and trans. Gillian T. W. Ahlgren (Chicago, University of Chicago Press, 2005).

On Protestant women in the seventeenth and eighteenth centuries, see Phyllis Mack, *Visionary Women: Ecstatic Prophecy in Seventeenth-Century England* (Berkeley, University of California Press, 1992), and Johanna Eleonora Petersen, *The Life of Lady Johanna Eleonora Petersen, Written by*

Herself, ed. and trans. Barbara Becker-Cantarino (Chicago, University of Chicago Press, 2005).

Quaker women have been especially well studied and their writings reprinted and analyzed: Bonnelyn Young Kunze, *Margaret Fell and the Rise of Quakerism* (Stanford, Stanford University Press, 1994); Catherine M. Wilcox, *Theology and Women's Ministry in Seventeenth-Century English Quakerism: Handmaids of the Lord* (London, E. Mellen, 1995); David Booy, *Autobiographical Writings by Early Quaker Women* (Burlington, VT, Ashgate, 2004); and Catie Gill, *Women in the Seventeenth-Century Quaker Community: A Literary Study of Political Identities, 1650–1700* (Burlington, VT, Ashgate, 2005).

The efforts of Catholic women to create an active life in the world have been examined in Elizabeth Rapley, *The Dévotes: Women and Church in Seventeenth-Century France* (Montreal and Kingston, McGill-Queen's University Press, 1990); Laurence Lux-Sterritt, *Redefining Female Religious Life: French Ursulines and English Ladies in Seventeenth Century Catholicism* (Burlington, VT, Ashgate, 2005); Susan Dinan, *Women and Poor Relief in Seventeenth-Century France: The Early History of the Daughters of Charity* (Burlington, VT, Ashgate, 2006); and Querciolo Mazznois, *Spirituality, Gender, and the Self in Renaissance Italy: Angela Merici and the Company of St. Ursula (1474–1540)* (Washington, DC, Catholic University Press, 2007).

On Jewish women, see Chava Weissler, *Voices of the Matriarchs: Listening to the Prayers of Early Modern Jewish Women* (Boston, Beacon Press, 1998), and Claudia Ulbrich, *Shulamith and Margarete: Power, Gender, and Religion in a Rural Society in Eighteenth-Century Europe,* trans. Thomas Dunlap (Boston, Brill Academic, 2004). On Muslim women, see Mary G. Giles, *Women in the Inquisition: Spain and the New World* (Baltimore, Johns Hopkins University Press, 1998); Gavin R. G. Hambly (ed.), *Women in the Medieval Islamic World: Power, Patronage, and Piety* (New York, St. Martin's, 1998); and Mary Elizabeth Perry, *The Handless Maiden: Moriscos and the Politics of Religion in Early Modern Spain* (Princeton, NJ, Princeton University Press, 2005). For women in the Ottoman Empire, see Leslie Peirce, *The Imperial Harem: Women and Sovereignty in the Ottoman Empire* (New York, Oxford University Press, 1993).

For more suggestions and links, see the companion Web site www. cambridge.org/womenandgender.

7   Witchcraft

As for the first question, why a greater number of witches is found in the fragile feminine sex than among men . . . the first reason is, that they are more credulous, and since the chief aim of the devil is to corrupt faith, therefore he rather attacks them . . . the second reason is, that women are naturally more impressionable, and . . . the third reason is that they have slippery tongues, and are unable to conceal from their fellow-women those things which by evil arts they know. . . . But the natural reason is that she is more carnal than a man, as is clear from her many carnal abominations. And it should be noted that there was a defect in the formation of the first woman, since she was formed from a bent rib, that is, a rib of the breast, which is bent as it were in a contrary direction to a man. And since through this defect she is an imperfect animal, she always deceives. . . . And this is indicated by the etymology of the word; for *Femina* comes from *Fe* and *Minus*, since she is ever weaker to hold and preserve the faith. . . . To conclude. All witchcraft comes from carnal lust, which is in women insatiable.

> *Malleus Maleficarum* (1486), translated and quoted in Alan C. Kors and
> Edward Peters (eds.), *Witchcraft in Europe 1100–1700: A Documentary*
> *History* (Philadelphia, University of Pennsylvania Press, 1972),
> pp. 114–27

It is commonly the nature of women to be timid and to be afraid of everything. This is why they busy themselves so much about witchcraft and superstition. One teaches the other, so that it is impossible to tell what kind of hocus-pocus they practice.

> Commentary by Martin Luther on I Peter, *Luther's Works*, vol. 30, edited by
> Jaroslav Pelikan (St. Louis, Concordia, 1968), p. 91

And then the Devil said, "Thee art a poor overworked body. Will thee be my servant and I will give thee abundance and thee shall never want."

> Confession of Bessie Wilson, quoted in Christina Larner, *Enemies of God:*
> *The Witch Hunt in Scotland* (Baltimore, Johns Hopkins University Press,
> 1981), p. 95

During the sixteenth and seventeenth centuries, Europeans hunted witches. Because so many records have been lost or destroyed, it is difficult to make an estimate for all of Europe, but most scholars agree that somewhere between 100,000 and 200,000 people were officially tried and between 40,000 and 60,000 were executed. These witch hunts are both fascinating and challenging. Most people in Europe (and elsewhere in the world) believed in witches for centuries before this era, and many continued to do so for long afterward. Other than a handful of cases, however, only during these two centuries were there large-scale hunts and mass executions. Why?

This question has puzzled people since the time of the witch hunts themselves, and many answers have been proposed. Learned authorities at the time, some of who were themselves hunting or trying witches, suggested that the flourishing of witchcraft and magic was a sign of the coming end of the world. The devil, they wrote, was more active and violent because he knows the last days are coming; he thus seeks out more people to do his bidding, and more people are tempted because of the moral decay that prophecy foretold would precede the apocalypse. Human agents could not stop this, but they were to resist the forces of darkness and work to rid their societies from evil as much as possible.

By the eighteenth century, this explanation had been turned on its head. The "forces of darkness," wrote Enlightenment philosophers, were the authorities who had persecuted generally harmless people for witchcraft, not the witches themselves. The witch hunts were the most extreme example of the misguided and irrational nature of religion, particularly that of the Catholic Church and its Inquisition, the power of which was slowly loosened with the advent of science and reason. Nineteenth-century historians generally ignored the witch hunts in their story of the political, economic, and intellectual changes of what they increasingly saw as the beginning of the "modern" era. Witch beliefs were an unfortunate remnant of a "medieval" past and had little to do with the rise of capitalism, the development of the nation-state, the Protestant and Catholic Reformations, and other changes that were truly important. Because witchcraft had no objective reality, they noted, it was not really the proper subject for historians or, at most, an aberration worthy of only the briefest mention.

The twentieth century demonstrated just how powerful ideas with no objective reality could be, and the last half of the century saw hundreds of studies of the witch hunts; this interest shows no signs of abating in the twenty-first century. As historians have delved into actual records of trials and the writings of those concerned with witches, they have discovered that many earlier ideas about the witch hunts – some of which continue to shape popular understanding and are now repeated endlessly on various Web sites – are simply wrong. The most intense period of witch-hunting was not the Middle Ages but rather the late sixteenth and early seventeenth centuries, clearly part of modern times. Protestants were just as active in hunting witches as Catholics, and skeptics about the power of witches included people from all Christian denominations. The Inquisition – whether Spanish, Portuguese, or Roman – actually tried relatively few witches and executed only a small number. Economic changes, including the development of capitalism, did play a role in many hunts. Rulers intent on creating nation-states were, in fact, often avid witch-hunters, and one – James I of England and Scotland – even wrote a treatise on demonology. The authors of other important works on witchcraft included leading political philosophers and scientists, who saw the power of witches as part of the natural world they were seeking to understand and explain. This research has made clear that the witch hunts were not marginal events involving ill-educated villagers and fanatical clergy but rather a central part of this era.

About 80 percent of those questioned, tried, and executed for witchcraft in Europe after 1500 were women. Thus, along with explanations for the great witch hunt itself, people who lived at the time and later have had to come up with explanations for this gender imbalance. The three statements at the head of this chapter, the first by two Dominican monks in the most influential witch-hunters' manual of the early modern period, the second by Martin Luther in a biblical commentary, and the third by a Scottish woman during her interrogation for witchcraft, represent widely varying explanations. Although they disagree, the three things they point to – sex, fear, and poverty – can in many ways be seen as the three most important reasons women were more likely to be accused of witchcraft.

Intellectual and Cultural Factors

In examining the witch hunts, some scholars have chosen to emphasize intellectual and cultural factors. During the late Middle Ages, Christian philosophers and theologians developed a new idea about the most important characteristics of a witch. Until that period in Europe, as in most cultures throughout the world, a witch was a person who used magical forces to do evil deeds *(maleficia)*. One was a witch, therefore, because of what one *did*, causing injuries or harm to animals and people. This notion of witchcraft continued in Europe but to it was added a demonological component. Educated Christian thinkers in some parts of Europe began to view the essence of witchcraft as making a pact with the devil, a pact that required the witch to do the devil's bidding. Witches were no longer simply people who used magical power to get what they wanted but rather people used by the devil to do what *he* wanted. (The devil is always described and portrayed visually as male.) Witchcraft was thus not a question of what one *did* but of what one *was*, and proving that a witch had committed *maleficia* was no longer necessary for conviction. Gradually, this demonological or satanic idea of witchcraft was fleshed out, and witches were thought to engage in wild sexual orgies with the devil; fly through the night to meetings called "sabbats," which parodied the Mass; and steal communion wafers and unbaptized babies to use in their rituals. Some demonological theorists also claimed that witches were organized in an international conspiracy to overthrow Christianity, with a hierarchy modeled on the hierarchy of angels and archangels constructed by Christian philosophers to give order to God's assistants. Witchcraft was thus spiritualized, and witches became the ultimate heretics – enemies of God.

Ideas about the activities of the devil, demons, and witches can be found in many types of writings from the fifteenth through the seventeenth centuries – biblical commentary, chronicles, almanacs, legal treatises, sermons, medical essays, scientific works, political theory, doctoral dissertations. They appear in their purest form in the hundreds of works specifically dealing with witchcraft and demonology that were penned – and then often published – by learned men. Demonology was not written in a vacuum nor by authors sitting in scholarly seclusion. Most of the authors of demonological works also wrote other things, and many were active as pastors, officials, university professors, lawyers, physicians, and even a few rulers. Some were also witch-hunters, judges, or officials involved in actual trials. They brought their ideas with them to the trials, framing questions based on their readings, and then used their experiences as the basis for their demonology. The fact that their questions often elicited the same or similar answers over broad geographic areas fueled the idea that witchcraft was an international conspiracy.

Historians in the nineteenth and much of the twentieth centuries who analyzed demonology generally regarded belief in witchcraft as an aberration when it appeared in the writings of highly learned men such as the political theorist, Jean Bodin. They viewed such beliefs either as remnants of earlier ways of viewing the world that intelligent men like Bodin had not yet been able to shake or as marginal to intellectuals' main concerns. Surely such people could not really have accepted the idea that thousands of people made pacts with the devil, through which they gained powers to harm their neighbors? More recently, however, intellectual historians have increasingly focused on connections and correspondences between witchcraft and other ideas held by educated Europeans. They have explored demonology as an intellectual system that made sense to those who accepted it and have been less concerned with highlighting the contrast between beliefs in witchcraft and an objective reality beyond those beliefs. Such studies have been part of the "linguistic/cultural turn" in history discussed in the Introduction, in which greater attention is paid to texts, language, and visual images – what is generally called "discourse."

Learned ideas gradually began to infiltrate popular understanding of what it meant to be a witch. Illustrated pamphlets and broadsides portrayed witches riding on pitchforks to sabbats where they engaged in anti-Christian acts such as spitting on the communion host and sexual relations with demons. Although witch trials were secret, executions were not; they were public spectacles witnessed by huge crowds, with the list of charges read out for all to hear. By the late sixteenth century, popular denunciations for witchcraft in many parts of Europe involved at least some parts of the demonic conception of witchcraft. Conversely, popular understandings of witchcraft also shaped demonology; charges such as witches entering cellars and storerooms to steal food and wine emerge first in local accusations and then later show up in formal demonological treatises. The spread of diabolism led to a greater feminization of witchcraft, for witches were now the dependent agents of a male devil rather than independently directing demons themselves, and it fit general notions of proper gender roles to envision women in this dependent position; even witches could not break fully with masculine norms. In areas of Europe in which the demonic concept of witchcraft never took hold, such as Finland, Iceland, Estonia, and Russia, witchcraft did not become female-identified and there were no large-scale hunts. In Finland and Estonia, about half of those prosecuted for witchcraft cases were male, and in Iceland and Muscovite Russia, the vast majority of those prosecuted were men charged with sorcery or using their skills as healers to harm people or animals instead.

Witch trials died down somewhat during the first decades after the Protestant Reformation when Protestants and Catholics were busy fighting each other, but they picked up again more strongly than ever about 1560. Protestants rejected many Catholic teachings, but not demonology, and may have felt even more at the mercy of witches than Catholics, for they rejected rituals such as exorcism that Catholics believed could counter the power of a witch. The Protestant and Catholic Reformations may have contributed to the spread of demonological ideas among wider groups of the population, for both Catholics and Protestants increased their religious instruction of lay people during the sixteenth century, and demonological ideas were a key part of such teaching.

As part of their program of deepening popular religious understanding and piety, both Protestants and Catholics attempted to suppress what the elites viewed as superstition, folk belief, and more open expressions of sexuality; some historians view the campaign against witches as part of a larger struggle by elite groups to suppress popular culture, to force rural residents to acculturate themselves to middle-class urban values. The fact that women were the preservers and transmitters of popular culture, teaching their children magical sayings and rhymes along with more identifiably Christian ones, made them particularly suspect.

Political, Economic, and Social Explanations

Whereas many historians have focused on demonology and related intellectual developments, others have highlighted the importance of political, economic, and social factors. The great witch hunts occurred at a time when monarchs in western and northern Europe were consolidating royal power, creating what would become nation-states out of more decentralized feudal territories. Even in areas where nation-states were not developing, such as the Holy Roman Empire in central Europe, rulers of smaller territories were consolidating their holds and determined to prove their power vis-à-vis both their neighbors and their subjects. With the Reformation, Christianity became a political ideology. Rulers felt compelled to prove their piety and the depth of their religious commitment to their subjects and other rulers; they did this by fighting religious wars and by cracking down on heretics and witches within their own borders. Witchcraft was thus used as a symbol of total evil and total hostility to the community, the state, the church, and God. Witches represented both a real internal enemy and a symbol of hostility to the ruler and the community.

Legal changes were also instrumental in allowing for massive witch trials. Historians have particularly highlighted the change from an accusatorial legal procedure to an inquisitorial procedure. In the former, a suspect knew the accusers and the charges they had brought, and an accuser could in turn be liable for trial if the charges were not proved; in the latter, legal authorities themselves brought the case. According to many historians, this change made people much more willing to accuse others, for they never had to take personal responsibility for the accusation or face the accused's relatives. Inquisitorial procedure involved intense questioning of the suspect, often with torture; areas in Europe that did not make this change saw few trials and almost no mass panics. Inquisitorial procedure came into Europe as part of the adoption of Roman law, which also (at least, in theory) required the confession of a suspect before she or he could be executed. This had been designed as a way to keep innocent people from death but, in practice, led in some parts of Europe to the adoption of ever more gruesome means of inquisitorial torture. Torture was also used to get the names of additional suspects because most lawyers trained in Roman law firmly believed that no witch could act alone.

The use of inquisitorial procedure did not always lead to witch hunts, however. The most famous Inquisitions in early modern Europe, those in Spain, Portugal, and Italy, were in fact lenient in their treatment of those accused of witchcraft: the Inquisition in Spain executed only a handful of witches, the Portuguese Inquisition only one, and the Roman Inquisition (which had jurisdiction in much of Italy) none, although in each of these areas there were hundreds of cases. Inquisitors firmly believed in the power of the devil, but they doubted whether the people accused of doing *maleficia* had actually made a pact with the devil that gave them special powers. They viewed them not as diabolical devil-worshippers but as superstitious and ignorant peasants who should be educated rather than executed.

In terms of the economy, Europe entered a period of dramatic inflation during the sixteenth century and continued to be subject to periodic famines resulting from bad harvests. Large-scale witch hunts often occurred after some type of climatic disaster, such as an unusually cold and wet summer, and came in waves. This was also a time when people were moving around more than they had in the previous centuries, when war, religious conflict, the commercialization of agriculture, enclosure, and the lure of new jobs in the cities meant that villages were being uprooted and the number of vagrants and transients increased. These changes led to a sense of unsettledness and uncertainty in values – and, in many places, a greater gap between rich and poor. Because most people accused of witchcraft came from the poorest level of society, economic factors may have played a role in witch accusations.

Social tensions are also important in understanding the development of the witch craze. Although there were "witch-hunters" who came into areas specifically to hunt witches, most witch trials began with an accusation of *maleficia* in a village or town. Individuals accused someone they knew of using magic to spoil food, make children ill, kill animals, raise a hailstorm, or do other types of harm. Local studies have shown that kinship stresses often played a role in these initial accusations, for tensions over property, stepchildren, or the public behavior of a relative or in-law were common in early modern families. In the intimate circle of the family, love and loyalty were often accompanied by hatred and hostility. Household or neighborhood antagonisms might also lead to an accusation, particularly those between people who knew each other's lives intimately, such as servants and their employers.

Demographic changes may have also played a part. During the sixteenth century, the age at first marriage appears to have risen, and the number of people who never married at all increased. The reasons for these changes are not entirely clear, but this meant that there was a larger number of women unattached to a man and, therefore, more suspect in the eyes of their neighbors. Female life expectancy may also have risen during the sixteenth century, either in absolute terms or at least in comparison with male life expectancy during this period when many men lost their lives in religious wars.

Medical issues have also been part of another area of investigation related to the witch craze. Witches were often accused of mixing magic potions and creams, leading some scholars to explore the role that hallucinogenic drugs such as ergot and belladonna may have played, particularly in inducing feelings of flying. Such hallucinogens could have been taken inadvertently by eating bread or porridge made from spoiled grain. A problem with this is that witches were rarely accused of eating their concoctions or rubbing them on their bodies but rather of spreading them on brooms or pitchforks, which they then rode to a sabbat. If delusions of flying came from eating spoiled grain, why was not the whole population of an area equally affected?

No one factor alone can explain the witch-hunts but, taken together, intellectual, religious, political, legal, social, and economic factors all created a framework that proved deadly to thousands of European women. In the rest of this chapter, I consider why the vast majority of European witches were women; to do this, we must first examine how the stereotype of witch-as-woman developed and then explore actual witch trials to develop a more refined view as to what types of women were actually accused and convicted.

The Stereotype

In central and western Europe, learned authors and unlettered villagers, male and female, generally agreed that most witches were women, and the gender balance among those accused, tried, and executed reflects this belief. Women were widely recognized as having less physical, economic, or political power than men so that they were more likely to need magical assistance to gain what they wanted. Whereas a man could fight or take someone to court, a woman could only scold, curse, or cast spells. Thus, in popular notions of witchcraft, women's physical and legal weakness was a contributing factor, with unmarried women and widows recognized as even more vulnerable because they did not have a husband to protect them.

Women also had close connections with many areas of life in which magic or malevolence might seem the only explanation for events. They watched over animals that could die mysteriously, prepared food that could become spoiled unexplainably, nursed the ill of all ages who could die without warning, and cared for children who were even more subject to disease and death than adults in this era of poor hygiene and unknown and uncontrollable childhood diseases. Because women often married at a younger age than men and female life expectancy may have been increasing, women frequently spent periods of their life as widows. If they remarried, it was often to a widower with children so that they became stepmothers; resentments about preferential treatment were common in families with stepsiblings, and the evil stepmother became a stock figure in folktales. If a woman's second husband died, she might have to spend her last years in the house of a stepson or stepdaughter who resented her demands but was bound by a legal contract to provide for her; old age became a standard feature of the popular stereotype of the witch.

The first person accused in many trials, especially in the German heartland of the witch craze, often closely fit the Halloween and Hollywood stereotype of a witch: female, old, poor, and in some way peculiar looking or acting. She was seen as motivated by envy and malice and accused of riding through the air to a sabbat where she had sex with the devil (although usually on a goat or pitchfork rather than a broom). She consorted with an animal familiar – often a dog rather than a black cat – and tempted children with sweets and delicacies, just like the evil stepmother in "Snow White" or the witch in "Hansel and Gretel."

We might assume that women would do everything they could to avoid a reputation as a witch but, in actuality, the stereotype could protect a woman for many years. Neighbors would be less likely to refuse assistance, and the wood, grain, or milk that she needed to survive would be given to her or paid as fees for her magical services such as finding lost objects, attracting desirable suitors, and harming enemies. This can help explain the number of women who appear to have confessed to being witches without the application or even threat of torture; after decades of providing magical services, they were as convinced as their neighbors of their own powers. Although we regard witchcraft as something that has no objective reality, early modern women and men were often absolutely convinced they had suffered or caused grievous harm through witchcraft.

This popular stereotype of the witch existed long before the upsurge in witch trials and would continue in Europe centuries after the last witch was officially executed; in some more isolated parts of Europe, people still mix magical love potions and accuse their neighbors of casting the evil eye. The early modern large-scale witch-hunts resulted much more from learned and official ideas of witchcraft than popular ones and, in the learned mind, witches were even more likely to be women than they were in popular culture.

Figure 13. Hans Baldung Grien, *The Witches*, 1510. In this woodcut, Grein depicts many elements of both the popular and learned stereotype of the witch: animal familiars, night-flying, the concoction of poisonous brews, and the link with female sexuality.

For learned authors, the link between women and witchcraft was supported by classical and Christian authorities. As we saw in Chapter 1, Aristotle regarded women as defective males, as more passive and weaker not just physically but also morally and intellectually, which to learned demonologists explained why they were more likely to give in to the devil's offers. Christian authors such as Jerome, Augustine, and Tertullian were often deeply suspicious of women, viewing them as seductive temptresses who lacked rational capacity. These attitudes were shaped by one of the primary underlying concepts in both Greek and Christian thought, a dichotomy between order and disorder, which was linked to other polarities including culture/nature, reason/emotion, and mind/body. In all of these, men were linked to the more positive first term and women to the more negative second. Witches were women who let these qualities – links with nature, their emotions, and their bodily drives – come to dominate them completely; they were both disorderly and actively bent on destroying order. Witches disturbed the natural order of the four elements and the four humors in the body by causing storms and sickness. They disrupted patriarchal order by making men impotent through spells or tying knots in a thread and subjecting their minds to their passions in a double emasculation. The disorder they caused was linked to the first episode of disorder in the Judeo-Christian tradition, the rebellion and fall of Satan.

The *Malleus Maleficarum (The Hammer of [Female] Witches)* (1486), traditionally attributed to two German Dominican monks, Heinrich Krämer (c. 1430–1505, also known by his Latinized name, Institoris) and Jacob Sprenger (c. 1436–95), is the classic expression of these ideas. In 1484, Pope Innocent VIII (pontificate 1484–92) authorized Krämer and Sprenger to hunt witches in several areas of southern Germany. Krämer oversaw the trial and execution of several groups – all of them women – but local authorities objected to his use of torture and his extreme views on the power of witches and banished him. While in exile, he wrote a justification of his ideas and methods, the *Malleus Maleficarum*; the treatise also gave Sprenger as an author, but recent research has determined that his name was simply added because he was more prominent and respected than Krämer and that Krämer was its sole author. A long, rambling, and difficult work, the *Malleus* draws on the writings of many earlier authors as it lays out Krämer's theories about the nature and danger of witchcraft and provides advice about how to identify and prosecute witches.

Many medieval authors believed that women were more superstitious and mentally weak than men and more likely to use magical means to get what they wanted. What was new in the *Malleus* was the authors' obsession with the sexual connection between witches and the devil. To them, the essence of witchcraft was an abjuration of faith by women and an abjuration directly connected to sex with demons; the women's unbridled lust led them to seek sexual intercourse with the devil, through which they gained power over men, particularly over men's power of procreation. Female sexual drive was viewed as increasing throughout a woman's life, making, in learned eyes, the postmenopausal woman most vulnerable to the blandishments of a demonic suitor. If this older woman was widowed or single, she, of course, had no legitimate sexual outlets, and even if she was married, sex with her husband was officially frowned upon because it could not result in children.

Male authors also worried about the effects of too much sexual intercourse on their own sex, for brain tissue, bone marrow, and semen were widely regarded as the same thing. Sexual intercourse was thought to draw brain tissue down the spine and out the penis, making all intercourse a threat to a man's reason and health. This worried even such leading intellectuals as Leonardo da Vinci and Francis Bacon, and men were advised to limit their sexual relations if they wished to live a long life. Intercourse with female demons (*succubi*) was especially threatening, for such creatures attempted to draw out as much semen as possible, thus drastically debilitating any man. (Because the devil and his demons were regarded as impotent, learned demonologists had to figure out where they got semen to impregnate witches; the theory developed that because demons could change shape, they would appear as a woman [*succubus*] to draw semen out of a human man, then change into a male demon [*incubus*] for intercourse with female witches. Because the semen had spent time in a devil's body, it produced demonic children.) In demonological theory, sex with the devil was not satisfying, for his penis was cold and hard, and so witches also had sex with other demons, their animal familiars, and with each other. These orgiastic sexual relations left their mark on a witch's body, which was either an extra nipple for the animal familiar to suckle or a place that did not feel pain; during trials, witches were "pricked," or poked with pins, to find the spot.

The *Malleus* is arguably the most misogynist of witchcraft treatises, and it became quite well known. It was written in Latin, and there were a number of Latin editions in the sixteenth and seventeenth centuries, printed in Germany and France. In these areas, the *Malleus* shaped ideas about witchcraft held by learned scholars and officials and the actual conduct of trials under their direction. The questions that it taught judges and lawyers to ask of witches were asked over a large area; the fact that they often elicited the same or similar answers fueled the idea that witchcraft was an international conspiracy. Recent historians have warned against overemphasizing its importance, however. In England, Scandinavia, eastern Europe, and southern Europe, the *Malleus* was much less influential, and the works of learned demonologists from these areas share some of Krämer's concerns but not all. Other than a Polish partial translation from 1614, the first translation of the *Malleus* into any vernacular language was an incomplete English translation made in 1928, so that only those who could read Latin (or Polish) could actually read it in the early modern period. Thus, it indirectly shaped popular notions of witchcraft in Germany and France through trial proceedings, but shorter works written in vernacular languages both shaped and reflected popular ideas more closely.

Sexual relations with the devil rarely (and in some parts of Europe, especially Scandinavia, never) formed part of popular ideas about witchcraft, and other aspects of the learned stereotype of the witch also never became part of the popular stereotype. The *Malleus* is convinced that witchcraft is particularly rampant among midwives, "who surpass all others in wickedness.... No one does more harm to the Catholic Faith than midwives."[1] This is not reflected in popular denunciations for witchcraft and, considering that most midwives were part of the population group from which the majority of witches were drawn – older women – their numbers are probably not overrepresented among the accused. As we noted in our discussion of midwifery in Chapter 2, female midwives remained the primary birth assistants throughout the early modern period, even in the areas of Europe such as the Holy Roman Empire where witch persecutions were most widespread.

One group of women involved with childbirth *were* more often charged with witchcraft: the lying-in maids who took care of the mother and infant immediately after birth. Lying-in maids were often accused by the mothers whose infants had suffered or died under their care; they were portrayed as inversions of good mothers, charged with actions that destroyed, rather than sustained, infants and children, such as drying up a woman's milk or menstrual flow or poisoning children with food. Anxieties surrounding childbirth and motherhood and images of bad mothers emerge often in witch trials, as do other portrayals of witchcraft as the inversion of the normal order. Witches were often portrayed riding backward on animals or their pitchforks to sabbats where they did everything with their left hand, ate nauseating food, and desecrated rather than honored Christian symbols; witches also often passed on their powers from mother to daughter, an inversion of the way property normally passed from father to son. The witch was also the inversion of a "good woman" and set a

---

[1] Translated and quoted in Alan C. Kors and Edward Peters (eds.), *Witchcraft in Europe 1100–1700: A Documentary History* (Philadelphia: University of Pennsylvania Press, 1972), pp. 114, 129.

negative standard for women; she was argumentative, willful, independent, aggressive, and sexual rather than chaste, pious, silent, obedient,
and married. As the indictment of Margaret Lister in Scotland in 1662
put it, she was "a witch, a charmer, and a libber."[2] The last term carried the same connotation and negative assessment of "liberated woman"
that it does today. The witch did not fulfill her expected social role as a
wife; the sixteenth-century scientist and physician Theophrastus Paracelsus described witches as "turning away from men, fleeing men, hiding,
wanting to be alone, not attracting men, not looking men in the eye, lying
alone, refusing men."[3]

Positive and negative standards for female behavior in early modern
Europe were set largely by men, but women internalized these cultural
values as well, which helps explain why women also joined and sometimes
led the attacks on witches. Women gained economic and social security
by conforming to the standard of the good wife and mother and by con-
fronting women who deviated from it. Witch-hunting was thus not simply
women-hunting but rather the tracking down of a certain type of woman.
Because this type of woman often used words as a weapon, witchcraft has
also been analyzed in the context of language, speech, and meaning, for
in witchcraft, words have the power of waging war. The language of the
witch-hunts provided a vocabulary for educated Europeans to describe
the natives of the New World; in 1585, for example, the French explorer
Jéan Lery described religious rituals of Brazilian women in words he had
taken from a contemporary French demonological guide. Like women in
Europe, the women of the New World were regarded as especially likely
to give in to demonic suggestion; linking their practices with those of
European women charged with witchcraft also made European witches
appear even more exotic and dangerous, representatives of a truly world-
wide conspiracy.

The Actualities of Persecutions for Witchcraft

How well did the people who were actually accused, charged, and executed for witchcraft fit the popular and learned stereotypes of the witch?
This question can only be answered by intensive local studies of actual

[2] Quoted in Christina Larner, *Witchcraft and Religion: The Politics of Popular Belief* (London,
Basil Blackwell, 1984), p. 85.
[3] *De sagis*, translated and quoted in Gerhild Scholz Williams, "On Finding Words:
Witchcraft and the Discourses of Dissidence and Discovery," in Lynne Tatlock and Christiane Bohnert (eds.), *The Graph of Sex and the German Text: Gendered Culture in Early
Modern Germany 1500–1700*, Chloe: Beihefte zum Daphnis, 19 (Amsterdam, Rodolpi,
1994), p. 55.

witchcraft trials. Court records can be both disturbing in their details and frustrating in their incompleteness. Records of arrests and questioning may never indicate the ultimate outcome; suspects are not completely identified, making it difficult to tell exactly who they are; or records from some years are missing or destroyed, so that it is difficult to trace patterns. Thousands of trial records do survive, however, some of them numbering many pages.

On the basis of such local records, historians now distinguish between two types of hunts: the isolated case or small hunt involving one or only a few suspects and the mass hunt in which the accused could number in the hundreds, often called a "witch panic." Isolated cases and, in fact, most hunts began with an accusation of *maleficia* in a village or town, and the persons accused most often closely fit the stereotype. They were female, over fifty, often widowed or single, poor, and in some way peculiar – they looked or behaved oddly or were known for cursing or scolding or aberrant sexual behavior. They were often on the margins of village society and dependent on the goodwill of others for their support, suspect because they were not under the direct control of a man. In some parts of Europe and in North America, they might also be women suspected of other types of crimes. They might be women who had been troublesome to authorities for various reasons as, for example, Doritte Nippers, who was convicted and executed for witchcraft in 1571 in Elsinore, in Denmark, despite refusing to confess even when tortured; she was the leader of a group of female traders who refused to stop trading when ordered to by the town council.

Local studies have shown that kinship stresses often played a role in these initial accusations for, as noted earlier, tensions over property, stepchildren, or the public behavior of a relative or in-law were common in early modern families. Women were in a more vulnerable position once such strains came out into the open, for marriage had often separated them from their birth families and they were dependent on their husband's family to protect them. Household or neighborhood antagonisms might also lead to an accusation, particularly those between women who knew each other's lives intimately such as servants and mistresses or close neighbors. Women number prominently among accusers and witnesses as well as those accused of witchcraft because the actions witches were initially charged with, such as harming children or curdling milk, were generally part of women's sphere. Witchcraft charges often arose in situations that were largely confined to women – food preparation and preservation, pregnancy and childbirth, the care of young children. As one English witch (speaking in the third person) confessed, "she touch[ed] the said John Patchett's wife in her bed and the child in the grace-wife's [midwife's] arms. And then she sent her said spirits to bewitch them to death, which they did."[4]

Often the incident that led to the charge was not the first, but for some reason the accuser decided no longer to tolerate the suspect's behavior. Once a first charge was made, the accuser often thought back over the years and augmented the current charge with a list of things the suspect had done in the past. The judges then began to question other neighbors and acquaintances, building up a list of suspicious incidents that might stretch for decades. Historians have pointed out that one of the reasons those accused of witchcraft were often older was that it took years to build up a reputation as a witch. Fear or a desire for the witch's services might lead neighbors to tolerate such actions for a long time, and it is difficult to tell what might finally drive them to make a formal accusation. Long pent-up emotions clearly played a role, just as they have in more recent examples of people's fantasies leading them to make spectacular accusations. (Organized campaigns against a particular group for reasons that prove to have no rational basis, such as that carried out by the American Senator Joseph McCarthy in the 1950s against "Communists" in government, are for this reason often called "witch-hunts.")

Once a formal accusation was made, the suspect was brought in for questioning by legal authorities, and the people whom she had implicated were brought in for questioning.

From this point, there were great regional differences in the likely outcome. In Spain, Portugal, and much of Italy, all cases of witchcraft were handled by the Spanish, Portuguese, or Roman Inquisitions, which continued to make a distinction between ritual magic and diabolic witchcraft. If there was no evidence the suspect had worshipped the devil or used Christian objects such as crucifixes or communion hosts in her magic, the case was most often simply dismissed. Even if the suspect was found guilty, judges of the Inquisition in many parts of southern Europe preferred punishments of public humiliation such as whipping or standing in the pillory to execution. There is no clear evidence that the Roman Inquisition ever executed any witches, nor that it allowed secular courts in the areas where it operated to handle witchcraft cases. The numbers from Spain are comparable – more than 4,000 cases of witchcraft from 1550 to 1700 and fewer than a dozen witches executed, most of them in a single trial in Navarre in northern Spain in 1610, when the area came briefly under the influence of the French demonologist Pierre de Lancre.

---

[4] *The wonderful discoverie of the witchcrafts of Margaret and Philippa Flower*, 1619, printed in Barbara Rosen (ed.), *Witchcraft in England 1558–1618* (Amherst, University of Massachusetts Press, 1991), p. 379.

Why, compared with other courts throughout the rest of Europe, was the Inquisition so lenient? We must base our answer on the record of the judges' comments, which may not necessarily represent their true sentiments, but it appears, as noted earlier, that they simply regarded the women and men charged with witchcraft as pawns of the devil, as misled by the "Father of lies" into thinking they had magical powers. They disagreed with the authors of the *Malleus*, which they never used as a guidebook for questioning as secular and ecclesiastical judges did in central Europe, and agreed with the few northern European commentators who opposed hunting witches that most witches were simply stupid or deluded old women suffering from depression who needed spiritual retraining and (earthly) male guidance. Their testimony was certainly not valid grounds to arrest anyone else, which means there were no mass panics. Inquisitors' attitude toward women was thus more condescending and patronizing than that of northern judges, but the effects of this attitude on women's lives was certainly more positive.

In Europe north of the Alps and Pyrenees, the initial accusation might also be dismissed if the judges regarded the evidence as questionable, but here there were wide regional differences. England, the northern Netherlands, and Scandinavia had fewer trials in total than areas on the Continent with similar populations and almost no mass panics. Several reasons have been suggested for this: the learned stereotype of witchcraft as a devil-worshipping international conspiracy was never fully accepted by English, Dutch, or Scandinavian judicial authorities, which both led to and resulted from a much more restricted use of torture. (Torture was generally used primarily to find out a witch's accomplices and learn the details of her demonic pact; it was employed most by those convinced of the reality of massive numbers of witches and, in turn, led to the denunciation of as many other people as the judges thought necessary, for torture was stopped only when the accused supplied what the judges thought was a sufficient number of names.) Witches were also tried by jury in England, which some analysts see as leading to milder sentences, although jury trials did not have this effect in Denmark. Witch-hunts in England were never begun by church or state officials but only after personal denunciations by neighbors, and they rarely grew into mass panics.

The geographic and cultural heartland of the witch-hunts, where both single accusations and mass panics were most common, was west-central Europe: the Holy Roman Empire, Switzerland, and eastern parts of France. There are a number of possible explanations for this: much of this area consisted of small governmental units, which were jealous of each other and, after the Reformation, divided by religion. The rulers of these small territories often felt more threatened than did the monarchs of western Europe and were largely unhindered in their legal or judicial moves by any higher authority. The parts of France that were under tighter control of the French monarchy and the centralized appeals court in Paris saw far fewer large witch-hunts than the areas that bordered Switzerland or the Empire.

Many of the deadliest hunts were in the prince-bishoprics in the Holy Roman Empire, such as Trier, Mainz, Würzburg, Ellwangen, Bamberg, or Cologne, where bishops were both the secular and religious powers in their territories. They saw persecuting witches as a way to demonstrate their piety and concern for order and were often founding hospitals and universities, building spectacular baroque churches, and modernizing their administrative bureaucracies at the same time that they were hunting witches. These modernized bureaucracies were quite efficient; in one hunt in Ellwangen, for example, more than 400 people were executed for witchcraft between 1611 and 1618, and nine prince-bishops were responsible for more than 6,000 deaths. One of the bishops of Bamberg later acquired the nickname, "burning bishop of Bamberg." They consciously used patriarchy as a model, describing themselves as firm but just fathers, ruling their subjects for their own benefit; a campaign in which most of the accused and convicted were women, and many of them women who did not conform to male standards of female behavior, fit their aims very nicely.

In these areas, inquisitors regularly asked about the witch's demonic sexual contacts. Suspects were generally stripped and shaved in a search for this "witch's mark"; if no wart or mole could be found that could be viewed as such a mark, she might be "pricked" with a needle in an attempt to discover a spot that was insensitive to pain, also regarded as a sign from the devil. These investigations were generally carried out by a group of male officials – judges, notaries who recorded the witch's answers, the executioner who did the actual pricking or other types of torture – with the witch at least partially naked, so that it is difficult not to view them as at least partly motivated by sexual sadism. Gradually, the circle of suspects widened, and small hunts sometimes grew into large-scale prosecutions. Large hunts spread in southern Germany and eastern France in the 1570s, 1590s, 1610s, and 1660s, the last spreading as far north as Sweden.

Women continued to be the majority of those accused in such mass panics – in 1585, two villages in Germany were left with one female inhabitant each after such an outburst – but when such large numbers of people began to be accused, the stereotype also often broke down. Wives of honorable citizens were taken in, and the number of male suspects increased significantly, although these were still often related to female suspects. Girls and boys as young as seven might be tried and children used as witnesses although their testimony was not normally accepted in law courts. It was generally only at this stage that witches were accused of causing widespread problems such as famine or disease; in smaller trials, they were charged only with *maleficia* directed against individuals or small groups. The men accused in mass panics were generally charged with different types of witchcraft than the women were – of harming things in the male domain such as horses or crops rather than killing infants or spoiling bread – and only rarely accused of actions such as night-flying or pacts with the devil. In Germany, Sweden, and perhaps elsewhere, they were wealthier than accused women and more likely to be defended successfully by friends and family so that their execution rate was lower.

This breaking down of the stereotype is perhaps the primary reason any mass panic finally ended; it suddenly or slowly became clear to legal authorities, or to the community itself, that the people being questioned or executed were not what they understood witches to be or that the scope of accusations defied credulity. Some from their community might be in league with Satan but not this type of person and not as many as this. This realization did not cause them to give up their stereotype but rather simply to become skeptical about the course of the hunt in their village or town and to call for its cessation.

In many ways, it was similar skepticism that led to the gradual end of the witch-hunts in Europe. In the sixteenth and early seventeenth centuries, the vast majority of judges and other members of the learned elite firmly believed in the threat posed by witches, but there were a few skeptics. The German physician Johann Weyer (1515–88) and the English gentleman Reginald Scot (1538?–99) questioned whether witches could ever do harm, make a pact with the devil, or engage in the wild activities attributed to them. In 1631, the Jesuit theologian Frederick Spee (1591–1635) questioned whether secret denunciations were valid or torture would ever yield a truthful confession. Such doubts gradually spread among the same type of religious and legal authorities who had so vigorously persecuted witches, and they increasingly regarded the dangers posed by the people brought before them as implausible. Older women accused by their neighbors or who thought themselves witches were more likely to be regarded as deluded or mentally defective, meriting pity rather than persecution. These intellectual changes resulted in the demand for much clearer evidence and a decreased use of torture, which in turn led to fewer accusations. By the end of the sixteenth century, prosecutions for witchcraft were already difficult in the Netherlands and the area under the jurisdiction of the Parlement of Paris; the last official execution for witchcraft in England was in 1682, the same year that trials for witchcraft were prohibited in France.

Skepticism about the extent of witches' powers or the possibility that the type of people normally accused of witchcraft could have such powers slowly grew into doubts about the reality of witchcraft in general. Such views emerged first in the writings of those who criticized the power of clergy, such as the English scholar John Wagstaffe (1633–77), who published *The Question of Witchcraft Debated* in 1669. Wagstaffe and others who expressed similar opinions were charged with being "atheists" because doubts about witchcraft or demonic power seemed to many to suggest doubts about divine power as well. Skeptical attitudes slowly spread, however, as increasing numbers of middle- and upper-class people expected religion and politics to be "reasonable" or saw witchcraft as a purely theological matter and not something for secular judges. People with at least some education gradually became convinced that natural explanations should be sought for things that had been attributed to the supernatural. Creating a godly society ceased to be the chief aim of governments and, in some parts of Europe, district and national judges fined local pastors or bailiffs for arresting and torturing accused witches.

By the eighteenth century, other countries in Europe followed the lead of France and forbade prosecutions for witchcraft: England in 1736, Austria in 1755, and Hungary in 1768. Sporadic trials continued into the late eighteenth century in other areas, but even in the Holy Roman Empire they were rare; the last execution for witchcraft in the empire was in 1775. At the popular level, belief in the power of witches often continued, but this was now sneered at by the elite as superstition, and people ceased to bring formal accusations when they knew they would simply be dismissed. This did not mean an end to demands for death to witches, however; lynchings for witchcraft or sorcery have been recorded in Europe within the last few decades and, as recently as 1998, calls for the pardon of a woman convicted of pretending to be a witch made headlines in London.

Although historians have investigated all aspects of the great witch-hunts, few have tackled what may be the central question for our investigation of the lives of early modern women: What broader effects might all of this have had on women? Earlier analysis of the witch-hunts thought they were especially directed at midwives and female healers by male authorities attempting to suppress women's traditional knowledge and healing practices. Actual trial records indicate that midwives were no more likely than other women to be accused, however, and that food played a much more important role in accusations than medicine or traditional healing practices. Male authorities limited midwives and female medical practitioners very effectively through direct prohibitions and licensing requirements and did not need to work indirectly through witch-hunts. Several other hypotheses may be more fruitful. The stereotype of the older woman from the late Middle Ages is one who is bawdy, aggressive, and domineering, whereas that of the nineteenth century is one who is asexual, helpless, passive, and submissive. Stereotypes are not reality, but they often influence people's real actions. Witch trials may have convinced some older women to change their behavior and act less "witchlike." At the same time that witchcraft accusations increased, accusations of women for other types of crimes also increased. As we saw in Chapter 2, these particularly involved sexual behavior, such as charges of fornication and prostitution, or the products of sex, such as charges of having a child out of wedlock or infanticide. This broader criminalization of women's behavior, of which witch accusations were a part, may have worked to shape the way that women acted, particularly in public. We can only speculate on the broader effects of witch-hunts, however. Female authors have surprisingly little to say about witches, and the voluminous records left by the witch-hunts include few comments about their effects on women as a group. The women who could have addressed this issue best, of course, were the women accused of witchcraft, but they had no way of leaving an answer for us to a question they were never asked.

For Further Reading

There is a huge literature on witchcraft, which continues to grow every year. The best place to start on any topic is the four-volume *Encyclopedia of Witchcraft: The Western Tradition*, ed. Richard Golden (New York, ABC-Clio, 2006). The most up-to-date general survey is Brian P. Levack, *The Witch-Hunt in Early Modern Europe*, 3rd ed. (London, Longman, 2006). Bengt Ankarloo, Stuart Clark, and William Monter, *Witchcraft and Magic in Europe: The Period of the Witch Trials* (Philadelphia, University of Pennsylvania Press, 2003), is part of a six-volume series covering witchcraft and magic in Europe from biblical and pagan societies through the twentieth century.

Darren Oldridge (ed.), *The Witchcraft Reader* (New York, Routledge, 2001), includes articles on a range of topics, as does my *Witchcraft in Early Modern Europe* (Boston, Houghton Mifflin, 2007); both of these books are designed for students. Brian Levack has edited two multi-volume collections of articles, *Articles on Witchcraft, Magic and Demonology*, 12 vols. (New York, Garland, 1992; volume 10 looks specifically at women), and *New Perspectives on Witchcraft, Magic and Demonology*, 6 vols.

(New York, Routledge, 2001). Other wide-ranging collections of articles include Bengt Ankarloo and Gustav Henningsen (eds.), *Early Modern European Witchcraft: Centers and Peripheries* (Oxford, Oxford University Press, 1989); Jonathan Barry, Marianne Hester, and Gareth Roberts (eds.), *Witchcraft in Early Modern Europe: Studies in Culture and Belief* (Cambridge, Cambridge University Press, 1996); and Stuart Clark (ed.), *Languages of Witchcraft: Narrative, Ideology and Meaning in Early Modern Culture* (London, Palgrave Macmillan, 2000).

There are several good collections of original sources: Barbara Rosen (ed.), *Witchcraft in England 1558–1618* (Amherst, University of Massachusetts Press, 1991); P. G. Maxwell-Stuart (ed.), *The Occult in Early Modern Europe: A Documentary History* (New York, St. Martin's, 1999); Alan C. Kors and Edward Peters (eds.), *Witchcraft in Europe 400–1700: A Documentary History*, 2nd ed. (Philadelphia, University of Pennsylvania Press, 2001); and Brian Levack, *The Witchcraft Sourcebook* (New York, Routledge, 2003). Marion Gibson has edited two collections of sources: *Early Modern Witchcraft: Witchcraft Cases in Contemporary Writing* (London, Routledge, 2001), includes scholarly editions of the surviving witchcraft pamphlets from Elizabethan and Jacobean England, sixteen in all, and *Witchcraft and Society in England and America, 1550–1750* (Ithaca, NY, Cornell University Press, 2003), includes many types of texts.

Hans Peter Broedel, *Malleus Maleficarum and the Construction of Witchcraft: Theology and Popular Belief* (New York, Manchester University Press, 2003), is the first book-length study in English of the most influential witchcraft treatise. Stuart Clark, *Thinking with Demons: The Idea of Witchcraft in Early Modern Europe* (Oxford, Oxford University Press, 1997), is an enormous work that analyzes hundreds of witch treatises and related writings. Robin Briggs, *Witches and Neighbors: The Social and Cultural Context of European Witchcraft* (New York, Harper Collins, 1996), provides extensive discussion of family and neighborhood relationships. Owen Davies and Willem de Blécourt (eds.), *Beyond the Witch Trials: Witchcraft and Magic in Enlightenment Europe* (New York, Manchester University Press, 2004), examines the era after the end of the witch-hunts.

Recent work on witchcraft has stressed the fact that patterns of persecution differed widely in different areas of Europe, and many of the best studies are those that focus on a specific city, country, or region. See Christina Larner, *Enemies of God: The Witch Hunt in Scotland* (Baltimore, Johns Hopkins University Press, 1981); Ruth Martin, *Witchcraft and the Inquisition in Venice 1550–1650* (London, Blackwell, 1989); David Gentilcore, *From Bishop to Witch: The System of the Sacred in Early Modern Terra d'Otranto* (Manchester, Manchester University Press, 1992); James Sharpe, *Instruments of Darkness: Witchcraft in Early Modern England*

(Philadelphia, University of Pennsylvania Press, 1997); Christine Worobec, *Possessed: Women, Witches, and Demons in Imperial Russia* (Dekalb, Northern Illinois University Press, 2001); Lyndal Roper, *Witchcraze: Terror and Fantasy in Baroque Germany* (New Haven, CT, Yale University Press, 2004); and P. G. Maxwell-Stuart, *An Abundance of Witches: The Great Scottish Witch-hunt* (London, Tempus, 2005).

Single case studies provide fascinating details that general surveys cannot. Michael Kunze, *Highroad to the Stake: A Tale of Witchcraft*, trans. William E. Yuill (Chicago and London, University of Chicago Press, 1987), provides a gripping narrative of a single case of otherwise obscure people charged with witchcraft in Bavaria; this is a book that is impossible to put down and, although slightly fictionalized in terms of details, is based on exhaustive archival research. Retha Warnicke, *The Rise and Fall of Anne Boleyn: Family Politics at the Court of Henry VIII* (Cambridge, Cambridge University Press, 1989), explores the case of one of the most prominent women ever accused of witchcraft. Gilbert Geis and Ivan Bunn, *A Trial of Witches: A Seventeenth-Century Witchcraft Persecution* (London, Routledge, 1997), traces an English case of two women hanged for witchcraft, with in-depth analysis of the court proceedings. Despite the sensational subtitle, James A. Sharpe, *The Bewitching of Anne Gunter: A Horrible and True Story of Football, Witchcraft, Murder, and the King of England* (London, Routledge, 1999), provides careful reconstruction of a case involving a young woman who claimed to be bewitched but was later tried for false accusations. Carol Karlsen, *The Devil in the Shape of a Woman* (New York, Norton, 1987), is only one of a score of books that look at the Salem case; it is important to recognize that Salem was the *only* mass trial in North America.

Some of the books that examine the issues of gender and witchcraft tend to emphasize misogyny and male control of female sexuality, such as Marianne Hester, *Lewd Women and Wicked Witches: A Study of the Dynamics of Male Domination* (London, Routledge and Kegan Paul, 1992); Anne Llewellyn Barstow, *Witchcraze: A New History of the European Witch Hunts* (New York, Pandora, 1994); and Sigrid Brauner, *Fearless Wives and Frightened Shrews: The Construction of the Witch in Early Modern Germany* (Amherst, University of Massachusetts Press, 1995). Deborah Willis, *Malevolent Nurture: Witch-Hunting and Maternal Power in Early Modern England* (Ithaca, Cornell University Press, 1995), examines the links between witchcraft and motherhood. Walter Stevens, *Demon Lovers: Witchcraft, Sex, and the Crisis of Belief* (Chicago: University of Chicago Press, 2002), analyzes the role that sex with demons played in concepts of witchcraft. Linda C. Hults, *The Witch as Muse: Art, Gender, and Power in Early Modern Europe* (Philadelphia, University of Pennsylvania Press, 2005), examines the visual imagery of witchcraft; and Diane Purkiss, *The Witch in History: Early Modern and Twentieth-Century Representations* (London, Routledge, 1996), provides a thorough and often witty analysis of contemporary representations of witches and the academic study of witchcraft.

For more suggestions and links, see the companion Web site www.cambridge.org/womenandgender.

8   Gender and Power

A woman promoted to sit in the seat of God, that is, to teach, to judge
or to reign above man, is a monster in nature, contumely to God, and a
thing most repugnant to his will and ordinance.

John Knox, *The First Blast of the Trumpet Against the Monstrous Regiment of
Women* (Geneva, 1558), fol. 16r

If all men are born free, how is it that all women are born slaves?

Mary Astell, *Some Reflections upon Marriage* (London, 1706), preface

In the preceding chapters, we have discussed many aspects of women's
lives in the early modern period, but you may have been struck by the
lack of a chapter on women's political role, a topic that would assuredly
be covered in a similar survey of women in the nineteenth or twentieth
centuries. The easiest explanation for this is the one that has traditionally
been used to justify ignoring women in discussions of the early modern
state or political theory of the period: other than a few rulers and a few
noblewomen and abbesses who chose delegates to representative institutions, women did not have a formal political role in early modern society.
They did not hold office, sit in representative institutions, serve as judges,
or in any other way participate in formal political institutions, except for a
few odd instances in which they served as sextons or churchwardens, very
minor offices. Their absence from political life was matched by an absence
from most works of political theory. Authors discussing political rights
and obligations, whether monarchical or republican, rarely mentioned
women at all, setting up the male experience as universal and subsum-
ing women's rights under those of the male heads of their household or
family. On this basis, political histories of the period have generally made
little mention of women, except for queens.

This has recently changed somewhat because of two historiographical trends. One is the broadening of political history to include not only
formal politics but also anything in a society having to do with power
relationships. Not only are the relationships between king and subject,
monarch and parliament now viewed as political but also those between

276

master and servant, landlord and tenant, father and son, husband and wife. The study of institutions of government is thus just one part of this broader political history, which also looks at other ways in which people expressed their opinions and shaped the world around them. As we saw in Chapters 1 and 4, historians of the early modern era have been particularly interested in the "public sphere" of scientific and literary societies, newspapers, magazines, salons, and coffeehouses, many of which involved women. In addition, many of the other aspects of women's lives we have discussed in previous chapters, such as their marriages, sexuality, work opportunities, and religious institutions, are now being examined politically, in both their internal power relationships and their connections with more formal institutions of political power or the public sphere.

Women's informal political power has also begun to receive more attention, in a more sophisticated way than older "power behind the throne" studies of queens and royal mistresses. Political historians make distinctions between power – the ability to shape political events – and authority – power that is formally recognized and legitimated – noting that while women rarely had the latter, they did have the former. Through the arrangement of marriages, they established ties between influential families; through letters or the spreading of rumors, they shaped networks of opinion; through patronage, they helped or hindered men's political careers; through giving advice and founding institutions, they shaped policy; through participation in riots and disturbances, they demonstrated the weakness of male authority structures. As we will see, none of these actions led in the early modern period to a call for formal political rights for women, but they are clearly part of the new wider concept of political history.

The second historiographical trend is the broadening of women's history into the history of gender, which has led to an exploration of the political context within which any society defines what it means to be female or male. As we noted in the Introduction, historians often distinguish between sex – physical or biological differences between men and women – and gender – socially constructed differences – although they also recognize that the boundaries between what is understood as "biological" sex and what is "cultural" gender are culturally created, not very clear, and historically changing. Contrasting our own era with the early modern period in Europe provides a good example of such changes, for behaviors that we would define as socially prescribed, such as dominance or dependence, were viewed as "natural" qualities in men and women, inherent in their bodies and beings.

Many historians, anthropologists, and sociologists have pointed out that the dichotomy male/female is linked in many societies, at least in theory, to the dichotomy public/private (or domestic) – that is, the male realm is defined as public, and the female realm as private. This understanding of "public" is broader than simply the "public sphere" of newspapers and salons but also includes all political, economic, and intellectual institutions that control people's lives. In this sense, "public" has existed from early in human history. Some theorists assert that men first created a public realm because they felt excluded from the most important human physical process – birth. The public/private split, in this view, is based on men's desire to control biological reproduction. Some scholars see this as a deeply internalized psychological process, whereas others locate it historically. Lisa Forman Cody, for example, has traced ways in which the emergence of the man-midwife as the dominant expert in childbirth in eighteenth-century Britain was linked with ideas about British national identity among male commentators.

Whatever the origins of this broader public realm, the public/private divide has varied in intensity throughout time and varied somewhat in its association with the gender dichotomy. At certain points, such as in classical Athens and Victorian England, the links between public/private and male/female are strong, and at other points, such as in early medieval Europe, they are less so. Consideration of these links formed part of the early modern debate about women discussed in Chapter 1 and the debate about women's education discussed in Chapter 4. It also formed part of the wider discussions of what we would term "gender roles" that I consider in this chapter, as learned and unlearned people debated the boundaries of women's and men's spheres: Did a woman's proper sphere extend beyond the household and family? Did a man's proper sphere require a household and family as its basis? What was the proper power balance between the sexes, and between individual men and women, in private and in public?

In this chapter, I shift the focus from women to gender to explore the ways in which masculinity and femininity were linked with broadly defined political power in the state and household, and then with other hierarchies and relationships that comprised what the early modern period termed the "social order" – that is, the proper functioning of society. Although other chapters have made comparisons between women's and men's situations, this chapter does so more extensively because considerations of power are always relational – that is, they involve power *over* someone or something, along with power *to* carry out a certain action.

Female Rulers

As we saw in Chapter 1, male and female writers in many countries of Europe wrote both learned and popular works debating the nature of women in the early modern era. Beginning in the sixteenth century, this debate also became one about female rulers, sparked primarily by dynastic accidents in many countries, which led to women serving as advisers to child kings or ruling in their own right – Isabella in Castile, Mary and Elizabeth Tudor in England, Mary Stuart in Scotland, Catherine de' Medici and Anne of Austria in France. The questions vigorously and at times viciously disputed directly concerned what we would term the "social construction of gender": Could a woman's being born into a royal family and educated to rule allow her to overcome the limitations of her sex? Should it? Or stated another way: Which was (or should be) the stronger determinant of character and social role, gender or rank?

The most extreme opponents of female rule were Protestants who went into exile on the Continent during the reign of Mary Tudor. From the safety of Strasbourg and Geneva, Anthony Gilby, Thomas Becon, Christopher Goodman, and John Knox all compared Mary with Jezebel, arguing that female rule was unnatural, unlawful, and contrary to scripture. Knox titled his treatise *The First Blast of the Trumpet against the Monstrous Regiment of Women* (1558), directing it against the Catholic queen of Scotland, Mary Stuart, as well as Mary Tudor. His sentiments can be seen in the quotation that opens this chapter, and the word "monster" was used by the other authors as well to describe female rulers (echoing Aristotle's notion that the female sex in general is monstrous) and asserting that both nature and Scripture placed all women under male authority, "excepting none" (fol. 15r). Thus, for these authors, being female was a condition that could never be overcome, and subjects of female rulers needed no other justification for rebelling than their monarch's sex. This suspicion of female rulers may have been influenced by the recent experiences of the German and Swiss cities in which these authors were exiled, against which noblewomen such as the Duchesses Bianca Maria Sforza of Milan or Elisabeth of Bavaria-Landshut led military actions, although this line of influence has not been investigated as thoroughly as those linking the Marian exiles' other political ideas with those of their Continental hosts.

Gilby, Goodman, and Knox all had the misfortune to publish their works in 1558, the very year that Mary Tudor died and Elizabeth assumed the throne, making their position as both Protestants and opponents of female rule rather tricky. A number of courtiers realized that defenses of female rule would be likely to help them win favor in Elizabeth's eyes and advanced arguments against viewing a woman's sex as an absolute block to rulership. Thomas Smith in *De Republica Anglorum: The Maner of Government or Policie of the Realme of England* (1583) stated bluntly that "an absolute Queene, and absolute Dutches or Countesse" had a clear right to rule, and John Aylmer, in a *Harborowe for Faithfull and Trewe*

Subjectes (1559), disputed both the scriptural and natural-law arguments against female rule. Aylmer argued that scriptural prohibitions of women teaching or speaking were only relevant for the particular groups to which they were addressed and that a woman's sex did not automatically exclude her from rule just as a boy king's age or a handicapped king's infirmity did not exclude him. He asserted that even a married queen could rule legitimately, for she could be subject to her husband in her private life yet monarch to him and all other men in her public – a concept of a split identity that Aylmer and other political theorists described as the ruler's "two bodies" and what we might describe as a distinction between the queenship and the queen. A queen might be thus clearly female in her body and sexuality but still exhibit the masculine qualities regarded as necessary in a ruler because of traits she had inherited or learned. Aylmer and other defenders of female rule were thus clearly separating sex from gender and even approaching an idea of androgyny as a desirable state for the public persona of female monarchs. It is perhaps not surprising that they were writing during the rule of Elizabeth, the early modern monarch who most astutely used both feminine and masculine gender stereotypes to her own advantage and expressed the idea of androgyny succinctly: "I know I have the body of a weak and feeble woman, but I have the heart and stomach of a king."[1]

Jean Bodin, the French jurist and political theorist, returned to Scripture and natural law in his opposition to female rule in *The Six Books of the Republic* (1576) but also stressed what would become in the seventeenth century the most frequently cited reason against it: that the state was like a household, and just as in a household the husband/father has authority and power over all others, so in the state a male monarch should always rule. Robert Filmer carried this even further in *Patriarchia*, asserting that rulers derived all legal authority from the divinely sanctioned fatherly power of Adam, just as did all fathers. Male monarchs used husbandly and paternal imagery to justify their assertion of power over their subjects, as in James I's statements to parliament: "I am the Husband, and the whole Isle is my lawfull Wife . . . By the law of nature the king becomes a natural father to all his lieges at his coronation. . . . A King is trewly *Parens patriae*, the politique father of his people."[2] Criticism of monarchs was also couched in paternal language; pamphlets directed against the Crown during the revolt known as the Fronde in seventeenth-century France,

---

[1] Queen Elizabeth I, Tilbury speech, quoted in Frances Teague, "Elizabeth I: Queen of England," in Katharine M. Wilson (ed.), *Women Writers of the Renaissance and Reformation* (Athens, University of Georgia Press, 1987), p. 542.

[2] *The Political Works of James I*, ed. Charles Howard McIlwain (New York, Russell and Russell, 1965), pp. 272–307.

for example, justified their opposition by asserting that the king was not properly fulfilling his fatherly duties.

Husbandly Authority

This link between royal and paternal authority could also work in the opposite direction to enhance the power of male heads of household. Just as subjects were deemed to have no or only a very limited right of rebellion against their ruler, so women and children were not to dispute the authority of the husband/father because both kings and fathers were held to have received their authority from God; the household was not viewed as private but as the smallest political unit and so part of the public realm. Jean Bodin put it succinctly: "So we will leave moral discourse to the philosophers and theologians, and we will take up what is relative to political life, and speak of the husband's power over the wife, which is the source and origin of every human society."[3]

Many analysts see the Protestant Reformation and, in England, Puritanism as further strengthening this paternal authority by granting male heads of household a larger religious and supervisory role than they had under Catholicism. The fact that Protestant clergy were themselves generally married heads of household also meant that ideas about clerical authority reinforced notions of paternal and husbandly authority; priests were now husbands, and husbands priests. Most Protestant writers also gave mothers a role in the religious and moral life of the household, but this was always secondary to that of fathers.

The split in Christianity created by the Protestant Reformation heightened male political authority in other ways in both Protestant and Catholic areas. During the sixteenth century, the citizens of many cities and villages increasingly added an oath to uphold the city's religion to the oaths they took to defend it and support it economically.

This annual oath swearing, which had begun when cities were first established in the Middle Ages, probably had never involved female citizens. (There is no explicit discussion of why women, who swore oaths of loyalty on first becoming citizens and were otherwise obligated to perform most of the duties of citizenship, did not participate in the annual oath swearing, nor are there any records of women who attempted to, as later women such as Susan B. Anthony would attempt to vote.) With the Reformations, however, the annual oath swearing created an even larger

---

[3] Jean Bodin, *Six Books of the Republic*, translated and quoted in Christine Fauré, *Democracy without Women: Feminism and the Rise of Liberal Individualism in France*, trans. Claudia Gorbman and John Berks (Bloomington, Indiana University Press, 1991), p. 40.

distinction between male and female citizens, and it also created a distinction between male and female *Christians*. (The vast majority of Europe's population was Christian, of course, and there was *never* any discussion of granting citizenship to non-Christians such as Jews or Muslims during this period.) For men, faith was a ritualized civic matter; for women, it was not. This led to uncertainty about how to handle the citizenship status of certain women. In Protestant cities, one of the key political effects of the Reformation was the integration of the male clergy into the citizenry, ending the distinction between clerical and lay status. In most cases, these priests also married, but this was not a requirement for obtaining citizenship. For nuns, however, it was. The only way they could become citizens was to marry, which meant, of course, they were no longer nuns. A priest could be both a citizen *and* a priest, but a nun could not be a citizen and a nun. Thus, *both* the public political community and the public religious community – which are regarded as the same in sixteenth-century Europe – were for men only, a situation reinforced in the highly gendered language of the Reformers, who extolled "brotherly love" and the religious virtues of the "common man."

The first elections in Europe since the time of the Greeks that involved common "people" rather than knights, nobles, or the residents of religious houses were in villages and towns of south Germany and Switzerland where, as early as the fourteenth century, the men of the parish elected their priest. Thus, in church as well as state, democracy marked a division between men and women that had not existed when priests were appointed, for noblewomen as well as noblemen often had the right to appoint priests. (Swiss democracy, so praised in the stories about William Tell, continued that gender division until very recently, for Switzerland was the last country in Europe in which women got the vote – they got the vote only in 1971, after 82 referenda.) Gender restrictions in electing clergy were eased in a few congregations among some radical Protestant groups in seventeenth-century England, where women as well as men raised their hands to approve or disapprove a new pastor. Even in congregations that allowed women to vote, however, positions as pastor or elder were reserved for men.

Protestant women such as Argula von Grumbach or Elinor James occasionally linked authority within the family to authority in the larger community for women as well as men. They argued that because the household was widely regarded as part of the public realm, women already had public duties even if they were not oath-swearing citizens; therefore, their speaking out on political or religious matters was simply an extension of their public role as mothers and wives. This line of argument was generally rejected in the early modern period, and when nineteenth-century women's rights advocates again spoke of their duties as wives and mothers, the terms of the debate had shifted. By this time, the household was regarded as part of the private sphere rather than the public, and women could not speak of political responsibilities as something they were already doing in the way that Grumbach or James had. Instead, they argued that only by gaining political rights would women truly be able to carry out their private familial duties because the political realm shaped family life so intensely in matters such as temperance, education, and health. These "domestic" or "relational" feminists, as they are termed, thus acknowledged the private nature of the household, although one wonders if in the long run a continued assertion of the public nature of women's domestic responsibilities might have proved a more secure base for the expansion of women's political rights.

Religious divisions were not the only development that enhanced the authority of many men. Rulers intent on increasing and centralizing their own authority supported legal and institutional changes that enhanced the power of men over the women and children in their own families. In France, for example, a series of laws were enacted between 1556 and 1789 that increased both paternal and state control of marriage. Parental consent was required for marriage, and severe penalties, including capital punishment, were prescribed for minors who married against their parents' wishes. (Minors were defined as men under thirty and women under twenty-five.) Marriages without parental consent were defined as *rapt* (abduction), even if they had involved no violence (such cases were termed *rapt de seduction*). Although in actuality they were not executed, young people who defied their parents were sometimes imprisoned by what were termed *lettres de cachet*, documents that families obtained from royal officials authorizing the imprisonment without trial of a family member who was seen as a source of dishonor. *Lettres de cachet* were also used against young people who refused to go into convents or monasteries when their families wished them to or against individuals whose behavior was regarded as in some way scandalous, such as wives whose husbands suspected them of adultery or men from prominent families who engaged in homosexual activities; this practice was often abused, and individuals were imprisoned for years if their families refused to agree to their release. These laws and practices were proposed and supported by French officials because they increased their personal authority within their own families and simultaneously increased the authority of the state vis-à-vis the Catholic Church, which had required at least the nominal consent of both parties for a valid marriage. This "family/state compact," as the historian Sarah Haley has termed it, dramatically lessened women's rights to control their own persons and property; these marriage laws would be one of the first things that French women's rights advocates in the nineteenth and twentieth centuries worked to change.

Such links between family patriarchs and the state were not limited to France. The historical sociologist Julia Adams has analyzed the ways in which family heads in the Netherlands built and maintained their power in both the Dutch East India Company and the government through marriage alliances and other familial arrangements. The "familial state" that they created extended beyond Europe itself, for they arranged the marriages of their children and engaged in other actions to build up their paternal rule in the Dutch East India colonies as well as in Europe. The family/state power structures that they created were instrumental in making the Dutch, for a short time, the most important commercial power in Europe and the most successful merchants abroad.

The power of husbands over their wives was rarely disputed in the sixteenth and seventeenth centuries, which was an important reason why women were not included in discussions of political rights; because married women were legally dependent, they could not be politically independent persons, just as servants, apprentices, and tenants could not. Thus, even the most eloquent defenders of women, such as Agrippa of Nettesheim, did not suggest practical ways to increase women's political rights and simply avoided the issue of marriage when promoting women's equality or superiority. The strongest supporters of a queen's right to rule, such as Thomas Smith, did not suggest extending political rights to other women: "In which consideration also do we reject women, as those whom nature hath made to keepe home and to nourish their familie and children, and not to medle with matters abroade, nor to beare office in a citie or commonwealth no more than children and infantes."[4]

Husbandly power was not simply a matter of theory. In France, men occasionally used *lettres de cachet* as a means of solving marital disputes, convincing authorities that family honor demanded the imprisonment of their wives, while in Italy and Spain, a "disobedient" wife could be sent to a convent or house of refuge for repentant prostitutes. Courts generally held that a husband had the right to beat his wife to correct her behavior as long as this was not extreme, with a common standard being that he did not draw blood, or that the diameter of the stick he used when beating her did not exceed that of his thumb. A husband accused of abuse in court was generally simply admonished to behave better and only on a third or fourth court appearance might stricter punishment be set. If the wife had left the household, she was ordered to return, although there are cases in many jurisdictions where this eventually led

---

[4] Thomas Smith, *De Republica Anglorum* (London, 1583), sig. D2r.

to a wife's death at the hands of her husband. The reverse situation, in which a wife killed her husband, was much rarer, but the few cases that did exist fascinated people and were often retold many times in illustrated pamphlets and broadsheets with titles such as *Murther, Murther. Or, a Bloody Relation How Anne Hamton... by Poyson Murthered Her Deare Husband* (London, 1641). In England, killing a husband was legally defined as "petty treason" and punishable by death at the stake. In the ballad "A Warning for All Desperate Women" (1628), a convicted wife warns others:

> Then hasty hairebraind wives take heed,
> of me a warning take,
> Least like to me in coole of blood,
> you burn't be at the stake.[5]

Accusations of adultery were taken far more seriously than those of domestic violence because adultery directly challenged the central link between marriage and procreation and impugned male honor and husbandly authority. In many ancient and medieval law codes, adultery was defined as sex between a married woman and a man who was not her husband; by the sixteenth century, sex between a married man and a woman who was not his wife was also legally defined as adultery. Because adultery by men did not threaten the family and lineage the way that adultery by a married woman did, however, the severity of penalties remained tied to gender. In the 1566 Genevan law, an adulterous married man and his lover were to be punished by twelve days in prison, but an adulterous married woman was to be executed; in the 1650 Adultery Act in England, adultery was made a capital offense for a married woman and her partner but was only punished by three months' imprisonment for a married man. In Geneva, the punishment set for the lover of a married woman explicitly links considerations of gender and class, for he was to be whipped and banished unless he was a servant, in which case he was also to be executed.

Political Actions and Protests

Women's dependence on their husbands was used as a reason not to listen to their demands in the few cases in which women other than queens actually carried out political actions in early modern Europe. Women's petitions to Parliament during the English Civil War provide

---

[5] Reprinted in Frances E. Dolan, *Dangerous Familiars: Representations of Domestic Crime in England, 1550–1700* (Ithaca, NY, Cornell University Press, 1994), p. 49.

the clearest example of this. Several times during the war, large groups of women petitioned Parliament to improve trade and end the debt laws, release the revolutionary Leveller John Lilburne from prison, or end the application of martial law in times of peace. Although their petitions were occasionally received respectfully, more often they were met with disdain and sarcasm, with Parliament commenting that such matters were beyond female understanding and that the women should go home and ask their husbands; using the standard argument that a husband represented his wife in public matters beyond the household, Parliament commented that women had no right to petition. Later women's petitions noted explicitly that "we are not all wives," and the 1649 petition against martial law contained the strongest language in the early modern period in favor of women's political rights:

Since we are assured of our Creation in the image of God, and of an interest in Christ, equal unto men, as also of a proportionable share in the Freedoms of this Commonwealth, we cannot help but wonder and grieve that we should appear so despicable in your eyes as to be thought unworthy to petition or represent our grievances to this honorable House. . . . Have we not an equal interest with the men of this Nation in those liberties and securities contained in the Petition of Right and the other good Laws of this Land? Are any of our lives, limbs, liberties or goods to be taken from us more than from men, but by due process of Law?[6]

We don't know who actually wrote these words, but the female petitioners answered their critics orally and spontaneously, so charges that the petition must have been written by a man are not warranted. It is also difficult to find out exactly what kind of women petitioned, for contemporary accounts are generally hostile and refer to them as fishwives or oysterwomen – in other words, lower-class women who were stepping outside their proper place in the class as well as the gender order. They were also labeled "bawds and whores," reflecting the common notion that women speaking in public must be of questionable sexual virtue. The content of their arguments was never seriously debated, with newspaper articles urging husbands to exert tighter control over their wives and increase their domestic duties so that they would not have the time to worry about politics.

The petitions by women to governmental authorities that *did* get a favorable hearing in the early modern period were those about strictly economic matters, such as the ability to work at a certain trade, and that used language emphasizing the women's domestic responsibilities and reflected the authorities' ideas about the proper roles of women and

[6] Quoted in Ellen A. McArthur, "Women Petitioners and the Long Parliament," *English Historical Review* 24 (1909), p. 708.

men. Women who were successful always stressed their obligations to their children or parents, their helplessness and the strength – tempered by charity – of the rulers. They did not couch their arguments in terms of rights or demand that their request be extended to other women, thus enabling authorities simultaneously to bend or break rules restricting women's actions while still feeling they were enforcing them. The frequency with which women brought individual petitions or cases to courts or other governmental bodies gradually declined during the early modern period, but women never stopped completely. Thus, although they had no political rights in theory and were never part of the bodies that decided such cases, women were actually to be found in courts and city council meetings much more often than we might expect.

Women's legal dependence might actually have been a factor increasing their participation in certain types of political activities, particularly riots and popular protests. A husband was legally responsible for many of his wife's actions in most parts of Europe, leading people to think women could not be prosecuted for rioting. For example, a crowd in Holland in 1628 protesting the renting out of what they viewed as common land chased the renter into the town hall, and then the women of the group cried, "Let us sound the drum and send our husbands home. We will catch the villain and beat him, as we cannot be tried for fighting."[7] Criminal records reveal that women actually were tried and even executed for their part in disturbances, but this did not lessen their participation. They were often the instigators of food riots, protesting scarcities of food and high prices, and took part in iconoclastic and other types of religious riots, threatening clergy, plundering churches, and carrying information.

Women also played a role in more purely political riots, for example, those over taxes in Holland and France in the seventeenth and eighteenth centuries. The women who led such riots were generally older with reputations for strength and strong connections to other women in their neighborhoods or through their occupations. In terms of the distinctions made previously between power and authority, these women had power but no legitimate political authority. Because they did not demand authority or political rights or, in fact, make any specific demands as women, their actions were less disturbing to authorities than those of the English female petitioners. Riots were also clearly extraordinary situations in which female leadership might occur without disturbing gender expectations; both the women activists and the authorities who responded

---

[7] Translated and quoted in Rudolf M. Dekker, "Women in Revolt: Popular Protest and Its Social Basis in Holland in the Seventeenth and Eighteenth Centuries," *Theory and Society* 16 (1987), p. 345.

to them were familiar with biblical and historical examples of women who took over in emergencies but then deferred again to men once the crisis had passed, a model all participants expected would be followed again.

When women's participation in political disturbances went beyond short-term riots to larger and more extensive political rebellions, male authorities were extremely threatened, and the response to such rebellions could be particularly brutal. Ireland offers a telling example. English men were horrified at Irish women's support of revolts against the English conquest of Ireland in the sixteenth century and used such women's influence over their husbands as a sign of Irish inferiority. Like the later English female petitioners, Irish women were accused of sexual misconduct, of being, in the words of the English observer William Camden in 1610, "more lewd than lewdness itself."[8] English military actions against the Irish were specifically directed at women as well as men, and their violence was justified with comments about the women's central role as instigators.

Women's subjection to their husbands may have made some women in early modern Europe more willing to participate in revolts because they might not be held legally liable for their actions, but it made others critical of marriage as an institution. Mary Astell, for example, built on the ideas of Anna Maria van Schurman and Bathsua Makin in advocating women's education but viewed the institution of marriage as well as women's inferior education as a prime cause of their secondary status:

> Though a Husband can't deprive a Wife of Life without being responsible to the Law, he may, however, do what is much more grievous to a generous Mind, render Life miserable, for which she has no Redress, scarce Pity, which is afforded every other Complainant, it being thought a Wife's Duty to suffer every thing without Complaint. . . . How can a Man respect his Wife when he has a Contemptible Opinion of her and her Sex?[9]

This theme was also part of the writings of Jane Barker, Sarah Fyge, Lady Mary Chudleigh, and Anne Finch (later Lady Winchelsea), who wrote poetry and polemics supporting women's rights to autonomous thought and celebrating female friendship.

Negative opinions about marriage were not limited to England, for Maria de Zayas y Sotomayor (1590?–1661?) in Madrid also wrote stories in which the main female character asserted her independence by

---

[8] William Camden, *Britain, or a Chorographical Description of England, Scotland, and Ireland* (London, 1610), p. 144.

[9] Mary Astell, *Some Reflections on Marriage* (1706), quoted in Moira Ferguson (ed.), *First Feminists: British Women Writers 1578–1799* (Bloomington, Indiana University Press, 1985), p. 193.

deciding to go into a convent rather than marry. This option was not open to women in Protestant areas such as England, and Astell's proposal to open a religious retreat for unmarried women was attacked as "Popish." In general, although they criticized marriage, English female writers recognized that most women would be forced to marry for economic reasons and so also gave suggestions about how to choose a husband wisely. They did note that those few who could afford to remain single should and suggested that such women should move to rural retreats to avoid other institutions that would compromise their independence.

Women such as Mary Astell and Maria de Zayas y Sotomayor have generally been termed "feminists" for their recognition and deploring of ideas and institutions that hindered women. They are also some of the first individuals to exhibit what we would call a consciousness of gender – that is, the realization that women as a group shared certain characteristics that resulted not from biology or "nature" but from social patterns. Early modern feminists recognized that such patterns could be changed but also came to feel the power of tradition and the force of misogyny. Marie le Jars de Gournay, for example, the protégée of Michel de Montaigne and editor of his works, asserted the equality of men and women in *L'Egalité des hommes et des femmes* (1622). Four years later, after being ridiculed and belittled, she realized its calls for equality would never be taken seriously and wrote despairingly in *L'Ombre (The Shadow)*: "Be happy, reader, if you are not of that sex to which is forbidden all good things inasmuch as it is forbidden liberty."[10] She went on to suggest that she and her male readers should simply separate to avoid arguing.

Gender and Political Theory

Men who otherwise broke with tradition in early modern Europe did not change their ideas about the proper roles of men and women, as we have seen with Martin Luther. In England, even the most radical groups in the English Civil War did not call for extending political rights to women or suggest that ending the power of the monarch over his subjects should be matched by ending the power of husbands over their wives. The former was unjust and against God's will, whereas the latter was "natural," as the words of the radical Parliamentarian Henry Parker make clear: "The wife is inferior in nature, and was created for the assistance of man, and servants are hired for their Lord's mere attendance; but it is otherwise in the State between man and man, for that civill difference . . . is for . . . the

[10] Translated and quoted in Constance Jordan, *Renaissance Feminism: Literary Texts and Political Models* (Ithaca, NY, Cornell University Press, 1990), p. 285.

good of all, not that servility and drudgrery may be imposed upon all for the pompe of one."[11] Political debates carried out in parliament, written treatises, and periodicals centered around the rights of the "free born Englishman," who was held to develop the qualities appropriate for a citizen and responsible adult through a maturation process that was specific to men. Mary Astell, among others, realized that no general discussion of the "rights of the citizen" ever concerned itself with women and criticized the parliamentarians for "not crying up Liberty to poor female slaves."[12] She eloquently pointed out the irony of their demands for rights in the second of the quotations that opens this chapter and, in part because of this, remained loyal to the monarchy.

By extending political power to a somewhat larger group of men, parliamentary governments in the early modern period, in fact, heightened the importance of gender as a determinant of political power. Once the decision of an all-male parliament became the most important factor in determining who would rule, women even lost the uncontrollable power over political succession they had through bearing children. The fact that parliamentary power over the choice of a monarch freed men from being dependent on women's biology was not lost on early modern advocates of limited monarchy. British writers during the reign of Queen Anne (1702–14), who had no children that lived to adulthood despite eighteen pregnancies, remarked – often in pamphlets published anonymously – on the problems created by depending on the bodies of women for political continuity.

Thus, although they disagreed on exactly how many men should have political power, royalists such as Filmer and parliamentarians such as Parker agreed that the limitation of political rights to men was grounded in the patriarchal power given to Adam by God. In *Two Treatises on Government* (1690), the political philosopher John Locke challenged this idea. Locke did not see the family and political society as analogous; property, not fatherhood, was the proper basis of political authority. God had given the world to humans in common, and individual property derived from applying labor and talents to that common inheritance. Locke uses the word "property" in several senses. Narrowly, he takes it to mean land, goods, and money. Only those who owned property, he argued, could be free enough to make political decisions without being influenced by others. More broadly, Locke uses "property" to mean "life, liberty, and estate," which he describes, somewhat vaguely, as "natural rights"

---

[11] [Henry Parker], *Observations upon some of his Majesties Late Answers and Expresses* [1642], p. 14.

[12] Mary Astell, *A Serious Proposal to the Ladies* (1694), quoted in Hilda Smith, *Reason's Disciples: Seventeenth-Century English Feminists* (Urbana, University of Iliinois Press, 1982), p. 10.

given to humans by God. Tyrannical monarchs could thus be legitimately opposed when they failed to protect individuals' property but also when they failed to uphold these broader natural rights.

John Locke's ideas offered some possibilities for a political role for women. Unmarried women and widows did own property on their own, and in a few local elections in some areas of Britain and eventually in some British colonies in North America, female property owners were allowed to vote. These anomalies did not last long, however, because they were not an intentional extension of voting rights to women but simply accidental. Because of these anomalies, however, laws that eliminated property ownership as a requirement for voting in the nineteenth century used the word "male" to describe eligible voters, thus explicitly excluding women on the basis of their gender. Locke also described marriage as a voluntary compact that could be terminated and whose conditions could be set by the two spouses; as long as the children were cared for, Locke did not see any "natural" necessity for following traditional patterns of authority in a marriage. He did not translate his theories about marriage into plans for change, however, nor did later thinkers who built on Locke's ideas, such as the leaders of the War of American Independence.

In a similar way, the thought of Thomas Hobbes could have offered women the possibility of greater political rights because he based male authority on social custom and agreements between the parties involved (what he terms a "contract") rather than on a notion of natural male superiority. In the *Leviathan*, Hobbes noted that in the state of nature, that is, before the development of civil society, mothers had absolute authority over their children; fathers' authority derived from the fact that men were the ones to have formed governments, not vice versa as Bodin and Filmer had argued. Hobbes does not consider the implications of this line of reasoning for the relationship between husband and wife, however, nor discuss how or why mothers had given up their authority and let men become sovereign within the household as well as the state. In his discussion of implicit contracts as the basis for the authority structure within a household, he refers only to a man and his children or a man and his servants and does not take into consideration the roots of women's inability freely to make contracts. Thus, both Locke and Hobbes are simply unable (or unwilling) to consider the implications of their thoughts for women.

Masculinity

We can clearly see the importance of gender when looking at women's political role during the early modern period, but it is perhaps less apparent when focusing on men. Men's level of participation in government ("political" in the narrow sense) appears to have been based on factors unrelated to gender, such as class, age, ethnicity, occupation, place of residence, and so on. Such factors created hierarchies in which some men had authority over other men (as well as over women): kings over their subjects, masters over their apprentices and servants, fathers over their sons. Thus, men as well as women were enmeshed in various patriarchal systems of dominance. All of these hierarchies, including those that only involved men, were shaped by notions and relations of gender, however, and in particular by concepts of masculinity. Men defined what it meant to be a man – the phrase often used by scholars is that they "constructed masculinity" – not only in relation to women but also in relation to other groups of men. They were taught appropriate masculine behavior in childhood and youth and then reinforced these lessons in their actions as adults. Historians of many periods have noted that men often seemed to be uncertain as to what was expected of them, however, and that masculinity was in "crisis" because of various types of social, political, and economic changes. The early modern period was one of these times of crisis, in which men were "anxious" about their masculinity, worried about contradictions that seem to have emerged in codes of manhood, and eager to assert and demonstrate their masculinity in a variety of ways.

Notions of masculinity were also important symbols in early modern political discussions. Queen Elizabeth was not the only ruler to realize that people expected monarchs to be male and that qualities judged masculine by her peers – physical bravery, stamina, wisdom, duty – should be emphasized whenever a monarch chose to appear or speak in public. The more successful male rulers recognized this as well and tried to connect themselves whenever possible with qualities and objects judged male, although sometimes with ironic results. French monarchs and their supporters, for example, used the image of a beehive under a "king bee" as a model of harmony under royal rule and a community whose existence depended on the health of its monarch; even scientists spoke of the beehive in this way, for they regarded nature as the best source of examples for appropriate political structures, which they then termed "natural." When the invention of the microscope made it clear the king bee was a queen, both royal propagandists and scientists tried to downplay her sex as long as possible, embarrassed that nature would provide such a demonstration of "unnatural" female power. (By the eighteenth century, the sex of the queen bee was no longer ignored, but her role was now described as totally maternal, a symbol of motherhood rather than monarchy.)

A concern with masculinity pervades the political writings of the Italian diplomat and political theorist, Niccolò Machiavelli (1469–1527), who used "effeminate" to describe the worst kind of ruler. Effeminate in the sixteenth century carried slightly different connotations than it does today, however, for strong heterosexual passion was not a sign of manliness but could make one "effeminate" (i.e., dominated by as well as similar to a woman). English commentators, for example, described Irish men as effeminate and inferior because they let both their wives and their sexual desires influence their actions. Strong same-sex attachments, on the other hand, were often regarded as a sign of virility, as long as they were accompanied by actions judged honorably masculine, such as effective military leadership, and not accompanied by actions judged feminine, such as emotional outbursts. For Machiavelli, effective rulers – and effective men – had the ability to shape the world around them according to their will and used whatever means necessary to preserve order and security. This included violence, although not utter ruthlessness: "It is much safer for the prince to be feared than loved, but he ought to avoid making himself hated."[13] Sometimes even the best-prepared and most powerful ruler could not escape the workings of fate (*fortuna* in Italian), however. *Fortuna* was personified and portrayed in Renaissance Italy as a goddess, and Machiavelli's advice to rulers about how to try to control fortune are expressed in highly gendered terms: "It is better to be impetuous than cautious, for fortune is a woman, and if one wishes to keep her down, it is necessary to beat her and knock her around some."[14]

Violence was an important aspect of masculinity for groups other than rulers as well. As we saw in Chapter 3, as their opportunities to become masters declined, journeymen in many crafts formed separate journeymen's guilds that vehemently opposed women's work and enhanced links among their members through meetings and ceremonies. They enforced their aims through violent riots and strikes and also gained status within the journeymen's guild itself through fighting and other types of physical force. Among other groups of men as well, insults could escalate into brawls or feuds, particularly when they involved affronts to other aspects of masculinity, such as sexual prowess or control over one's wife. Violence was used by men in authority to discipline subordinate men and also to challenge men who were seen as not living up to expected standards of masculinity. To put this issue in the terms of cultural history, men communicated their anxieties about status through the language of violence.

Notions of masculinity among journeymen included other qualities along with the ability to use physical force effectively. Journeymen were

[13] Niccolò Machiavelli, *The Prince*, trans. Leo Paul S. de Alvarez (Prospect Heights, IL, Waveland, 1980), p. 101.
[14] Ibid., p. 149.

often prohibited from marrying and were required to travel from master to master learning their craft. They turned these restrictions imposed from the outside into virtues and made them important aspects of manhood. For them, a real man was one who was loyal to his comrades in the all-male journeymen's organization but otherwise free of political duties. He had seen much of the world and was free of family responsibilities. Real men, in fact, had few contacts with women but proved their masculinity and gained status through drinking, fighting, and buying drinks for their comrades. (Many of these ideas about what made a "real man" are passed down from journeymen's organizations to trade unions and other institutions of working-class culture.)

Journeymen's ideal of masculinity separated them from women, but it also separated them from other groups of men. For craft masters, merchants, and other middle-class men, the qualities of an ideal man increasingly centered on their role as heads of household: permanence, honesty, thrift, control of family members and servants. Their masculinity included responsible use of political power; as Jean Bodin put it, "To be a good man is also to be a good citizen."[15] Manhood was thus linked to marriage, a connection that in Protestant areas even included the clergy. This notion of masculinity became increasingly dominant (or what is often termed "hegemonic") and was enforced by law as well as custom. Men whose class and age would have normally conferred political power but who remained unmarried did not participate to the same level as their married brothers; in some cities, they were barred from being members of city councils. As we have seen, unmarried women were increasingly suspect in early modern Europe but so were unmarried men, for they were also not living up to what society viewed as their proper place in a gendered social order. By the eighteenth century, reason was added to the list of qualities expected of a true man in this hegemonic masculinity. As secular virtues became more important for men, religious virtues such as piety and charity became increasingly feminized, part of the feminization of religion discussed in Chapter 6.

Thus, in many of Europe's cities, two distinct notions of masculinity developed: that of journeymen and that of their middle-class employers. In fact, there were other masculinities as well, especially in large cities: thieves and other criminals had their own ideas about what made a true man, homosexual subcultures presented yet another variant, as did religious and ethnic minorities.

Competing notions of masculinity can be seen in other contexts as well. The English Civil War, for example, is often portrayed as a battle between

---

[15] Bodin, *Six Books*, in Fauré, *Democracy*, p. 39.

Royalist cavaliers in their long hair and fancy silk knee-breeches oppos-
ing Puritan parliamentarians with their short hair and somber clothing,
clearly two conflicting notions of masculinity. Parliamentary criticism
of the court was often expressed in gendered and sexualized terminology, with frequent veiled or open references to aristocratic weakness and
inability to control the passions. Men of other nations, as well as other
classes, were frequently judged insufficiently manly. In the eighteenth
century, men in Britain worried about the effects of French culture on
British masculinity, particularly among well-to-do gentlemen. They created a distinctly British version of the gentleman, who dressed in a more
subdued way, rarely showed his emotions, and spoke little. Such con-
structions of national masculinities were accompanied by a disparage-
ment of the masculinity of other nations; in this case, French men were
increasingly described as effeminate and knowledge of the French language viewed as appropriate only for English women (an idea that has
been remarkably long-lived, judging by the gender balance in secondary
school French classes). Jews were also increasingly judged to be effeminate sissies who would not stand up for themselves, in contrast to Christian British gentlemen.

Recent research has increasingly shown that notions of masculinity
among any group were always constructed in opposition to some other
group of men and that the masculinity of those other groups was regarded
as wanting. For middle-class men, the masculinity of journeymen was
violent, dangerous, deviant; for English men, the masculinity of French
and Jewish men was insufficient and shallow. As we will see in Chapter 9,
European men took these ideas with them when they created colonial
empires, for critiques of the masculinity of men in other parts of the
world are common features of the colonial process.

Gender and the Social Order

Once we begin to investigate all relationships of power ("political" in
its broadest sense), we find that gender was a central category in the
thinking of early modern Europeans. The maintenance of proper power
relationships between men and women served as a basis for and a symbol
of not only the larger political system but also for the functioning of
society as a whole. Relations between the sexes often provided a model
for all dichotomized relations that involved authority and subordination,
such as those between ruler and subject. Women or men who stepped
outside their prescribed roles in other than extraordinary circumstances,
and particularly those who made a point of emphasizing that they were
doing this, were seen as threatening not only relations between the sexes

but also the operation of the entire social order. They were "disorderly," a word that had much stronger negative connotations in the early modern period than today and had two somewhat distinct meanings: outside of the social structure and unruly or unreasonable.

Women were outside of the social order because they were not as clearly demarcated into social groups as men. Unless they were members of a religious order or guild, women had no corporate identity at a time when society was conceived of as a hierarchy of groups rather than a collection of individuals. One can see women's separation from such groups in the way that parades and processions were arranged in early modern Europe: if women were included, they came at the end as an undifferentiated group, following men who marched together on the basis of political position or occupation. *The Athenian Mercury*, a periodical designed to provide scientific knowledge for the general public, noted that its mission was to "all men and both sexes"; by "all" it meant all classes, ages, stations, and occupations – divisions that were not essential when reaching out to include women, for whom sex was the only significant variable.

Rather than deny that women were less divided by class or occupation than men, a few feminist authors celebrated it. The Venetian writers Moderate Fonte and Lucrezia Marinelli both created models of societies based on cooperation and egalitarian relationships, which they saw as the essence of relationships between women; a feminized society, in their opinion, would be one without rank – and infinitely preferable to the hierarchies that prevailed among men. For most authors, however, such lack of hierarchy was a threat. When a few women in London appear to have adopted slightly masculine dress in the early seventeenth century – wearing shorter gowns, cutting their hair, and perhaps carrying small daggers – a host of pamphlets immediately attacked them for being "Men-women," and James I ordered the preachers of London to preach against the practice. The pamphlets were not especially concerned with the women's sexuality – they regarded them as aggressive man chasers, not lesbians – but that such dress would lead to a breakdown in distinctions of social class as well as gender because a woman in man's clothing did not reveal her class affiliation the way she would with her normal dress. To male eyes, middle-class wives and noblewomen all looked the same in doublet and hose.

Women were also more "disorderly" than men because they were unreasonable, ruled by their physical body rather than their rational capacity, their lower parts rather than upper. As we saw in Chapter 7, this was one of the reasons they were more often suspected of witchcraft; it was also why they were thought to have nondiabolical magical powers in the realms of love and sexual attraction. At the same time that the number of witchcraft accusations grew, there was also an increase in accusations and trials for love magic, another way in which women could gain power over men's bodies and minds. This same period saw an increase in accusations and punishment of women for scolding, name-calling, and other types of verbal abuse, particularly when it was directed against their husbands. Through these legal sanctions, communities disciplined women who used words to gain power in their households or neighborhoods.

Disorder in the proper gender hierarchy was linked with other types of social upheaval. Groups and individuals intent on some alteration in political or social hierarchies were also charged with wanting to change the proper hierarchy of the sexes. This charge was leveled at Anabaptists speaking about spiritual equality, Levellers advocating fewer economic disparities, and Quakers unwilling to take off their hats for social superiors. Only in the case of the Quakers was this charge justified at all, for, as we have seen, most Anabaptists on the Continent and revolutionary groups in England had very traditional views on gender roles. In cases where it was clear the group did not advocate equality between the sexes, charges of destroying the proper gender structure were still often made but, in these instances, the charge was holding or wanting to hold wives in common. "Community of wives" appeared even more shocking to early modern Europeans than community of goods, requiring harsh suppression in the few instances it actually did appear – such as the Anabaptist community at Münster – and provoking scandal when simply mentioned as part of a mythical utopia – such as Tommaso Campanella's *City of the Sun* (1602). ("Community of husbands" would be still more shocking, of course, which is perhaps why even those attacking Campanella could not mention that the arrangements for procreation in his utopia would have meant this as well.)

Women dominating men were connected with other ways in which the expected hierarchy might be overturned – the unlearned leading the learned, the young controlling the old – in both learned and popular literature and popular festivals. Carnival plays frequently portrayed domineering wives in pants and henpecked husbands washing diapers alongside professors in dunce caps and peasants riding princes. These figures appear in woodcuts and engravings and in songs, stories, and poems. Shakespeare and other learned authors used gender inversions, especially women in men's clothing, as plot devices with both serious and comic intent; but, by the end of the plays, the women are back in women's clothing, generally happily married, and the proper social order has been restored.

Judging by court cases, popular customs, family records, and all types of literature, reversals of the gender hierarchy were the most threatening way in which the world could be turned upside down. Literature and art provided examples of strong women, but their independence was usually restricted in the end, or they voluntarily chose to restrict it through marriage or entering a convent. Men and women involved in relationships in which the women were thought to have power – an older woman who married a younger man, or a woman who scolded her husband – were often subjected to public ridicule, with bands of neighbors shouting insults and banging sticks and pans in their disapproval. Adult male journeymen refused to work for widows, although this decreased their opportunities for employment. Fathers disinherited disobedient daughters more often than sons. The derivative nature of an adult woman's authority – the fact that it came from her status as wife or widow of the male household head – was emphasized by referring to her as "wife" rather than "mother" even in legal documents describing her relations with her children. Of all the ways in which society was hierarchically arranged – class, age, rank, ethnicity, occupation – gender was regarded as the most "natural" and therefore the most important to defend. As Europeans developed colonies, gender hierarchies became increasingly interwoven with hierarchies of race as well as those of class, occupation, age, and level of education, as we see in the following chapter.

For Further Reading

An excellent place to begin for theoretical discussion is R. W. Connell, *Gender and Power: Society, the Person and Sexual Politics* (Oxford, Polity, 1987). Joan Landes (ed.), *Feminism, the Public and the Private* (Oxford, Oxford University Press, 1998), includes important essays about the public/private split in many eras. Works that focus on public/private in the early modern period include Susan Cerasano and Marion Wynne-Davies (eds.), *Gloriana's Face: Women, Public and Private in the English Renaissance* (Detroit, Wayne State University Press, 1992); Robert Shoemaker, *Gender in English Society 1650–1850: The Emergence of Separate Spheres?* (London, Longman, 1998); Michael McKeon, *The Secret History of Domesticity: Public, Private, and the Division of Knowledge* (Baltimore, Johns Hopkins University Press, 2005); and Lisa Forman Cody, *Birthing the Nation: Sex, Science and the Conception of Eighteenth-Century Britons* (Oxford, Oxford University Press, 2005).

The debate about female rulers has been surveyed in Constance Jordan, *Renaissance Feminism: Literary Texts and Political Models* (Ithaca, NY, Cornell University Press, 1990); Amanda Shephard, *Gender and Authority in Sixteenth-Century England: The Knox Debate* (Keele, UK, Keele University Press, 1994); Carole Levin and Patricia A. Sullivan (eds.), *Political*

Rhetoric, Power, and Renaissance Women (Albany, State University of New York Press, 1995); and Regina Schulte (ed.), *The Body of the Queen: Gender and Rule in the Courtly World from the 15th to the 20th Century* (New York, Berghahn, 2005). Lisa Hopkins, *Women Who Would Be Kings: Female Rulers of the Sixteenth Century* (London, St. Martin's, 1991); Sharon L. Jansen, *The Monstrous Regiment of Women: Female Rulers in Early Modern Europe* (New York, Palgrave, 2002); and Theresa Earenfight (ed.), *Queenship and Political Power in Medieval and Early Modern Spain* (Burlington, VT, Ashgate, 2005), discuss both ruling queens and queen consorts (wives of kings). Clarissa Campbell Orr (ed.), *Queenship in Europe 1660–1815: The Role of the Consort* (New York, Cambridge University Press, 2004), focuses on consorts, and Katherine Crawford, *Perilous Performances: Gender and Regency in Early Modern France* (Cambridge, MA, Harvard University Press, 2004), on regents.

Because of her peculiar status as an unmarried queen, Elizabeth I has merited the most attention, both in the early modern period and today. Some of the most important analyses are Carole Levin, *The Heart and Stomach of a King: Elizabeth I and the Politics of Sex and Power* (Philadelphia, University of Pennsylvania Press, 1994); Helen Hackett, *Virgin Mother, Maiden Queen: Elizabeth I and the Cult of the Virgin Mary* (New York, St. Martin's, 1996); and Carole Levin, Jo Eldridge Carney, and Debra Barrett-Graves (eds.), *Elizabeth I: Always Her Own Free Woman* (Burlington, VT, Ashgate, 2003). Recent biographies include Wallace MacCaffrey, *Elizabeth I* (London, Edward Arnold, 1994), and Susan Doran, *Elizabeth I* (New York, New York University Press, 2003). Leah S. Marcus, Janel Mueller, and Mary Beth Rose (eds.), *Elizabeth I: Collected Works* (Chicago, University of Chicago, 2000), includes nearly all of Elizabeth's writings, with excellent introductions.

For discussions of other female rulers, see Michael Lynch (ed.), *Mary Stewart: Queen in Three Kingdoms* (Oxford, Basil Blackwell, 1988); Magdalena S. Sánchez, *The Empress, the Queen, and the Nun: Women and Power at the Court of Philip III of Spain* (Baltimore, Johns Hopkins University Press, 1998); Susan E. James, *Kateryn Parr: The Making of a Queen* (New York, Ashgate, 1999); Barbara F. Weissberger, *Isabel Rules: Constructing Queenship, Wielding Power* (Minneapolis, University of Minnesota Press, 2003); Barbara Stephenson, *The Power and Patronage of Marguerite de Navarre* (Burlington, VT, Ashgate, 2004); and Leonie Frieda, *Catherine De Medici: Renaissance Queen of France* (New York, HarperCollins Publishers, 2006). For noblewomen who wielded great authority, see Natalie R. Tomas, *The Medici Women: Gender and Power in Renaissance Florence* (Burlington, VT, Ashgate, 2003); Helen Nader (ed.), *Power and Gender in Renaissance Spain: Eight Women of the Mendoza*

Family, 1450–1650 (Urbana, University of Illinois Press, 2003); and Caroline P. Murphy, *The Pope's Daughter: The Extraordinary Life of Felice della Rovere* (New York, Oxford University Press, 2005).

Links between public political power and the power of the male head of household have been explored most innovatively by Sarah Hanley, "Engendering the State: Family Formation and State Building in Early Modern France," *French Historical Studies* 16 (1989), 4–27, and other essays; Julie Hardwick, *The Practice of Patriarchy: Gender and the Politics of Household Authority in Early Modern France* (University Park, Pennsylvania State University Press, 1998); and Julia Adams, *The Familial State: Ruling Families and Merchant Capitalism in Early Modern Europe* (Ithaca, NY, Cornell University Press, 2005).

Women's participation in revolts and extraordinary political activities during times of unrest have been discussed in Sharon L. Jansen, *Dangerous Talk and Strange Behavior: Women and Popular Resistance to the Reforms of Henry VIII* (New York, St. Martin's, 1996); Alison Plowden, *Our Women All on Fire: The Women of the English Civil War* (London, Sutton Books, 1999); James Daybell (ed.), *Women and Politics in Early Modern England, 1540–1700* (Burlington, VT, Ashgate, 2004); and Diane Purkiss, *Literature, Gender, and Politics during the English Civil War* (New York, Cambridge University Press, 2005).

Discussions of gender in early modern political theory include Gordon Schochet, *Patriarchalism in Political Thought: The Authoritarian Family and Political Speculation and Attitudes especially in Seventeenth Century England* (New York, Basic Books, 1975); Christine Fauré, *Democracy without Women: Feminism and the Rise of Liberal Individualism in France*, trans. Claudia Gorbman and John Berks (Bloomington, Indiana University Press, 1991); Genevieve Fraisse, *Reason's Muse: Sexual Difference and the Birth of Democracy* (Chicago, University of Chicago Press, 1994); Jodi Mikalachki, *The Legacy of Boadicea: Gender and Nation in Early Modern England* (London, Routledge, 1998); Hilda L. Smith, *All Men and Both Sexes: Gender, Politics, and the False Universal in England, 1640–1832* (University Park, Pennsylvania State University Press, 2002); and Mihoko Suzuki, *Subordinate Subjects: Gender, the Political Nation, and Literary Form in England, 1588–1688* (Burlington, VT, Ashgate, 2003).

Studies that focus on women's own ideas about their political position include Hilda L. Smith, *Reason's Disciples: Seventeenth-Century English Feminists* (Urbana, University of Illinois Press, 1982); Ruth Perry, *The Celebrated Mary Astell: An Early English Feminist* (Chicago, University of Chicago Press, 1986); Erica Harth, *Cartesian Women: Versions and Subversions of Rational Discourse in the Old Regime* (Ithaca, NY, Cornell University Press, 1992); Hilda L. Smith (ed.), *Women Writers and the*

Early Modern British Political Tradition (Cambridge, Cambridge University Press, 1998); Megan Matchinske, *Writing, Gender and State in Early Modern England: Identity Formation and the Female Subject* (Cambridge, Cambridge University Press, 1998); Theresa Ann Smith, *The Emerging Female Citizen: Gender and Enlightenment in Spain* (Berkeley, University of California Press, 2005); Christine Sutherland, *The Eloquence of Mary Astell* (Calgary, Canada, University of Calgary Press, 2005); and Hilda L. Smith, Mihoko Suzuki, and Susan Wiseman (eds.), *Women's Political Writings 1610–1725* (London, Pickering and Chatto, 2007).

Editions of women's feminist works include Moira Ferguson (ed.), *First Feminists: British Women Writers 1578–1799* (Bloomington, Indiana University Press, 1985); Mary Astell, *The First English Feminist: Reflections on Marriage and Other Writings*, ed. Bridget Hill (New York, St. Martin's, 1986); *Astell, Political Writings*, ed. Patricia Springborg (Cambridge, Cambridge University Press, 1996); Moderata Fonte (Modesta Pozza), *The Worth of Women: Wherein Is Clearly Revealed Their Nobility and Their Superiority to Men*, ed. and trans. Virginia Cox (Chicago, University of Chicago Press, 1997); Lucrezia Marinella, *The Nobility and Excellence of Women and the Defects and Vices of Men*, introduction by Letizia Panizza and Anne Dunhill, trans. Anne Dunhill (Chicago, University of Chicago Press, 2000); and Marie de Gournay, *The Equality of Men and Women and Other Writings*, ed. and trans. Richard Hillman and Colette Quesnal (Chicago, University of Chicago Press, 2001).

The social construction of masculinity has become an extremely hot topic in historical research. For studies that focus on the early modern period, see Mark Breitenberg, *Anxious Masculinity in Early Modern England* (Cambridge, Cambridge University Press, 1996); Elizabeth Foyster, *Manhood in Early Modern England: Honour, Sex and Marriage* (London, Longman, 1999); Tim Hitchcock and Michele Cohen (eds.), *English Masculinities* (London, Longman, 1999); Michele Cohen, *Fashioning Masculinity: National Identity and Language in the Eighteenth Century* (London, Routledge, 1996); Tim Hitchcock and Michele Cohen, *English Masculinities, 1660–1800* (London, Addison Wesley, 1999); David Kuchta, *The Three-Piece Suit and Modern Masculinity: England, 1550–1850* (Berkeley, University of California Press, 2002); Kathleen P. Long (ed.), *High Anxiety: Masculinity in Crisis in Early Modern France*, Sixteenth Century Essays and Studies Series (Kirksville, MO, Truman State University Press, 2002); David M. Turner, *Fashioning Adultery: Gender, Sex, and Civility in England, 1660–1740* (New York, Cambridge University Press, 2002); Alexandra Shepard, *Meanings of Manhood in Early Modern England* (Oxford, Oxford University Press, 2003); Valeria Finucci, *The Manly Masquerade: Masculinity, Paternity, and Castration in the Italian Renaissance* (Durham, NC, Duke University Press, 2003); Matthew Biberman, *Masculinity, Anti-Semitism and Early Modern English Literature: From the Satanic to the Effeminate Jew* (London, Ashgate, 2004); Margaret A. Gallucci, *Benvenuto Cellini: Sexuality, Masculinity, and Artistic Identity in Renaissance Italy* (New York, Palgrave Macmillan, 2005); and Allison Levy, *Remembering Masculinity in Early Modern Florence* (Burlington, VT, Ashgate, 2006).

Relations between gender and the social order have been discussed in Hannah Pitkin, *Fortune Is a Woman: Gender and Politics in the Thought of Niccolò Machiavelli* (Berkeley, University of California Press, 1984); Susan Dwyer Amussen, *An Ordered Society: Gender and Class in Early Modern England* (London, Basil Blackwell, 1988); Carole Pateman, *The Sexual Contract* (Stanford, Stanford University Press, 1988), and *The Disorder of Women* (Stanford, Stanford University Press, 1989); Mary Elizabeth Perry, *Gender and Disorder in Early Modern Seville* (Princeton, Princeton University Press, 1990); Anthony Fletcher, *Gender, Sex, and Subordination in England 1500–1800* (New Haven, CT, Yale University Press, 1995); Pavla Miller, *Transformations of Patriarchy in the West, 1500–1900* (Bloomington, Indiana University Press, 1998); A. Lynn Martin, *Alcohol, Sex, and Gender in Late Medieval and Early Modern Europe* (New York, Palgrave Macmillan, 2001); Emlyn Eisenach, *Husbands, Wives, and Concubines: Marriage, Family, and Social Order in Sixteenth-Century Verona* (Kirksville, MO, Truman State University, 2004); and Will Fisher, *Materializing Gender in Early Modern English Literature and Culture* (Cambridge, Cambridge University Press, 2006). Mary Lindemann, *Liaisons Dangereuses: Sex, Law, and Diplomacy in the Age of Frederick the Great* (Baltimore, John Hopkins University Press, 2006), explores a fascinating murder case that brings together politics and sexuality.

For more suggestions and links, see the companion Web site www.cambridge.org/womenandgender.

9   Gender in the Colonial World

As we traveled inland, we discovered lush plains teeming with countless almond trees, like those in Spain, along with olive trees and other fruit. The governor got it in his head that we should plant crops here, in order to make up for what we had lost, but the infantry wouldn't go along with it, saying we didn't come here to be farmers but to conquer and take gold. . . . We pressed on, and on the third day we came to an Indian village whose inhabitants immediately laid hold of their weapons, and as we drew nearer scattered at the sound of our guns, leaving behind some dead . . . we fell at them again with such spirit that blood ran like a river across the plaza, and we chased them to the Dorado River, and beyond, slaughtering all the way.

> Catalina de Erauso, c. 1628, in *Lieutenant Nun: Memoir of a Basque Transvestite in the New World*, trans. Michele and Gabriel Stepto (Boston, Beacon Press, 1996), pp. 33, 34

We are asked why we prefer to be vagabonds rather than cloistered, the cloister being a protection for persons of our sex. Why do we not make solemn vows which are conducive to greater perfection and which draw women to religious life? Why do we go on missions that put us in danger of suffering greatly and even of being captured, killed or burned by the Indians? . . . The state we embrace and to which we commit ourselves in this uncloistered community is the same as that of the Blessed Virgin, our foundress, our mother and our queen. Having received from God this country as her domain in accordance with the prayers of the first settlers, she planned to have the little girls taught to be good Christians so that they would later be good mothers of families. For this she chose the poor women of the Congregation without brilliance, skill, talents or goods; just as Our Lord chose men who were not refined or held in high esteem by the world to teach everyone his doctrine and his Gospel.

> Marguerite Bourgeoys, 1695, *The Writings of Marguerite Bourgeoys*, trans. M. V. Cotter (Montreal: Congrégation de Notre-Dame, 1976), pp. 49, 52

In the early modern era, the lives of European women were shaped by developments beyond Europe more than they had been in earlier times, and European notions and patterns of gender were spread throughout much of the world. This was a time of dramatically increasing global

303

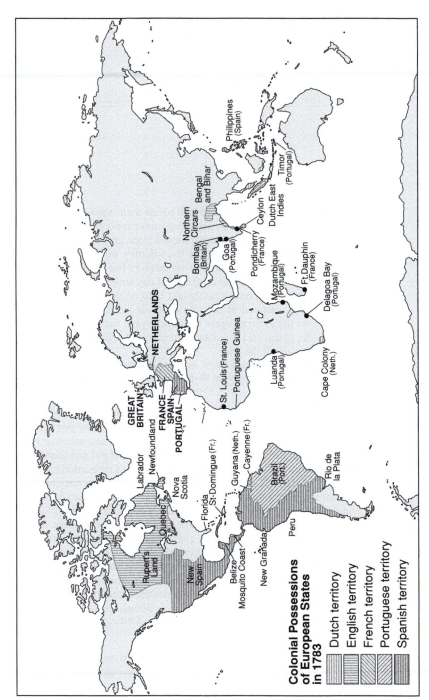

Colonial Possessions of European States in 1783

- Dutch territory
- English territory
- French territory
- Portuguese territory
- Spanish territory

GREAT BRITAIN
FRANCE
SPAIN
PORTUGAL
NETHERLANDS

Rupert's Land

Labrador
Newfoundland
Nova Scotia
Quebec

New Spain

Florida
St-Domingue (Fr.)
Belize
Mosquito Coast
New Grañada

Guyana (Neth.)
Cayenne (Fr.)

Peru

Brazil (Port.)

Rio de la Plata

St. Louis (France)
Portuguese Guinea

Luanda (Portugal)

Cape Colony (Neth.)

Mozambique (Portugal)
Ft. Dauphin (France)
Delagoa Bay (Portugal)

Bombay (Britain)
Northern Circars
Goa (Portugal)
Pondicherry (France)
Bengal and Bihar
Ceylon
Dutch East Indies
Timor (Portugal)

Philippines (Spain)

Map 1. Colonial possessions of European states in 1783.

interaction, with new contacts between peoples brought about primarily – although not only – by European voyages. The major push for overseas empires by European powers came in the nineteenth century but, by the middle of the eighteenth century, the Americas, much of southeast Asia, and some coastal parts of Africa and south Asia were ruled by European countries. Colonies saw varying degrees of immigration; some had large European populations and some only a few merchants, soldiers, and missionaries. Even if the number of European immigrants was small, however, European family forms, legal systems, religious beliefs and practices, political institutions, and economic systems confronted and blended with existing ideas and structures in colonial areas, creating new types of hybrid forms. European men (and sometimes women) also married and had other forms of sexual relations with indigenous people and with immigrants from other areas, creating populations, as well as ideas and institutions, that were mixed.

During the Middle Ages, the largest trading network in the world was the Indian Ocean basin, where Indian, Arab, Malay, Persian, and Turkish merchants controlled the trade in spices and other luxuries, and ships carried Muslim pilgrims on their way to Mecca. A few Italians had contacts with this cosmopolitan and wealthy trading world, but Europe was largely on the fringe. This began to change in the mid-fifteenth century, when Portuguese ships inched around Africa. By the middle of the sixteenth century, the Portuguese had established fortified trading posts along the coasts of Africa, India, and southeast Asia and were carrying goods and a few Christian missionaries throughout the area. At the same time, explorers and conquerors sent by Spain went west, establishing colonies in the Caribbean, Central America, South America, the southern part of North America, and the Philippines. Missionaries brought Christianity and merchants brought African slaves, especially to work on plantations growing sugar and other tropical crops.

French, Dutch, British, and even a few Danish and Swedish colonies followed. By the end of the 1780s, Spain and Portugal had effective control of much of South America, and Spanish holdings in Central America stretched into North America; Portugal had several trading colonies on the African coasts and at Goa in India. The French empire around the world had been significantly reduced by its losses in the Seven Years' War (1756–63) but still included well-populated islands in the Caribbean, French Guiana in South America, and smaller colonies around the Indian Ocean and the Pacific and along the coast of Africa. The Dutch held most of the East Indies and a flourishing colony in South Africa. Britain had the largest empire. It had recently lost some of its well-populated North American holdings in the War of American Independence (1775–83), but

Figure 14. William Blake's engraving of "Europe Supported by Africa and America," 1796. Blake's engraving was designed to accompany John Gabriel Stedman's account of slavery in Surinam, *Narrative of a Five Year's Expedition Against the Revolted Negroes of Surinam, in Guiana, on the Wild Coast of South America; from the Year 1772 to 1777*... (London, 1796). As was common, Blake used female forms to symbolize the

it still held much of North America, many of the islands in the Caribbean, and Belize in Central America. A British company had direct rule of part of India and indirect rule of more. Britain claimed islands in the Pacific, controlled North America north of the forty-ninth parallel all the way to a fort on Vancouver Island on the West Coast, and had just established the first colony in Australia.

Every aspect of the process of colonization was gendered. Letters, reports, and other documents by explorers, missionaries, and government officials describe territories they were seeing for the first time in highly sexualized metaphors. European explorers and colonizers described their conquests in sexualized terms, portraying themselves as virile, powerful, and masculine. Indigenous peoples were often feminized, described or portrayed visually as weak and passive in contrast to the dynamic masculine conquerors, or they were hypersexualized, regarded as animalistic and voracious (or sometimes both). In his description of the discovery of the South American country of Guiana, for example, the English explorer Sir Walter Raleigh described the land as "a country that hath yet her maidenhead [that is, still a virgin]. . . . It hath never been entered by any armie of strength."[1] The gendering included visual imagery as well as written works; in a number of woodcuts and engravings from the sixteenth and seventeenth centuries, for example, America was depicted as a naked woman in a feather headdress.

Colonial ventures often involved the movement of large numbers of people over vast distances, such as Europeans traveling to the Americas and later to Asia and Australia to conquer and settle or Africans being taken as slaves to the Americas or to parts of Africa far from their homelands. In all of these movements, the gender balance between men and women was never equal so that traditional patterns of marriage and family life were disrupted and new patterns were formed. In the Americas, Europeans brought devastating new diseases; demographers estimate that within several decades after Spanish conquest, 90 percent of

[1] Walter Raleigh, cited in Louise Montrose, "The Work of Gender in the Discourse of Discovery," *Representations* 33 (Winter 1991): 27.

Figure 14 (*cont.*) continents, though his inclusion of a nude Europe was unusual, and resulted from his desire to highlight ways in which the wealth of Europe (the necklace of imported pearls) was linked to the slavery of Africa and America (the gold armbands). Stedman's book, for which Blake and other artists did engravings, detailed brutality against enslaved people and became part of the growing body of anti-slavery literature.

the population of Central America died, and similar numbers in some parts of South America. Disease often attacked local populations before soldiers or settlers arrived, for only one person who had made contact could spread disease to a whole village. When European troops came into an area, they found people were already weak and fewer in number and families and kin groups dislocated by death.

The vast majority of merchants, conquerors, slaves, and settlers who traveled great distances were men. Although there were attempts to keep groups apart, this proved impossible, and in many parts of the world a *mestizo* (mixed) culture emerged in which not only ethnicity but also religions, family patterns, cultural traditions, and languages blended. Indigenous women acted as intermediaries between local and foreign cultures, sometimes gaining great advantages for themselves and their children through their contact with dominant foreigners, although also sometimes suffering greatly because their contact with foreigners began when they were sold or given as gifts by their families or were taken forcibly.

European men in some colonial areas learned local ideas and practices of gender from these women and occasionally adapted their own behavior to these, marrying in indigenous ceremonies and raising children according to local norms. In Southeast Asia, for example, European men were sometimes integrated into long-standing systems of temporary marriage by which foreign merchants made alliances with local families. When the man returned to his home country, whether China or Portugal, the marriage ended, just as marriages between local spouses ended if there was conflict or one spouse disappeared for a year or more. In North America, French fur traders married American Indian women, who constructed mixed-blood kinship networks that facilitated the trade in furs and other goods. Some of these women converted to Catholicism and were often stronger in their devotion than their spiritually lackadaisical husbands. Aramepinchieue, for example, the daughter of Chief Rouensa of the Kaskaskia, refused to marry the French trader her father wanted her to marry until both her father and the trader affirmed allegiance to the church. The men both did, and her child was the first to be baptized in what later became Illinois (in 1695, at Peoria). This marriage became the model for subsequent marriages between French men and Native American women in the Illinois area, for, although Jesuits and other missionaries initially opposed intermarriage, they gradually came to support it if both partners were Catholic.

The migration of large numbers of men also had an influence on gender structures in the areas they left. Two-thirds of the slaves carried across the Atlantic from Africa were male, with female slaves more likely to become part of the trans-Saharan trade or stay in West Africa.

This reinforced polygyny in Africa, because slave women could join households as secondary wives, thus increasing the wealth and power of their owner/husbands through their work and children. They were often favored as wives over free women because they were far from their birth families who could thus not interfere in a husband's decisions. In parts of Europe, male migration also led to a sexual imbalance among certain social groups. Because Christianity and Judaism did not allow polygyny, solutions were more difficult than in Africa. Male migration may have contributed to the entry of more women into convents in Catholic areas or to dowries reaching the stratospheric heights they did for wealthy families in Italian cities. (Which itself, as we saw in Chapter 6, resulted in more women being sent to convents.) In Protestant areas, male migration reinforced an existing pattern of late marriage and large numbers of women who remained single.

Consumer goods such as sugar and coffee required vast amounts of heavy labor and are most profitably worked on a large scale, leading to the development of plantation economies in tropical areas with largely male slave workforces. These slaves wore clothing made from cloth that was often produced in European households, speeding up the adoption of new forms of proto-industrial techniques of production in some parts of Europe. As we saw in Chapter 3, this sometimes broke down traditional gender divisions of labor so that men, women, and children all spun and wove. New consumer goods, both imported ones such as coffee and porcelain cups to serve it in and locally produced ones such as window glass and lace curtains to go over it, were purchased by middle- and upper-class Europeans and their descendents in North America. Women's role in such households gradually became more oriented toward consumption rather than production. Class status was signified by the amount and quality of goods in one's home, all of which required purchase, cleaning, care, and upkeep, which became the work – although unpaid – of the women of a household, aided perhaps by a servant or two. Along with their roles as producers and consumers, European women also participated in the growing commercial system as investors. Wealthy women, especially widows and unmarried women, invested in trading companies such as the Dutch and British East India Companies, receiving profits in return. Thus, women in Europe who were far from an ocean and never left their village or town were increasingly enmeshed in the global economy.

Many women *did* leave Europe, however, and this chapter focuses first on those who did, who went to growing colonies for opportunities, for God, or because they had no choice. It then examines the racial hierarchies that Europeans developed as they encountered other peoples, hierarchies that were interwoven with those of gender and enforced by regulating sexual relationships.

European Women in the Colonies

The initial voyages of exploration and military ventures to establish colonies were carried out almost exclusively by men, although there were a few women, including the wives and daughters of conquerors, as well as female servants and slaves. There were a handful of women on Columbus's third voyage in 1498, on Hernan Cortés's conquest of the Aztec Empire in the 1520s, and on Spanish expeditions into South America. Records often label such women "ladies of games" or "women of love," thus focusing on their sexual role; but, like the women who accompanied armies in Europe, women who accompanied Spanish conquistadores also found food, cooked, did laundry, and carried out all types of work. Some of these women were slaves but some came of their own accord, and by the 1530s, they probably included many mixed-race women who had been born in the Americas. Mixed-race women also played an important role in other frontier areas as well, serving as traders in French Canada and the Dutch-held island of Curaçao.

Many of the women involved in European conquests stepped outside prescribed gender roles to some degree, and a few did so spectacularly. Catalina de Erauso (1592–1650?), a Basque woman from northern Spain whose memoir is quoted at the beginning of this chapter, was sent to a convent when she was four, escaped when she was teenager, dressed as a boy, and found work on a ship going to South America. In the colonies, she passed as a man, and (as she later relates) engaged in masculine activities, serving as an agent for business transactions, drinking and brawling, and leading troops of soldiers against native peoples. In one of her brawls, she killed her own brother, was arrested, and only then revealed her true sex. She went back to Europe, where she received papal permission to continue to wear men's clothing and then returned to Mexico, where she apparently continued to live and work as a man. Erauso's story would be limited to what we could know from a few brief comments in colonial records about the "lieutenant nun" had she not written or dictated a memoir while she was in Europe. She describes her own life as long and adventure-filled, with danger and violence, similar to the stories about male adventurers that were popular among seventeenth-century readers. There is no way to know how much of what she relates actually happened, although her cross-dressing is noted in other sources. Her memoir reveals little about her inner life, so it is difficult to say anything about her sexual orientation or sense of gender identity. Dressing as a man provided her with opportunities – and dangers – that were largely unavailable to women (and certainly to cloistered nuns). Many people used the great distances of the colonial world to remake their identities, and, as records of military forces and trading companies indicate, Erauso was not the only cross-dressing woman. Given the close quarters on ships and general lack of privacy, it is hard to see how the men working alongside these women would not have known; most scholars assume that they did know but perhaps decided not to inform superiors because it did not really matter to them or they themselves also had secrets they did not want made public.

Erauso's exploits were largely in frontier areas, where there was little control on anyone's activities. As colonies became more established, officials tried to re-create the institutions that regulated people's conduct, especially relating to sexuality and marriage. Spanish authorities tried to separate women who sold sex from other women, just as governments were doing in European cities in the sixteenth century. In 1527, the Spanish Crown issued licenses to one man in Puerto Rico and another in Santo Domingo to open "a house for public women . . . in a suitable place, because there is a need for it in order to avoid (worse) harm."[2] The Crown worried about the type of Spanish women who were immigrating when it received reports that they were running brothels as well as working in them and attempted – with little success – to examine their background. Because of such worries, the Crown in the 1530s outlawed immigration by single women on their own, but illegal immigration continued.

In many colonial areas, political authorities tried a variety of measures to encourage (or force) more of the right kind of European women to immigrate. They hoped to increase the permanent European population and moderate the behavior of the rough and violent soldiers who predominated among colonial forces. Women's dowries would augment investment in the colonies, authorities hoped, especially in Spanish and Portuguese areas where unmarried women and widows could control their own property. European women were to serve as models of proper female behavior for indigenous and mixed-race women.

Although it tried to stop independent immigration by unmarried women, the Spanish Crown actively promoted the immigration of married European women, ordering all men who had been married when they immigrated to send for their wives or it would send them back to Spain. In Mexico, the bishop was in charge of enforcing these policies, and he sometimes ordered searches for single men and then arrested and deported them; only those who were too old or were physically impaired (a condition determined by the bishop) were exempt from the marital

---

[2] Translated and quoted in C. R. Boxer, *Mary and Misogyny: Women in Iberian Expansion Overseas 1415–1815* (New York: Oxford University Press, 1975), p. 51.

312 Women and Gender in Early Modern Europe

requirement. In general, however, these laws were difficult to enforce, and the wife could also certify in writing that the husband's presence in the New World was necessary to support her, so there were ways to get around them. Such laws did eventually lead to more immigration by women, especially given that married women often brought their unmarried daughters, nieces, and servants, and employment possibilities attracted other unmarried women despite prohibitions. By the 1570s, women comprised perhaps as much as 30 percent of the immigrants to the Spanish American colonies.

Spanish policies promoting the immigration of European women to the Americas centered on married women, but other colonial authorities devised schemes to bring in unmarried women. Beginning in the mid-sixteenth century, the Portuguese Crown sent white orphan girls and reformed prostitutes (who had often been housed in the same institution in Portugal) to its colonies in Goa in India, Brazil, and West Africa. It provided them with dowries in the form of an office or a piece of land for their future husbands, and ordered them to marry. In 1586, Spanish residents in the Philippines petitioned the royal council for transport and dowry funds so that "ten, fifteen, or twenty women [be] brought from Spain, to be married to the common people of these islands, such as soldiers and others, that this country may secure an increase of population – which it has not at present, for lack of women and marriages."[3] In the early seventeenth century, officials of the Dutch East India Company arranged for orphan girls, who they termed "Company daughters," to be brought from the Netherlands to the East Indies, giving them clothing and a dowry. In 1619, the new legislative assembly in Virginia asked that women be sent as wives for colonists, with their passage paid for by tobacco. Between 1646 and 1715, the French Crown sent a few young women, called the *filles du roi* (king's girls), to New France (now Quebec in Canada) to be wives of soldiers, fur traders, and other French men.

The numbers of young women transported in any of these schemes was never great, however, and, as the Spanish had discovered, the unmarried girls and women who were willing to leave Europe were often not the sort that authorities favored. Peter Both, the first Dutch governor-general of the East Indies, suggested that the East India Company ban further female immigration because the "light [meaning frivolous, not light-skinned] women" who had come were a "great shame to our nation."[4]

---

[3] Memorial to the Council by the citizens of the Philippines, July 26, 1586, in Emma Blair and James Robertson, *The Philippine Islands 1493–1898* (Cleveland, OH, Arthur C. Clark, 1902–), 6:172.

[4] C. R. Boxer, *The Dutch Seaborne Empire, 1600–1800* (New York: Knopf, 1965), p. 216.

In 1632, the company stopped sponsoring women as immigrants to any Dutch settlement east of Africa.

Because colonies housed large numbers of unmarried men or men whose wives were far away, informal sexual arrangements of all types were largely tolerated, despite official support for Christian norms of monogamy. The households of wealthier European and European-background men born in Latin America (termed "creoles") tended to include a hierarchy of women and children: one official wife and her children, who were regarded as legitimate, and several other women, slave and free, whose children were not regarded as fully legitimate. White elites generally married within their extended families, favoring distant cousins. For high-status white women, the group of suitable spouses was often small and, as in Italian cities, many were sent into convents instead of making what the family regarded as a disadvantageous marriage. For poorer whites, persons of mixed race, and slaves, family and property considerations did not enter into marital considerations and, in most cases, people simply did not get married. These relationships were not always short term, however, for a large number of what the Catholic Church termed "irregular unions" or "concubinage" lasted for years and were recognized by the community. Actual concubinage – in which a man paid for the exclusive companionship and sexual services of a woman – was also common, as was prostitution.

As in Catholic Europe, Catholic colonial authorities attempted to encourage women to change their ways by opening asylums for repentant prostitutes and other – in the words of the Count of Lemos, the viceroy of Peru who established such a house – "women accustomed to living licentiously [who] have decided to reform and act in a modest and penitent manner."[5] These houses – termed *recogimientos* – subsequently came to be used as places where a variety of women was housed: wives whose husbands were traveling, wives seeking separation from their husbands, women accused of scandalous behavior, and even women who simply wanted a secluded life without the vows of a convent. The various types of residents were supposed to be housed separately, but being sent to such a place marked one as a woman whose honor was in question, whatever one's ostensible reason for going, and they thus served to blur the very border between honor and dishonor they were established to enforce.

---

[5] Letter of Count of Lemos to Queen Regent Mariana (1669) translated and quoted in Nancy E. van Deusen, "Defining the Sacred and the Worldly: *Beatas* and *Recogidas* in Late-Seventeenth-Century Lima," *Colonial Latin American Historical Review* 6 (1997): p. 464.

Figure 15. Giambattista Tiepolo, *Saints Catherine of Siena, Rose of Lima, and Agnes*, 1740. This altarpiece, designed for the Dominican church Maria del Rosario in Venice, shows Rose of Lima (carrying the Christ Child) with two other female saints important to the Dominican order. Rose was often included in European Catholic paintings after her

Along with prospective wives and "scandalous" women, another type of unmarried woman quickly immigrated to the colonies after initial European conquests: nuns. The first New World convent was founded in Mexico City in 1540, and the first convent in South America was founded in Cuzco, Peru, in 1558. Convents mirrored the society around them: professed nuns (who took final vows) were wealthier and of European background, lay sisters were poorer and of mixed race, servants and slaves were still poorer and of indigenous or African background. This hierarchy was also true in the Philippines, where there were several convents; most of the Filipino women who lived in them were servants or lay sisters rather than professed nuns. The first convent especially for indigenous women in the Philippines was founded in 1721 and in Mexico City in 1728. Particularly in larger cities, convents were increasingly popular solutions for housing unmarried women. One-fifth of the female population of Lima, Peru, in the seventeenth century, for example, lived in convents, although most of these were servants, slaves, and lay sisters, not professed nuns. Some of these were young women who were boarders, sent to convents until they married, but many stayed their whole lives. It was often difficult for high-status European-background women to find a spouse acceptable to their families, and the convent was the only honorable alternative; in the Portuguese colony of Bahia, for example, more than three-fourths of the daughters of leading families went into convents. They often took their servants and furniture with them and paid little or no attention to the rules of the Council of Trent on enclosure; bishops throughout Latin America complained regularly about the number of servants employed by nuns and the number of visitors in convents at all hours, but they could do little to control this.

There were a few women whose spiritual practices were more stringent, of whom the most renowned was the mystic Rose of Lima (1586–1617). Rose was the daughter of a Spanish soldier and at least partly indigenous mother who began engaging in intense pious practices and severe bodily penance as a child. She persuaded her parents to allow her to live as a recluse and had regular visions, often while praying and meditating. Rose joined the Dominican order, gathered around her a group of spiritually devout women, and at her early death was viewed by many as a living saint. Eight years later, religious authorities cracked down on her

---

Figure 15. (*cont.*) canonization, particularly, as here, in locations linked to the rosary, a set of prayer beads associated with the Virgin Mary that became an increasingly common form of devotional practice in the early modern period.

followers, calling them deluded and demonic. Criticism of her followers did not dent Rose's great public following, however, and in 1671 she was made a saint, the first person born in the Western Hemisphere to be canonized.

In Canada, Jesuit missionaries established a separate community for Indian converts at Sillery outside Quebec in 1637, where they were joined by several Augustinian nursing nuns two years later. In the same year, Marie de l'Incarnation (1599–1672) and several other French women established an Ursuline house in Quebec, which soon took in both native women and European immigrants. Ursuline and Augustinian houses for women grew to seven by the eighteenth century, which meant there were more religious houses for women in French Canada than for men. By 1725, one of every 100 European residents in New France was a nun. (Western Canada remained a frontier area ruled primarily by fur-trade companies; European women were banned from most fur-trading areas until the 1820s, and intermarriage between French traders and native women continued to be common.) In 1665, enclosed convents were joined by another type of religious community for women, when Marguerite Bourgeoys (1620–1700) established a teaching congregation modeled on those being founded in Europe in the frontier town of Montreal. Bourgeoys, whose words describing her mission are at the beginning of this chapter, took in Canadian-born and immigrant French girls, including some of the *filles de roi* brought in by the French Crown. Later, American Indian and mixed-race girls were admitted as well, both as temporary residents before marriage and as full members.

There was no institution for women corresponding to convents or teaching congregations in Protestantism, so most Protestant women who immigrated came either with their families or hoping to start one. Soon after the first English colonies in North America were established, most of them became settler societies in which people planned on permanent settlement rather than simply the extraction of natural resources such as gold or furs. In New England, family groups of religiously inspired English Protestants, such as Puritans, established communities beginning in 1620. Immigration continued throughout the rest of the seventeenth century, and this, combined with a high birth rate and early marriage, meant a rapidly expanding European population. American Indians were pushed out or killed or died of disease, so few European men were integrated into indigenous gender systems through intermarriage the way they were in Southeast Asia or French Canada.

The early New England colonies were regarded by their founders as religious communities bound to God by a special contract or "covenant." Political participation was limited to men who had undergone a personal conversion experience and were church members. Women became church members independently through their own conversion experiences and were regarded as part of the religious covenant, although this did not give them political rights.

The Puritans had left England seeking a place to practice their religious faith without encumbrance, but this did not make their leadership willing to give others the same freedom. Religious dissenters were whipped, expelled, or even executed. Anne Hutchinson (1591–1643) was one of these. Hutchinson held prayer and religious discussion meetings for women in her home, which soon attracted men as well as women. She was charged with unauthorized religious teaching and "lewd conduct"(because women and men were there together) and banished. Along with Roger Williams, she founded Rhode Island colony. Among the group banished with Hutchinson was Mary Dyer (1611–60), who later became a Quaker. As we saw in Chapter 6, Quakers were treated particularly harshly; religious authorities in New England, as in Old England, regarded their teachings of pacifism and social equality as especially threatening. Quaker women preachers were put in the stocks, whipped, and banished. A few, including Mary Dyer, were executed when they returned after being exiled. Women's religious independence was linked with sexual deviancy in the minds of church and political officials. Both Anne Hutchinson and Mary Dyer were accused of adultery, lascivious conduct, and bearing deformed children; these "monstrous births" were interpreted as clear signs of God's displeasure with their "monstrous" ideas.

English settlers began to arrive in the Chesapeake area of Virginia and Maryland in the early seventeenth century, although most of these were men, and many of them were indentured servants. The first Africans came in 1619 and, although in the early decades some Africans were indentured servants, most of them became permanent slaves. By 1720, 30 percent of the Virginia and 70 percent of the South Carolina populations were black; by 1776, 20 percent of total United States population was black, of which 96 percent were slaves. American Indians were also enslaved in many parts of the South, but their numbers were soon dwarfed by those of Africans. Only in New England were marriages between slaves recognized; because the gender balance among slaves was highly skewed in favor of men before 1750, there was little possibility of marriage or permanent heterosexual relationships for many slaves.

Laws regulating interracial unions began in the 1660s, at the same time that colonial governments declared that all children born of a slave mother would be slaves. Between 1700 and 1750, all of the Southern states, and also Pennsylvania and Massachusetts, passed laws prohibiting all interracial marriage, with steep fines set for any minister who performed such a ceremony as well as for the individuals themselves. White women who gave birth to mixed-race children were to be punished severely through imprisonment, whipping, fines, and banishment. White men's fathering of mixed-race children was not recognized legally and rarely spoken about publicly in polite society, although men occasionally made private arrangements for their children by slave women, just as men occasionally did in European households when they fathered children by servants or slaves. Ignoring the father reinforced laws that based a child's "condition of servitude" on the mother and increased the likelihood that childbearing, along with agricultural labor, would be a central part of slave women's lives. This was true in every American slave economy, although the number of children who survived to adulthood varied greatly. In Brazil, fewer slaves were women, and the conditions on sugar plantations were especially brutal; thus, many more slaves died than were born, and importation continued at a high rate. In North America, "natural increase" came to be more important than continued importation in increasing the slave population; of all the people who were taken from Africa to be slaves in the New World, only 5 percent went to North America.

A year after the first Africans came to Virginia, the Virginia Company began to import women from England as brides for men to purchase, hoping to encourage the growth of families and population. These occurred very slowly, however, and throughout the seventeenth century, the gender balance among both whites and blacks in Virginia and Maryland was skewed in favor of men. Many of the white women who did come were indentured servants rather than wives or daughters and, like male indentured servants, were prohibited from marrying during the term of their service. This prohibition of marriage led to an incidence of pregnancy out of wedlock that was far higher than elsewhere in the English-speaking world; one of five female servants bore a child outside of marriage. The punishment was originally set at a fine and an extra year or two of service, until authorities discovered that masters were intentionally impregnating their female servants to gain this extra time. The law was revised, and a servant who became pregnant by her master "shall, after her time by indenture or custom is expired be by the churchwardens of the parish where she lived when she was brought to bed of such bastard, sold for two years, and the tobacco [which served as money in Virginia] from the sale to be imployed by the vestry for the use of the parish."[6] Only the

[6] William Waller Hening (ed.), *The Statutes at Large; Being a Collection of All the Laws of Virginia, from the First Session of the Legislature* (1823; facsimile reprint, Charlottesville: University of Virginia Press, 1969), II: 166–67.

servant and not the master was to be punished, for her original period of service with him was not shortened. Servants were also prohibited from engaging in secret marriages or promising themselves to one another, although this was impossible to stop.

Clandestine or extra-legal marriages were not limited to servants in the colonial South, because people often lived great distances from a church, visits by pastors were infrequent, and marriage licenses cost money (or tobacco). Thus, although English marriage customs were supposed to be followed, in actuality people often married themselves and began living together in what became known as "common-law" marriages, accepting – in the words of one Maryland man in 1665 – that "his marriage was as good as possible it could be made by the Protestants he being one because before that time and ever since there has not been a Protestant minister in the province and that to matrimony it is only necessary the parties consent."[7]

In the eighteenth century, proportionately more women immigrated to the European colonies in the Americas than had earlier, and they often had more children and more who survived than did women who stayed in Europe. This was especially true in the British North American colonies, which by 1750 had at least a million and a half inhabitants, 80 percent from Europe or of European background and 20 percent of African. By contrast, the population of New France in 1750 included only 100,000 Europeans and a small number of Africans; this much smaller population was an important reason that France lost almost all of its North American holdings to Britain in the Seven Years' War.

European women's lives in colonial areas were as varied as they were in Europe. Women whose husbands or fathers owned plantations were often extremely isolated, but they were also sometimes left to manage the estate while the men went to London, Madrid, or colonial capitals on political or business matters. A few women did this brilliantly, including Eliza Pinckney (1722–93), who began running the family estate in the West Indies when she was sixteen and introduced the profitable new crop of indigo, used to make blue dye. Just as they did in Europe, wealthy women invested in trading companies. In cities, elite women tried to create the cultural and social life that they learned about from trips to Europe or from reading. They wore clothing made of English wool or Chinese silk, ate off Chinese porcelain dishes or the European ones that copied them, drank sweet Portuguese wine, and worshiped in churches designed by

[7] William Brown et al. (eds.), *Archives of Maryland* (Baltimore, 1883–1912), cited in Sylvia R. Frey and Marian J. Morton, *New World, New Roles: A Documentary History of Women in Pre-Industrial America* (New York: Greenwood Press, 1986), p. 10.

Italian (if they were Catholic) or English (if they were Protestant) architects.

Among Moravians and Methodists in the eighteenth century, women occasionally taught and preached to indigenous people and European immigrants. Educated women in a few colonial cities, such as Bogotá, developed small salons on the model of those in Paris, where they discussed new ideas in poetry, science, and politics. In the British North American colonies, a few women, including Abigail Adams (1744–1818), criticized men's domination of women just as Maria de Zayas y Sotomayor and Mary Astell did in Europe. Such criticism did not influence the formation of new institutions of government after the American War of Independence, however. By 1784, every state except one had ended the voting rights of the few propertied women who had earlier been allowed to vote and, in 1807, the last state – New Jersey – forbade women to vote as well.

Most European-background women in colonies were not flamboyant cross-dressers, wealthy property owners, or preaching missionaries, of course, but rather poor or middling-status women in cities, small towns, and rural areas. They worked in shops and in cloth production, as merchants, domestic servants, and on small farms. Their lives were filled with hard physical labor, often while dressed in the heavy clothing that was designed for the colder European climate. If they lived in the countryside, they produced everything that they ate, wore, and lived in. In frontier areas, women, along with men and children, were sometimes captured by indigenous tribes. Generally, captives were returned to white society – and their stories were sometimes told in published "captivity narratives" that became popular reading – although occasionally they remained with their captors and gradually assimilated into native groups.

The Development of Gendered Racial Systems

Although their stories became well known through books and songs, the number of white women who were captured by or otherwise had direct contacts with indigenous groups was very small. By contrast, the number of indigenous women enslaved, raped, and abducted by European men was great. Indigenous women were used for labor, sexual relations, and as hostages. Many women resisted, but others became cultural intermediaries, go-betweens linking their own people with the colonial powers. They learned European languages, taught European men about local customs and food, and sometimes converted to Christianity.

Several of these women were central figures in the earliest history of different nations, although judgments about their role have varied. Doña

Maria, also known as Malinche (d. ca. 1530), was given along with other women as a gift to the Spanish conqueror Cortés by the Maya noble in whose court she was a slave. Gifted in languages, she translated for Cortés when his forces conquered the Aztec Empire and later bore him a son. For a long time, she was judged to be a "race traitor" who had helped destroy her own culture, although she was also seen as a victim; recently, several authors have celebrated her as the founder of Mexico's distinct *mestizo* culture. Pocahontas (1595?–1617), the daughter of the Algonquian Chief Powhatan in Virginia, may or may not have saved the English captain John Smith from being killed by her tribe. (There are many doubts about the story.) She was definitely captured by English colonists, served as a hostage, converted to Christianity, and married an English man, John Rolfe. The couple had a son and went to England, where they became celebrities; Pocahontas (then known as Rebecca Rolfe) died on the ship back to Virginia. Although Rolfe wrote in a letter to the governor of Virginia asking permission to marry her that his "hearty and best thoughts" toward Pocahontas were "entangled and enthralled in so intricate a labyrinth," their marriage was insufficiently romantic for later writers, who invented a love affair between Pocahontas and Smith as well.[8] In South Africa, Eva (born Krotoa 1640?–74), a Khoikhoi woman who lived near the tiny new Dutch settlement, went into service in the household of the Dutch commander as a girl and became a key interpreter for merchants and in peace negotiations between the Dutch and native groups. She married a Danish surgeon who lived in the colony and had several children, although after he died and relations between the Dutch and the Khoikhoi grew increasingly hostile, Eva no longer had a respectable position and died in poverty. Like Doña Maria, she has been viewed as both victim and collaborator.

These three women became cultural icons (for a long time, Pocahontas was the only woman whose name appeared regularly in histories of the colonial United States), and other stories involving love, sex, or both between indigenous women and European men also captured people's imaginations in the early modern era. One of these was the story of Thomas Inkle, an English trader, and Yarico, a young Indian woman, which was told in at least sixty different versions in ten European languages during the eighteenth century. According to the story, Inkle was rescued by Yarico after he was shipwrecked; the two became lovers, and he promised to take her back to England and marry her. When she hailed a passing ship, they sailed to Barbados, where he sold her into slavery. The

---

[8] John Rolfe, Letter to Thomas Dale (1614). Reprinted in *Jamestown Narratives*, ed. Edward Wright Haile (Champlain, VA, Roundhouse, 1998), p. 851.

account was first told in a single paragraph in *A True and Exact History of the Island of Barbados* (1657) by the Englishman Richard Ligon, who reported that he heard it directly from Yarico, now a slave in the house in which he was staying; he describes her as "of excellent shape and colour... with small breasts, with the niples of a porphyry colour." The story was retold in 1711 by Richard Steele in an essay in *The Spectator*, a very widely read periodical, who fleshed it out considerably; he transformed Yarico into a princess (a detail he may have taken from the story of Pocahontas) and made her pregnant with Inkle's child at the time he sold her, which caused him to demand more for her. Steele used the story primarily to argue that women were more constant in love than men, but in its later incarnations – as poetry, essays, several plays performed in Paris and Philadelphia, and even a comic opera (in which it was given a happy ending) – it was often used to criticize the slave trade, with Yarico sometimes changed into an African or referred to as both Native American and African in the same text.[9]

Steele and later authors do not go into the details that Ligon does about Yorico's breasts, but they generally make it clear that she was naked or nearly naked. European accounts of exploration and travel almost always discuss the scanty clothing of indigenous peoples, which was viewed as a sign of their uncontrolled sexuality. Hot climate – which we would probably view as the main influence on clothing choice – was itself regarded as leading to greater sexual drive and lower inhibitions. By the eighteenth century, leading European thinkers such as Adam Smith and David Hume divided the world into three climatic/sexual zones: torrid, temperate, and frigid. (Words that still retain their double climatic/sexual meaning.) They – and many other European writers and statesmen – worried about the effects of tropical climates on the morals as well as the health of soldiers and officials and devised various schemes to keep Europeans sent to imperial posts from fully "going native," adopting indigenous dress, mores, and who knew what else. They also linked this climatic/sexual schema with the advancement of civilization; in the torrid zones, heat made people indolent and lethargic as well as lascivious, whereas a temperate climate (like Britain) encouraged productivity and discipline along with sexual restraint. The British ideas about masculinity that we traced in Chapter 8 were part of these judgments, although men from others parts of Europe agreed. Men who lived in hot climates

[9] Many of the texts that retell the Inkle and Yarico story have been collected in Frank Felsenstein (ed.), *English Trader, Indian Maid: Representing Gender, Race and Slavery in the New World* (Baltimore, Johns Hopkins University Press, 1999).

were effeminate and have a "servile spirit," wrote the French Enlightenment thinker Baron de Montesquieu, while those in colder climates (like
France) "have a certain vigor of body and mind, which renders them
patient and intrepid." Women in hot climates were more passionate than
European women and so should marry when they were still in a "state
of dependence" lest their fathers have to worry about their virtue and
be so suspicious of other men that "the kingdom overflow with rivers of
blood."[10]

Ideas about a hierarchy of climate were linked with developing notions
of racial difference, which were deeply gendered. Notions of race shaped
laws regarding marriage and sexual behavior in the colonial world, and,
conversely, actual sexual activity shaped the racial systems that developed.
Ideas about racial difference grew out of earlier ideas about religious and
class difference, all of which were conceptualized as "blood." In many
cultures, "blood" had long been a common way of marking family, clan,
and eventually class differences, with those of "noble blood" prohibited
from marrying commoners and taught to be concerned about their blood
lines. This has been studied most extensively in Europe, but high-status
people in other parts of the world were also thought to have superior
blood. In several European languages, the word "race" was also used to
mean family line or lineage; both French and English dictionaries in the
seventeenth century define race in this way, as does Samuel Johnson's
enormous *Dictionary of the English Language* published in 1755. Both
"blood" and "race" also came to be used to describe national boundaries, with those having "French blood" distinguished from those having
"German blood," the "English race" distinguished from the "Spanish
race." Religious beliefs were also conceptualized as blood, with people
regarded as having Jewish, Muslim, or Christian blood and, after the Reformation, Protestant or Catholic blood. The most dramatic expression
of this was in early modern Spain, where "purity of the blood" – having
no Jewish or Muslim ancestors – became an obsession, but it was also
true elsewhere. Fathers choosing a wetnurse for their children took care
to make sure she was of the same denomination lest, if he was a Catholic,
her Protestant blood turn into Protestant milk and thus infect the child
with heretical ideas. Children born of religiously mixed marriages were
often slightly mistrusted, for one never knew whether their Protestant
or Catholic blood would ultimately triumph. Describing differences as

---

[10] Montesquieu, *Spirit of the Laws*, Book 16, "How the Laws of Political Servitude Bear
a Relation to the Nature of the Climate," at http://www.constitution.org/cm/sol_17.
htm#002.

blood naturalized them, making them appear as if they were created by God in nature.

As Europeans developed colonial empires, these notions of blood became a way of conceptualizing ethnicity as well as religion, social status, and nation. In some cases, religious and ethnic differences were linked. English Protestant authorities, for example, regarded the Catholicism of Gaelic-speaking Irish as one sign of the "natural" barbarity and inferiority of the "Irish race." Christian suspicions of those with "Jewish blood" or members of the "Jewish race" were not limited to Spain, with Jews throughout Europe increasingly regarded as a separate race as well as religion. Religion was also initially a marker of difference in colonial areas outside Europe, where the spread of Christianity was used as a justification for conquest and enslavement. As indigenous peoples converted, however, religion became less useful as a means of differentiation and skin color became more important. Laws in the British colony of Virginia regarding sexual relations, for example, distinguished between "christian" and "negroe" in 1662 but, by 1691, between "white" men and women and those who were "negroe, mulatto, or Indian."

Ideas about differences created by social status, nation, religion, and ethnicity in the early modern period were often understood – sometimes by the same person – to be both culturally created and inherent in the person. Thus, the same religious reformers who warned against choosing the wrong wetnurse also worked for conversions and did not think about whether adopting a new religion would also change a woman's milk. Rulers who supported nobles' privileges because of their distinction from commoners regularly ennobled able commoners who had served as generals and officials. French royal officials with authority over colonies spoke about the superiority of "French blood" but also advocated assimilation, in which indigenous peoples would "become French." Catholic authorities limited entrance to certain convents to "pure-blooded" white or native women, thus excluding mixed-race people, but were more willing to allow a light-skinned mixed-race person than a "full-blooded" native marry a white person. Such contradictions did not generally lessen people's convictions that racial, social, or religious hierarchies existed, however.

These hierarchies differed from one colonial area to another. In the earliest colonial empires, the Spanish and Portuguese Crowns hoped to keep various groups – Europeans, Africans, and indigenous peoples – apart, but the shortage of European and African women made this impossible, and there were sexual relationships across many lines. The children of these relationships challenged existing categories, but the response of colonial authorities was to create an even more complex system of categories for persons of mixed ancestry, who were called *castas*; about one-quarter of the population was *casta* by the end of the eighteenth century. The Catholic Church and Spanish and Portuguese officials defined as many as fifteen or twenty categories and combinations that were in theory based on place of birth, assumed geographic origin, and status of one's mother, with a specific name for each one. In practice, whether one was a "mestizo" or "mulatto" or "caboclo" or another category was, to a large extent, determined by how one looked, with lighter-skinned mixed-ancestry persons accorded a higher rank than darker, even if they were siblings. New laws passed after 1763 in the French Caribbean colonies set out a similar system, with various categories based on the supposed origin of one's ancestors.

The social structure that developed in colonial Spanish and Portuguese America, including the Caribbean (and later in the French Caribbean) was thus a system based partly on physical appearance but intricately linked to concepts of honor and virtue as derived from class, family status, and the behavior of one's parents. One's social status rested on a precarious balance of moral, physical, and class judgments that frequently shifted within the regional and social hierarchy. Because one's ability to marry or inherit, enter a convent or the priesthood, or attend university relied on official determination of ancestral purity, individuals sought to "whiten" their social status to obtain privileges in society. In many areas, families of property and status bought licenses to pass as descendents of Europeans, regardless of their particular ethnic appearance and ancestry. In frontier areas of Spanish America, or during times of political and social transitions, family members classified their children as "Spanish" or "Castellano" (Castilian) on baptismal records, often in open defiance of the presiding priest's observations about the actual appearance of the child. In addition, individuals might define themselves, or be defined, as belonging to different categories at different points in their life so that the hierarchy became increasingly confused and arbitrary over generations.

While Spanish and Portuguese authorities were developing hierarchies of classification, Dutch authorities were taking a less systematic approach to ethnic mixing in their colonies in Southeast Asia. They initially encouraged sexual relations and even marriage between European men and indigenous women as a means of making alliances, cementing colonial power, and increasing the population. The directors of the Dutch East India Company, which ran the colonies, gave soldiers, sailors, and minor officials bonuses if they agreed to marry local women and stay in the Dutch colonies. This policy was opposed by some Dutch missionaries

Figure 16. "Casta" painting from colonial Mexico. This anonymous painting shows sixteen different couples of varying ancestries, each with their child, all labeled by category – for example: "Spanish father and African mother produces a mulatto." Inspired by Spanish concepts about the mixing of various types of blood and Enlightenment ideas about classification, such paintings became very common in the eighteenth century and were often sent or brought home to Spain as gifts or souvenirs.

but accepted by others, who hoped marriage with local women would not only win converts but also give missionaries access to female religious rituals. There were limits to this acceptance of intermarriage, however. Rijkloff von Goens, the Dutch East India Company governor-general in the 1670s, supported mixed marriages but then wanted the daughters of those marriages married to Dutchmen so that "our race may degenerate as little as possible."[11] (By "our race," von Goens probably meant the "Dutch race" because he worried about mixed marriages with Portuguese-background women as well.) By the second and third generation, many European men preferred women of mixed race as marital partners. The pattern in Dutch colonies was repeated in those of other European nations in the Indian Ocean basin. The directors of the English East India Company, for example, generally approved of intermarriage in the seventeenth century; in 1687, they even decreed that any child resulting from the marriage of any soldier and native woman be paid a small grant on the day of its christening. As more white women moved to British South Asian colonies in the eighteenth century, however, official encouragement and even toleration of mixed marriages generally ceased because the European communities worried about what they termed "racial survival," although informal relations ranging from prostitution through concubinage continued.

At the same time that Dutch and British authorities in the East Indies tolerated or even encouraged intermarriage, British colonies in North America forbade it. Laws similar to the 1691 Virginia law forbidding mixed-race marriages mentioned earlier were passed in all the southern colonies in North America and also in Pennsylvania and Massachusetts between 1700 and 1750. (They were struck down by the U.S. Supreme Court in 1967 but remained on the books in some states for decades after that; the last of such "miscegenation" laws was rescinded by Alabama voters in a statewide referendum in 2000.) The relatively large number of women among white settlers and the increasingly small number of indigenous women in coastal areas where settlements were located meant that marriages or even long-term sexual relationships between white men and indigenous women were rare in the British North American colonies. As the slave population in southern colonies increased, sexual relations between white men and black women did as well, but these were never marriages. In contrast to the hierarchy of categories found in Spanish, Portuguese, and French colonies, the British North American colonies and later the United States developed a dichotomous system, in which in

---

[11] Quoted in Charles Boxer, *The Dutch Seaborne Empire, 1600–1800* (New York: Knopf, 1965), p. 221.

theory one drop of "black blood" made one black, although in practice lighter-skinned, mixed-ancestry individuals may have passed over without notice into the white world.

Whether the racial system was a hierarchy or dichotomy, white skin put one at the top. In this, Europeans drew on polarities of white and black that had existed in Western culture since ancient times. Whiteness was viewed as particularly important for women, for early modern writers often equated it with beauty, purity, and sexual virtue. Portraits of elegant European women in the seventeenth century sometimes showed them with young black servants, whose black skin was understood to highlight the sitter's "fair beauty." Not surprisingly, people used physical measures to maintain or enhance their whiteness. European women who lived in tropical areas tried to keep their skin light by using umbrellas, gloves, and masks, and in the eighteenth century some also used bleach and caustic chemicals that peeled off the top layer of skin. Commentators often ridiculed these efforts, and they also worried that they might be used by mixed-race individuals of both sexes trying to pass as white. Such efforts were jeered at as vain attempts, as the West Indian planter Edward Long put it, to "wash the Black-a-moor white," a critique that became particularly vehement in the later eighteenth century by defenders of slavery such as Long and others who saw permanent essential differences between black and white "species."[12]

Laws regarding intermarriage were usually framed in gender-neutral language, but what lawmakers were most worried about was, as the preamble to the Virginia law states, "negroes, mulattoes, and Indians intermarrying with English, or other white women" and the resultant "abominable mixture and spurious issue." Such worries about "spurious issue" that is, the out-of-wedlock children whose fathers might be black or were in any case not the husband's, were grounds for restrictions on European-background women's mobility and activities. Thomas Jefferson, for example, sets out certain groups as excluded from having a political voice, among them, "Women, who, to prevent depravation of morals and ambiguity of issue, could not mix promiscuously in the public meetings of men."[13] Such concerns led to gender-specific laws in many

---

[12] A Planter [Edward Long], *Candid Reflections upon the Judgement lately awarded by the Court of the King's Bench, in Westminster-Hall, on what is commonly called the Negroe-cause* (London, T. Lowndes, 1772), p. iii. The expression "washing the Black-a-moor white" was a common metaphor for an impossible task but also used in a nonmetaphorical way, as in Shakespeare's play *Othello*.

[13] Thomas Jefferson, Letter to Samuel Kerchival (1816), in Paul Leicester Ford (ed.), *The Works of Thomas Jefferson* (New York: G. P. Putnam's Sons, 1904), 10: 46. The other

colonial areas. Unmarried white women who bore mixed-ancestry children were more harshly treated than those who bore white children, and in places where intermarriage was allowed, European women who married indigenous men often lost their legal status as "European," whereas men who married indigenous women did not. (A similar disparity became part of the citizenship laws of many countries well into the twentieth century; even today in some countries, a woman automatically loses her citizenship on marrying a foreign national but a man does not.) The story of Inkle and Yarico would have been told much differently if their races had been reversed. Instead of a noble symbol of love and loyalty, she would have been regarded as degraded and dissolute, as were the white creole women in the West Indies who the English traveler Charles Leslie noted "coquette much, dress for Admirers" and tended "to run away with their black servants."[14]

Worries about racial mixing were most pronounced in the colonies, but Europe itself was also threatened, in the minds of some observers. Edward Long, for example, warned that "the lower class of women in England are remarkably fond of the blacks." Like Jefferson, he worried about the "mixture" that would result, through which "the English blood will become so contaminated" until the "whole nation resembles the *Portuguese* and *Moriscos* in complexion of skin and baseness of mind."[15]

At the time that Long and Jefferson were writing, many educated Europeans were seeking to create a system in which all human differences could be arranged in a single schema and the reasons for them explained. They settled on "race" as this key category of classification, positing four or five basic human groups, although differed as to whether these had been created separately by God or had emerged after creation. This intense concern with race developed in a society dependent on large-scale plantation slavery but at a point at which opposition to slavery, or at least the brutality of the slave trade, was slowly leading to prohibitions in a few countries and slave revolts in others. It would be another 100 years before slavery was abolished more widely, however, and notions of essential racial differences have been even longer-lived. Today, scientists who study the human species as whole, such as biologists and anthropologists,

---

groups he excludes are "Infants [by which he means male children], until arrived at years of discretion" and "Slaves, from whom the unfortunate state of things with us takes away the rights of will and of property."

[14] [Charles Leslie], *A New History of Jamaica* (London: I. Hodges, 1740), p. 35, as cited in Kathleen Wilson, *The Island Race: Englishness, Empire and Gender in the Eighteenth Century* (London: Routledge, 2003), p. 144.

[15] [Long], *Candid Reflections*, p. 48.

avoid using the word "race" because it has no verifiable meaning, but the racial categories created in the early modern era are still powerful.

As Europeans created social meanings for racial hierarchies and debated their source, they also, as we have seen in several chapters, debated the source of the gender hierarchy in their own society. Were gender differences the result of divine creation? Education? Nature? Did women and men have the same capacity for religious devotion, reason, or moral virtue? These were exactly the same questions being asked about race, but linking the two hierarchies in these debates appeared to be more disturbing than most people could contemplate. Writers often debated whether social status could outweigh gender for female rulers and, by the eighteenth century, whether nonwhite men had the capacity for reason that white men did, but they rarely explicitly discussed whether it was easier for a white woman or a nonwhite man to show the characteristics judged to be those of an ideal man. Perhaps theoretical contemplation of the intersection of gender and racial hierarchies was too disturbing in a world in which actual intersection of those hierarchies in the form of sexual relationships across racial lines happened regularly and were imagined even more regularly. If they became common enough, of course, such sexual relationships (or at least those that resulted in children) would ultimately make maintaining systems of racial difference impossible. This would truly turn the world upside down, perhaps even more fundamentally than would commoners lopping off the heads of kings or "disorderly" women gaining power over men. The early modern colonial world was one in which the transgression of gender norms, especially for women but also for men, could have momentous consequences. This may be one reason why men were anxious about their masculinity, and why court records, marriage manuals, dramas, paintings, songs, sermons, and the variety of other sources we have traced in this book so regularly reinforced gender hierarchies and patriarchal structures.

Gender hierarchies appeared fragile to many observers for other reasons as well. The inherited traditions about gender we traced in Chapter 1 were still dominant at the end of this era, when even revolutionaries such as Thomas Jefferson used the same justification as Aristotle had 2,000 years earlier to limit political life to men. This was not the only voice, however, for some women were acting in ways that at least appeared to be breaking down gender hierarchies, and some women (and a few men) were arguing that these hierarchies were not essential, divinely created, or natural. Yet even the most radical voices arguing for greater gender egalitarianism could probably never have imagined what has happened in the last thirty years. Elizabeth I was conceivable; Vigdís Finnbogadóttir,

Margaret Thatcher, Gro Brundtland, Mary Robinson, Vaira Vike-Freiberga, Tarja Halonen, and Angela Merkel were not.

For Further Reading

Older literature on early European colonization generally pays no attention to gender and discusses only a few iconic women, such as Pocahontas. One of the few older studies that focused on women and is still very valuable is C. R. Boxer, *Mary and Misogyny: Women in Iberian Expansion Overseas, 1415–1815* (New York, Oxford University Press, 1975).

Maria Beatriz Nizza da Silva (ed.), *Families in the Expansion of Europe, 1500–1800* (Burlington, VT, Ashgate, 1998), presents legal, religious, and demographic aspects of the transfer of European family organizations to new environments. Natalie Zemon Davis, *Women on the Margins: Three Seventeenth-Century Lives* (Cambridge, MA, Harvard University Press, 1995), includes discussion of two European women who left extensive records of their travels to the New World. Richard Trexler, *Sex and Conquest: Gendered Violence, Political Order, and the European Conquest of the Americas* (Ithaca, NY, Cornell University Press, 1995), analyzes sexualized language in European conquests.

Collections of essays that focus on European women's religious activities in the colonial world include Mary G. Giles (ed.), *Women in the Inquisition: Spain and the New World* (Baltimore, Johns Hopkins University Press, 1998); Susan E. Dinan and Debra Meters (eds.), *Women and Religion in Old and New Worlds* (London, Routledge, 2001); and Nora E. Jaffary (ed.), *Gender, Race, and Religion in the Colonization of the Americas* (Burlington, VT, Ashgate, 2007). Two books by Patricia Simpson look at the life of the remarkable Marguerite Bourgeoys: *Marguerite Bourgeoys and Montreal* and *Marguerite Bourgeoys and the Congregation of Notre Dame* (Montreal and Kingston, McGill-Queens University Press, 1997 and 2005). For Spanish America, see Nora E. Jaffary, *False Mystics: Deviant Orthodoxy in Colonial Mexico* (Lincoln, University of Nebraska Press, 2004). Studies of the religious activities of indigenous Christian converts include Allan Greer and Jodi Bilinkoff (eds.), *Colonial Saints: Discovering the Holy in the Americas, 1500–1800* (New York, Routledge, 2003). For further readings on gender and sexuality in the expansion of Christianity, see the bibliographies in my *Christianity and Sexuality in the Early Modern World: Regulating Desire, Reforming Practice* (London, Routledge, 2000).

Scholarship on women in the Spanish American colonies increasingly emphasizes the active participation of women of all social groups, both religious and lay, in many aspects of life. See Luis Martín, *Daughters of the Conquistadores: Women of the Viceroyalty of Peru* (Albuquerque, University of New Mexico Press, 1983); Patricia Seed, *To Love, Honor and Obey in Colonial Mexico: Conflicts Over Marriage Choice, 1574–1821* (Stanford, Stanford University Press, 1988); Asuncion Lavrin, *Sexuality and Marriage in Colonial Latin America* (Lincoln, University of Nebraska Press, 1989); Kathryn Burns, *Colonial Habits: Convents and the Spiritual Economy of Cuzco, Peru* (Durham, NC, Duke University Press, 1999); Susan Socolow, *The Women of Colonial Latin America* (Cambridge, Cambridge University Press, 2000); Nancy E. van Deusen, *Between the Sacred and the Worldly: The Institutional and Cultural Practice of Recogimiento in Colonial Lima* (Stanford, Stanford University Press, 2001); Kimberly Gauderman, *Women's Lives in Colonial Quito: Gender, Law, and Economy in Spanish America* (Austin, University of Texas Press, 2003); and Jane E. Mangan, *Trading Roles: Gender, Ethnicity, and the Urban Economy in Colonial Potosí* (Durham, NC, Duke University Press, 2005). Studies that focus primarily on the responses of indigenous women to colonization include Irene Silverblatt, *Moon, Sun and Witches: Gender Ideologies and Class in Inca and Colonial Peru* (Princeton, NJ, Princeton University Press, 1987), and Ramón A. Gutiérrez, *When Jesus Came, the Corn Mothers Went Away: Marriage, Sexuality, and Power in New Mexico 1500–1846* (Stanford, Stanford University Press, 1991). Alida C. Metcalf, *Go-betweens and the Colonization of Brazil, 1500–1600* (Austin, University of Texas Press, 2005), explores the roles of male and female cultural intermediaries.

Studies of encounters between Europeans and indigenous men and women in North America discuss subjugation, resistance, and increasingly adaptation as well. See Carol Devens, *Countering Colonization: Native American Women and Great Lakes Missions, 1630–1900* (Berkeley, University of California Press, 1992); Karen Anderson, *Chain Her by One Foot: The Subjugation of Women in Seventeenth-Century New France* (London: Routledge, 1991); Susan Sleeper-Smith, *Indian Women and French Men: Rethinking Cultural Encounter in the Western Great Lakes* (Amherst, University of Massachusetts, 2001); and Katie Pickles and Myra Rutherdale, eds., *Contact Zones: Aboriginal and Settler Women in Canada's Colonial Past* (Vancouver, UBC Press, 2005). The many works of James Axtell, such as *Natives and Newcomers: The Cultural Origins of North America* (New York, Oxford University Press, 2000), have been influential on the ways encounters are understood. Camilla Townsend, *Pocahontas and the Powhatan Dilemma* (New York, Hill and Wang, 2004), provides a different look at Pocahontas than did earlier biographies.

For European women in colonial North America, the best place to start is Mary Beth Norton, *Founding Mothers and Fathers: Gendered Power and the Forming of American Society* (New York, Alfred A. Knopf, 1996). Kathleen Brown, *Good Wives, Nasty Wenches and Anxious Patriarchs: Gender, Race, and Power in Colonial Virginia* (Chapel Hill: University of North Carolina Press, 1996), examines many types of colonial relationships, whereas Terri L. Snyder, *Brabbling Women: Disorderly Speech and the Law in Early Virginia* (Ithaca, NY, Cornell University Press, 2003), looks at issues of social disorder.

Jennifer Morgan, *Laboring Women: Reproduction and Gender in New World Slavery* (Philadelphia, University of Pennsylvania Press, 2004), traces the ways that expectations regarding gender and reproduction were central to racial ideologies and the organization of slavery. Her book builds on the earlier work of David Barry Gaspar and Darlene Clark Hine, *More than Chattel: Black Women and Slavery in the Americas* (Bloomington, Indiana University Press, 1996).

Encounters between women and men of many ethnic groups in Southeast Asia are increasingly the focus of study. See Leonard Blussé, *Strange Company: Chinese Settlers, Mestizo Women and the Dutch in VOC Batavia* (Dordrecht, Foris, 1986); Barbara Watson Andaya (ed.), *Other Pasts: Women, Gender and History in Early Modern Southeast Asia* (Honolulu, Center for Southeast Asian Studies, University of Hawai'i at Mânoa, 2000); Leonard Blussé, *Bitter Bonds: A Colonial Divorce Drama of the Seventeenth Century*, trans. Diane Webb (Princeton, NJ, Markus Wiener Publishers, 2002); Carolyn Brewer, *Shamanism, Catholicism and Gender Relations in Colonial Philippines, 1521–1685* (Burlington, VT, Ashgate, 2004); and Barbara Watson Andaya, *The Flaming Womb: Repositioning Women in Early Modern Southeast Asia* (Honolulu, University of Hawaii Press, 2006).

For the development of ideas about race, Ivan Hannaford, *Race: The History of an Idea in the West* (Washington, DC, 1996), is a good place to start. More specialized analyses include Sue Peabody, *"There Are No Slaves in France": The Political Culture of Race and Slavery in the Ancien Régime* (New York, Oxford University Press, 1996); Roxann Wheeler, *The Complexion of Race: Categories of Difference in Eighteenth-Century British Culture* (Philadelphia, University of Pennsylvania Press, 2000); Sue Peabody and Tyler Stovall (eds.), *The Color of Liberty: Histories of Race in France* (Durham, NC, Duke University Press, 2003); Sujata Iyengar *Shades of Difference: Mythologies of Skin Color in Early Modern England* (Philadelphia, University of Pennsylvania Press, 2005); and Colin Kidd, *The Forging of Races: Race and Scripture in the Protestant Atlantic World* (Cambridge, Cambridge University Press, 2006).

For work that brings together race and gender, see Margo Hendricks and Patricia Parker (eds.), *Women, "Race" and Writing in the Early Modern*

Period (London, Routledge, 1994); Kim F. Hall, *Things of Darkness: Economies of Race and Gender in Early Modern England* (Ithaca, NY, Cornell University Press, 1995); Felicity Nussbaum, *Torrid Zones: Maternity, Sexuality, and Empire in Eighteenth-Century English Narratives* (Baltimore and London, Johns Hopkins University Press, 1995); Ann Laura Stoler, *Carnal Knowledge and Imperial Power: Race and the Intimate in Colonial Rule* (Berkeley, University of California Press, 2002); Margaret Ferguson, *Dido's Daughters: Literacy, Gender, and Empire in Early Modern England and France* (Chicago, University of Chicago Press, 2003); Kathleen Wilson, *The Island Race: Englishness, Empire and Gender in the Eighteenth Century* (London, Routledge, 2003); and Tony Ballantyne and Antoinette Burton (eds.), *Bodies in Contact: Rethinking Colonial Encounters in World History* (Durham, NC, Duke University Press, 2005).

For more suggestions and links, see the companion Web site www. cambridge.org/womenandgender.

Index

NEW APPROACHES TO EUROPEAN HISTORY